# Postcolonial Legality: Law, Power and Politics in Zambia



This book interrogates the ideology and practices of liberal constitutionalism in the Zambian postcolony. The analysis focuses on the residual political and governmental effects of an imperial *form of power*, embodied in the person of the republican president, termed here *prerogativism*. Through systematic, long-term ethnographic engagement with Zambian constitutionalist activists – lawyers, judges and civic leaders – the study examines how prerogativism has shaped the postcolonial political landscape and limited the possibilities of constitutional liberalism. This is revealed in the ways that repeated efforts to reform the constitution have sidelined popular participation and thus failed to address the deep divide between a small elite stratum (from which the constitutional activists are drawn) and the marginalized masses of the population. Along the way, the study documents the intimate interpenetration of political and legal action and examines how prerogativism delimits the political engagements of elite actors. Special attention is given to the reluctance of legal activists to engage with popular politics and to the conservative ethos that undermines efforts to pursue a jurisprudence of transformational constitutionalism in the findings of the Constitutional Court. The work contributes to the rising interest in applying socio-legal analysis to the statutory domain in postcolonial jurisdictions. It offers a pioneering attempt to deconstruct the amorphous and ambivalent assemblage of ideas and practices related to constitutionalism through detailed ethnographic interrogation. It will appeal to scholars, students and practitioners with an interest in theorizing challenges to political liberalism in postcolonial contexts, as well as in rethinking the methodological toolbox of socio-legal analysis.

**Jeremy Gould** is Professor Emeritus of Development Studies, and an Adjunct Professor in Social and Cultural Anthropology based at the University of Helsinki, Finland.

# Postcolonial Legality: Law, Power and Politics in Zambia

Jeremy Gould

Routledge
Taylor & Francis Group
LONDON AND NEW YORK

First published 2023
by Routledge
4 Park Square, Milton Park, Abingdon, Oxon OX14 4RN

and by Routledge
605 Third Avenue, New York, NY 10158

*Routledge is an imprint of the Taylor & Francis Group, an informa business*



*British Library Cataloguing-in-Publication Data*
A catalogue record for this book is available from the British Library

ISBN: 978-1-4724-8908-1 (hbk)
ISBN: 978-1-032-28830-7 (pbk)
ISBN: 978-0-429-19898-4 (ebk)

DOI: 10.4324/9780429198984

Typeset in Galliard
by Deanta Global Publishing Services, Chennai, India

For the grandchildren

# Contents

# Foreword

Two themes run through the case studies that form the substance of this book. The first concerns the postcolonial form of governmental power, or what I call prerogativism, and the ways 'unfettered' presidential powers – rooted in colonial government – both presume and sustain the political and economic exclusion of huge swaths of the Zambian population. The second theme explores how the highly educated, politically conscious middle classes have responded to the grossly skewed distribution of power and wealth in their society. The efforts of legal professionals (lawyers and judges) to promote a more democratic dispensation in Zambia come under close scrutiny.

The issues discussed here resonate far beyond Zambia. Similar questions about accountable leadership and the juridification of politics are being posed with increasing frequency and concern in democratic jurisdictions on every continent. It is fair to say that debates concerning the alleged crisis of democratic leadership occupy citizens in nearly every country on the planet.

Nor are these novel concerns. Progressive African scholarship since Kwame Nkrumah and Franz Fanon has exposed the exclusive and predatory class nature of the (post)colonial state and has called for popular movements and even revolution to redress the marginalization and exploitation of the masses. Acknowledging these seminal anticolonial contributions, I hope to contribute to resurgent efforts to rethink the political conditions for social progress in the Global South. Indeed, cultivating the political and epistemic prerequisites for social, economic and environmental justice have never been more crucial, and urgent, than they are today.

This does not mean that everything is getting worse in Africa, that all African governments are failing or that African politics are intrinsically corrupt or ineffective. The past two decades have witnessed the emergence of an entitled, enlightened and empowered middle class, and with it many robust voices for a more liberal democracy. These thin strata are increasingly integrated into global economic and professional elites, and have benefitted markedly from capitalist globalization. Despite this, it is clear that Africa has seen neither a commensurate trickling down of the accumulated wealth of the privileged postcolonial elites, nor effective efforts at empowering the voices of the structurally excluded.

This study, I believe, explains why the exorcism of systemic injustices through legislative means has had so little success. The sustained efforts to enhance constitutional democracy by the Zambian civil society coalition that calls itself the Oasis Forum provide the raw material for my analysis. Rather than arguing for abandoning the quest for justice, or calling for more substantial constitutional reform, the ideas, events and processes dissected in the following chapters suggest that democrats in Zambia and elsewhere in postcolonial Africa might be wise to focus on harnessing prerogativist means to just ends. Conventional (neo)liberal defenses of the rule of law often merely shore up entrenched illiberal tendencies in the status quo. The analysis presented here suggests that a progressive postliberalism may best transform the politico-legal order to better serve equality and justice. This path involves harnessing the constituent power of the *demos* to overcome entrenched elite interests rooted in postcolonial legality.

## Outline of the volume

This book has been conceived in such a way that it serves two, or perhaps three, distinct purposes. First of all, *Postcolonial legality* is political sociology, focussed on the actors, sites and processes that together maintain the politico-legal scaffolding for Zambia's Third Republic. That description encompasses an unwieldy number of people, places and events – far too many for a lone ethnographer to cover — and I have narrowed my purview to the specific matrix of people, ideas and events involved in so-called constitution-making. By this I mean the politico-legal process that began immediately after the hurried ratification of the multi-party constitution of 1991, and culminated in the compromise constitutional reforms of 2016.

That too is a huge field and, of necessity, my coverage of this period is hardly comprehensive, as will be evident to the informed reader. What's more, much of what went into constitution-making during this period had its impetus long before 1991, and extended beyond the ratification of the Constitution of Zambia Act of 2016, Zambia's most recent constitutional legislation. (The workings of the new Constitutional Court, discussed in the penultimate Chapter 10, being a case in point.) This has made it necessary to indulge in some well-worn historical narratives in Chapters 5 and 6. Readers pressed for time may choose to skim over some of the more detailed historical sections.

At the same time, constitution making is not a world unto itself; many actors connected to efforts to create a constitution for Zambia that would 'stand the test of time' were also otherwise active in the politico-legal realm. Following these men and women as they pursued their careers led me to sites which seemed, at first glance, to be quite unrelated to constitution-making, but which gave me new and important insights into the politico-legal stakes which motivated their impassioned views about Zambian constitutionalism. The most productive of these sites was the Task Force against Corruption, erected to indict and prosecute President Chiluba for abuse of office, as well as the two drawn-out court cases against him that followed. The key actors in all of these processes were elite lawyers, often in the headlines and frequently close to power at some point of their careers. Two lawyers figure centrally in the later chapters of the book. These are Mutembo Nchito and Wynter Kabimba, neither of which took active part in the extended tug-of-war over constitutional politics between President Mwanawasa and his pet antagonists, the Oasis Forum. Despite their relative disinterest in constitutionalism, I gradually realized that the actions of these men – and the dramatic rise and fall of their political careers, revealed something essential about a hidden, inner logic of Zambian government.

I may be the only one who thinks that Mr Nchito — a ruthless crusader to bring President Chiluba's to justice, who became the Director of Public Prosecutions under President Michael Sata — shares some essential qualities with Mr Kabimba, Secretary General of the Patriot Front and President Sata's Minister of Justice. In zooming in on these exceptional men, I don't suggest that they have similar personalities, capacities or values. Rather, their similarity lies in their role as avatars of a certain paradoxical *form of power* at the core of constitutional power, one which is deeply rooted in colonial politics and Imperial jurisprudence.

Outlining and illustrating this argument about postcolonial law, politics and power is one of the book's key aims. Its second driving ambition is to offer contemporary and future cohorts of scholars and students an extended example of how and why to carry out detailed, first-hand empirical analysis of the postcolonial politico-legal domain — the consequential matrix of actors, ideas, values and institutions where what is law, and what is politics cannot be fruitfully disentangled from one another. *Postcolonial legality* is not a blueprint or a handbook. Rather, I hope that this example, with its extensive bibliography of empirical and theoretical resources, might inspire others to use socio-legal analysis to better understand why the majority of Africans have so little amidst such abundance.

I am not a citizen of Zambia, and I am not a judge. I have lived in Zambia long enough to have made some dear and lasting friendships. But I don't own land, or vote. I don't have a Zambian passport. My ancestors are all interred across a vast ocean.

These facts suggest why I am hesitant to pass moral judgment on local politics. Its not so much that I am afraid that foreign biases will distort my moral compass. Rather, I prefer to relegate moral assessment to the countless individuals and institutions dedicated to that purpose. For my part, I have chosen to scrutinize select several high-profile instances in order to unravel mysteries concerning the nature of power itself. In doing so, I learned an important lesson: The alleged Absolutism of African political leaders, and their purported imperviousness to liberal norms comes into novel relief when looked at through fleeting cracks in the armor.

This suggests a third aim for my book: to promote lines for future research. One line of inquiry implied in my findings stems from recognizing that we are far from achieving an adequate understanding of the lasting effects of empire on the webs and hierarchies of social relations established and sustained through the practices of postcolonial government. The second point is that there is a vital difference between focussing on how power is *used* and sustained, which is the grist of most political science, and looking hard at how power is *constituted*. Together, such investigations promise to reveal how 'the people', that sacred fount of all democratic legitimacy, are consistently denied their rightful share.

The first chapter offers an overview of the book's arguments and motivations. The study's analytical tools are developed in Chapters 2 and 3, as well as in an Excursus. (These sections may be of less interest to readers primarily interested in the dynamics of Zambia's recent politico-legal history.) Chapter 4 highlights the voices of Oasis Forum activists and their fellow travelers. The book's main historical chapter (Chapter 5) describes the colonial roots of Zambia's politico-legal order. Chapter 6 scrutinizes the fraught and protracted struggles over constitutionalism between 1991 and 2016. Subsequent chapters flesh out the contested meanings of Zambian constitutionalism by scrutinizing a number of high-profile politico-legal incidents. Chapter 7 examines the two abuse-of-office trials of President Frederick Chiluba, as well as Levy Mwanawasa's concomitant 'war on corruption.' Chapters 8 and 9 further apply the perspective of political legality to an analysis of the political dynamics of prerogativist power during the brief reign of reformist President Michael Sata. Chapter 10 brings the analysis up to date by examining the emerging jurisprudence of the new Constitutional Court after 2016. The final chapter seeks to offer constructive dialogical tools, based on the study's key findings, for rethinking Zambian democracy.

## Acknowledgments

Funding for the fieldwork informing this study was provided by the Research Council for Culture and Society of the Academy of Finland (grant 111794). Support for the write-up also came from the Academy (grants 288998 and 318762). My sincere thanks to research support personnel at the Universities of Helsinki and Jyväskylä for their excellent administrative support.

Sections of an earlier essay (Gould 2012) have found their way into Chapter 5. I am grateful to Cambridge University Press for permission to reprint that material.

Earlier versions of various chapters have been presented at a number of venues. These include a workshop on Political Liberalism and Postcolonial Africa in Berder, France, in May 2009, convened by Terence Halliday; an Anthropology Department Seminar at the University of North Carolina, in May 2012, convened by Arturo Escobar; a workshop on Political Culture in Africa – The Narrative Foundations of Authority and Leadership, held in Point Sud, Bamako, Mali, in October 2014, convened by Elísio Macamo and Georg Klute; a Community Law Centre seminar in discussion with Lukas Muntingh at the University of the Western Cape, in May 2015; an African Studies Seminar at the University of Cape Town, in May 2015, convened by Grasian Mkodzongi; a workshop on Africa as a New Frontier? Lawyers, Extractive Economies and Global Reconfigurations of Political Authority, at Goethe University Frankfurt/Main, in June 2016, convened by Sara Dezalay; a panel on The Role of Methodology in Socio-legal Studies, at the Law Society Association Annual Meeting in D.F., Mexico, in June 2017; an EASA Lawnet workshop in Helsinki, in May 2019, convened by Reetta

Toivonen, Miia Halme-Tuomisaari and Jane Cowan; a University of Helsinki Anthropology Department Brown Bag Lunch in October 2018, convened by Anni Kajanus; and a Helsinki Socio-Legal Initiative webinar, in April 2021, convened by Panu Minkkinen. Many thanks to convenors and participants for their critical support.

I owe sincere gratitude to my many colleagues in the departments of anthropology and development studies at the University of Helsinki, and in the Faculty of Social Sciences and the Humanities at the University of Jyväskylä. Thanks also to Eeva-Maija Henriksson at the University of Helsinki library, and to the specialist librarians at the African Studies Center in Leiden and at the Nordic Africa Institute in Uppsala, the unsung heroes of my scholarly struggles.

During fieldwork in Lusaka, I benefited at critical junctures from the support of the staff of the Embassy of Finland, and from employees of the now defunct Finnish Service Centre for Development (Kepa). Colleagues at the University of Zambia were immensely generous with their time, among them Jotham Momba, Bizeck Phiri, Chrispin Matenga and Derrick Elemu. The good graces of Ilse Mwanza and Marja Hinfelaar; of my dear friends Misael Kokwe, Ben Zimba and their families; and of my musical compatriots Maureen Lilanda and James Mumba elicit heartfelt appreciation. My deepest debt is to Päivi Takala, who put her life on hold for a year to come and kept me company in Lusaka. Natotela mukwai!

Discussions with the following colleagues have been formative for my thinking about postcolonial law and politics: Marisol de la Cadena, Ina Conradie, Sara Dezalay, Rachel Ellett, Harri Englund, Arturo Escobar, James Ferguson, Terence Halliday, Karen Tranberg Hansen, Saana Hansen, Miles Larmer, Vito Laterza, Elísio Macamo, Lalli Metsola, Panu Minkkinen, Greg Moore, Patience Mususa, Muna Ndulo, Franklin Obeng-Odoom, Liina-Maija Quist, Jothie Rajah, Chris Tapscott, Neo Simutanyi, Aili Tripp, Katja Uusihakala, Peter vonDoepp, Mariana Valverde, Fiona Wilson and Wolfgang Zeller – my sincere thanks to all. Saija Ohtonen and Noora Rikalainen shared in the joys and tribulations of fieldwork in Lusaka, and their insightful Masters theses (see Bibliography) have been an important source of inspiration. Daria Wadsworth and Daisy Charlesworth provided skillful and conscientious help in keeping track of my voluminous sources. Thank you.

Not least, I must also express my especial indebtedness to the following people who selflessly provided me with information and guidance during my fieldwork: James Banda (LAZ); the late Professor Alfred Chanda (University of Zambia); Chomba Chellah (Oasis Forum); Mark Chona (Oasis Forum, Task Force Against Corruption); Rodgers Chongwe, Beatrice Grillo (NGOCC); Professor Michelo Hansungule, Eva Jhala (National Assembly of Zamia); Wynter Kabimba (Patriotic Front); Valentine Kabonga (Zambia Institute for Advanced Legal Education); Mwangala Kamuwanga (Zambia Law Development Commission); Grace Kanyanga (NGOCC); Fr Joeseph Komakoma (Zambia Episcopal Conference); Reuben Lifuka (Transparency International Zambia); Fr Cleophas Lungu (Zambia Episcopal Conference); Fred M'membe (*Post* Newspaper); Mumba Malila (Zambia Human Rights Commission); Patrick Matibini (PatMat

Legal Practitioners, National Assembly of Zambia); Fr Ignatius Mbewe (Zambia Episcopal Conference); Nalukui Milapo (Oasis Forum); the late Dr Gilbert Mudenda, the late Mukelebai Mukelebai (Director of Public Prosecution); Palan Mulonda (Institute of Human Rights, Intellectual Property and Development); Christopher Mundia (LAZ); Fabian Muneku (LAZ); the late Wila Mung'omba (Mung'omba Constitutional Review Commission); Justice Philip Musonda (High Court of Zambia); Bishop Paul Mususu (Evangelical Fellowship of Zambia); Nellie Mutti (LAZ); Lucy Muyoyeta, (NGOCC); Professor Patrick Mvunga, William Mweemba (LAZ); Musa Mwenye (LAZ); Mutembo Nchito (Task Force Against Corruption, DPP); Dipak Patel, Justice Gregory Phiri (High Court of Zambia); John Sangwa (Legal Resources Foundation); Sakwiba Sikota, Caroline Sokoni (DPP); and Senior Chief Inyambo Yeta.

With humble apologies to the many people and places I have neglected to mention, rest assured that I am solely responsible for errors in the accounts and interpretations offered herein.

I

# Preliminary issues

# 1 Problems and paradoxes

This is a book about the complex intercourse of law and politics in Zambia's recent history. The book's main case studies, laid out in Chapters 4 through 10, suggest that the practices of Zambia's postcolonial legality entwine law and politics in complex and unorthodox ways.

Modern liberal democracies are predicated on respect for the rule of law. This principle implies that legal processes should be independent of political interference. Courts are expected to pass judgment purely on legal grounds – as prescribed in legislation, by constitutional provisions or, in common-law jurisdictions, based on judicial precedent. It is no secret, though, that in practice, law and politics are intimately entwined. Courts can be compliant with the perceived or explicit demands of political leaders; they can be sensitive to the political ethos of the moment (especially when judges and state attorneys are elected officials). At the same time, some judges are known for their activist mien, seeking to promote extra-juridical ends through rulings based on "transformative" readings of the law. I argue here that this variable interpenetration of legal and political agendas is not simply the effect of individual personalities and propensities; rather, there are structural factors at play rooted in Zambia's colonial history.

This study engages with only one limited domain within the legal realm – the specific field which concerns how the political and administrative power of the state is constituted and deployed. The law of state power is rooted in Zambia's republican constitution, core provisions of which concern the scope of presidential discretion. The legislative foundations of presidential discretion are slim, but these provisions reflect and sustain a particular culture of postcolonial legality, one which presumes, rather than spells out, the 'unfettered' character of governmental power. My aim is to provide an account of ideas, values and institutional practices anchored in this legal culture.

The *politics* under scrutiny here is also of a specific kind. Of immediate concern here are various forms of public co-action among Zambian citizens which seek to shape the constitutional powers of the president. For my purposes here, the exemplar of this sort of politics is represented by a non-partisan alliance of lawyers, clergy and activists called the Oasis Forum. It follows from this understanding of politics that my lens is trained less on the usual venues of political contestation – elections, parliamentary debates – and more on the sites that my

DOI: 10.4324/9780429198984-2

primary sources – priests, politicians, traditional leaders, activists, journalists and, above all, legal practitioners – have struggled to shape the trajectory of constitutional outcomes. The modes and sites of cooperation and contestation and the concepts and justifications that these actors characteristically deploy are central to this account. As a result, the empirical case analyses at the heart of my discourse involve issues, settings and debates which strictly legal analyses conventionally eschew. This approach obliges me to try and think outside of many conventional boxes. In this, I find inspiration in the words of Nobel laureate Sir Arthur Lewis, who wrote (1965, 16) '[p]olitical writing is full of stereotypes which have to be cleared from one's thoughts if one is to make progress in studying particular cases.'

The operational term that encompasses this conjuncture of law and politics is *constitutionalism.* Here, constitutionalism is neither a legal theory nor a political program, but the site of politico-legal contestation about the ways that Zambians wish to be governed. Every historical state has a constitution, even if that constitution is comprised of only one rule: the unlimited power of *Rex*, the ruler (Waluchow 2018). Proponents of political liberalism, descended from 18th-century legal philosopher Montesquieu, generally see constitutionalism as a defense of the idea that 'government can/should be limited in its powers and that its authority depends on its observing these limitations' (ibid.). From this perspective, 'unless we think that somebody needs protection against somebody else, there is no point in being concerned with constitutionalism' (Sartori 1962, note 10). In many situations, however, constitutionalism is invoked to defend the powers that liberalism seeks to constrain. The juxtaposition between unfettered and limited governmental power is especially prevalent in postcolonial Africa. It is, one could say, the specific dilemma of postcolonial constitutionalism. This dilemma derives from an essential historical paradox: Colonial legislation laid the legal foundations of Africa's independent nations, but at the same time colonial constitutions were predicated on the legitimacy of the absolute subjectification of its non-White subjects. Contemporary rulers embody this paradox – the African nation is presumed to be governable only under the auspices of what I will term an "Imperial" form of power with the potential to suspend liberal legality. The dispute at the heart of postcolonial constitutionalism thus involves the nature of the norms that should define the social relations of government and, most particularly, the role of 'the people' vis-à-vis government, in the independent era.

My concern with constitutionalism in this study is not driven so much by a desire to test a philosophical premise about legitimate power, but by the need to make sense of first-hand empirical observations. This is an ethnography of constitutionalism which implies documenting the dynamics of an *empirical* arena of discursive contestation at a particular time and place (Zambia's capital city of Lusaka, during the reign of President Levy Mwanawasa), about how the power to govern is constituted, distributed and deployed. The first years of this millennium saw an intense and prolonged tug-of-war between the Oasis Forum and the Zambian government of the day, embodied in two consecutive presidents of the

Movement for Multiparty Democracy (MMD): Frederick Chiluba (1991–2001) and Levy Mwanawasa (2001–8). In the course of these struggles, the notion of *constitutionalism* emerged as a site and object of politico-legal contestation involving key players of Zambian political society. Both parties to the contestation, the MMD government and the non-partisan Oasis Forum (and its various constituencies in so-called civil society), felt entitled to define the parameters of the constitutionally enshrined ideals and procedures by which the nation should be governed. To simplify somewhat, the government promoted the view that constitutionalism implies respect for an order in which virtually limitless discretion is vested in the president. The Oasis Forum, for its part, insisted that the prevailing constitution harbored undemocratic residues of the one-party state of Zambia's Second Republic under President Kenneth Kaunda and his United National Independence Party (1973–91), and required fundamental reframing. These divergent understandings of constitutionalism played out in a drawn-out process of constitutional reform which began with the appointment of a Constitution Review Commission in 2003 and concluded, at least for the time being, with the Constitution of Zambia (Amendment) Act of 2016.

This long decade of constitution-making spawned a number of subsidiary skirmishes in which the parameters of constitutionalism were tried and tested. Careful analysis of these incidents has provided an opportunity to learn how constitutionalism shapes the interaction of law and politics in real life. The most important of these incidents involves the indictment of Frederick Chiluba for abuse of office, the establishment of a Task Force against Corruption to investigate and prosecute the former president, and the two trials (one in Lusaka and one in London) in which the charges against him were weighed. Another fertile area for examining real-life constitutionalism resides in a series of presidentially appointed tribunals to investigate high-profile legal actors. A third arena where the politics of constitutionalism come into focus is in the workings of the newly established Constitutional Court. These various politico-legal contestations over the substance of constitutionalism provide the grist for this book's analysis.

In recounting these skirmishes, *Postcolonial Legality* seeks to tell a critical story about the fleeting past in order to provoke reflection about the future. The main question the book poses is: What sort of democracy do Zambians want their children and grandchildren to inherit? Is it a democracy that truly lives up to the constitution's promise that 'sovereign authority vests in the people of Zambia,'[1] one in which the welfare of all Zambians constitutes the government's first priority – no matter where they live, what language they speak, how they make a living or how wealthy they are, and irrespective of gender, age, education or physical abilities? Or, conversely, will Zambians continue to abide by a politico-legal order that privileges autocratic discretion, reserves the fruits of land and labor for the few and leaves it to the marginalized many to bear the costs of climate change, elite malfeasance and unfettered globalization?

1 Constitution of Zambia (Amendment) Act 2016, §5.

## Problems

Despite decades of scholarly inquiry, the character of governmental power in postcolonial democracies remains an enigma.[2] Postcolonial jurisdictions invoke the will of the people to shore up their legitimacy, govern through procedures and practices that remain largely invisible to the citizenry at large and then systematically constrain opportunities for 'the people' to express their views on the form of power that governs them. This ambivalence toward empowering the *demos* to shape and contain sovereign state power is so pervasive among postcolonial elites that it often entraps even the staunchest champions of liberal constitutionalism.

The thematic focus of this study is the growing impact of statutory legal institutions on how political power is constituted and deployed. The time frame highlights the Third Republic (1991 to present) but draws on older sources as well. Academically, it contributes to an ongoing critique of a paradigm, described aptly by Nic Cheeseman (2018a), of Africa as an 'institutionless' continent. The foregrounding of judicial acts in the current study aligns with Cheeseman's view (ibid., 4) that 'it is no longer possible – if it ever was – to understand Africa without factoring in the role played by constitutions, judiciaries, electoral systems and the like.' This book is not, however, a simple celebration of formal rules and rule-making, but argues that the rules themselves – even those framed by ostensibly modern, liberal jurisprudence – can be deeply problematic. This may seem counterintuitive: As already noted, Zambia's recent political history has exhibited several peaceful transitions of power at the polls. In the case of Frederick Chiluba, political society as a whole, encompassing elected representatives and non-partisan civic leaders, acted to constrain the president's unconstitutional political ambitions. It is tempting to argue that Zambia offers a counter-paradigmatic example of a society evincing effective institutional checks and balances on presidential power (ibid., 17). The evidence, however, suggests something different.

Zambia is a constitutional democracy. The constitution provides for freedom of expression and assembly, a multiparty electoral system, a professional and nominally autonomous judiciary and so on. Over the past 30 years, Zambia has seen three relatively smooth and orderly changes in the ruling party. Successive generations of elected leaders have maintained overall peace and stability among the nation's diverging economic classes and 80-odd language groups. If Westerners know little about the country, it is because Zambia has avoided the strife and conflict that too often propels African nations into mass media headlines.

And yet ... Ask a Zambian in the street and she will tell you that all is not well. This, she will say, is because *they* are running the country for *their* own benefit, at the expense of 'the people.' Who *they* are is not a mystery. Zambia is near the top of the list of countries with the highest level of inequality among its citizens. The

2 Cheeseman (2018a) provides a meticulous overview of these debates over the past 60 years; see also Chapter 3.

richest 10% of the population controls 50% of the wealth, while the poorer half of Zambian households account for a mere 6% of the economy's aggregate income (Bhorat et al. 2017, 33). An extended run of robust growth between 1998 and 2010 lifted Zambia into the global club of 'lower-middle income economies,' and yet 'gains from growth were largely captured by a growing class of high-skilled formal workers, leaving few rewards for both the urban and rural poor' (ibid., 6). In other words, despite the economy's upward bump, the structural injustice of skewed asset distribution has persisted, and may even have become sharper.

The years since the demise of Zambia's single-party dispensation in 1991 have seen the emergence of a prosperous elite, an urban upper crust far removed from the rural austerity of their parents' and grandparents' generations. One influential segment of those thriving in the neoliberal economic order is a motley class of well-educated professionals whose actions and interests shape the way the nation is governed. In many ways, lawyers[3] epitomize this group, and while their influence is inevitably subsidiary to that of the ministers and the presidents they inevitably serve, it is nonetheless substantial.

The lawyers who feature in this study are men and women whose support, compliance, manipulations and acts of resistance animate the politico-legal domain. They are players whose personal and professional fortunes are, in many ways, contingent upon the continuity and stability of state power. The growing prominence of courts, judges and lawyers in sustaining the prevailing form of power has increasingly eroded the autonomy liberal theory envisions between law and politics. Struggles over the meanings of constitutionalism are central to this blurring of the legal and political spheres. As the University of Zambia (UNZA) law don Carlson Anyangwe (1997, 25) observes, the constitution is not simply law; it is 'a politico-legal document.' Nowhere is this intermingling of politics and legality more evident than in the prescription of presidential powers. Central to this domain, as we will see, is the legal apparatus responsible for maintaining presidential power itself. Judging by the empirical record (Chapters 5 and 6), Zambia's presidents have seen constitution-making – a politico-legal act par excellence – as critical to preserving their discretionary prerogatives. This explains, I hope, why what began as an ethnography of constitution-making evolved into an attempt at theorizing the political contours of postcolonial legality, and its concomitant form of power.

Lawyers were largely mute bystanders to the consolidation of political legality in the Second Republic. That said, a tension simmered between the liberal legalism of the lawyers trained in the common-law tradition, and the "prerogativist" (see below) conventions of the politico-legal domain.[4] This tension burst into the

3 Unless context clearly indicates otherwise, I use the term 'lawyers' to refer to anyone with formal legal training, including judges, state officials and private practitioners.

4 This was evident, for example, by the role of rising lawyers Edward Shamwana and Pierce Annfield in the 1980 coup attempt against the Kaunda government. John Mwanakatwe (2003, 311–52) provides a detailed account of the coup trial from a defense lawyer's perspective.

public realm as a full-blown contradiction with the demise of the one-party state in 1991. Fueled by the mushrooming of lucrative conveyancing work connected to the dismantling and privatization of the parastatal sector, and by the concomitant emancipation of the legal profession from reliance on state contracts, a stratum of ambitious lawyers was newly untethered from the endorsement of the ruling party. It was these developments, discussed in Chapter 6, which saw the emergence of a segment of the legal profession as a class *for* itself with interests distinct from those of the ruling party. This shift in the self-awareness of the legal elite has important implications for our narrative; it precipitated a paradox within the politico-legal domain, the effects of which continue to play out in both law and politics.

By virtue of their direct stewardship over the constitutional rules governing the deployment of state power, the legal profession is a pivotal overseer of the status quo. Legal professionals, while nominally dedicated to all-inclusive justice, serve as gatekeepers of a politico-legal order predicated on a deep social gulf between the haves and the have-nots. In order to understand the source and mechanisms of this conundrum, this study seeks to illuminate the ways a particular culture of legalism (Shklar 1964) has colonized elite political strategies in postcolonial Zambia. The role of Zambia's trained legal experts in contestations over the meaning of constitutionalism has not been studied before and is thus the central focus of this study.[5]

## *Sources and resources*

The intellectual resources I bring to this analysis are not those of the legal historian, much less those of an academic lawyer (I am neither), but rather those of a politico-legal anthropologist interested in what Upendra Baxi (2013, 43) has termed the ethnography of constitutionalism. In a wider sense, this study falls within what Paul Blokker and Chris Thornhill (2017, 6; original emphasis) have recently called 'a *constitutional turn* in sociology and of a *sociological turn* in constitutionalism.' From their perspective, 'both sociology as a whole and constitutional law as a whole are increasingly shaped by reciprocal interest and cross-fertilization.'[6] What a sociological perspective means for this study is that I am less interested in constitutionalism in terms of its underlying jurisprudence (philosophy of law) than in the political means and ends that drive different actors' interaction in the process, and in the political outcomes of these elite struggles. In other words, then, this book examines a particularly volatile politico-legal zone where the 'judicialization of politics' (Hirschl 2008) and the 'politicization of law' (i.e., Klug 2021) are virtually indistinguishable.

This book represents an extended case study (Burawoy 1998). In it, I privilege empirical depth over geographic breadth. Attempting the systematic study

5 For an overview of the emerging scholarship on African lawyers, see Chapter 3.

6 While political sociology has shaped my theoretical perspective, my primary methodological tools are ethnographic. I give an account of my research strategy in Chapter 3.

of comparable constitution-making processes in other Anglophone African jurisdictions has been tempting but beyond my means. Instead, I have tried to map the networks of ideas, values and social relations engendered by the fraught politics of Zambian constitutionalism in all their complexity. No single case can represent the myriad ways by which postcolonial power is constituted and executed. Indeed, each constitution, and each governmental apparatus, is unique. While constitutional liberalism implies a set of general tenets, noted above, all of these principles find empirical expression within singular contexts.

Ethnography is the social scientific methodology best attuned to context, and the data undergirding this inquiry is ethnographic, based on first-hand observation and extended immersion in the flow of daily engagements between the constitutional activists and the government of the day during the Mwanawasa presidency. The bulk of the material analyzed in subsequent chapters revolves around events and personalities connected with the Oasis Forum. The Forum has only been the starting point, however, for a research strategy that has pursued the trajectories of these events and agents into other corners of the politico-legal domain. The interpretation of this ethnographic data (supplemented by an extensive archive of secondary sources) has required detachment from first-hand, everyday observation and recourse to more abstract conceptualization in order to flesh out the patterns and lacunae in my case materials.

To grasp continuities and shifts in context, it has also been necessary to think structurally and historically. The emphasis on *structure* implies that the role that lawyers play in defending the status quo is less a matter of personal choice than an effect of governmental design. Indeed, the study shows how the preponderant weight of Zambia's politico-legal culture often overrides individual agency. It is, in any event, rare for trained legal professionals to step outside their designated institutional roles to reflect on the political effects of the juridical apparatus as a whole. It is naturally the main concern of responsible lawyers whether the 'rule of law' is operating, not whether these operations have unintended, or potentially nefarious consequences. Tracing these effects is a task for a detached scholar.

The design of governmental institutions, and the ways that power is distributed – legally by the constitution and practically by complex human actors – is a deeply rooted *historical* fact. I take as given that the power embodied in republican rulers – like the politico-legal mechanisms that bind rulers and ruled together – has a deep and partially buried history. Institutional design evolves slowly, and past configurations of power (along with the concomitant ideas and values that have given them the semblance of inevitability) leave lasting traces in subsequent state formations. In particular, my analysis suggests that the *form* that power takes – its corporal manifestations, and the privileges that accrue to a leader by virtue of this embodiment of power – is singularly stable. Even revolutionary upheaval may fail to wholly exorcise core aspects of an entrenched form of power. In the case of Zambia, as I will argue, perceiving the continuities that survived emancipation from colonial domination via postcolonial law is paramount to understanding the present.

The coherence of the narrative I have constructed about struggles over Zambian constitutionalism relies on a set of conceptual innovations. At the core is the notion of the *politico-legal domain* which, I argue, has been colonized by an imperial *form of power* (termed here *prerogativism*). This form of power is evident in acts of *political legality*, i.e., routine practices of 'lawful illegalities' at the core of state power.[7] Postcolonial power, of course, has other effects as well; however, routine acts of African statecraft are not the focus of this analysis (but see Bierschenk & Olivier de Sardan 2014). I believe that these tools belong to an as yet to be assembled framework for better understanding the ongoing transformations within postcolonial democracies bearing the legacy of British imperialism.

What these concepts reveal has naturally been shaped by the 'detached' observer's affective and intellectual calibrations. In most work on African politics, liberal ideals provide the filter, the vocabulary and the normative ordering that frame the analysis. In other words, political studies of contemporary African realities are routinely guided by the expectation that postcolonial democracies *should* emulate an idealized model of political liberalism (cf. Halliday et al. 2012). As my work progressed, I realized that the Oasis Forum activists invoked this very same normative template, highlighting a liberal understanding of the rule of law and the constitutionalism of presidential constraint, to justify their own political strategies. The overlapping of labels used by analysts and the objects of analytical scrutiny made me increasingly uneasy – I was trained to seek critical distance between explanation and what was to be explained. This uneasiness deepened as I reflected on the role that liberal activists played in sustaining the status quo. I understood that I had initially seen my task as one of documenting the unprecedented emergence of a progressive strain of legal activism in postcolonial Zambia, and that story is indeed central to the analysis in Chapter 6. As the constitution-making process dragged on, and as I dug deeper into proximate patches of the politico-legal domain, I realized that contestations over constitutionalism were more complicated than a struggle between progressive and reactionary politics. Beneath the tug-of-war between assertive lawyers (and their allies) and a defensive political class was an issue that neither party articulated. This was the problem of prerogativism – the status of unfettered power in a constitutional democracy.

## Paradoxes

### *Politico-legal paradoxes*

The dual conundrum of unfettered democratic power and of illiberal liberalism constitutes Zambia's *politico-legal domain.* This domain is not a formal institution of government or an organized body. It is an analytical abstraction, useful inasmuch as it helps reveal the source and dynamics of such contradictions.

7 The term 'lawfully illegal' was used by former President Frederick Chiluba to defend his actions when under prosecution for abuse of office (see Chapter 7).

As understood here, the politico-legal domain is an immaterial assemblage of relationships and effects, constituted and bound together by the cultural dispositions and conventions of political and legal actors. The politico-legal domain comes into view through the scrutiny of acts of power – by presidents, government ministers and judges – in which the law and politics of power interact. These acts, and the conventions that make them possible, are real, empirical facts, but a theoretical construct is required to render their inter-related character visible and open to systematic analysis. Changes in the constitution can alter the culture of the politico-legal domain, but its overall transformation cannot be legislated. Changing politico-legal conventions depends upon shifts in the incentives that guide the work of politicians, lawyers and significant shapers of public opinion. Transformations in the conventions of the politico-legal domain involve maneuvers very different from those of statutory constitution-making. However, such changes do happen, both spontaneously and due to the purposeful actions of influential jurists and politicians.

History, again, is the key to understanding the ways the contradictory conventions of the politico-legal domain evolve. The contours of the politico-legal domain were cast under the auspices of colonial government, when legal dictates faced no overt political challenges. This situation continued under independent Zambia's first president, Kenneth David Kaunda (1924–2021), who assumed the presidency with a state of emergency already in force. This state of exception then persisted for the 27 years of Kaunda's incumbency, amplifying the president's already extensive powers to derogate basic civil rights in the name of national security (Parker 1980). Kaunda further subordinated the legal to the political with the constitutional reforms of 1973, which outlawed political competition and, in effect, rendered the judiciary an extension of 'the Party and its Government' in matters of state administration.

Kaunda's legacy weighs heavily on the politico-legal domain; the implicit conventions of the politico-legal domain have a self-perpetuating character. Yet, they are not immutable. Their transformation may be possible, but elite rallying around demands for rule of law or for more accountable governance will not in itself hasten change. Rather, fundamental change requires a radical shift in the structure of incentives driving the practices and actions of political and legal actors. Above all, it demands profound changes in the status of the *demos* in the government of the nation. Zambia has yet to experience such a radical transformation. The three main obstacles to such a transformation are the paradoxes of the presidency, of the constitution in which presidential powers are anchored and of the ideology of imperial liberalism that frames the instantiation of power.

## *Paradoxes of liberalism*

European colonialism and the emergence of the ideology of liberal government are in effect two sides of a single historical process (Losurdo 2011). As historian Dipesh Chakrabarty (2000), among others, has shown, the development of modern social science is also an integral part of this history. The self-serving coincidence of imperial exploitation, state formation and conceptual history is reflected in the ways that contemporary theories of 'the state' and 'political power' cloak the localized experiences of Euro-American jurisdictions in the guise of universal theoretical constructs. Indeed, the persistent tendency of contemporary political theory to view non-Western forms of government as not yet arrived versions of modern liberal democracies continues to express the epistemic habits of European empire.

Historian Partha Chatterjee (1993, 5) enunciates the consequences of these epistemic habits for the ways non-Western politics are conceived:

> Europe and the Americas, the only true subjects of history, have thought out on our behalf not only the script of colonial enlightenment and exploitation, but also that of our anticolonial resistance and postcolonial misery. Even our imaginations must remain forever colonized.

Few dispute that colonialism had a significant impact on postcolonial state formation. Although, as Crawford Young (1994, 283) once noted "we commonly describe the independent polities [in Africa] as 'new states,' in reality they were successors to the colonial regime, inheriting its structure, its quotidian routines and practices, and its more hidden normative theories of governance." How then to acknowledge these continuities while at the same time respecting the agency of the subsequent stewards of independent postcolonial states?

To be clear, it is *not* my claim that the political imaginations of the postcolonial world are defined in their totality by the colonial experience. By the same token, it is *not* the case that Zambia's colonial legacy has pre-empted the political creativity of Zambian leaders, politicians, lawyers, intellectuals and activists. One might fruitfully relate the story of Africa's relationship to the colonial past as one which highlights the autonomy and ingenuity of African leaders and their constituencies. My focus here, however, is on persisting continuities between colonialism and contemporary trends in the constitution of power. The reason for this choice of perspective is not to bind Zambia to an irrevocable legacy. On the contrary, highlighting the persistent impact of empire on the politico-legal domain aims at exorcising the tenacious spirits of the colonial past by bringing them into the light of day.

Colonial rule, as is well known, was an order of sanctimonious hypocrisy, humiliation and violence. Colonial government was premised on the denial of basic human dignity to non-White African subjects. It worked through a web of power woven around a scaffolding of racist deceits and of capitalist, as well as quasi-feudal, exploitation. Africans across the continent fought bloody wars of liberation from the inhumanity of colonial rule. In light of these facts, how, then, can one claim that Zambia's postcolonial leaders, the contemporary heirs to the freedom fighters, have perpetrated the legacy of colonialism?

This is not a trite concern. How one approaches the legitimacy of a constitutional order has a strong political dimension. This is what makes the liberal frame of reference so problematic. As legal scholar Makau Mutua (2008, 19) declares, 'with an alarming frequency, liberalism's key tenets have been deployed to advance narrow, sectarian, hateful, and exclusionary practices and ideas.' The liberal framing of the postcolonial state is steeped in what Gayatri Spivak (1988, 282) termed epistemic violence, i.e., the suppression of the knowledge of marginalized or 'subaltern' subjects. It also does nothing to assuage the frustration of many critics, channeled by Ndlovu-Gatsheni (2013, viii), that stems from 'the continued use of imported Euro-American ideas and institutions in Africa.' Liberal scholarship thus fails to respond constructively to those who 'have unanimously called for the reconstitution and reconstruction of African postcolonial states on the basis of African history, African knowledge and African positive values if these states are to be considered legitimate and to serve their African constituency fully' (ibid.). Rather the contrary. All of this, of course, is a sobering censure for any metropolitan scholar of postcolonial politics, myself included, and clearly defines what is at stake when discussing the imperial legacy of postcolonial law.

Ndlovu-Gatsheni's frustration is both intellectual and political. His critical insights, however, do not offer a clear alternative to the distorted solutions offered by political liberalism – neither as an analytical perspective nor as a practical model of government. Well before Paulin Hountondji (1970) launched his critique of colonial ethno-philosophy, scholars had attempted to rethink how a postcolonial order might better accommodate autochthonous aspirations and identities in Africa (e.g., Deng 2008; cf. Hessebon 2013). Such projects are aesthetically compelling, but their translation into practical politics within established (post) colonial boundaries is difficult, and can be tragically divisive. Despite eloquent celebrations of *ubuntu*, a political philosophy extolling indigenous African values (e.g., Ramose 1999), a jurisprudence based on African autochthony has found little resonance in recent constitution-making processes. Designing practical political alternatives would require, as Ndlovu-Gatsheni suggests,

> a thorough knowledge of the operations of the present-day colonial matrix of power that made it impossible for decolonization to be carried to its logical conclusion of creating a new Africa imbued with new humanism and inhabited by truly free and liberated African people. (op cit., 6)

This study seeks to contribute to the decolonization of debates about constitutional design along these lines. That said, I think it is fair to say that the articulation of an alternative framework for a post-liberal constitutionalism (e.g., Arditi 2008) is still a work in progress.

Since the early years of the 20th century, liberalism has long generated intellectual and political controversy; I review some of the debates in Chapter 3. These debates have gained momentum in the new millennium via the resurgence of challenges to principles of political liberalism. Challenges not only from the Right (a resurgence of blatantly autocratic politics in established liberal democracies like the United States, Hungary and Poland), but also from the Left (in several South American countries), where myriad social movements call for greater space for popular participation in government by excluded groups (the indigenous, the poor, the invisible), and for commensurate changes to their republican constitutions. Tellingly, the Left and the Right critiques of liberalism both tend to endorse enhanced and discretionary executive powers. I will argue that there is a fundamental methodological flaw inherent in the conflation of an analytical frame with an ideological mindset. The predisposition of scholars to side with self-proclaimed liberal constitutionalists has led academics to underplay the coloniality of liberalism and, by extension, to ignore the traces of imperial law in postcolonial politics. These themes are clearly evident in my Zambian materials, and also have broader resonance across Africa and elsewhere.

These paradoxes of Zambia's ostensibly illiberal liberal constitutionalism suggest that the notion of liberalism itself has an enigmatic quality, and needs to be dismantled and scrutinized as an assemblage of mutually contradictory elements.[8] Quite clearly, the principles of liberal constitutionalism have different meanings, and are mobilized differently by different actors. Liberal constitutionalism, as we will see, is the fallback ideology of social forces invested in state stability, regardless of their commitment to democratic principles. Constitutionalism (like the kindred slogan of 'law and order') is a particularly compelling agenda in situations where state stability is threatened by the mobilizations of marginalized social forces.

In the West, liberal rhetoric has been historically associated with movements opposed to arbitrary, autocratic rule; its banners of freedom and equality suggest an emancipatory political agenda. One can argue that this is true of Zambia in the first decade of the Third Republic when liberal constitutionalism became a rallying point for elite groups freed from the autocratic dictates of the one-party state. The scrutiny of the politics of constitution-making during that period thus begs the question, posed by Portuguese socio-legal scholar Boaventura de Sousa Santos (2002, 439), 'Can law be emancipatory?' In his meticulous analysis, Santos notes that the question of the emancipatory potential of law can be traced to a very specific historical context. It initially emerged in the struggle of the rising European merchant classes for a regulatory order that would protect their trade from arbitrary taxation by the aristocracy. That

8 A number of authors (e.g., Phiri 2006, Macola 2010, Larmer 2011) have argued for the importance of a liberal tradition in Zambian politics. Reviewing some of this literature, Harri Englund (2013, 673) identifies an antiauthoritarian impetus behind this scholarship and asks whether such sensibilities provide 'reliable guides to what the liberal values of freedom and equality might mean under Zambia's historical conditions.'

As we will see, versions of liberalism have been a significant element in the design of Zambia's politico-legal order; imperial liberalism, in particular, has been a persistent pillar of Zambia's several constitutions. But this is not the liberal tradition that these political historians are invoking. Rather, they suggest that genuine ideals of equality and freedom stood in insistent opposition to both colonial rule and the one-party state. There may well have been elements of this in the colonial-era Capricorn Society (Phiri 2006, chapter 3) or in Harry Nkumbula's African National Congress (ANC) (Macola 2010, 73–94), but a platform of political liberalism in this sense has not defined the constitution or the deployment of state power at any stage of Zambia's history.

scenario differs fundamentally from the context framing constitution-making in postcolonial Zambia. As we will see, liberal constitutionalism provided the basis for an unprecedented alliance between lawyers (who see professional benefits in the rule of law), anti-patriarchal feminist activists (inspired by liberalism's enmity toward discrimination) and a liberationist clergy; the aims of this alliance (the Oasis Forum; see Chapter 6) had nothing to do with freeing up the market for capitalist consolidation.

What then made this unlikely coalition of elite Zambian professionals rally around liberal constitutionalism? How did they find themselves enmeshed in fraught political contestation with leaders with whom they share, to no small degree, very similar socioeconomic and cultural backgrounds and who, for the most part, also pay lip service to principles of political liberalism? Santos suggests that contemporary struggles for emancipatory law in the Global South, of which the saga of the Oasis Forum is arguably an exemplar, relate to meta-trends on a planetary scale. As Santos puts it (ibid., 445),

> neo-liberal hegemonic globalization has advanced a political and legal paradigm that is global in scope. Inspired by a highly selective view of the Western [liberal] tradition, it is being imposed throughout the world system. This means that the question of the relationship between law and social emancipation [i.e., politics], albeit historically a Western one, may now become a global question – one that fits in the political and scientific agenda of both Western and non-Western countries

Central to this process is the way in which 'the highly politicized tension between social regulation and social emancipation' is being supplanted by 'a depoliticized conception of social change whose sole criterion is the rule of law and judicial adjudication by an honest, independent, predictable and efficient judiciary' (ibid.).

Santos' remarks on the depoliticization of liberal constitutionalism will be good to keep in mind when considering the kinds of political strategy that the Oasis Forum adopts in its struggles with the president (Chapter 6). In Zambia's case, postcolonial liberalism has indeed been a successful resource for legitimizing a certain form of governmental power. The constitution provides rulers with a repertoire of governmental tools. It creates an apparatus for the exercise of power, as well as for the constitution of subjects to that power, while also providing institutional tools with which to rule: taxation, policing, adjudication. The constitution embodies the idea of national unity, and poses virtually no limits on the ways state power can be deployed to ensure that unity, or to repel any threats, real or perceived, to national security – a notion which is defined in only the vaguest of terms. What this suggests is that while constitutionalism appears attractive as a tool to resist autocracy, it has also proved useful in enabling Zambia's (often autocratic) political leaders to consolidate their power.

The challenges of governing a young nation economically gutted by colonial exploitation and systemically disadvantaged in its dealings with the global capitalist order are immense. The job of the president, while coveted and not without substantial rewards, cannot be easy. Is it, then, justified that leaders entrusted with resolving these challenges not be unduly constrained by the details of statutory law? Is it not reasonable to ask what kinds of political privileges are adequate, or necessary, to ensure that leaders' can protect the welfare of their democratic subjects? More cogent still is the question of the ends to which these powers are exercised. Zambia's inherited constitutional framework and its concomitant governmental infrastructure – line ministries; a judiciary; intelligence, security and law enforcement agencies – have served the long-term stability of Zambia as a nation with considerable success. Whether these same politico-legal resources have also served the task of building an inclusive, equitable and just democracy is at best debatable.

## *Presidential paradoxes*

Zambia's politico-legal order has been fundamentally shaped by its roots in British imperial government. As is well known, British imperial rule over Northern Rhodesia (as Zambia was then known) from 1924 to 1964, was designed to maximize the exploitation of the territory's natural resources – above all copper – and the labor of the colony's indigenous population (i.e., Rotberg 1966). It is less well understood that colonial rule was an embattled form of government, predicated on the basic need to protect the lives and interests of a small White population in the face of a disenfranchised, and largely hostile Black majority. At the same time – and this similarly under-acknowledged fact is crucial – colonial government was a constitutional order grounded in an ideology of imperial liberalism (e.g., Pitt 2005). Colonial power was beholden, at least rhetorically, to the liberal values of good governance and the rule of law. This fundamental contradiction – the tension between liberalism and violence, and between lawfulness and existential political insecurity – found expression in the institution of the colonial governor, an office mandated to exercise unfettered power in defense of an embattled minority on behalf of the Imperial Crown.[9] Governors were civil servants appointed by the Crown. This imperial form of power – a liberal façade enfolding the potential for harsh racist violence – was a core facet of the imperial constitutional order, and was passed on via the independence constitution of 1964, to Zambia's newly minted presidency (see Chapter 5).

Ghanaian legal scholar Kwasi Prempeh (2008, 809–10) has argued that the 'Imperial' presidencies of the postcolonial era were 'purposefully and systematically constructed at the dawn of African independence by Africa's nationalist elites to answer certain specific regime needs at the time.' Indeed, an imperial form of power was sustained across the continent by a generation of nationalist leaders. Rather than abandon the absolutist trappings of the colonial executive, it was more useful to test and refine them. It was, in any case, far easier to mobilize

9 I return to these arguments in Chapter 2.

opposition to colonial injustice than to assemble political consensus concerning how to reconstruct the politico-legal scaffolding of the state. The colonial legacy persisted, to no small degree, because the exceptional powers of the imperial presidency were well-aligned with the new nationalist leaders' political aspirations, as well as the needs of the former colonial powers.

These leaders, like Zambia's founding president Kenneth Kaunda and his cohort of like-minded nationalist sovereigns (Kwame Nkrumah of Ghana, Julius Nyerere of Tanzania, Jomo Kenyatta of Kenya), willingly and creatively embodied and deployed the 'exceptional' forms of sovereign power that were encoded in colonial constitutions. They also worked diligently to domesticate them in ways that were ideologically more palatable to their anti-colonial sensibilities and constituencies. The philosophies of Consciencism (Nkrumah), Ujamaa (Nyerere), Harambee (Kenyatta) and Humanism (Kaunda) all sought to remake the postcolonial world into a domain of dignity and justice for African peoples, and thus distinguish the anti-colonialism of the nationalist movements from the racism upon which imperial liberalism was founded. That said, colonial forms of power were retained in the new republican constitutions and, in Kaunda's case, assertively mobilized in defense of his independent regime.[10]

The illiberalism of African government is most commonly linked to the unbridled powers of the postcolonial president, relatively immune to the 'checks and balances' imposed by a vigilant judiciary. As Prempeh (ibid., 829) has noted,

> even if judicial independence in contemporary Africa were secure, reliance on the judiciary to restrain presidential power would run into yet another problem. This is... a 'jurisprudence of executive supremacy' – a jurisprudence that is unduly deferential to executive power and, at best, skeptical of 'novel' claims rooted in modern conceptions of constitutionalism

Unfettered presidential discretion is enabled, then, by both explicit constitutional provisions and a tacit culture of deference. Discretion in the exercise of executive power is not, of course, a new phenomenon. Republican constitutions around the world include provisions for the removal from office of leaders deemed guilty of overstepping their statutory powers. While such mechanisms are rarely invoked, they signal the awareness among democratic citizens and legislators everywhere that no form of power is beyond abuse. At the same time, it is central to the republican tradition to routinely endow heads of state with a wide range of discretionary powers that evade both 'the written restraints of the Constitution and the unwritten restraints of the republican ethos' (Schlesinger 1973).[11]

10 Even before Zambia's official independence, then Prime Minister Kaunda called out the army to punish members of the Lumpa cult of Alice Regina Mulenga (better known as Alice Lenshina) who refused to demonstrate their loyalty to Kaunda's United National Independence Party (Mulenga 1998).

11 Historian and one-time White House advisor Arthur Schlesinger Jr was writing in the context of the constitutional crisis unleashed by US President Richard Nixon's Watergate scandal.

A paradox, then, is central to the essence of a liberal democratic order: This paradox is often seen as the dilemma of ensuring that 'a President is strong enough to protect the people's rights and liberties, but not so strong as to threaten them' (Chambers 1977, 21). In popular debates, this paradox is often cast as a trade-off between 'freedom' and 'security' (Dinh 2002). Political liberalism promises to ensure democratic subjects with both benefits in equal measure. In practice, however, real or alleged threats to a nation's security commonly trump concerns with citizens' liberties.

Prerogativism by which executive action is not effectively constrained by law poses a hard problem for the liberal mindset. Indeed, the political legality of postcolonial jurisdictions constrains liberal constraint. This is not a question so much of 'constitutions without constitutionalism' (Okot-Ogendo 1991) – Zambian prerogativism is indeed enshrined in law, and defended by a constitutionalist judiciary. The problem for liberal critique, rather, is that the culture of political legality rooted in a prerogativist form of power appears to distort the liberalism espoused by the constitution's principles and values. The premise underlying this perception is that prerogativism is a politico-legal flaw which can be redressed by greater respect for the rule of law, and/or by consolidating the provisions of liberal legality through democratic constitutional reform. These are mistaken premises; they may make sense within the universe of liberal theory, but in order to do so, they must bracket the historical legacy of imperial liberalism.

The premise of the state's political embattlement is not spelled out in the Zambian constitution. The illegitimacy of colonial occupation was repressed in imperial ideology, and obscured in legal documents via euphemistic references to the 'pleasure' of the Crown. Zambia's postcolonial constitutions express the principles and values of the republican order via promises of unity, equality and justice. By the same token, the most fundamental aspects of presidential power do not reside in explicit provisions of executive authority. Rather, they lie to some extent between the lines of the constitution, in the capacity of the president to step outside legal provisions, to derogate from black letter law. Since independence, Zambia has seen four comprehensive reviews of the constitution. All of these constitutional reviews have left the president's discretionary powers intact. Herein lies a crucial paradox of postcolonial power – the explicit constitutional provisions which create executive prerogative do not define its limits. Rather, explicit constitutional provisions create the possibility of an opaque realm of power, beyond democratic scrutiny, where absolute discretion reigns.

Unfettered power is nominally linked to the president's responsibility as the final authority in defense of national security. Concerns related to national security are invariably invoked when the contours of presidential powers are debated, as when the National Constitutional Conference (Republic of Zambia 2010, 404) contended that 'Zambia needed a strong President who would inspire confidence and a sense of security whenever problems beset the nation.' This sentiment echoed a long-standing tenet of Zambian political culture. Indeed, the government's response to the report of the first constitution review commission 40 years earlier acknowledged that 'Zambia has many enemies surrounding her and therefore the implementation of the One-Party Participatory Democracy as well as Humanism, together with the attendant problems, require a ***unified Command*** under an Executive President' (Republic of Zambia 1972, 4; emphasis added).

This notion of the necessity of a unified command, a direct residual of imperial jurisprudence, provides the conceptual and normative basis for the president's constitutional power to invoke a state of emergency, and to exercise exceptional powers, beyond those explicitly stipulated by law. The prerogative both constitutes and reflects a particular culture of government established under imperial rule – an epistemic habit of empire, so to speak – which deposits the capacity for legitimate yet illiberal violence in the body of the governor. There is nothing specifically African or Zambian about this predilection for autocracy. The postcolonial presidency is not a super-chief so much as a purposively modern instantiation, in quasi-democratic form, of imperial despotism.

The discretionary prerogatives of the Zambian president have been tenaciously sustained and protected in each of Zambia's five constitutions, and by the nation's highest courts, across two changes of regime and the tenures of six individual presidents.[12] Ex-President Chiluba's indictment in 2002 for abuse of office was a watershed event in the growing tensions within the politico-legal domain. Established conventions were increasingly under pressure, as at least some aspects of the president's discretionary powers no longer appeared sacrosanct. This shift in public perception reflected a growing tension within the politico-legal domain between a 'jurisprudence of executive righteousness' (Kaaba & Sambo 2020, 5) and ideals of liberal legalism. This contradiction was not new – indeed, I have argued that it is constitutive of the postcolonial order – but it has had an incremental effect on the relationship between law and politics in the management of public affairs.

Successive constitutional amendments since 1991 have introduced nominal limitations on presidential authority.[13] In practice, these provisions are more ritualistic than real. It is taken for granted, at all levels of Zambian society and throughout the politico-legal domain, that presidential authority will inevitably prevail. The unwritten conventions of postcolonial politics have made it inconceivable that the legislature or the judiciary would obstruct presidential intentions. This does not mean that presidents are immune to political strife. The tendency for Zambian leaders to turn to constitutional reform to resolve political crises does not rule out the seemingly contradictory fact that these crises, as will be shown, are often triggered by attempts to bracket, bend or abuse constitutional provisions.

12 There is, as yet, scant evidence of how prerogativist provisions will fare under the neoliberal presidency of Hakainde Hichilema, elected in 2021.

13 The 2016 constitution, for example, obliges the president to 'consult' with parliament, the speaker, one of the higher courts or another government agency (such as the judicial service commission) in connection with specific decisions, appointments or measures. In certain instances, a presidential appointee is subject to ratification by the National Assembly.

## *Paradoxes of constitutionalism*

Citizens rarely need to think about the provisions of their national constitutions. The rare exception is when political crises – impeachment proceedings or the failure to form a viable government – call the basic premises of the politico-legal order itself into question. In the contemporary world, most constitutions embody an ethos of republicanism, whereby elected representatives manage public affairs (Latin: *res publica*) on behalf of the population.[14] As Martin Loughlin (2003, 46) puts it '[C]onstitutionalism rests on the principle that constituent power resides in the people, who delegate a limited authority to government to promote the public good.'

Republican constitutions in today's world generally espouse a philosophy of political liberalism, characterized by the explicit acknowledgment of citizen's rights (to private property, freedom of expression, assembly, faith, etc.); the separation of powers between different branches of government (executive, legislative and judiciary); and respect for the rule of law. In the classical liberal canon, it is the task of a constitution not to overly constrain individual freedoms. In a republican order, the constitution creates the locus of representative power, such as a president or prime minister, which is assumed to both aggregate and transcend individual interests. Having created this transcendental locus of power, a liberal constitution must simultaneously constrain it. Liberal constitutionalists, in the tradition of John Rawls (1993), argue that this dual act of constituting and constraining power is achieved through political consensus. Jeremy Waldron (1987, 140), for example, claims that a liberal social and political order must be 'rooted in the consent of all those who have to live under it; the consent or agreement of these people is a condition of its being morally permissible to enforce that order upon them.'

A countervailing understanding of constitutionalism – termed agonist – denies the necessity, or even the possibility of political consensus. From this perspective (Sleat 2011, Mouffe 1993), constitutional legitimacy must cater to the fact of intrinsic conflict among citizens and subjects. Where liberals tend to take a legalist view of constitutions as fundamental law that, when enforced by a judiciary, lays 'the foundations of public order' (Loughlin 2003, 47), agonistic approaches see constitutions (and constitutionalism) as a means to political ends. It follows that the point of critical scholarship is not to seek the 'best' version of constitutionalism, but rather to examine how legal actors and their political allies evoke the constitution to justify their political strategies.

The Zambian constitution provides a template for the operations of the state. It defines where the power to govern resides, and how it may (or should not) be deployed (Ndulo & Kent 1996). The practices of Zambian constitutionalism examined here suggest that the liberal and agonist views are not mutually

14 Loughlin (ibid.) invokes Montesquieu's (1748) distinction between republicanism, monarchy and despotism. For Montesquieu, republicanism can take two forms: democracy ('when the people as a body possess sovereign power') and aristocracy ('when that power is held only by a portion of the people').

exclusive. As will be evident throughout this study, the Zambian constitution is used by different parties and at different times to advance both liberal ideals and political expediency. That said, the cases examined here indicate that recourse to legal means to resolve political disputes, i.e., what Hirschl (2008), among others, terms the judicialization of politics, appears to have steadily gained prominence in Zambia. This seems to be true in many other parts of Africa (Isanga 2016), and elsewhere.

Republicanism and political liberalism are variables, not absolutes; constitutions differ greatly in the ways political power and rights are defined and distributed. Mechanisms of political representation and accountability can fluctuate markedly from country to country, and even within a given jurisdiction.[15] The stability of a constitution's core provisions can also vary. This reflects the fact that, on the one hand, constitutions are commonly the outcome of political processes, involving a range of social actors (politicians, legal experts, pressure groups), and are embedded in political economies and legal cultures with specific histories (Elster 1995). On the other hand, constitutions can provide for the incremental reworking of the law on a case-by-case basis. This is true of Zambia's constitution, originally designed in the British common-law tradition (a legal culture disseminated across the planet as a fundamental pillar of British imperial government). The case-wise recasting of law occurs through judicial precedent or so-called judge-made law (Depoorter & Rubin 2017). In this tradition, a court ruling – especially one tested by appeal to a higher court – can alter the way a bit of law or legislation is understood. For the most part, constitutional orders change slowly – unless (or until) a revolution sweeps away one constitution and supplants it with a new one.

Amid apparent stability, the legal orders of some states can be the object of persistent dispute. For such nations, constitutions are not so much the immovable bedrock of government as a site of incessant contestation, prone to remaking and manipulation by successive regimes. The postcolonial constitutions of young democracies in particular seem to invite contestation. Across Africa, endemic constitutional reformism was exacerbated by the proliferation of multiparty political systems, often called the 'third wave of democracy' (Huntington 1991), following the end of the Cold War. Indeed, countless African states have remade their constitutions, some more than once, in the past 30 years (Fombad 2008). Zambia, the case in point, has been engrossed in more-or-less continuous constitution-making since the birth of the Third Republic in 1991.[16] The politics of

15 Jurisdiction, from the Latin for law (*iuris*) + to speak (*dicere*), refers to the authority of a court or comparable official body to make decisions and judgments. It can also (as in the above sentence), denote the space or domain within which a (constitutional) authority is intended to prevail, i.e., a state.

16 Each of Zambia's three republics have been inaugurated by the enactment of a new constitution. Chapter 5 offers a broader historical context by sketching Zambia's constitutional history from the advent of Northern Rhodesia's colonial occupation in the late 19th century. A chronology of the key events in Zambia's constitutional history is provided in Annex B.

constitution-making (see Chapters 4–6) involves complex interactions of actors, ideas and processes.

The tendency for Zambians to frame constitution-making via the rhetoric of liberal constitutionalism is a pivotal expression of their colonial legacy. As Fareed Zakaria (1997, 29) has noted, 'British rule meant not democracy – colonialism is by definition undemocratic – but constitutional liberalism.' In any event, a political obsession with constitutional reform has wavered little in the five long decades since independence, across three major changes of regime to date and six presidencies. Zambia is not the only former British jurisdiction in which liberal constitutionalism plays a key political role; it may, however, be an exemplar of this trait.

While a tradition of constitutionalism is a cornerstone of Zambia's politico-legal framework, this alone tells little about the kind of jurisdiction Zambia is today, or about how it became that way. It doesn't explain how or why Zambia's constitutional liberalism conceals – albeit only barely – a paradoxical, prerogativist form of power at its politico-legal core. Dissecting this core dilemma reveals a slew of more specific questions: How shall we reconcile the premise of constitutional liberalism with virtually unfettered presidential discretion? How shall we grasp the ways that the rule of law accommodates itself to the persistence of what one former Zambian president termed his 'lawfully illegal' behavior (see Chapter 7)? How shall we explain the centrality of constitutionalism for a politico-legal order in which fundamental operations occur in shadowy realms, beyond public scrutiny? Why the massive public investments in constitution-making, with so few results? Why are so many disputes of a political nature fought in court? Is the political elite's recurrent recourse to constitutional reform, and the pronounced role of the courts in maintaining political order merely maneuvers designed to maintain the *impression* of legality, while shadowy governmental business proceeds unabated? Is, indeed, the "entire constitutional performance… an elaborate confidence trick, in which governing elites invent and deploy this idea of 'the people' to bolster their oligarchical arrangements of government" (Loughlin & Walker 2007, 3)?

These, briefly, are the issues that this book seeks to clarify through a series of detailed analyses of Zambia's politico-legal domain. The constitution and the political rhetoric of constitutionalism run as a red thread throughout these empirical cases. This prevalence of legalist rhetoric reflects the fact that the constitution has been both a key tool of government and a site of sustained contestation between those in power and members of civil society dedicated to a more democratic and just social order. The Oasis Forum's lawyers invoked liberal legalism as justification for the legitimacy of their demands, but these liberal gestures could not undo the lawyers' ultimate complicity with the status quo. Rather than mobilize the emancipatory potential of the law, elite legalism has served to trivialize the 'will of the people' in constitution-making. Rather than rally support around bread-and-butter issues like improved credit facilities, accessible health services and quality education, contestation focused on procedural concerns (a constituent assembly or a national constitutional conference?)

and obscured technical provisions (must a presidential petition be filed within 14 or 30 days?).

The politico-legal maneuvers of the elite classes never assuage the underlying dissatisfaction for long, however, and political discontent has the tendency to resurface in unpredictable ways – hence the incessantly provisional and recurrent character of constitution-making. The will of the people has consistently performed a perfunctory role in the validation of authority, and the verification of popular support for the prevailing form of power has been relegated to the vagaries of a deeply flawed electoral system. Given the failure of constitutional politics to defuse the standoff between elites and the *demos*, one is left wondering whether there might be other means available to exorcise these colonial survivals? What might a 'post-liberal' alternative look like, and what forces and processes might bring such a state into existence?

# 2 Unthinking the postcolonial state

This chapter argues that the critique of postcolonial rule needs to be anchored in the historical analysis of the *form of power* upon which governmental practices are predicated. This perspective takes its inspiration from Michel Foucault's observation (1982, 780–1), that an effort to

> go further toward a new economy of power relations… consists of taking the forms of resistance against different forms of power as a starting point… The main objective of these struggles is to attack not so much 'such or such' an institution of power, or group, or elite, or class but rather a technique, a form of power.

Writing more than a decade ago, Jean and John Comaroff (2006, ix) declared the indispensability of postcolonial Africa as a site for theory production. The reason for this, they claimed, 'lies in the fact that many of the great historical tsunamis of the twenty-first century appear to be breaking first on [African] shores… thence to reverberate around the Northern Hemisphere cosmopoles.' The roots and consequences of one such tsunami –unfettered presidential power, nearly ubiquitous across postcolonial Africa – appear now to foreshadow a global crisis of liberal democracy. This Zambian case study seeks to offer inputs into the ways that the conventional antidote to despotism, political liberalism, needs to be reconsidered in order for us to find the means to protect democracy. But, as Immanuel Wallerstein (2001, ix) has advised, 'to make those inputs intelligent, we need to unthink our intellectual fetters.' This chapter attempts to do precisely that.

## Imperial liberalism and postcolonial illiberalism

Liberalism is intrinsically ambiguous, a veritable 'mark of ambivalence' (Bell 2016, 62). It purports to empower the free, autonomous individual, while at the same time condoning the vagaries of impersonal markets and discretionary authority, both of which undermine justice, equity and welfare. The form of power entrenched in Zambia's postcolonial constitution claims fealty to political liberalism. And yet it rules in ways that systematically ignore the interests of the

DOI: 10.4324/9780429198984-3

common people who remain the objects, as against the subjects of government. In this, postcolonial constitutionalism conforms to a general historical pattern by which, in the words of Achille Mbembe (2019, 162), 'liberal democracy has always needed a constitutive Other for its legitimation, an Other who is and is not at the same time part of the polis.'

Due to its fluid character, the critical appraisal of liberalism's effects needs to be set in context. The notion of liberalism, as understood here, is rooted in a specific historical and institutional setup – the conjuncture that emerged in the late 17th century when an emergent bourgeois class struggled against arbitrary regulation of their enterprise by the British Crown and its allied aristocracy. This moment of liberalism's ascent to the predominant ideology of government coincided in complex and entangled ways with the birth of Britain's global empire. Liberalism, then, is for my purposes, a cornerstone of an imperial ideology embedded in a configuration of social, political and cultural factors that have subsequently been recognized as the onset of European modernity.[1]

Jennifer Pitts (2005), among others, has termed this ideology imperial liberalism. The liberalism that today sets itself apart from, and against, forms of authoritarian government would seem to have a tenuous relationship with the imperial liberalism of the 18th and 19th centuries. An absolutist form of power (denoted by 'the Crown') was central to overseas colonization, and thus to the consolidation of the British Empire. This does not mean that the Crown exercised absolute control over day-to-day affairs in its imperial territories. As Stern and Wennerlind (2014, 13) note of early modern Britain,

> [n]o matter how determined monarchs and ministers were to overcome [various] political and ideological obstacles, their states remained far too weak, and ideologies of statecraft too conflicted, to exercise supreme and complete authority, in particular over English subjects conducting their affairs overseas.

That said, in matters of imperial jurisprudence, colonial governors ruled explicitly 'at the Regent's pleasure' (a phrase inscribed in countless imperial documents); this obligation persisted right up to the final independence of African territories from colonial rule.

A paradox, then: empire, established to advance the glory of the monarchy, was the midwife of liberalism and vice versa. The liberalism of this provenance sought protection from arbitrary regulation, and espoused a bourgeois obsession with private property and profit, and an innate faith in the moral and cultural superiority of what was termed European civilization – legitimizing the exclusion, exploitation and, if required, annihilation of non-European peoples. This imperial liberalism was not a pacific creed. Its proponents understood that the success of the imperial mission hinged on wresting wealth from a hostile environment

1 For a nuanced examination of the ideologies of empire, see Bell (2016), especially chapter 4.

(and from 'savages' trapped in a premodern state of nature); a civilized man's profit may thus require the dispossession of the native's lands and possessions, and the discipline of native labor into the routines of industry.

How is this ancient history relevant to the task of understanding contemporary law and politics? After all, contemporary champions of liberalism do not typically identify themselves with imperial ambitions. And yet, as we will see, the liberal constitutionalism we find alive and well in Zambia encompasses indelible traces of its colonial legacy. To pinpoint the continuities between colonial and postcolonial power, I will show how forms of liberal constitutionalism that frame postcolonial law and politics derive directly from the imperatives of imperial government. Indeed, imperial liberalism engendered a specifically colonial form of sovereign power, assembled from legal and theological provisions of early modern English monarchy. This imperial form of power found expression in particular practices of colonial government – ostensibly liberal, but at once encompassing a deeply embedded fount of discretionary, and illiberal exceptions to colonial legality. These practices coalesced, over time and under the prevailing epistemic hegemony of European liberalism, into constitutional orders, comprising both the written articles and unwritten conventions of imperial rule. This chapter sets out a conceptual scheme for interrogating these continuities. Chapter 5 will show how, in Northern Rhodesia (as Zambia was called under the British rule), these colonial constitutional foundations survived the transition from colonial territory to independent postcolonial nation-state virtually intact.

## *Constituting (post)colonial government*

Colonial governments were commonly run by small numbers of aliens who sought to govern huge indigenous populations. At the end of World War II, some 50 territories of the British Empire comprised almost two million square miles and roughly 77 million people (Lee 1967, 36). Yet, in terms of administrative manpower, colonial government was 'exiguous to the point of disbelief' (Kirk-Greene 1980, 38, cited in Ranger 1980, 349). Kirk-Greene (ibid., 29, citing Jefferies 1972) estimated that 'the thin white line' of colonial administrators in Northern Rhodesia, with a 'native' population of around two million, numbered 160 in 1947, and 210 a decade later.[2] Colonial government was well-armed, of course, but historian L.H. Gann (1977, 459) insists that 'British authority rested on a minimum of force.' In Northern Rhodesia, 'the colonial military establishment amounted to barely one African infantry battalion commanded by a handful of Britons' (ibid.). On top of this, the colonial police force – recruited largely from the local population – was, according to a 1957 government report, 'years away' from being 'strong enough to be able

2 'Europeans,' including non-African settlers of many nationalities amounted to less than 2% of the Northern Rhodesian population in 1951 (*Digest of Colonial Statistics*, September–October 1953).

to accept responsibility for enforcing law and order throughout the Territory' (Killingray 1986, 423).

This is not to infer that Africans were blindly acquiescent to colonial domination. For the bulk of the Black population, colonial coercion took the form of brutal taxation and endless restrictions to private and household enterprise – forms of repression against a rural population which was unable to mount organized resistance. Colonial violence was quite direct; however, it was in the small, if financially important domain of copper extraction. It was here that protest manifested itself most clearly. In 1935, most notably, a combination of factors spurred a spontaneous miners' strike at three locations on the Copperbelt. Despite the "exiguous" scale of colonial firepower, worker resistance resulted in the arrest of dozen of protesters, the deaths of six miners and serious injury to 22 more (Perrings 1977, 33).

Nevertheless, brute material force cannot fully explain the maintenance of colonial hegemony. While "disciplinary" violence in the mines was an everyday occurrence, this affected a relatively small share of the colonial population. What characterized colonial rule was not so much ubiquitous brutality but the evident willingness of the colonial administration to resort to unfettered violence when threatened in order to sustain itself. Behind the façade of colonial legality, it was this intrinsic capacity to overstep the limits of liberal government that defined the character of imperial power. As we shall see, this capacity for illiberal action was embodied in the person of the colonial governor. It was this capacity for violence that was crucial to rendering the colonial territory governable.

British colonialism was, in most of its territories and for much of its duration, a constitutional order. Government was predicated on explicit legal provisions which the rulers and ruled alike were nominally obliged to follow. These rules were framed, as noted earlier, by a normative disposition in support of Britain's global expansion. Imperial liberalism came to be embraced over the course of the 19th century by the leading lights of British (and French) liberal theory. Imperial liberalism was ideological in the commonplace pejorative sense that it masked the brutal enslavement, displacement and dispossession of indigenous populations in the interests of commercial profit and territorial domination. It can be difficult, from this historical distance, for today's reader to grasp the hypocrisy and cynicism that imperialism's self-serving ideology enabled. But imperial ideology was not merely a smokescreen for colonial plunder (Kostal 2005); to no small degree, the operational functionaries of colonial administrations were themselves ensnared in the normative justifications that liberalism provided for their actions. Colonial administrations were, for example, often at loggerheads with settler populations over the government's leniency toward 'native' labor (e.g., Rotberg 1977). That said, the liberal champions of European imperialism (i.e., Adam Smith, Jeremy Bentham, James and John Stuart Mill, Alexis de Tocqueville) were committed to 'an increasingly secure belief that Europe's progressive civilization granted Europeans the authority to suspend, in their relations with non-European societies, the moral and political standards they believed applied to themselves' (Pitt 2005, 11).

Imperial liberalism thus espoused both liberal entitlements and their exceptional derogation. This paradox provided the normative template for Britain's colonial constitutions. The liberal inspiration for these constitutions encompassed a dual irony: The first irony was that the rights and freedoms guaranteed to White settlers under the imperial social contract were not generally available to a colony's non-European populations. The second irony was that the justification for colonial annexation, advanced as an antidote to 'oriental despotism,' disguised a form of rule which resembled nothing so much as the despotism it allegedly opposed (Hussain 2003; see also Muthu 2003, Losurdo 2011). One should not be surprised, then, to find iconic liberal J.S. Mill (1963 [1859], vol 18, 224; in Pitts 2005, 1) proclaiming that '[D]espotism is a legitimate mode of government in dealing with barbarians, provided the end be their improvement, and the means justified by actually effecting that end.'

Mills' point reveals the anxious heart of the imperial form of power – it was, and saw itself, as *embattled* government. The threat of popular resistance to colonial taxation, forced labor and the ubiquitous indignity of racial discrimination was omnipresent. Great consideration was given to the means of quelling or pre-empting a potential uprising. Colonial government's embattled status legitimized, for the governors, a slew of opaque and illiberal practices revolving around security agencies and the organized coercive might of the army, police and the special forces.

Struggles for independence from colonial rule were fueled by precisely these illiberal abuses of imperial power. Independence brought the unconditional deracialization of postcolonial biopolitics. Nevertheless, the embattled nature of colonial government remains woven into the fabric of postcolonial constitutions. Under the Zambian constitution, for example, exceptional powers are linked to the prospect of a national emergency – such as a foreign invasion or an environmental crisis. But these caveats mask a more fundamental anxiety. Each state of emergency declared by an incumbent Zambian president has been in response to a perceived (or alleged) threat to his party's rule. Indeed, Benjamin Constant's observation from more than 200 years ago continues to resonate: 'Every time constitutions have been violated it is not the constitutions that are saved but the governments.'[3] The postcolonial form of sovereign power is as alert to the fragility of its embattled legitimacy as was the imperial form of power it inherited.

## Misreading liberal power

The residual effects of imperial liberalism, then, continue to inform the notions of legality and sovereignty – i.e., of legitimate power – encoded in postcolonial Zambian constitutions. These colonial traces are mapped in Chapters 5 and

3 From Constant, Benjamin 1814. *De la suspension et de la violation des constitutions*, cited in Negretto and Rivera (2000, 1800).

6. The purpose of this chapter is to 're-describe' (Rorty 1989) ways in which the postcolonial form of power extends the legacy of imperial liberalism. This attempt at a critical re-description seeks to illuminate a specific problem of politico-legal theory and practice in mainstream conceptualizations of postcolonial power. The problem in question is the empirical legitimacy of unaccountable discretionary practices within the framework of a nominally liberal constitutional order. Empirical legitimacy refers here not so much to popular acquiescence to allegedly illiberal acts, as to the fact that systemic instances of exceptional powers, privileges and prerogatives appear to survive persistent attempts to repress them – through judicial review, popular movements, constitutional reform or any other means. One cannot say that the postcolonial form of power would have undivided support among the Zambian citizenry; the views of democracy activists recounted in Chapter 4 make this abundantly clear. But opposition to its abuses has never mobilized sufficient power to replace it with something else. The saga of the Oasis Forum's campaign to democratize the constitution (see Chapter 6) provides an extended case study of the potential and limitations of such efforts.

The postcolonial form of power, in the sense employed here, does not refer to a particular regime (such as that of Kenneth Kaunda's United National Independence Party [UNIP] or of Frederick Chiluba's Movement for Multiparty Democracy [MMD]), to a type of government (democratic, neoliberal or socialist) or to a particular style of rule (populist, authoritarian, libertarian). Rather, it is an assemblage of politico-legal capacities and normative dispositions embodied in the person of the sovereign ruler – in Zambia's case, the republican president. These proclivities are anchored in the constitution and shaped by institutional cultures that have become established conventions over the course of political and constitutional history. Veteran legal scholar B.O. Nwabueze[4] (1974) invoked the term *presidentialism* as a synonym for the postcolonial form of power in Africa.[5] Presidentialism is, in many instances, an accurate portrayal of a constitutional model that emerged with decolonization, wherein 'both the complex task of nation-building and the urgent demands of economic and social development called for clear, decisive, and legitimate political leadership' (Fix-Fierro & Salazar-Ugarte 2012, 637). This certainly applies to how many postcolonial African regimes justify their modes of government (Ndulo 2002, van de Walle 2003). Presidentialism, in Nwabueze's sense, describes how executive power is

4 Nigerian-born academic lawyer Benjamin Obi Nwabueze became a forerunner professor of law at the University of Zambia in 1970. In 1972, President Kaunda appointed Nwabueze to the Chona Constitution Review Commission set up to draft and legitimize the single-party constitution of 1973.

5 Presidentialist regimes are commonly contrasted with parliamentarian systems (e.g., Stepan & Skach 1993). Outside of Africa, presidentialism is the dominant regime type in Latin America and the United States. The mainstream literature has tended to underscore the 'perils' of presidentialism (e.g., Linz 1990). Recent work by Chaisty et al. (2014, 2018) has taken a more constructive approach, focusing on the political strategies of presidentialist rule.

organized and deployed in a given jurisdiction.[6] The concept was not designed to illustrate how the powers embodied in the presidency are *constituted*. For this task, a different conceptual apparatus is required. Instead of viewing political power through the lens of presidentialism as an attribute of the postcolonial state, I propose a perspective that identifies a *prerogativist form of power*, anchored in a specific *politico-legal domain*. To justify this conceptual move, and to lay the foundations for its elaboration, I turn next to examine the principle debates currently in circulation concerning the nature of power in the African postcolony.

## *The neopatrimonial stain*

The most prevalent explanation for unaccountable discretionary practices in both the scholarly and popular literatures on African politics employs the elastic catchword of 'neopatrimonialism.'[7] Neopatrimonialism, based on terminology made popular by German legal scholar Max Weber in the early 20th century, has three inter-related dimensions: First, neopatrimonialism channels a *culturalist* perspective, according to which the 'traditional African leader' has incontrovertible transcendental powers, grounded in the chief's charismatic authority. The president represents an extrapolation, or up-scaling of this primordial despotism to the national level. Conventional political norms of interdependence, which connect leaders and subjects via bonds of vertical reciprocity, are seen to be unavoidably despoiled when transposed onto a modern state order. Second, there is the presumption that the extensive powers constitutionally conferred on the person of the president are so 'sweet' (a much-used simile) as to be *innately corrupting*. A social contract rooted in vertical reciprocity and care thus deteriorates into predatory rentierism. Third, neopatrimonial behavior is seen as a *failure of individual character*. Political scientists, in particular, give these premises an institutionalist spin: The 'personalized' nature of presidential powers exploits a bundle of perverse incentives that undermines weakly institutionalized checks and balances in the constitution.

Weber (1968, 226–41) originally proposed the notion of patrimonialism to describe premodern forms of 'traditional' authority. In Weber's model, patrimonial princes made no distinction between their own private assets and those of the public coffers. Twentieth-century Africanists extended Weber's idea to characterize modern Africa government as a predatory institution driven by a 'politics of the belly' (Bayart 1993). In this view, alleged executive pressures on, for example, court decisions and legislative acts are viewed as evidence of political

6 Thus, Chaisty et al. (2014, 72) argue that in presidentialist regimes, 'presidents use a toolbox of five key tools when constructing legislative coalitions: agenda power, budgetary authority, cabinet management, partisan powers, and informal institutions.'

7 There is a vast literature on neopatrimonialism, with countless new books and articles appearing every year. An influential early theorization is that of Israeli sociologist S.N. Eisenstadt (1973). For astute critical reviews, see Olivier de Sardan (2014), Wai (2012) and Erdmann and Engel (2007).

patronage and of a judiciary compromised by political bribes, or of 'semi-authoritarian' (Olcott & Ottaway 1999) coercion. Judges and lawmakers are allegedly so dependent for their sustenance and security on executive favor that they dare not indulge in measures that may be taken as an affront to the head of state. This view of postcolonial power has been ubiquitous in mainstream comparative politics for some time. Already a quarter of a century ago, British anthropologist Jonathan Spencer (1997, 13) remarked that "political science has a special subset of dustbin categories for politics like this – 'personalistic,' 'parochial,' 'primordial.' But, needless to say, these sound more like terms of admonishment than possible sources of enlightenment." More recently, the ubiquity of such 'dustbin' categories prompted Thandika Mkandawire (2015, 563) to observe that neopatrimonialism has been 'taken up by non-Africanist development scholars as an accurate characterization of the state of Africa so much so that even for otherwise meticulous comparative politics scholars …, Africa provides prototypes of the predatory state that require no further examination.'

Neopatrimonial presidentialism appears, then, as a blight perpetuated by an endless parade of flawed politicians crippling an entire continent. Granted, the neopatrimonial thesis is not blatantly false. As the empirical cases scrutinized below reveal, leaders do embezzle state funds; presidents do ignore constitutional constraints; and judiciaries do, on occasion, overlook these transgressions. That said, these exceptional practices are not the norm everywhere. Neopatrimonialism has a valid domain of application, but what began as a rigorous effort to understand the material and ideal reciprocities that tether together governors and governed (Médard 1982) evolved in the triumphalist milieu of the post–Cold War era into a moralizing discourse of illiberal transgression. Neopatrimonialism as a *model* of African government reduces the relationship between rulers and subjects to a pathological interdependence between a predatory ruler and a deformed or unwitting *demos.*

The rhetoric of neopatrimonialism along these lines flourished in Zambian political analysis in the first decades of the Third Republic. The regime of President Frederick Chiluba (1991–2001), in particular, inspired much academic writing in this mode (e.g., Mutesa 2005, Momba 2007). Van Donge (2009) and Lewis (2009) both highlight the predatory nature of President Chiluba's behavior. Judging from the evidence laid out in Chapter 7, Mr Chiluba may, indeed, have been relatively unconcerned with distinguishing between what was his and what belonged to the state. And yet, as van Donge (2009) notes, labelling a regime like Zambia under Chiluba as neopatrimonial does little to increase our knowledge of the concrete social practices through which government and politics actually function. Instead of undertaking the arduous work of mapping intricate reciprocities and complex political practices, or of probing the structural/historical roots of politico-legal exception, neopatrimonial analysis invokes liberal clichés that do little more than reaffirm the initial presumption of the immaturity of postcolonial politics. This gesture cements the smug certainty that Euro-American liberalism represents a political order that is both technically and morally superior to the generalized illiberalism of the Global South (Verheul

2013, 766). But what if liberalism – the hidden cornerstone of prerogativism – is part of Africa's governmental dilemmas, and not their (relentlessly unattainable) solution? Perhaps the more fruitful approach is not to rush to moral judgment, but to reflect with a cool heart and mind on the conditions of possibility for the paradoxical nature of postcolonial sovereignty.

## *Exception as an art of government*

Neopatrimonial theory has dominated the analysis of African politics, but it is not the only model in circulation. A parallel discourse frames postcolonial government as a 'state of exception' to similar effects. The recent resurgence of interest in states of exception reflects a response to the specter of 'illiberal democracy' in post–Cold War Europe (e.g., Lazar 2009, Ramraj 2008), in Trump's America (Carbado 2019) and, most recently, to the use of emergency powers to corral the COVID-19 pandemic (Zinn 2020).

Political liberalism espouses a paradoxical commitment to constrain the discretionary elements of political power that it both requires and enables. The conventional counterargument to this premise was articulated forcefully by German constitutional theorist (and Nazi fellow traveler) Carl Schmitt (1922).[8] Schmitt argued that there exist conditions under which strict adherence to liberal values threatens the integrity of the state and, by inference, the security of its peoples (cf., Gross & Ní Aoláin 2006, Ramraj 2008, Lazar 2009). Under such conditions, state survival demands recourse to 'exceptional' means. For Schmitt, these exceptional measures included the suspension of legality. The power to decide when to step outside the legal order lies, in Schmitt's (1922, 1) widely cited axiom, solely with the sovereign. In Schmitt's view, this prerogative cannot be legally codified; the power to decide on a state of exception is intrinsically exceptional, the prerogative of the sovereign leader.

In his radical critique of political liberalism, 'Schmitt's main weapon… is the inevitable existence of the exception' (Gross 2000, 1827). The political makeup of societies governed by liberal constitutionalism, argued Schmitt, was not immune to exceptional circumstances, i.e., 'sudden, urgent, usually unforeseen events or situations that require immediate action, often without time for prior reflection and consideration – i.e., without allowing for pre-planned responses' (ibid.). The Achilles' heel of liberal constitutionalism, in this view, is the conceit that 'pre-established general norms cover and apply to all possible situations' (ibid.). Schmitt asserted, quite convincingly, that this liberal premise is an illusion, and that exceptional measures arise in all juridical orders, and must be catered to in jurisprudence.

Schmitt's notion of the state of exception provides a legal justification for a politics of decisionism that German Chancellor Adolf Hitler appropriated from 1933 onward, and which became the foundation of Fascist National Socialist rule

8 For a comprehensive intellectual biography of Schmitt, see Balakrishnan (2000).

in the Third Reich. Of course, Schmitt did not invent unfettered, arbitrary power – colonial governors had been practicing it in colonial territories since the dawn of empire. Schmitt's anti-liberal texts are a response to Germany's loss in World War I, which catalyzed the fall of the imperial reign of Kaiser Wilhelm. From the ashes of German monarchy rose the Weimar Republic, rooted in a new order of liberal constitutionalism, the collapse of which predicated the rise of Hitler to power. Schmitt's railings against the ascent of liberalism in Weimar Germany not only reflected an evident nostalgia for the monarchy, but also highlighted fundamental dilemmas of democratic government. Schmitt was concerned with the relationship of law to politics, and sought to theorize the nature of the popular or 'constituent' power upon which a politico-legal order draws its legitimacy. Schmitt's theorization of constituent power earned him a place in the canon of 20th-century political theory, but his 'ethno-nationalist' view of constituent power, according to which the legitimacy of a political order depended on the extent to which it embodied the will of the dominant *Volk*, was explicitly racist and complicit with German Fascism.

Contemporary political theorists like Giorgio Agamben (2005) do not read Schmitt in order to rehabilitate his racist justifications for totalitarianism. Rather, Schmitt's significance for our age, it is said, is in his problematization of 'sovereign dictatorship.' In his central texts, Schmitt problematized the mechanisms by which political power is deemed legitimate, and he anticipated the emergence of a dictator armed with the power of the exception as a kind of revolutionary power, an 'embodiment of the popular sovereignty that determines the new political order and therefore cannot be judged as legal or illegal since there are no criteria to do that' (Smoleński 2012, 272). In this, Schmitt foreshadowed contemporary debates about the blurring of politics and legality in the conceptualization of means by which 'the people' express their constituent power in democratic dispensations.[9] Such debates are central tools for a critique of prerogativism.

Giorgio Agamben's critical elaboration of Schmitt's prescription for a state of exception has opened fertile ground for examining political legality as an art of government. In his influential essay on the state of exception, Agamben (2005) is largely concerned with the biopolitical dimension of Schmitt's thought – that is, with the way that immigrants and other politically volatile parts of a population can be 'managed' productively through bureaucratic practices. The primary thrust of Agamben's argument is to highlight the nature of Schmitt's state of exception as a theoretical apology for Nazi concentration camps and, by extension, for the contemporary encampment of refugees in the EU and elsewhere. Agamben's reading of Schmitt has thus fueled concern about the propensity of state violence to produce 'zones of exception' within nominally liberal polities.[10]

9 I return to these debates about constituent power in Chapter 4.

10 There are vast literatures on liberalism, democracy and states of exception inspired by Schmitt, in particular. For an overview see, for example, Dyzenhaus (1998), Kalyvas (2008) and Smoleński (2012).

As Sheila Nair (2011, 390) points out, Agamben 'has little to say about how or whether colonial and imperial modalities of sovereignty matter in the way the exception is conceptualized and contextualized.' This suggests the necessity of moving from an abstract notion of 'exception' to an understanding of the post-colonial form of power firmly rooted in the specificities of time and place: history, law, politics and culture.

Approaching postcolonial power via Schmitt's notion of exception has the merit of highlighting the relationship of law to politics. Yet, a focus on states of exception has a tendency to conflate extreme oppression and the banal abuse of power. This can be problematic for the theorization of governmental practices in which banal forms of abuse are routine, but violent oppression is not. Postcolonial governments have been widely scrutinized as states of exception. Schmitt and Agamben are not the immediate sources for such accounts, however. Rather, portrayals of postcolonial totalitarianism come largely through the work of Cameroonian anthropologist Achille Mbembe. Mbembe's major work *On the Postcolony* (2001) continues to be among the most-cited analyses of contemporary African politics, and thus presages both the strengths and the shortcomings of current political debates.

Like the study at hand, Mbembe derives his understanding of postcolonial sovereignty from the scrutiny of colonial power. Mbembe elaborates on the essence of colonial sovereignty via the notion of *commandement* (ibid.). Anticipating the original Italian edition of Agamben's *Lo Stato di eccezione* by several years, Mbembe's treatment of (colonial) sovereignty clearly resonates with the Schmittian themes that provoked Agamben's critique. Colonial *commandement* is, for Mbembe (ibid., 29–31), 'based on a régime d'exception' that works through a system of 'privileges and immunities.'[11] Indeed, Mbembe places exceptional powers and their arbitrary and unconditional deployment at the core of colonial government. He also explicitly underscores its continuity across the colonial/postcolonial divide: 'Postcolonial state forms have inherited this unconditionality and the regime of impunity that was its corollary' (26). Many facets of this study corroborate this claim.

The central arguments of *On the Postcolony* appeared as an article nearly a decade before the book. That article (Mbembe 1992) was an evident reaction to the systemic state violence perpetrated by figures like Mobutu in the Congo (Zaïre), Bokassa in the Central African Republic and Biya in Mbembe's native Cameroon. In linking *commandement* to such exceptional and violent autocracies, Mbembe evokes, without citing him, what Schmitt (op. cit.) termed a 'commissarial' form of dictatorship.[12] Comparable forms of constitutional autocracy became

11 Mbembe is well read in continental political philosophy and deftly cites Schmitt's contemporaries and commentators (Heidegger, Arendt). His mainstay, however, is French poststructuralism (Derrida, Lacan and, above all, Foucault). It is somewhat surprising that despite its focus on the genealogy of sovereign power, there is no reference to Schmitt, nor to Agamben's *Homo Sacer* (1995/1997 in French, 1998 in English) in Mbembe's *On the Postcolony.*

12 'A commissarial dictatorship is one where the preservation of an already existing constitutional order is the aim of its suspension, and where this suspension occurs according to this

a trademark of Cold War–era despots in Africa and elsewhere. Commissarial dictators like Mobutu, Bokassa and Biya were legally immune to democratic oversight (and buoyed up, in turn, by Western and Soviet financial and military support). Subsequent authors have taken Mbembe's notion of *commandement* to authorize their analyses of the continuities between colonial and postcolonial government. Sheila Nair (2011, 390), for one, argues that

> [p]ostcolonial sovereignty... appears as an imitation or mimicry of the forms of rule and order enacted by colonial power and equally repressive... [while] the insistent regulation of third world spaces and their production as crisis-prone, terror-ridden, disease-bearing, anarchic, corrupt, non-rational, and ungovernable reaffirms the postcolonial exception. (ibid.)

In such accounts, the commissarial regime (such as that of Biya, or of Robert Mugabe in his last decades) becomes a synecdoche for postcolonial power in general.

Drawing a link between colonial totalitarianism and postcolonial *commandement* is not a recent maneuver. Writing 70 years ago, German political theorist Hannah Arendt also raised the specter of authoritarian violence in Africa. In her path-breaking study *The Origins of Totalitarianism* (first published in 1951), Arendt showed how Hitler's Nazi regime appropriated and systematized Republican Germany's racialized murder of African peoples in its nascent colonial empire. Arendt (1951, 197) argued that Fascists learned from Imperial Germany's colonial precedents. In particular, they adopted the insight that 'absolute European supremacy... could hardly be maintained except through racism [alone] because the permanent European settlement was so hopelessly outnumbered.' Jews – the primary victims of Nazi genocide – did not outnumber non-Jews in post–World War I Germany, but in Arendt's analysis anti-Semitism became the '"amalgamator" around which the other elements of totalitarianism crystallized' (Canovan 2000, 33).

German totalitarianism also emulated the ways that the local administrators of the British Empire subverted morality and law to imperial necessity:

> When the European mob discovered what a 'lovely virtue' a white skin could be in Africa, when the English conqueror in India became an administrator who no longer believed in the universal validity of law, but was convinced of his own innate capacity to rule and dominate, ... the stage seemed to be set for all possible horrors. (Arendt 1951, 221)

order's own rules' (Arato 2000: 927; citing Schmitt 1924: 136–7). Schmitt distinguishes a commissarial dictatorship from a 'sovereign' one, wherein "a dictator... does not defend an already existing constitution but attempts to create a new one and... does so not by his own authority but in the name of the people" (Vinx 2019; citing Schmitt, op. cit., 112–31). The elected dictators Mbembe criticizes do not, however, seek to create a new constitution, but merely suspend elements of the prevailing one.

The horrors of central concern to Arendt, who herself fled Hitler's terror in the 1930s, were those perpetrated by the Nazi regime in Germany. Some observers have seen parallels between Nazi genocide and the behavior of certain present-day African despots. Christine Sylvester (2006), for example, has reapplied the notion of totalitarianism to postcolonial Africa. Witness, for example, her insistence that Agamben's re-theorization of Schmitt's state of exception allows us to appreciate the fundamentally 'fascistic' character of the postcolonial African state, in which citizens have been reduced to 'bare life,' i.e., to mere biological entities without rights or political personhood (for a similar assessment, see Patel & McMichael 2004). Sylvester (2006, 76n) conveys an image of postcolonial Africa as one huge site of territorialized state violence, a concentration camp within a regime of 'global fascism' where 'exception and norm have become indiscernible.'

Sylvester's account is a credible picture of the ways that many African countries are the targets and victims of global corporate extractivism, and of the complicity of rich-country governments in abusing African labor and the continent's natural environment. The reduction of local communities to the status of 'bare life' is indeed condoned and facilitated by elected governments eager to secure foreign investments. But postcolonial autocracy comes in very different forms. Zambia, even during its single-party heyday, was far from an overtly totalitarian state along the lines of Hitler's Germany.[13] In drawing such parallels, the notion of exception is no longer 'exceptional,' but becomes a simile for generalized state violence, and is invoked as a cliché of postcolonial government *tout court*. In such accounts, the postcolonial African government is conceived of as pervasively illiberal and fundamentally lawless. This singularly undialectical rendering of the relationship between legality and exception (a problematic central to both Schmitt and Agamben) misrepresents contemporary forms of power by reducing the messy and internally inconsistent domain of government to a single, coherent, albeit an opaque form of oppressive intentionality. It also occludes the possibility of even considering the productive possibilities of exceptional powers in postcolonial contexts.

Commissarial dictatorship is certainly not the whole truth – not even an 'average' truth about the African government. Much of the literature on neopatrimonialism and states of exception conflate diverse African governments, and in doing so recall Mbembe's (2001) remarks about the way Africa is characteristically portrayed as 'absolute otherness,' a state of absences that exists only to affirm the West's iconic stature as the universal moral standard. Such blanket reductionism deprives Africans of a sense of 'true lawfulness,' and denies them a role as peoples 'in relation to nothing other than themselves' (Mbembe 2001, 5, citing Bayart 1989). The exclusions, privileges and exceptions of the political landscape that emerged with the end of the Cold War are not those of the 1980s. Contemporary analysis needs to come to terms with this fact.

13 Disclosure: I worked as donor-funded "technical assistance" in Zambian provincial administration for an extended period in the final decade of the Second Republic.

The lack of access of huge numbers of Africans to clean water, health and educational services, traversable roads and dignified livelihoods can be reasonably seen as a structural form of state violence. Such structural abuse, however abhorrent, is not necessarily the consequence of *commandement* – the intentional policies of heartless autocrats. Complex interactions of internal politics and external forces conspire to deny the *demos* enjoyment of the surpluses national economies generate. In itself, a model of postcolonial government as *commandement* tells us little about the far more common incidents of 'banal' exception, where the exercise of exceptional powers is one integral tool of statecraft among others. In thinking about the possibilities for democracy and justice, these latter cases – of which Zambia is an exemplar – challenge intellectually lazy juxtapositions of liberal and illiberal legality, and are thus productive sites for re-describing postcolonial power.

## A prerogativist form of power

Neo-Weberian neopatrimonialism situates a failed moral person at the crux of postcolonial government, while neo-Schmittian exceptionism posits an inefficient legal system, unable to exercise constitutional checks on the executive. Both well-established conceptualizations posit sovereign monsters at the helm of African states – leaders who are outrageous precisely because they are not ideal-typical liberal governors. Both models operate on a terrain defined by a stark juxtaposition between the corrupt and the predatory leader, on the one hand, and the transparent, liberal sovereign on the other. Neither approach has much interest in the middle ground between these two ideal types; moreover, both are weakened by a sentimental tendency to ignore how liberalism is fundamentally tainted by its imperial past.

But how to theorize this ambivalent political entity? De Roeck and van Rossem (2015, 6) portray the middle ground between authoritarianism and democracy as a 'grey zone' comprising political configurations ranging from 'illiberal democracy,' 'delegative democracy,' 'exclusive and tutelary democracy,' 'partial democracy' to 'competitive authoritarianism,' 'electoral authoritarianism,' 'semi-authoritarian regimes' and 'illiberal autocracy,' among others. Clearly, as the authors note (ibid.), such a proliferation of labels 'precipitates conceptual confusion.' Indeed, the theorization of myriad hyphenated formations is undermined by the unexamined assumption that such regimes are flawed liberal democracies and that the task of analysis is to explain their failures, rather than pay attention to the division of labor between the exceptional and the liberal exercise of power in achieving governmental outcomes. Perhaps an even graver problem is the firmly entrenched propensity to approach postcolonial power via the category of 'the state.' It is, I believe, an effect of adopting 'the state' as the object of theorization that has nurtured the hegemonic literature on neopatrimonialism, as well as that echoing neo-Schmittian states of exception.

'The state' has such a canonical status in the study of postcolonial Africa that it requires some effort to unthink the ways we conceptualize core sites of power. To be sure, the state's empirical facticity seems uncontroversial. For most countries, one can easily identify what Steinmetz (1999, 9) terms the 'structural features' of a state. These comprise

> the entire set of rules and institutions that are involved in making and implementing policies: the arrangement of ministries or departments, the set of rules for the allocation of individual positions within these departments, systems for generating revenues, legal codes and constitutions, electoral rules, forms of control over lower bodies of government, the nature and location of boundaries between state and society, and so forth.

Indeed, as one who has needed a visa, a study permit and a driver's license, among other public services, I cannot dispute the existence of a Zambian state. The institutions of the state are defined by the constitution, which creates the presidency, the cabinet, an army, a revenue authority and an annual budget, as well as an administrative apparatus, including a range of security agencies, responsible for the government of Zambia's populations. International conventions, agreements about bilateral and multilateral development loans and grants, etc., presuppose a state as a principle actor, capable of engaging in and enforcing contractual provisions. Seen from the outside, the Zambian state appears as a relatively coherent regulatory force. For the purpose of understanding particular forms of power at work in the government of Zambia's peoples and territories, 'the state' explains little.

I find three distinct problems with thinking about power as an aspect of the state. The first problem is empirical. In everyday practice, the efficacy of the postcolonial government's regulatory apparatus remains, as already noted for colonial Northern Rhodesia, strikingly thin. Public administration is tragically underresourced and citizens are obliged, in nearly every aspect of their lives, to seek 'informal' solutions to the provision of basic welfare services. The inefficiency of public authority lies in stark contrast to the brisk efficacy by which political challenges to the ruling party's hegemony are dealt with. Power is real when it needs to be, but its effects do not match the scope of the state's territorial claims.

The second problem is conceptual – the notion of the state is generally assumed to correspond to the systemic qualities enumerated by Steinmetz (above). This is an epistemic error; empirical states do not possess such institutional tidiness and coherence. On the contrary, as authors like Philip Abrams (1988) and Timothy Mitchell (1999, 76) have argued, the image of institutional coherence that prevails in both popular and academic conceptualizations of the state is an illusory 'state effect,' produced through the processes by which citizens are subjugated to political power. In its pursuit of scholarly tidiness, the academic analysis of the state 'is liable to… misrepresent the incoherence of state practice' (ibid.). We must beware, then, of conflating the state's 'symbolic identity' – the illusory effects of political subjugation – with an alleged institutional reality. This implies, as Philip Abrams advised (1988, 82; cited in Mitchell, 76), 'attending to the sense in which the state does not exist rather than those in which it does.'

A third problem with the state is political. Conflating normative authority with the centralized governmental apparatus suggests that redressing the epistemic and institutional ballast of the imperial past must focus on reforming that apparatus. Or, to put it differently, privileging 'the state' implies that the struggles aimed at decolonizing the prevailing form of power, and of the social contract derived from it must take the form of constitutional reform. This premise, associated with the theory of 'transformative constitutionalism' (Klare 1998; see also Shai 2019), undergirds the political controversies analyzed in the empirical chapters that follow. It is reasonable to argue that constitutional provisions are an important pillar of the political order, but it may also be true that a decolonized constitution implies the *prior* transformation of the contract between governed populations and the rulers in whom they invest their trust. I return to this theme in the concluding chapter.

One response to these analytical dilemmas has been to train scrutiny away from centralized forms of government to the manifestations of power in the 'margins' of the state (e.g., Das & Poole 2004). This approach counsels attention, among other things, to the 'spaces, forms, and practices through which the state is continually both experienced and undone through the *illegibility* of its own practices, documents, and words' (ibid., 9–10). Such attention has opened up rich and novel perspectives on the microphysics of political contestation in the everyday lives of citizens and other postcolonial subjects. And yet, in looking away from the constitution of power at its core sites, something is lost. Indeed, while the scripts of power can appear indecipherable in the spatial and social margins of society, there is a realm of power where extreme fastidiousness prevails about both the coherence and legibility of power. I term this assemblage of sites and practices the *politico-legal domain* and suggest that it is through its problematization, rather than that of 'the state,' that we can best come to terms with the constitution and dynamics of postcolonial power.[14] This approach involves attenuated attention to legal institutions and practices, not as expressions of 'the state,' but as a 'semi-autonomous field' (Moore 1972) constituted via intentionalities that are irreducible to any singular logic.

In order to illustrate the substance and implications of the conceptual move from state to politico-legal domain, let us look further into the politics of another embattled post-imperial democracy – that of Germany in the 1930s – the same context that inspired Carl Schmitt's prescription for decisionist leadership. The point of reference is Ernst Frænkel's[15] (1941) study of the dual state that he

14 There are other 'sub-state' theorizations of the law/politics interface in circulation – most proximately, that of the 'legal complex' (Halliday, Karpik & Feeley 2007). This notion is useful for examining the political effects of postcolonial law through its primary emissaries – lawyers and judges (Halliday et al. 2012). For my purposes, however, the analytical utility of the legal complex is constrained by an implicit legalist bias that largely limits its focus to the legal professions above others, while approaching law and politics as relatively autonomous realms.

15 Ernst Frænkel (1898–1975) was a German Jew, Weimar Social Democrat and labor lawyer (Scheuerman 2000). Despite Frænkel's Jewish heritage, his status as a World War I veteran

saw taking shape under the reign of Hitler and his National Socialist party.[16] By contrasting Frænkel's analysis of the prerogative state in Nazi Germany with the notion of a prerogativist form of power in Zambia's struggling democracy I seek to clarify the specificity of the latter concept for the analytical (re)description of political legality as an extension of imperial liberalism. At the same time, I hope to specify how political legality works in an autocratic, but decidedly non-totalitarian setting.

## *Prerogativism and the politico-legal domain*

Working as a labor lawyer in Nazi Germany, Ernst Frænkel (1941, xiii) documented the operations of what he called a 'prerogative state.' The prerogative state that administered exceptional jurisprudence in matters of political concern, co-existed with a 'normative state' responsible for the adjudication of non-political cases. In Frænkel's words, the prerogative state refers to 'that governmental system which exercises unlimited arbitrariness and violence unchecked by any legal guarantees,' while the normative state is 'an administrative body endowed with elaborate powers for safeguarding the legal order as expressed in statutes, decisions of the courts and activities of the administrative agencies.' This duality characterized the legal maneuvers of Hitler's National Socialist government following the *Decree of the President of the Reich for the Protection of the People and the State* of 28 February 1933.[17] From then on (Frænkel 1941, 57),

---

allowed him to practice law in Berlin until late 1938, when he fled Germany, eventually settling in the United States. In the United States, Frænkel studied American law at the University of Chicago. After an academic stint at the New School in New York, Frænkel returned to Germany, where he became a professor of political science at Freie Universität Berlin.

There has been a resurgence of interest in Frænkel's work of late, including two intellectual biographies (see Meierhenrich 2018, Morris 2020; see also Suntrup 2020). Part of the interest in Frænkel's notion of a dual state under Fascism dovetails with ongoing debates about what Suntrup (ibid., 18) terms the 'bifurcation of the legal system' in contemporary 'illiberal democracies.'

16 Frænkel's work has subsequently influenced more contemporary discussions of the so-called deep state. The current academic discussion of the deep state is much indebted to an essay by Hans Morganthau (1962[1955], 400; cited in Tunander 2009, 56), in which Morganthau argues that the 'security state' – the assemblage of opaque intelligence and military agencies tasked with defending elected government – is able to exert 'an effective veto over the decisions' of state officials governed by the rule of law. Morganthau linked the deep state to Frænkel's dual state in his original essay, and this connection resonates in recent empirical work on illiberal politics with a Frænkelian framework by, among others, Meierhenrich (2008, for apartheid South Africa), Mérieau (2016, for Thailand) and Tunander (2009, for Sweden).

17 This ordinance (known as the Reichstag Fire Decree) was in response to the burning of the German Parliament the previous day, an alleged act of arson by a Dutch Communist. Recently appointed Chancellor Adolf Hitler invoked the incident as proof of a Communist plot against the state, and used it as a pretext to restrict civil liberties. The decree is seen as having laid the juridical foundations for Nazi tyranny (Mommsen 1985).

> [w]hether the decision in an individual case is made in accordance with the law or with "expediency" is entirely in the hands of those in whom the sovereign power is vested... The jurisdiction over jurisdiction rests with the prerogative state.

It is unclear how Frænkel intended us to understand the relationship between the normative state and the prerogative state. Frænkel notes that the normative state is not the old *Rechtsstaat* of pre-Nazi Germany but rather, like the prerogative state, is a strategic creation of the Nazi regime: The more predictable *Normenstaat* was a functional precondition for the arbitrariness of the *Maßnahmenstaat.* While the two states were interdependent, Frænkel (ibid., 70) insists upon a 'qualitative difference' between them.

> 'A decisive distinction between the administrative agencies of the normative state and the organs of the prerogative state rests on the difference between their respective sphere of jurisdiction and is not a problem of varying degrees of discretionary power.'

Discretionary power in the normative state could only be exercised within the administrative purview of a specific agency.[18] In contrast, 'the organs of the Prerogative State are characterized by their unlimited jurisdiction.' In Frænkel's (ibid., 46) view, under Nazi rule '[t]he Rule of Law no longer exists. It has been supplanted by the Dual State, which is the joint product of the Prerogative State and the Normative State.'

Frænkel's 'ethnography of Nazi law' (Meierhenrich 2017) was an attempt to theorize his professional encounters with the incursion of Fascist politics into the German judiciary. This specifically Fascist mode of political legality aimed at weeding out Social Democratic and Communist resistance to Hitler's authoritarianism, and to promote the National Socialists' ethno-nationalist agenda of exterminating Germans of 'non-Aryan,' i.e., Jewish and Roma, extraction. It is evident from Frænkel's writings that by the time of his flight, in 1938, any distinction between the National Socialist party and government administration had disappeared, and that the Nazis exercised complete control over the judicature of all cases the party deemed 'political.'

There is little doubt, of course, that the subjugation of law in the service of Nazi ideology was state policy, and that it was both intentional and systematic. Frænkel (ibid., 74) quotes key Nazi minister Hermann Göring as saying that Nazi law was the 'promulgation of the Leader's will,' and that will, for all its abhorrent cruelty, was not erratic, but adhered to a consistent logic. The fact that Frænkel assembled his model of the dual state on the basis of official Nazi-era court documents also suggests that the political legality of Fascist Germany was neither arbitrary nor clandestine. By the same token, the actions Frænkel attributes to the

18 Frænkel (ibid.) cites the Foreign Exchange Control Office as an example.

prerogative state were systematic acts of a security agency dedicated to political repression, not sporadic aberrations within a nominally liberal legal order. There was no possibility of legally challenging the party-state for its politico-legal brutalities.[19]

In light of this context, and given the resurgence of *Staatstheorie* in the Weimar period,[20] it is understandable that Frænkel cast the burgeoning politicization of the law as a function of 'the state,' rather than, say, as a perversion of the legal system.[21] Understandable, but unfortunate – especially given the resurgence of Frænkel's model. In theoretical terms, conflating political legality with 'the state' is misleading in that it misrepresents the diversity of governmental intentionalities (a vital source of political change), and overstates the hegemony of law, even within authoritarian jurisdictions. Indeed, it is clear from Frænkel's account that the suppression of *habeas corpus* and other principles of natural law in the service of Nazi politics was not a function of an abstract 'state.' Rather, the exercise of Fascist political legality was managed specifically by one dedicated agency, the *Geheime Staatspolizei* (the *Gestapo*, i.e., the secret police) and its leadership. This is an important point, because defining the nature and locus of prerogativist power is a crucial political precondition for containing its excesses. What is at stake is grasping the limits of law (and of its professional elites) to salvage democracy when, yet again, 'the boundaries between dictatorship, illiberal democracy and exceptional legality become blurred' (Mérieau 2019).

Frænkel's prerogative state thus describes a condition of Schmittian exception where political legality has been weaponized as a dedicated art of government. Can Frænkel's model help us understand the 'exceptional legality' of postcolonial democracies like Zambia? Yes, and no. It is clear, as the testimony of President Chiluba presented in Chapter 7 shows, that the politico-legal domain in Zambia has a 'dual' quality – the law is read differently for presidents than for other citizens. And yet, Zambia is not, and has never been, a Fascist polity. Its ostensibly liberal constitutionalism is entwined with imperial residues, but the Zambian legal system has no 'parallel' jurisdiction for political incidents.[22] The key, I suggest, is in how we describe the similarities and differences between modes of autocracy in distinct post-imperial setups – that is, in the wake of the British Empire as against the denouement of the *Kaiserreich*. Germany's prerogative state denoted a total annulment of liberal constitutionalism, while the deployment of postcolonial prerogativist power in Zambia represents an accommodation between liberal and autocratic tendencies rooted in colonial politico-legal culture.

19 According to Meierhenrich (2017, xxxiv), often the only legal strategy available for Frænkel to protect his clients' lives was having them convicted on a non-political charge.

20 Epitomized by the debates between prominent legal theorists Hans Kelsen and Carl Schmitt (see Vinx 2015).

21 Cf. Francis Lucey's (1941) contemporary notion of 'totalitarian jurisprudence.'

22 There exists, of course, a parallel jurisdiction for breaches of 'custom,' but this is not intrinsically repressive.

Historical context also matters. While the brutality of the Third Reich clearly overstepped that of the *Kaiserreich*, there was a striking continuity in the form of power at work: 'Germany in the era 1871–1945 had an uncomfortably persistent tendency' to elevate autocrats to power and to 'submit to their rule' (Evans 1983, 486). I would go further and argue that Frænkel's theorization of Nazi dictatorship reveals the persistence of a form of power grounded in the imperial legacy of Germany's recent past. Carl Schmitt's Weimar-era theory of exceptional rule exuded nostalgia for the imperial monarchy, and Frænkel's autopsy of the prerogative state provides a stark critique of this same legacy. At the core of Frænkel's prerogative state, then, is a specifically imperial form of power – one cloaked in unbridled authority, with the capacity to transcend constitutional constraints at the whim of Schmitt's proverbial sovereign.[23] In order to harness the imperial form of power, Hitler was obliged to nullify the liberal constitutionalism of the Weimar Republic and declare a new Reich based on the absolute power of the National Socialist party-state. One might argue that in reinstating a one-party regime in 1973, President Kenneth Kaunda opted for a similar strategy (see Chapter 5). The difference is that where Hitler overturned the constitution, Kaunda's Second Republic involved only minor alterations to the independence constitution wherein a prerogativist form of power lay latent. This subtle difference is important – where Hitler essentially abolished and even lavished scorn on the *Rechtsstaat*, Kaunda strategically sustained it.

Thus, while Frænkel's nuanced analysis of Nazi political legality helps grasp the contours of prerogative power taken to its extremes, his model of the dual state has only limited value for understanding the postcolonial politico-legal domain. Indeed, the internal complexity and paradoxical essence of the postcolonial governmental apparatus are obscured rather than illuminated when approached via the bifurcation of legality at the level of the state. Frænkel identifies a prerogativist form of power at the core of the National Socialist government, and a similar agency is at work in postcolonial Zambia. In both instances, and perhaps more generally, the residual effects of imperial government are apparent. These effects can be seen in the uncontainable character of power in response to an endemic sense of embattlement, in the constitutional roots of this power and in the continuity of its embodiment in the persons of the imperial Kaiser and the post-imperial chancellor, as well as that of the colonial governor and the republican president. What Frænkel described with great insight – and what I seek to re-describe for postcolonial Zambia – is the workings of a singular, albeit paradoxical, prerogativist form of power that works through, and not against the prevailing constitutional order.

23 Some caveats are in order: Frænkel himself did not make this connection between imperial and Nazi power and seems to treat Hitler's prerogativism as a *sui generis* phenomenon. Further, experts in late 19th-century German history will protest that executive power was not wielded so much by the monarch (i.e., Wilhelm I and II) as by the Kaiser's 'imperial' chancellor, especially Otto von Bismarck.

## *The paradoxical* demos[24]

Zambia's transition to political independence took shape via the enactment of a constitution, i.e., 'a Statutory Instrument made by the British executive' (Sipalo 1978, 132). Independent Zambia's first constitution of 1964 was the *sine qua non* of the nation's political, administrative and legal statehood. The framework of Zambia's founding constitution represented to no small degree what British imperial liberals thought would be best for the new nation. Indeed, Zambia's independence constitution was essentially the final colonial constitution purged of explicit racial discrimination (see Chapter 5); the form of power once embodied in the colonial governor was reassigned intact to the republican president.

The new constitution endowed Zambia's peoples with substantial rights and liberties, but it also had practical political, legal and administrative consequences far beyond the provision of independence. In reproducing many of the trappings of colonial rule, the postcolonial constitution exercised an agency over democratic subjects that was to some degree independent of the conscious intent of both the governors and the governed. What was unclear from the outset, and remains so, is the role of 'the will of the people' in institutionalizing the form of power at the heart of the new independent constitution.

The ineffable 'will of the people' lies at the heart of modern constitutional theory. Its initial problematization can be traced to two tumultuous anti-monarchical uprisings of the late 18th century, the American and French revolutions. These historical upheavals gave birth to the modern constitution and to the notion of republican, representative government (Loughlin 2007, 32–39). These trans-Atlantic revolutionary moments also begat the notion of 'constituent power' (Sieyes 1789), expressed through a representative gathering – a constituent assembly in France, a constitutional conference in America – through which the population of a territory could seize the mandate to frame a new social order in law. This same historical epoch, we should recall, saw the consolidation of liberalism as the ideological engine of European empire.

The Zambian constitution, like republican constitutions generally, is predicated on the liberal notion that it embodies the will of the people; in practice, 'the people' have had little impact on the form of power the constitution creates. Making sense of this paradox is hindered by the inadequacy of the intellectual tools available to analyze postcolonial African politics, and is compounded by the fact that even among Western-educated political theorists, no consensus prevails concerning the role of the 'constituent power of the *demos*' in constitution-making (e.g., Loughlin 2017, Colón-Rios 2010, Frank 2010, Oklopcic 2014, Arato 2016). This ambivalence concerning a foundational premise of political liberalism is the source of much confusion.

One prevalent view emphasizes the 'transcendental' character of constituent power and celebrates its revolutionary potential as an 'extra-legal absolute' (Frank

24 From the classical Greek δῆμος, or 'people.'

2010, 54). The French Revolution of 1789, for example, was self-consciously based on such a transcendental notion of constituent power.[25] French revolutionaries saw in the will of the people the means by which to bridge the rupture in law between the abrupt revolutionary dissolution of the old legal foundations, and the moment when a new form of legitimate legality was effectively restored. Thinkers of a 'realist' bent, on the other hand, have been skeptical about this metaphysical framing of constitution-making. Such theorists prefer to understand the power legitimizing a constitutional order in terms of the pragmatic politics surrounding its drafting and ratification. From this perspective, the transcendental notion of an 'absolutely' empowered *demos* is seductively akin to political absolutism, rendering the transcendental essence of constituent power conducive to appropriation by a tyrant (Arato 2016).[26]

German-American philosopher Hannah Arendt[27] straddled transcendental and realist views of constituent power. For Arendt, politics were, ideally, a process of mutual action and debate among free equals in a public domain. The making of a constitution was, at its best, an act of what Arendt termed 'natality' (1958, 8–9) – an expression of the fundamental human capacity to give birth to something entirely new, and which she suggested 'may be the central category of political, as distinguished from metaphysical, thought.' Arendt noted (1963, 144), however, that it is often 'difficult to recognize the truly revolutionary element in constitution-making.' This has certainly been true for Zambia. The exorcism of colonial domination in Zambia did not come about through the revolutionary fervor of the *demos*. Granted, the final years of colonial rule saw organized resistance (e.g., the anti-colonial Chachacha campaign) and localized violence against British rule (i.e., Zukas 2002, 111–23). Nationalist leaders, like founding President Kenneth Kaunda,[28] spent extended periods in prison (Mwanakatwe 1994, 33). Nevertheless, Zambia's postcolonial political order was forged, not in the fire of revolutionary upheaval, but in staid deliberation in Lusaka and London, between an elite team of nationalist leaders and a group of colonial administrators repre-

25 The intellectual architects of the French Revolution, including Abbé Sieyès (1789), who coined the notion of *pouvoir constituant*, were inspired by Rousseaux's notion of the *volonté général* (popular will) of the French nation (see Baczko 1988).

26 Political absolutism derives from the medieval theory of the Divine Right of Kings (e.g., Figgis 1914, Graeber & Sahlins 2017).

27 I have found the work of political theorist Hannah Arendt to be particularly helpful for thinking about the form of power embodied in postcolonial constitutions. Arendt, a German exile active in the United States in the latter part of the 20th century was hardly a postcolonial thinker in any strict sense, but she espoused a refreshingly non-doctrinaire skepticism about liberalism that resonates with my own experience.

28 First republican president, candidate of the United National Independence Party, Kenneth David Kaunda was born on 28 April 1924. He served as president from 1964 to 1991. Kaunda did not reinvent the Zambian nation on his own. His comrades in arms, Simon Kapwepwe and Harry Nkumbula, among others, were pivotal contributors to the birth of Zambia as is evident from a recent collection of essays on late colonial Zambia (Gewald et al. eds. 2011).

senting the British Crown (Phiri 2006, 118). This fact belies the impression of Zambian constitution-making as a foundational act of 'natality.' It also begs the question of the source and nature of the power that underwrote the social contract upon which the new nation of Zambia was predicated.

### *Constituent vs constituted power*

The essential character of postcolonial power is an enigma. It invokes the will of the people to shore up its legitimacy, governs through procedures and practices that remain largely invisible to the citizenry at large and then systematically constrains opportunities for 'the people' to express their views on the form of power that governs them. This ambivalence toward empowering the *demos* to shape and contain sovereign state power is so pervasive among postcolonial elites that it entraps even the staunchest champions of liberal constitutionalism. This paradox is not specifically Zambian. In the abstract, it reflects what legal theorists Martin Loughlin and Neil Walker (2007, 1) term the 'paradox of constitutionalism' – a tension between the source of legitimacy of democratic states (*constituent* power) and the institutional regime with which power is exercised (*constituted* power). The authors characterize this tension in these general terms:

> Modern constitutionalism is underpinned by two fundamental though antagonistic imperatives: that government power ultimately is generated from the 'consent of the people' and that, to be sustained and effective, such power must be divided, constrained, and exercised through distinctive institutional forms. The people, in [revolutionary-era French lawyer] Maistre's words, 'are a sovereign that cannot exercise sovereignty'; the power they possess, it would appear, can only be exercised through constitutional forms already established or in the process of being established.

In her study *On Revolution* (1963), Hannah Arendt notes that the constitutional orders that emerged from the American Revolution of 1776 and the French Revolution of 1789 both established novel forms of republican power to replace the monarchy. While the architects of both revolutions claimed to have harnessed the will of the population to give their constitutions legal legitimacy, only the American constitution, in Arendt's view, was a sustainable expression of the popular will (see Kalyvas 2008, Frank 2010, Muldoon 2015). In this assessment, Arendt's concern with natality as the foundation of genuine politics nudged her toward a transcendental understanding of constituent power. In the end, however, she argued that it is not the *source* of constitution-making power that determines the course of a revolution, but the way in which that power is *institutionalized* – the source of constitutional power is less important than the ways that power is incorporated in a form of government.

For Arendt, the protagonists of the French Revolution failed to institutionalize their aims and values. She links this failure to its leaders' penchant for an absolute, and quasi-theological, grounds for legitimacy. The French became, in her view (1963, 144), bogged down in a 'permanent' revolution – of the kind which 'do not come to an end and do not produce their end, the foundation of freedom.' In contrast, she argued, the success of the American republic was rooted in the American colonies' century-and-a-half history of pre-revolutionary self-government. The American republic and its constitution persevered, Arendt (1963, 181) claimed, not due to the people's revolutionary passions and ideals, but because of the long-term institutionalization of 'promises, covenants and mutual pledges' that bound together the colonial settlements in British North America.[29] It is precisely such forms of grassroots cultural experience that Zambian constitution-making has consistently disregarded.

The issue of constituent power resurfaced in Europe from the rubble of World War I. Debates around the role of 'the people' in legitimizing state power were in the spotlight as the Imperial German Reich gave way to the liberal Weimar Republic. In this fleeting moment, from the abdication of Kaiser Wilhelm II in 1918 to Hitler's rise to power in 1933, German legal and political theorists debated the parameters of the new republican state. Legal theorist Carl Schmitt, in particular, underscored the importance of the notion of constituent power in assessing the legitimacy of the new constitutional order. Schmitt's liberal contemporaries defended a legalist notion of constitutionalism, according to which law should remain relatively autonomous from politics (Vinx 2019). Schmitt, in contrast, defended a dispensation that retained the prerogativist powers of the imperial sovereign. Schmitt argued that the revolutionary moment that emerged at the end of World War I, and the subsequent birth of the new republican order, represented a transition from the constituent power of the monarch to that of the people (Cristi 1998, 186–9). In highlighting the continuity of the form of state power from the imperial to the republican regime, Schmitt reveals the absolutist concept of power central to his thought (Scheuerman 1996). In his view, the absolute power of the Kaiser had been supplanted, through revolutionary action, by the absolute sovereignty of *das Volk* (the people). To put it in the terms of this study, Schmitt retains an absolutist, imperial form of power at the core of his theory of the state; only the *source* of constituent power undergirding state legitimacy has been reassigned, from the Crown to the *demos*.

Schmitt felt that the liberal democracy of the post-war Weimar constitution was based on a misunderstanding of the role of the *demos* in state formation. As John McCormick (2007, 108) has noted, 'constitutions of the modern republics almost invariably treat the people as a homogenous unit: the people are a unitary and socio-economically anonymous collection of individual citizens, formally equal under the law.' Schmitt (1985, 11; cited in Mouffe 1998, 162) rejected this view of the *demos* as an embodiment of abstract 'humanity,' and argued that '[i]n

29 Arendt has been justifiably faulted with romanticizing the political outcomes of the American Revolution (e.g., Disch 2011, Frank 2010), but this does not, I feel, negate the validity of her general observations about the institutionalization of power (but cf. Honig 1991).

the sphere of the political one cannot abstract out what is political, leaving only universal human equality.' Indeed, the liberal vision of the Weimar Republic was anathema to Schmitt's understanding of the political, which 'begins only with the battle between conflicting, ethnically homogenous entities' (Volk 2017, 90). As Mouffe (1998, 163) points out, Schmitt's conception of democracy 'consists fundamentally in the identity between rulers and ruled,' and is 'linked to the fundamental principle of the unity of the *demos* and the sovereignty of its will.' Liberalism's penchant for individual freedom cannot embrace this subordination of the citizen-subject to a collective ethos, embodied in a prerogativist leader. Liberal democracy, with its emphasis on individualism and pluralism was thus incompatible with Schmitt's ideals.

Belgian political theorist Chantal Mouffe concedes that Schmitt has identified a genuine problem in democratic theory. Mouffe's 'agonist' understanding of politics is aligned with Schmitt's conflictual model in that both see a real tension between democratic consensus and the defense of individual interest. Mouffe (1998, 164) points out that 'Schmitt highlights the fact that democracy always entails relations of inclusion/exclusion. This is a vital insight that democrats would be ill-advised to dismiss simply because they dislike its author.' Indeed, Mouffe continues, '[t]here is an evident opposition between the liberal grammar of equality which postulates universality…, and the practice of democratic equality, which requires the political moment of discrimination between us and them.' At the end of the day, the governors and the governed are not equal. An elected government's monopoly over political power precludes the day-to-day exercise of power by the rest of the population.

From an agonist perspective, the *demos* is intrinsically plural, and internally divided. The ethos of universal equality is incompatible with the necessity of governing, which ascribes rights and implements laws (military conscription, a wealth tax) which are prejudicial to some sections of the *demos*, and not others. The merits of liberalism lie not in the possibility of installing an inclusive regime of universal equality; Mouffe agrees with Schmitt that this makes little practical sense. Rather, in Mouffe's (1998, 165) view, liberal values of universality and humanism can and should afford important checks on "the forms of exclusion that are necessarily inscribed in the political practice of… defining 'the people' who are going to rule."

While there is sufficient conceptual overlap in Mouffe's and Schmitt's respective views of politics to allow for a dialogue (Beckstein 2011), the differences between them are fundamental. Like Arendt (see Volk 2017, 37), Mouffe (1998, 172) eschews Schmitt's 'metaphysical approach to politics and its need for an Archimedean point.' There is, in other words, no need in Mouffe's agonist thought for an omnipotent *demos* to leverage, anchor or stabilize the constitutional order. In contrast to Schmitt's obsession with stability engendered through the absolute identification of sovereign and *demos*, Mouffe implies 'not only the irreducibility but the centrality of conflict to democratic politics' (Thomson 2009, 149). For Mouffe, the identification of the ruled with the rulers is neither desirable nor possible.

Mouffe's fundamental political problem is the inverse of that expressed by Chambers (1977; see Chapter 1), of how to ensure that a president is strong enough to govern, but not so powerful as to endanger basic rights and freedoms. Again like Arendt,[30] Mouffe forefronts the 'constitutional' aspect of power, which both thinkers approach from the ground up. For Mouffe, the basic question of politics is that of how we can 'envisage a form of commonality strong enough to institute a demos but nonetheless compatible with certain forms of pluralism: religious, moral and cultural pluralism as well as a pluralism of political parties?' In this formulation, there is no place for an 'Archimedean' fulcrum of power, whether in the form of a divinely ordained monarch or a mythical *demos*.

The tension between constituent and constituted power in Zambia's constitution-making processes is not hard to see. '[I]n the modern world,' as Loughlin and Walker (ibid., 38) assert, 'constitutional struggles have arisen from the competing claims of various groups authentically to represent the constituent power of the people.' In analyzing the politico-legal dynamics of Zambia's postcolonial situation, the problem is indeed one of identifying the people in whose name power is constituted. In many respects, struggles over representing the elusive Zambian *demos* has, in Ernesto Laclau's (2005, 132) terms, mobilized a 'floating signifier' encompassing "two antagonistic ways of constituting the 'people' as a historical actor." For government, the people is a latent social category – a largely dormant electorate whose periodic, and often unenthusiastic, visits to the polls give a party in power its political legitimacy. For the liberal constitutionalists of the Oasis Forum, the people are a volatile social force, potent with the capacity to re-engineer the very structure of government. In the fervor of political campaigns, these distinctions merge and blur. The entity signified by 'the people' not only 'floats,' but also vacillates unpredictably between the poles of latency and volatility. This will be evident in Chapter 6, which documents arguments between Mwanawasa and the Forum around the need for a constituent assembly to render the constitution legitimate.

## The elusive exception

Over the course of the case analyses that make up the backbone of this study, I argue that political legality is an effect of prerogativism. The postcolonial prerogativism identified in Zambia is a form of power lodged in the body of a president. The prerogativist president claims to possess a transcendent, seemingly

30 Several authors have noted a contradiction within Arendt's view of politics. On the one hand, she appears to write from an agonistic perspective (Honig 1993, Schaap 2007); while others (Benhabib 1996, 200–1) cite her in support of a dialogical or deliberative theory of democracy. It is argued (see Ballacci 2019, 2) that in *The Human Condition* (1958), Arendt is an agonist thinker, while her analysis in *On Revolution* (1963) represents a more deliberative approach. Others (e.g., Lederman 2014, Ballacci 2019) have argued that this 'self-contradiction' is not an unwitting paradox in Arendt's thinking but that, on the contrary, Arendt offers a way of reconciling these opposed conceptions of democratic politics.

miraculous capacity to act outside of the prevailing law with impunity. This capacity resides in the *letter* of postcolonial Zambia's liberal constitution, as well as in the law's *spirit* (the unarticulated norms of politico-legal culture), rooted in the legacy of imperial liberalism.

A key element of postcolonial power is the president's ability to declare a state of emergency (Chanda 1986, Lazar 2009, Ramraj 2008). While this power is critical, it does not exhaust the absolutist character of postcolonial prerogativist rule. Constitutional provisions limit the president's authority to use a state of emergency to abrogate constitutional codes of liberal legality. The Zambian president must, in principle, seek parliament's ratification of his declaration of a state of emergency and even then, it cannot be prolonged indefinitely. While the power to 'decide on the exception' is ideologically important for how the presidency is perceived, focusing on these explicit constitutional capacities conceals the more fundamental locus of the postcolonial president's unfettered powers. Presidential powers encoded in the constitution – however vast – cannot support the implicit *culture* of prerogativism, wherein the 'genuine tyranny' (as Locke put it) of the postcolonial prerogative resides.

Despite the prerogativist entitlements conferred on Zambia's presidents, the most fundamental aspects of presidential power do not rest on explicit constitutional provisions alone. As Craig (1973, 139) points out, in Zambia 'the totality of Presidential power is not in fact restricted to the accumulation of grants of authority expressed within the formal confines of the constitution.' Indeed, presidential powers transcend the constitution, and accumulate in the elite cultural conventions of the politico-legal domain.

The true crux of prerogativist powers lies between the lines of the constitution, in the capacity of the president to step outside legal provisions, to derogate from black letter law. All constitutional reviews have left the president's discretionary powers intact. Herein lies a crucial paradox of postcolonial power – the explicit constitutional provisions which create executive prerogative do not define its limits. Rather, these explicit constitutional provisions merely create the possibility of an opaque realm of power, beyond democratic scrutiny, where absolute discretion reigns.

Prerogativist power, then, does not imply or presuppose a totalitarian regime. *Absolute* prerogativism, or what Schmitt (1931, 79) termed 'qualitative totalitarianism' does, however, and the possibility that 'sporadic' prerogativism may transmute into an absolute dictatorship cannot be dismissed.[31] Unlike a full-blown state of exception, postcolonial prerogativism operates largely in the shadows, in a piecemeal fashion. Its maneuvers are not well-honed and systematic arts of government; rather, they occur in ad hoc fashion, resembling cleverly concealed

31 In basing my notion of prerogativism on debates surrounding Schmitt's work, I am not offering homage to Schmitt's problematic legacy. Rather, my intent is to *reclaim* the notion of presidential prerogative from its association with Fascistic dictatorship and resituate it firmly within a (post-)liberal canon.

ploys, rather than polished political maneuvers.[32] Quite unlike a Fascist dictatorship, Zambian prerogativism requires constitutional foundations, and is not entirely free from an obligation to justify its ends and means. That said, prerogativism is, by nature, largely beyond legal constraint. Transparent or opaque, sporadic or methodical, the prerogativist form of power is the mortar that solidifies and stabilizes Zambia's postcolonial politico-legal order. Its potency resides less in its illiberal excesses, than in the ways it shapes the conditions of possibility for more just and democratic government or, to put it somewhat differently, the political horizons accessible to the Zambian imagination.

It is also important to distinguish between the explicit decisionism associated with absolutist autocracies (like that of Nazi Germany), and the postcolonial prerogativism it resembles in many ways.[33] Decisionism, in the sense originally suggested by Schmitt, is exercised in public, justified by a timely emergency and is targeted at specific policies. Prerogativism, in contrast, finds expression in private actions, out of the public eye; it has no specific temporal triggers; and relates to politics, in the broadest possible sense, as against specific governmental measures. Both decisionism and prerogativism involve the discretionary exercise of power, and both express the sovereign's 'will.' Where decisionist acts are often performative ploys to expand or consolidate a leader's political status, prerogativism eschews scrutiny. From a legal perspective, full-blown decisionist government signals the blatant breakdown of liberal principles. A prerogativism form of power, on the contrary, is rooted in the cracks in the liberal façade of post-imperial government. Inasmuch as the current crises of 'illiberal democracy' proliferate via the expansion of private political powers – as against overt shifts of public policy – Zambia can provide a mirror in which political liberalism's repressed history is reflected – a reminder of how much, and in how many ways, so much of the modern world is postcolonial.

32 Indeed, without the quite inadvertent exposure of the incriminating 'Zamtrop' bank records (see Chapter 7), President Chiluba's allegedly lawfully illegal actions may have never come to light.

33 In Zambian constitutional language, 'prerogative' has a very specific meaning, related to clemency and the commutation of sentences (the 'prerogative of mercy' – see Republic of Zambia 2016: §§96-7). While the Schmittian notion of decisionism has become well-entrenched in the literature on autocracy and illiberal democracy in Europe and North America (e.g., Bessner & Guilhot 2018), I want to stress the specificity of the post-imperial power I have studied in Zambia and feel that 'prerogativism' best expresses that essence.

# 3 Constitutionalism as an ethnographic object

I arrived in Zambia in 2003 with a grant to carry out research about law, politics and state formation in postcolonial Zambia. The plan was to study the participation of the Law Association of Zambia (LAZ) in the Oasis Forum as a unique and unprecedented expression of judicial activism – an evident blurring of a once pristine divide between legal and political agency in Africa. As my fieldwork progressed, I found myself intrigued by the intensity of contestation around constitutional reform. I hadn't anticipated that bickering over principles of constitutionalism between the Oasis Forum and the president, Levy Patrick Mwanawasa, would dominate the front pages of the independent press for several years running.

I was already familiar with many aspects of civil society activism from earlier research (e.g., Gould & Ojanen 2005), and through a network of activist friends and acquaintances accumulated over the course of my work in Zambia since 1983. What was new for me, and for Zambia, was the way that political disputes around constitutionalism had inspired prominent lawyers to harness their 'juridical capital' (Bourdieu 1987, 823) to overtly political ends. It became clear that in order to understand what was at stake in these unusual and very public struggles, it was necessary to map the formal and the informal ways that legal authority was organized and performed in the Third Republic.

Power largely eludes the kind of direct observation ethnography thrives on. Lacking the opportunity to observe the exercise of executive power first hand, I have sought to study how power shapes legality by identifying the *effects* of state authority in the ways state actors think and act. The people I have interviewed and observed are members of an elite professional class, a diverse and unstable stratum of urban Zambian society. These are individuals whose professional lives revolve to a great extent around navigating the effects of state authority in politico-legal processes impinging on elements of administrative law, or via engagement in public processes of constitution-making. By studying the thoughts and actions of such actors, I found, the effects of public authority can become ethnographically accessible.

Against this backdrop, this chapter introduces the contours of the Zambian politico-legal domain. Central to this portrayal of law and how it works is a description of *how* I came to my particular understanding of Zambia's distinct

DOI: 10.4324/9780429198984-4

form of postcolonial legality. I am not a lawyer and never studied for a law degree. My understanding of Zambian law is a direct product of my methodology – the primary element of which is extended immersion in everyday interactions between legal and political actors – or better, between lawyer-politicians and political lawyers – at a particular time and place. An ethnographic approach accepts the premise that objects of interest – be they legal disputes, activist strategies or presidential privileges – are in some respect an effect of the process of trying to understand them. Ethnographers come to their understandings of the world differently than, for example, lawyers, economists or journalists. By the same token, two ethnographers will seldom be in complete agreement with one another about the nature of an object of common concern – a reflection of the fact that ethnographic encounters are unique events that cannot be replicated.

Source-based descriptions of events or interviews are as flawed or precise as the original source material. In most cases, factual accounts can be checked for accuracy. Interpretations are a different matter. Readers and publishers require that, on the whole, books like this make sense, and the interpretative tools and moves authors employ are expressions of the quest for coherence. Abstract conceptualizations and related theoretical elements constitute the main tools scholars use to coax a credible story from a patchwork of contradictory and inconclusive materials. At the same time, abstract conceptual schemes – such as the one outlined in Chapter 2, and in the Excursus (in Part III, below) – allow readers and researchers familiar with other situations to scrutinize a case study such as this one for common characteristics and differences.

Ethnography and social theory are thus irrevocably bound together, but they have a complicated relationship. There are two specific tensions worth mentioning. The first tension relates to the role of general concepts in the process of ethnographic fieldwork. Obviously, it is not possible for a trained scholar to enter the field with an empty mind. All researchers have accumulated epistemic habits (Liljeström & Peltonen 2017) over the course of their lives and careers, and ethnographic observation is inevitably filtered through a cognitive framework of tacit, intuitive assumptions about the field and its inhabitants (Gould & Uusihakala 2016, 9-37). Acts of ethnographic selectivity (the sites one visits, the things one pays attention to, the people one talks to, the questions one asks) can easily tend to reinforce rather than destabilize one's unreflected intuitions. The antidote to being blinded by one's personal and professional calibrations is to exercise *reflexivity*, a sort of systematic auto-analysis involving relentless challenges to one's interpretation of a situation or bit of information, questioning how feelings of sympathy, repulsion or confusion may be based in the ethnographer's training or personal history.[1] No amount of reflection can guarantee objectivity in ethnographic research, but reflexivity can provide a safeguard against ethnocentric distortions of culturally distant realities. In this project, which relates so intimately to the impact of Western interests and justifications on African politico-

1 For discussions of ethnographic reflexivity see Lichterman (2017) and Davies (2012).

legal institutions, it has felt especially important to keep my own interpretative scheme distinct from the normative orientations of the actors under observation. It is particularly problematic, in my experience, when a conceptual system, such as political liberalism, informs ethnography as both an interpretative tool and a normative framework (cf. Cheesman 2018b).

The second tension between ethnography and theory is the inverse of the potential for being blinded by unreflected assumptions. At its most successful, ethnographic immersion aims at attaining a perspective on the world as close as possible to that of one's informants.[2] Sometimes, an ethnographer's identification with the 'native' viewpoint is so complete that it proves impossible for them to 'get back' to an 'outside' vantage point on the situations they have studied. The 're-externalization' of one's perspective is, nonetheless, necessary in order to translate one's findings into generalizations that can be shared with people who have never been 'there.' Despite much hard work, and the generosity of one's informants, a case study will not be of interest to others – scholars and lay readers alike – unless a compelling argument can be made for its more general relevance.

The fact that I came to the dynamics of Zambian constitutionalism without a systematic versing in American or European constitutional theory (the default canons of the field) means that I have not been predisposed to judge the various strains of Zambian constitutionalism with respect to external legal standards. Given the overwhelming hegemony of Euro-American constitutional theory as a template for comparative constitutional studies, this lacuna in my preparation might be seen as an asset. Of course, it follows that I will have inadvertently rediscovered the wheel at some junctures. I pray this doesn't distract from the sense of discovery I have felt.

## The Zambian context

Like most large African states, Zambia is a difficult territory to govern (Herbst 2014). With a land area of 743,390 km$^2$, Zambia is slightly larger than France, and much of the country is sparsely populated (24 residents per km$^2$, compared with France's 119). The population's median age in 2020 was 17.6 years, meaning that the majority of Zambians can be considered economically dependent on

2 'Informant' is a conventional term used in ethnographic literature to describe members of a group, community or institution under study who voluntarily provide their experiences and insights to the ethnographer. In my case, the people who generously shared their time and wisdom were many; some of them became what is commonly termed 'key' informants, i.e., people I got to know better and spoke with numerous times. Due to the nature of this study, which recounts well-publicized events in the public realm, many of my informants were, and are, prominent public figures, and a few have subsequently risen to positions of considerable authority. None of the sources cited herein requested anonymity, and I have not tried to anonymize such sources which, and by virtue of their prominent public roles, would have been virtually impossible.

a working adult. About 45% of the people now live in cities, double the figure at independence in 1964.

Zambia has no known fossil fuel deposits, and given the high cost of petroleum imports, human muscle power is the primary source of energy. From the perspective of global capitalist markets, the country's main economic asset is its non-renewable minerals, above all copper (Fraser & Larmer 2010). The challenges of government are exacerbated by variable climate patterns, overworked soils and the predatory quest for land and minerals by unaccountable and often irresponsible international corporations. In recent decades, Zambia's economic growth has been robust albeit uneven, lifting the country into the bracket of lower-middle income countries.[3] But, as in much of Africa, rapid population growth and decades of meager investment in health, education and social services have overwhelmed efforts to convert economic growth into social equity. Indeed, according to one comprehensive review (World Bank Group 2018, 25), 'hunger, undernourishment, and malnutrition rates for Zambia have been reported as among the highest in the world,' and 'while [r]ecent economic growth has brought some benefits to urban areas … poverty in rural areas remains widespread and increasing' (ibid., 27). Even with robust growth, as was the case between 2004 and 2014, '[i]mprovements in many indicators of living standards benefited only urban areas, and often just the wealthiest among the urban population (ibid., 23). On the whole, the Third Republic status quo has been much kinder to urban professionals than to the self-employed *demos.*

For the past century, Zambia's wealth in labor and minerals has sufficed to sustain a lifestyle based on an energy-intensive level of material consumption for a small minority of the population. Founding President Kaunda and his United National Independence Party (UNIP) hoped to find the means to expand the sphere of modern consumption to the entire nation, but could not, for reasons too complex and numerous to portray here, break the pattern of elite asset appropriation established under colonialism (Bates & Collier 1995, Bigsten & Kayizzi-Mugerwa 2000). Nationalist leaders believed that colonial racism explained why the indigenous population did not partake equally in Northern Rhodesia's wealth; of course, this was true, in part. But it is also arguable that copper revenues were never adequate to sustain the lifestyle enjoyed by the White colonial classes for a population larger by two orders of magnitude. Agricultural economists have consistently advised the Zambian government to diversify the economy away from its singular dependence on copper (Dodge 1977, Kydd 1988, Oya 2007). This implied a push to improve smallholder productivity and to invest in primary commodity processing. This has not happened to any decisive degree. The

3 The World Bank defines the threshold for lower-middle income status as a gross national income (GNI) per capita of more than $1,006 per annum. Zambia attained this status in 2011. Zambia's GNI per capita hit a historical peak in 2014 of $1,770, but slipped back down to $1,300 in 2017. In 2022, the World Bank reclassified Zambia as a low income country.

burgeoning financial and service sectors that have boosted growth in the 21st century have barely kept apace with population growth. Another obstacle to economic diversification is the unquestioned political premise that greater equity should be achieved among Zambians by raising the consumption of the masses by overall growth in output, rather than by redistributing the wealth accruing to the elite.

Zambia has enjoyed a long history of relative political stability (Burnell 2005), and for the duration of its independent history, there has been virtually no violent strife among the nation's many sociolinguistic groups. This relative tranquility is in sharp contrast to the endemic chaos afflicting the Democratic Republic of the Congo and Angola, across Zambia's northern and eastern borders, and Zimbabwe, to the southeast. What distinguishes Zambia in the southern African context, aside from its mineral wealth, is the extreme concentration of the population along the north/south railway line that divides the country in half, and which sports several major urban settlements. These include the main Copperbelt towns of Ndola and Kitwe at the railroad's northern terminus and Livingstone on the southern border with Zimbabwe. The nation's capital and its largest city, Lusaka, the fastest-growing metropolis in Southern Africa, lies roughly halfway between these two points. An important factor contributing to Zambia's exceptional stability may be the high level of intermarriage among different groups along the Line of Rail. Zambians themselves claim that they are a peaceful nation.

The economy's relatively robust growth reflects, to a large extent, the rewards of a bullish (if volatile) copper market over the past decade. Increased economic dynamism may also be attributed to socially painful adjustment policies in the 1990s, though the causal relation between austerity and subsequent growth is not straightforward (Scott 2002). Neoliberal reforms do not entirely explain the sharp rise in gross national income in the 2000s, nor the dramatic rise in life expectancy at birth, from less than 45 years in 2000, to nearly 62 years in 2016 (World Bank Group, op cit.). But there is no denying that President Chiluba's efforts to reorganize the moribund public economy (dominated by lethargic parastatal firms) infused the economy with a vitality that single-party management and pervasive state monopolies had failed to muster.

That said, Zambia's poor economic performance under UNIP's 27-year monopoly was not simply the consequence of Kaunda's quasi-socialist/humanist policies. Surrounded by hostile racist regimes, Zambia in the Second Republic was attacked and sanctioned by these apartheid regimes for its generous support to national liberation struggles in South Africa, Zimbabwe and Namibia (Hall 1969). Apartheid South Africa's allies in the United Kingdom and the United States, and the international agencies they controlled, were also hostile toward Kaunda's socialist experiments. This campaign had strong geopolitical aspects in the Cold War landscape of the day, but the main prize at stake was arguably Zambia's rich copper deposits and the mining infrastructure Kaunda's government had nationalized in 1968 (Sardanis 2003, Fraser & Larmer 2010). In Kaunda's words (in Kydd 1988, 227),

> 'It was not socialist principles which ruined the Zambian economy, but unfavourable economic terms which the North has imposed on the South … I have no power … We agreed to the IMF reform programme much against out better judgement.'

The end of the Cold War thrust Zambia into a radically different realm of political economy. With the collapse of the Berlin Wall and the implosion of the Eastern European socialist empire, an economic Big Bang shook the foundations of many postcolonial African states and societies. The Zambian economy underwent radical deregulation, the era of single-party elections ended and the public arena saw the burgeoning of private actors and interests. A major beneficiary was the corps of non-profit associations (self-termed civil society), as was the increasingly independent legal profession. In the wake of these tumultuous reforms, it was evident that many of the problems that political and economic liberalization were supposed to resolve, persisted. A burst of economic growth, technological renewal, new avenues for upward mobility and constitutional reform brought an array of new rights and liberties. Yet, wealth and power continue to accumulate in the hands of a few; vulnerable citizens have been dispossessed of their basic economic entitlements (land, water, housing, employment) in the scramble for profits. Despite profound structural changes over the past generation in terms of living standards, for most Zambians much has remained the same.

## Ethnographic encounters

My most intensive stint of fieldwork, about 18 months all told, took place in Lusaka during the reign of President Levy Mwanawasa (2001–8).[4] This was an unusual period in Zambia's political history: neither before nor since has ostensible non-partisan political rhetoric, emanating from civic alliances like the Oasis and Citizen Forums (see Chapter 6), gained such visibility and influence on public affairs. The uniqueness of this moment has become increasingly evident in hindsight. At the time, the public media portrayed the ongoing campaigns for a 'people-driven' constitution as an inevitable phase in the evolution of Zambia's young democracy. In retrospect, the linearity of Zambia's political evolution is not so self-evident. All the more reason, then, to apply critical reflection on the nature of the knowledge my informants and I collaborated in producing.

My fieldwork coincided with a phase in which law and legal actors in Zambia appeared to wield immense authority, both within the political domain and among citizens at large. That said, it was evident on close inspection that law is an endlessly pliable tool, not only for judges and lawyers, but also in the hands of social engineers, political entrepreneurs, activist clergy and other self-styled champions of justice, not to mention Zambia's prerogativist president.

4 On-site data collection began in 2003 and continued until 2013.

The power of law is to enable not to effect; law does not do anything on its own, it must be deployed. This is a key limitation on law's political utility. In practical terms, plaintiffs seeking relief for damages stemming from illegal actions must employ a lawyer to bring their complaint before a judge. Only under exceptional conditions can lawyers initiate legal processes on their own – and even then, they must be able to establish 'standing' – a personal stake in the outcome. Law, then, must be invoked in its own particular institutional setting, and in accordance with stringent procedural rules, for its power to become effective and visible. Attaining relief from damages – whether of a civil, criminal or administrative nature – requires a court and a bench with requisite jurisdiction, representatives of the bar (accredited lawyers) and a plaintiff with standing. Sometimes, high-profile cases are resolved dramatically, by purposive judges with an extra-legal agenda. More often, legal claims dissipate in a blur of banal technicalities; a huge number of cases founder because of the late or improper filing of crucial documents, and other procedural missteps. That said, courts have an imperative to deliver an unambiguous ruling on cases which fall within their jurisdiction. Judges are obliged to determine 'the truth' in any given dispute, to pass judgment concerning guilt and innocence, the lawful and the illegal. Judicial rulings can, of course, be overturned on appeal, but at no level of the judiciary do judges issue provisional or conditional judgments. Each ruling is supposed to represent the truth based on the evidence and the applicable statute.

This legal imperative to speak the truth implies a fundamental distinction between law and politics. Hannah Arendt, as Chantal Mouffe (1993, 14) notes, 'was absolutely right to insist that in the political sphere one finds oneself in the realm of opinion, or "doxa", and not in that of truth.' The provisional nature of political opinions – which are valid only until a more 'learned' or expedient opinion emerges – makes legal certainty an important ally. Under the UNIP party-state, there was no possibility for challenging the constitutionality of an executive action, or the validity of an electoral outcome. In the Third Republic, since 1991, applications for the judicial review of executive actions and of electoral petitions have increased markedly, enhancing the political agency of lawyers and judges, and laying the foundations for new forms of symbiosis between law and politics – various forms of political legality.

Clearly, the ends to which law (and the authority of lawyers) can be used are many, not all of them strictly speaking legal (there will be many examples of this in the chapters to follow). The boundary between allegedly legitimate law and political legality is porous and shifting. The intrinsic instrumentality of law – the requirement that it responds to and resolves practical legal problems – implies the need to pay special attention to the nature of the incentives, disincentives and justifications that inform the labors of lawyers, as well as the rules of attraction which play out in the formation of alliances and networks.

Law is not just any source of authority, and lawyers are not typical social agents. Law encompasses an undeniably metaphysical aspect, in the sense that the historical origins of law – like those language or of human society itself – are hidden from empirical scrutiny. In all known human societies, law-like forms of both explicit and implicit normative code exert a force which is crucial to the accomplishment of social order. However, there is no consensus on how this force has come about. In modern societies, it is 'somehow' encoded in the constitution, which derives its authority from the quasi-mythic 'will of the people.' It follows from law's ineffable origins that there is no clear or identifiable source of legal or of constitutional authority. It exists – in varying degrees under different political dispensations – but its roots have a quantum nature; the closer one looks, the harder they are to pin down. Law's indeterminate origins do not prevent lawyers and constitutional theorists from conjuring up competing justifications for particular forms of jurisprudence, and for commensurate forms of power. For the ethnographer, however, the point is not to agree or disagree with any particular interpretation, but to understand how and why, in a given context, certain positions gain credibility, and to map how these epistemic politics predicate certain kinds of effects beyond the chambers or the courtroom.

In 2004, I settled in a walled-in compound managed by the Finnish Embassy in the upscale neighborhood of Kabulonga. My neighbors were upper-middle-class professionals, lawyers, businessfolk and diplomats. The election of lawyer Levy Mwanawasa to the presidency in 2001 marked a new phase in Zambia's evolution from a tattered humanist outpost to a bustling neoliberal metropole. President Mwanawasa's decision to investigate Frederick Chiluba, his predecessor, on corruption charges suggested that Zambia's democracy had turned a new leaf. The Mwanawasa government's successful campaign for international debt cancellation under the Heavily Indebted Poor Countries initiative in 2005 infused the economy with a fresh wave of liquidity,[5] while also contributing to the rising ethos of civic optimism. Private, non-profit bodies – calling themselves civil society – with close ties to foreign donor agencies and international non-governmental organizations, were awash with project assistance. A generation of young, upwardly mobile professionals was emerging as a significant political and economic factor, fueling the proliferation of new shopping malls, restaurants, cinemas and upmarket 'watering holes.' For example, one such bar – Rhapsody's, located in the high-end Arcades shopping mall, a short distance from the University of Zambia's main campus – was one of several popular meeting places for a diverse array of stylish urban professionals enjoying afterwork sundowners. On any given evening, I could usually count on running into any number of acquaintances with valuable information (and juicy gossip) for my project.

Such public spaces were important sites for ethnographic networking, but not with the legal community. Lawyers working for well-appointed legal chambers were a pivotal source of knowledge and opinions for my study, but they are also notoriously aloof and private persons. Lawyers also run on the clock. With the exception of a handful of legal practitioners who generously shared their time with me, it was virtually impossible to find opportunities for ethnographic 'deep hanging out' (Geertz 1998) with lawyers or judges. Other groups

5 Zambia's debt burden decreased by half a billion dollars in 2005 (Zulu 2006, 4).

were more accessible. The managers and employees of the non-governmental organizations working on constitutional reform and related issues often had university degrees and a personal situation quite similar to mine. We shared a common vocabulary and an interest in the political gossip of the day. Members of the activist clergy, though not seen at bars like Rhapsody's, were open and welcoming.

Early on, I made a consequential strategic choice not to embed myself in any one specific site, say a private law firm, but to take a 'multi-sited' (Marcus 1995) approach to gathering research data. In this case, multi-sitedness implied not only attention to a variety of different organizations and processes, but also an increasing reliance on internet resources, especially for court documents and online journalism. My ethnographic 'sample' was determined by my focus on the Oasis Forum – a dispersed network of autonomous organizations. The Forum was a consortium of organizations comprising the Law Association of Zambia, Zambia's main Christian bodies, as well as the Non-Governmental Organization Coordinating Committee, itself a consortium of women's non-profits. Following paths radiating out from the Forum, my research took me to non-profits like Women for Change, the Zambia Civic Education Association, Transparency International Zambia, Citizens for Poverty Reduction and the Jesuit Centre for Theological Reflection; as well as to state agencies including the Human Rights Commission, the Director for Public Prosecution and the ad hoc Task Force against Corruption. I was particularly well received at the Catholic Commission for Justice and Peace, a bastion of liberal activism. At each of these sites, I encountered individuals and initiatives that revealed different aspects of the ongoing disputes around constitutionalism.

As my presence in the field lengthened, my store of information (and gossip) grew, and the campaign strategists I befriended shared their perspectives on timely events with me more freely. These visits and conversations often generated the need to triangulate around a new development or a bit of information with another key informant or to seek out a new source of data. This strategy is highly prone to errors of omission and amplification. An extended process of post-field reflecting, analyzing and writing has helped redress some of my more blatant errors of perception and interpretation, but it is not possible to second-guess the real-time choices one makes (to invest time and energy in validating some succulent piece of gossip, for example) while in the field.

My days in the field were spent driving around Lusaka from office to office, seeking out informants and new information. As friction deepened between the government and constitutional activists, the frequency of campaign workshops and seminars accelerated. These public events were informative and fruitful for securing meetings with potential informants. Many contacts found my curiosity about their work both flattering and surprising. (How, some wondered, could anyone have so much time for so much seemingly random conversation?) Informants were forthcoming and applied themselves to answering my questions seriously. They were also keen to ensure that the information I gathered was reliable.

As my research progressed, many contacts were eager to learn whether I had information useful for their particular endeavors. Recruitment into one's informants' personal projects is always a concern in ethnographic research. I experienced expectations from constitutional activists to side with them in their efforts to wrest concessions from the government, but this pressure was neither explicit nor overbearing. For the most part, people were open to discussing their work and seemed confident that any even-minded observer would grasp the justice of their actions.

At the same time, some facts were maddeningly elusive. There was always a variety of explanations for the ceaseless maneuverings of the president and his political allies. Informants would speculate extensively about who was behind the day's juiciest media leak, and what this revealed about hidden alliances and secret agendas. Some of these leaks, alliances and agendas appeared to be relevant to my evolving inquiry and I would often spend days trying to verify a rumor, only to find new ones awaiting me at every juncture. I have done my level best to ensure that none of this fake news has ended up in this study.

In the course of my fieldwork, I encountered many diverging and mutually contradictory accounts of constitutional politics. Parties to these incidents and outside observers alike had different understandings of the facts underlying prominent incidents of the day. Key points of contention were President Frederick Chiluba's alleged theft of public funds, and his unconstitutional attempt at prolonging his stay in office; the legality of President Levy Mwanawasa's subsequent 'War on Corruption,' and his many skirmishes with the Oasis Forum over constitutional reform. Equally controversial were President Michael Sata's later attempts at fomenting a populist revolution, and the chaotic political machinations which accompanied his untimely death in office. These incidents are explored in detail in subsequent chapters.

In constructing these accounts, I have combined my 'primary,' or first-hand data with so-called 'secondary' materials (court records, newspaper articles and so on). The research materials, both primary and secondary, are rife with contradictions and lacunae. I have not attempted to paper over the cracks and crevices in my materials; at the same time, I have done my best to provide the most coherent account possible of what I learned. I cannot claim to have achieved an objective reckoning with these materials. It is in the nature of politics that discussions about political issues are framed from a partisan perspective. The conversations I had with key informants, or with casual acquaintances, were virtually always about who was right and who was wrong, about the likely consequences of a particular incident for 'our side.' I cannot claim that my analysis is unwaveringly neutral in all its aspects – certainly, I was swayed (and repelled) by some of the arguments and personalities that figured centrally in these conversations. Nonetheless, I have, as best I can, sought to look beyond partisan considerations to the way that postcolonial liberalism underwrites democratic activism and contributes to its successes and failures. I read the testimony of my informants, like the court judgments I discuss in subsequent chapters, against the backdrop of the complex political processes in which they are embedded, as evidence of the ways that the form of sovereign power shapes the contours of legality itself. Inevitably, the story I am telling about Zambia's politico-legal domain is only one of many possible versions. While I have tried to ensure that this account is empirically valid, it is not *the* Truth; it is not intended as the final word, but as an overture to further conversation.

## A makeshift toolkit

My methodological strategy was initially inspired by a research agenda termed constitutional ethnography, first proposed by Kim Lane Scheppele (2004, 2017). Scheppele's (2004, 395) proposal for 'the study of the central legal elements of polities using methods that are capable of recovering the lived detail of the politico-legal landscape' succinctly captured the spirit of what I was attempting. My attraction to socio-legal studies, and to the study of constitutionalism in particular, reflects a dissatisfaction with existing anthropologies of the state. As my work progressed, I felt increasingly constrained by the way that anthropological analyses of state institutions tended to be delimited not only by the human scale of the ethnographer (which is inevitable), but also more decisively by the implicit perspective of the individual citizen/subject central to this literature. For example, an influential introduction to state anthropology (Gupta & Sharma 2009) advocated approaching the 'cultural constitution of the state' in terms of 'the experience of everyday practices' and the circulation of public 'representations' of state power. While it is interesting and important to understand how citizens experience state authority, anthropologies of the state have largely ignored the thoughts and practices of those who exercise that power. Path-breaking studies (e.g., Das 2011, Gupta 2012, Li 2007, Chalfin 2010, Olivier de Sardan 2014) have opened up anthropology to fresh ways of seeing postcolonial states. But, for the most part, works in this vein are concerned with revealing the dynamics, and injustices, of how sovereign power is *deployed*; they have little to say about how it is *constituted*. Their focus, in other words, is on what Philip Abrams (1988, 65) terms the 'output side of the political process.' How the 'force of the law' (Bourdieu 1987), i.e., legality itself, is constituted seems similarly to be taken for granted. Scheppele's original agenda (2004, 391; emphasis added) pointed to a broader purview when she proposed constitutional ethnography as a means of determining 'the *mechanisms* through which governance is accomplished and the strategies through which governance is attempted, experienced, resisted and revised, taken in historical depth and cultural context.'

Fieldwork led me to a series of encounters with lawyers who were drawn into associations with politicians, media moguls, private bankers, men of the cloth and donor-sponsored democracy activists. A constant thread running through my inquiries was the extended constitution-making process, spanning a long decade from 2003 to 2016. This process of constitution-making, analyzed in Chapter 6, revealed how the politico-legal principles undergirding these alliances were disputed, tested and ultimately bent in ways that seemed to have none of the intrinsic 'logic' that Scheppele's agenda had promised to reveal. As data accumulated and I rehearsed numerous cycles of interpretation, it became clear that I could not make sense of the cases and personal trajectories I had scrutinized and mapped in detail solely by reference to these actors' intentions – be they driven by self-interest or ideological commitment. I needed to go beyond a focus on intent to an analysis of the barely visible historical structures – encoded in university curricula, professional codes, juridical protocols and the 'spirit of the law' – that shape individual priorities and practices. But a bracketing of intent cannot dispense with individual purpose altogether. How, then, to invoke the structural determination of social action without collapsing the agency of my real-life actors into the blind performance of a pre-composed script?

This begs the question of how to make sense of the relationship between law and politics in the aftermath of colonial government, where power continues to be centralized and buffered from political regulation by an arsenal of 'exceptional' prerogatives, shrouded in veils of concealed practices and countenanced by both legal script and convention. Achille Mbembe (2001, 11) formulates the dilemma succinctly:

> There thus arises the purely methodological question of knowing whether it is possible to offer an intelligible reading of the forms of social and political imagination in contemporary Africa solely through conceptual structures and fictional representations used precisely to deny African societies any historical depth and to define them as radically other, as all that the West is not.

The task then, as I understood early on, could not be merely to document an elusive and largely illusory 'justice cascade' (Sikkink 2011), i.e., the progressive deepening of liberal legality in the politico-legal domain. Making sense of the acts and intentions of politico-legal players demanded the (re)theorization of power itself, based on the careful scrutiny of alignments and discrepancies between individuals and institutions aims and empirical outcomes of their actions.

An ethnographic approach to constitutional politics does not guarantee privileged insights into the politico-legal domain, and especially to the 'opaque and murky' (Mbembe 2001, 14) regions where exception thrives and discretion is the rule. As with any ethnographic endeavor, such access is an outcome of previous field experience, a certain amount of audacity and a substantial dose of luck. But penetration beyond the veil of discretion is not the only way to reveal the mechanisms by which constitutional spirit becomes flesh (so to speak). One can reasonably expect that the constituent elements of sovereign power should be evident in its everyday deployment, if one only knows where and how to look. For the purposes of this study, court records have been an important site for interrogating the ways a prerogativist form of power is sustained. An understanding of how sovereign power is legally constituted has informed the scrutiny of political outcomes and the concomitant struggles around them. In this way, my constitutional ethnography has involved a constant circulation between historical-theoretical reflection, ethnographic immersion and the close reading of politico-legal documents, such as the court rulings and tribunal reports central to the narrative in Chapters 7 through 10.

The methodological issue at stake here is this: Inasmuch as the postcolonial form of power is assembled, as Agamben (1998) puts it, around a paradox of public visibility and private concealment, of accountability and discretion, of liberal legality and illiberal exception, how should this be reflected in a first-hand, ethnographic engagement with the politico-legal domain? One answer can be read from the above: A genuinely ethnographic study of constitutional politics must look beyond conventional concerns with the ways that contests over the deployment of power enhance or degrade liberal tenets, to the foundations of the form of power itself. This involves anticipating conceptual elaborations in the Excursus, seeking out manifestations of the sovereign's 'body politick' in the myriad associations and mundane practices that sustain Zambia's postcolonial politico-legal domain. In other words, an ethnography of constitutionalism must begin – as does all ethnography – with the everyday, while aspiring to excavate the foundations of constitutional history that have made observable varieties of contemporary thought and action possible. As it turns out, I found myself digging up not one, but two bodies. But now I am getting ahead of myself.

## Domains of legal knowledge

When planning my initial fieldwork, I found no previous attempts to interrogate the nature of postcolonial statutory legality ethnographically. The field has developed rapidly in the last decade.[6] By virtue of Zambia's received constitutional order, there are common points of reference in the institutional design and legislation between the edicts of occidental liberal legality, and those of Zambia's domestic legal system. From a socio-legal perspective, however, English and Zambian law are quite different entities.[7] Despite procedural similarities and a shared technical vocabulary, the basic premises underlying Euro-American liberal legalism apply poorly to the empirical field of Zambian law as I observed it. Among many other, less fundamental discrepancies, liberal legal theorists assume an institutionalized liberal polity, shaped by relatively stable legislative precedents, and a functioning, competitive market within which the legal profession is firmly embedded. Zambia does not exhibit these properties. On the contrary, the real-life contingencies and specificities of Zambia's politico-legal institutions and the workings of its market differ so markedly from comparable institutions in the United Kingdom, or in other comparable common law jurisdictions, that

6 A growing literature on legal actors and professions in the postcolonial world is renewing the field of postcolonial law substantially. The work of Zimbabwean scholar G.H. Karekwaivanane (2011, 2016, 2017) is particularly significant. See also Verheul (2013), Ellett (2013), Dezalay and Karekwaivanane (2015), Cooper-Knock and Karekwaivanane (2016) and Oloka-Onyango (2017).

7 These differences are illustrated clearly in Chapter 7, where English and Zambian court rulings based on virtually identical case materials are compared.

the generalities of conventional legal theory fail to connect with empirical reality in productive ways.

In light of the disjuncture between (occidental) legal theory and (postcolonial) legal practice, it is necessary to rethink the nature of postcolonial law anew. Postcolonial legality, however, remains a small, backwater district, tucked away in the sprawling continent of contemporary legal theory. The heyday of empirical enquiry into the politico-legal systems of (former) colonial jurisdictions, once a bustling site of imperial knowledge production, had largely passed by the 1980s. The empirical domain of postcolonial jurisprudence as an object of theorization in its own right is scant (cf. Douzinas & Geary 2005), which has led to much misunderstanding.[8] It is commonplace, for example, to characterize Zambia as a 'weak' rule-of-law jurisdiction in comparison with the 'strong' jurisdictions of the United Kingdom and other Euro-American court systems.[9] This description is valid in a banal quantitative sense: In my estimation, the ratio of lawyers to the general population in England and Wales was roughly 1:420 in 2017. In Zambia, the comparable ratio was 1:16,100 – there are, in other words, about 40 times more lawyers per resident in the United Kingdom than in Zambia. Similar differences pertain with respect to firm size and financial turnover; to fees, licensing and regulatory practices; and so on. But to term Zambia's legal system as categorically 'weak' presumes a universal standard of jurisdictional strength which channels unsettling imperial undertones.

Many of my Zambian informants, it bears noting, saw much room for improvement in the Zambian legal apparatus. As one senior constitutional scholar told me:

> The problem that we have in Zambia is this: We live in an environment where archaic laws, which are basically unconstitutional, still exist. Now, throughout the history of this country, there's never been a law review. [Not] even ... at the time of Independence, as happened in Namibia and South Africa. What they did, when they had a new constitution in place was to review all the *apartheid* laws ... Those that were not consistent with the constitution were repealed.
>
> In Zambia that has never happened. Even though we have gone through various constitutional dispensations, that exercise has never been carried out, largely because there is lack of political will on those who have political power to carry out those changes ... These oppressive laws are useful for them, as and when they need them. So it's just good to keep them there.

8 Karekwaivanane's recent work on Zimbabwe's legal history (2011, 2015, 2017) has productively revived and rejuvenated this tradition. In his magisterial *The Struggle over State Power in Zimbabwe* (2017), Karekwaivanane's focus is on the legitimacy of 'the law,' which he situates within a tension between state coercion and popular resistance. This study differs from Karekwaivanane's work in that my focus is on the constitution of legality itself. Absent self-evident (liberal) standards, this has required bracketing the extent and mechanisms of law's legitimacy.

9 See, for example, the UK Supreme Court's ruling in *Vedanta v Lungowe* (UKSC 20, Hilary Term 2019), which makes precisely this distinction.

This authoritative account has merit, but it does not follow that the Zambian judiciary is simply a flawed or immature version of UK law. For all of its shortcomings – and given its chronic underfunding – Zambia's politico-legal system is, in many respects, both competent and predictable, with its own particular jurisprudence and institutional practices, including robust agents of enforcement. These institutions, while prone to the human failings that plague judiciaries everywhere, have served the basic ends of state stability and security for half a century.[10] To understand the system's strengths amid its flaws – and to devise realistic and effective strategies for judicial reform – requires achieving cognitive distance from the normative assumptions of colonial epistemology.

Zambia's legal code has deep roots in British law, which Zambian lawyers commonly refer to as 'received' law. This is evident from the Zambian constitution itself. According to the 1996 version (cited in Munalula 2004, 2):

> 'existing law' means all law, whether a rule of law or a provision of an Act of Parliament or of any other enactment or instrument whatsoever (including any Act of Parliament of the United Kingdom or Order of Her Majesty in Council), having effect as part of the law of Zambia or part thereof immediately before the commencement of this [Constitutional Amendment] Act.

This definition offers a distinction that separates statutory law from 'custom' – normative codes ostensibly based on precolonial jurisprudence. Such a distinction has profound consequences for attempting to unravel what is *post*colonial about Zambian law. This understanding of the law also implies, among other things, that contemporary Zambian legal institutions reproduce a model initially designed to serve imperial rule. As noted by Catholic priest and activist Father Joseph Komakoma (interview, 2005):

> The constitution is critical since we are building a nation, [but] it is not something that we created. It was an imposed reality. If you consider the 1884 Berlin conference, that's where these states come from. We have [a state], and we have to make sense with it. How we make sense with it is that we have to have some guiding principles of how we are going to relate with each other, and how the state is going to function. We haven't done that yet as a nation, and we have been grappling with this for the past forty years.

Now, it is *not* true, strictly speaking, that prior to our conversation in 2005, Zambians had never debated how the state should function. There had been four substantial constitutional reviews since independence (in 1972, 1991, 1993–5

10 Assessing whether or not Zambian courts deliver *justice* as well as, for example, English courts is beyond my purview. That said, it is not controversial that the Zambian court system is under-resourced and over-worked. Judging by the ancient axiom, 'justice delayed is justice denied,' achieving genuine justice for all in the Zambian judicial system would require substantial investment.

and 2003–5) and four constitutional texts (1964, 1973, 1991 and 1996), all of which were enacted with public debate – in parliament and elsewhere. Indeed, Zambian constitution-making has been a recurrent and tenacious enterprise. Given the expense and effort involved, it seems curious that Zambia – a relatively poor and stable nation – would find the need to revisit its supreme law with such frequency. What Father Komakoma meant, I believe, is not that Zambians haven't debated constitutionalism, or the terms of their social contract, but that from the beginning, the procedure for defining how they should relate to one another has been flawed.[11]

To understand the contours of the politico-legal domain, it will be useful to flag two sets of conceptual distinctions that guided my path into this inquiry. It is, first, necessary to identify what is distinct about a socio-legal approach to law, in comparison with the 'doctrinal' (or legalist) one that dominates legal discourse in Zambia.[12] At first glance, doctrinal and socio-legal analysis appears to focus on different objects – doctrinal analysis typically applies to state (statutory, formal, official) law, while customary (informal, native, folk) law is commonly the subject of legal anthropology, a major strand of socio-legal studies. Since this study is based on a socio-legal analysis of the legal foundations of governmental power, it will be helpful to clarify how 'law' and 'custom' are juxtapositioned in Zambian discourses about legality. This distinction becomes crucially relevant later on when problematizing the role of 'the people' (whose lives straddle the formal and the informal realms) in the legitimation of existing law.

### *Doctrinal legality*

Like official statute, the academic analysis of contemporary African legal systems displays deep colonial roots. The colonial juxtaposition of European vs Native, echoed in the distinction between official and informal law, is sustained in the study of contemporary African legalities. Indeed, a distinction between the discrete domains of 'customary' norms and the 'statutory' law largely determines what is recognized as proper legal scholarship. The theory and methodology of established legal scholarship draw on the conventions of doctrinal analysis.

Doctrinal analysis is bound to the internal logic of established jurisprudence, reflecting the pragmatic interests of the legal institutions of the day. Its standardized methodology, as taught in the University of Zambia's School of Law, is absolutely central to the establishment of a distinct identity among Zambian legal professionals.[13] The methodology and style of reasoning that inform the doctrinal

11 Zambia's experience with constitution-making is the focus of Chapters 5 and 6.

12 A doctrinal approach to the study of law focuses 'exclusively on traditional legal materials and the techniques required to interpret them' (Cownie & Bradley 2013, 34).

13 The prevailing hegemony of doctrinal analysis was not inevitable. Writing in the early years of the UNZA School of Law, academic lawyer Philip Thomas (1971, 36) believed that "the Law School will become even further involved in sociological and empirical research. The

analysis of an academic lawyer and that of a judge scrutinizing a case before the bench are, in principle, identical. The similarity is most striking when considering a case under appeal. An appeal judge's research, like that of an academic lawyer, typically involves 'a critical conceptual analysis of all relevant legislation and case law to reveal a statement of the law relevant to the matter under investigation' (Hutchinson 2015, 131). Such analysis is based (ibid.) on

> an understanding of the rules of precedent between the court jurisdictions, the rules of statutory interpretation, the tacit discipline knowledge such as the difference between civil and criminal jurisdictions, and various tests of liability, along with the acknowledged reasoning methods, borrowed from philosophy and logic, such as induction and deduction.

Doctrinal analysis thus seeks (ibid.) 'through the production of general and defeasible theories, legal doctrine … to present the law as a coherent net of principles, rules, meta-rules and exceptions, at different levels of abstraction.' Its epistemic habits are ubiquitous in judicial texts. The incentive structures of the academic world have also encouraged scholars interested in legal phenomena to internalize the self-referential logic of doctrinal analysis. While useful for the day-to-day work of bench, bar and the legal academy alike, a doctrinal approach to law nonetheless reveals little about how law shapes or expresses the ways that law participates in shaping the relationships of citizens to the state. Doctrinal analysis focuses on semantic issues of textual coherence and consistency. To do so, it must bracket both the legitimacy of the law and the competence of its execution. These questions are the starting point for socio-legal analysis (e.g., Singhal & Malik 2012).

### *Socio-legal alternatives*

There are many different strands and styles of socio-legal analysis. Within these various strains can be found, as Banakar (2015, 5) notes, 'conflicting epistemological assumptions and social theoretical suppositions about the study of law.' Socio-legal studies also engage with a diverse range of objects and topics. In Banakar's view (ibid., 43),

---

doctrinal approach, through examination of judicial opinions, legislation and scholarly writing, though valuable, must be prepared to augment the empirical methodology that should emerge on an inter-disciplinary basis within the university. The 'armchair scholar' has a limited role to play within a developing society."

The fact that this trajectory did not materialize may be attributed to the government's emphasis on the law school's vocational function, i.e., producing as many qualified lawyers as quickly as possible. Not only was there a shortage of Black legal practitioners, but also Zambia's young public administration was severely lacking in Zambians with legal skills. This was both a practical and a political problem. At independence, 'of 7,000 positions designated as requiring a general certificate of education, more than 6,000 were occupied by whites, of whom many hailed from, or sympathised with, areas south of the Zambezi' (ibid., 10).

> Law provides sociologists with a standpoint from which they may view and study a range of theoretical and substantive issues such as social differentiation, socio-cultural integration, forms of authority, legitimacy, the role of rationality, the exclusion or criminalisation of groups, the rise of professions, equality of access to wealth and resources or the significance of gender, sexuality and race in social organisation.

Arguably, these various socio-legal sites and interests have two things in common. One is a commitment to empirical substance (as against purely abstract, conceptual elaboration). The second is a concern with the socio-political effects of law. In other words, socio-legal analysis interrogates versions of legality linked to the prevailing form of power; it does so in order to reveal how real-world efforts to promote and sustain legality create, empower, marginalize and discipline various categories of political subjects. Indeed, the fundamental difference between doctrinal and socio-legal analysis of legal orders relates to how power is linked to law.

Despite Zambia's rich colonial tradition of legal anthropology, socio-legal scholarship has left few traces in Zambian academia.[14] That said, law's political effects are widely debated in informal conversation among practicing lawyers. I found many lawyers willing to step back from the doctrinal concerns of the immediate moment to ponder the relationship between law and politics in their everyday professional practices. They also reflect strategically on how politics shape their businesses and careers. When looking at the bigger picture, reflexive lawyers consider factors which socio-legal scholars also find interesting: power, prestige, social relations and windows of political opportunity. Where conventional doctrinal analysis entertains little interest in the political contingencies of the law, activist lawyers in particular are concerned with the overall impact of their activism on the future of Zambian society, and on the law itself. From a methodological point of view, it is the rich curiosity of activist lawyers about their working environment – about the politics of the courts, or the strategic options facing social movements – that provides an ethnographer of constitutionalism with an approach to the politics of constitution-making from a diverse, socio-legal perspective. At the same time, professional lawyers largely circumvent the topic of uncodified custom, despite the fact that this is the form of legality by which the vast majority of disputes among Zambians are resolved.

14 This anthropological tradition was in any case exclusively concerned with customary law. Max Gluckman (1955; see also Gordon (2018) for a comprehensive biography) and Martin Chanock (1985), among others, made significant, original contributions to socio-legal scholarship based on work in Zambia. Contemporary scholarship sustaining or enhancing their legacy is thin, although Cambridge anthropologist Harri Englund's (2015) work on Zambia connects constructively with Gluckman's interest in indigenous legal concepts. Recent work by Melvin Mbao (2010), Sishuwa Sishuwa (2019, 2020), as well as O'Brien Kaaba and Pamela Sambo (2020), however, suggests a possible renaissance of socio-legal studies of the statutory realm in Zambia.

### *Custom vs law*

The divide between formal (state) and informal (customary) law is as much an administrative as an academic distinction. Colonial administrators and legal scholars were similarly obsessed with the mysteries of indigenous jurisprudence.[15] This curiosity was motivated, above all, by the need to discipline and control life in indigenous communities, while not conferring justiciable rights upon colonial subjects. As a result, norms and conventions prevailing in African communities were appropriated and codified as tribal 'custom' in an effort 'to define Africans as custom-bound ethnicized subjects' as against 'rights-bearing citizens' (Karekwaivanane 2016, 61). The colonial codification of custom resulted in a quasi-legal code, overseen by locally administered Native courts. Far from sustaining traditional jurisprudence, argues legal historian Martin Chanock (1985; see also Karekwaivanane 2017, 8), the resulting normative system represented the convergence of the biopolitical obsessions of colonial government with those of embattled indigenous male elders, who felt threatened by the liberties proffered to young men and women by the emerging capitalist economy. Customary adjudication – overseen by chiefs or lay magistrates – was administratively cordoned off from statutory law. Indeed, to this day, parties to a customary hearing in Zambia may *not* be represented by a lawyer. This logic, according to one Zambian law professor with considerable experience in the field of customary law,[16] derives from colonial policy.

> Colonialists in Zambia wrote … that if you are appearing before a local court you cannot be allowed to be defended by a counsel of your choice … The reason that was used by the colonialists … was the understanding that [custom] was not a subject that should be subjected to specialized study by experts. This is a matter that is known only by [local] custodians. There are certain people who have the knowledge, skills and experience in accordance with their culture and traditions, and those are the ones who should adjudicate in cases. If we brought in lawyers, they might confuse the set-up. And so, up to now, we [lawyers] cannot appear before the local courts.

The Zambia Law Development Commission (established in 1996 under Cap. 32 of the Laws of Zambia) is mandated, among other things, to 'codify unwritten laws in Zambia,' but the commission's efforts have fallen short of harmonizing the plurality of normative codes in the national jurisdiction. The ban on lawyers entering customary hearings, along with the legal marginalization of traditional authority, has sustained the gulf between 'law' and 'custom,' and

15 It is a curious fact that while there is a rich sociological literature concerning 'customary' law during colonial rule, the comparable socio-legal analysis of statutory courts is virtually non-existent.

16 Subsequent quotes are from this same conversation.

hindered the integration of the two normative systems into a uniform code of national law, applicable to all Zambians in all places.

The problem is not necessarily that of reconciling two incommensurable sets of principles. The normative systems of statutory law and customary norm are, in practice, intricately intertwined. Alongside the legislated statutes of formal law that Zambians are expected to adhere to, everyday life is shaped by countless conventions, overseen and enforced by state-recognized authorities in local communities. Statute does, in fact, intervene in many aspects of local custom – intestate inheritance, for example, falls under statutory law (Himonga 1991). The main obstacle to legal integration may not hinge so much on problems of jurisprudence, as on unsurmountable practicalities of homogenizing the juridical domain. Indeed, the overwhelming majority of disputes among Zambians are adjudicated by peers – chiefs, village headmen and lay magistrates – with no formal legal training. Providing formal certification of legal competence to everyone carrying out some sort of a judicial function is unlikely within any imaginable timeframe. Such a move would also undermine the legal monopoly of certified lawyers and their 'disproportionate influence ..., both individually and as a class, in the agitation for reform and the ensuing process of constitution-making and revision' (Prempeh 2008, 827).

The fragmentation of empirical legality has immense consequences, however. Denying justiciable rights in land, for example, goes to the heart of the colonial legacy. For the members of indigenous rural communities, land is not simply a 'factor of production.' As the living domain of ancestral spirits and supernatural forces, the lived-in landscape of forests, hills, streams, rivers and lakes embodies community history and identity. Marginalizing the claims and obligations incumbent on the politico-legal domain of 'custom' was central to the colonial project of dehumanization and labor extraction. In the postcolonial order, the residues of this endeavor continue to frame the relationship between urban elites and 'the people' in Zambia's myriad villages and small rural towns in whose name the legitimacy of the prevailing constitutional order is predicated.

After independence, prominent Zambian politicians defended their newly established political legitimacy by, among other things, portraying the main guardians of custom – chiefs (and allied 'earth priests' – as complicit with colonial rule and/or as threats to the legitimacy of the nascent party-state government. Politicians and lawyers jealously patrolled the boundary between the formal law of the state and the informality of custom. The distinction was both normative and hierarchical, with state law trumping customary norms and practices in virtually every instance. As a politically prominent chief explained:

> The new leaders were not subtle. They acted coldly, and used bully tactics: 'You [chiefs] cannot assert yourselves!' Any reference to colonial times was anti-nationalistic. It was not fashionable, or stylish, to refer to colonial times. Even though chiefs enjoyed a lot of authority, the politicians usurped and centralized power. Decentralized decision-making was taken away. Not

> because the previous arrangement was less efficient, or in order to administrate better, but just to supplant the chiefs.

Under colonial rule, in the chief's view, power was shared between the state and traditional authority:

> During the colonial period, the role of the chiefs was very localized, limited to a specific area of jurisdiction (and to some extent this still holds true). Except that in colonial times power was more decentralized. Power was never in Lusaka, it was out in the Districts and chiefdoms. Colonial District Commissioners [DCs] were more important administrators than Provincial or National government. DCs *were* government. Decisions were made at that level and chiefs were fully occupied running their areas. There was no need for them to spread their wings. They had Native Treasuries under the DCs that catered to development issues, clinics, etc. Work was being done. In the Local Courts only some matters went to the DC. Chiefs had the authority to adjudicate to a certain level.

Turning to the postcolonial present, the professor offers a complementary view of the legitimacy of custom. In his view,

> [W]hichever spectrum you look at in Africa, there are two types of states running side by side, with a lot of tensions among them. You have the modern state imposed by colonial rule and perpetuated after Independence in the name of the new modern state, and then you have the customary system. Sometimes they complement one another, sometimes they reinforce one another, but often enough there is perpetual conflict between them.

Over time, he argues, things have changed:

> In the precolonial states, principles of equality, etc., were applied because they were believed in, because they were coming from [the communities]. But now, [when] as a state we are writing constitutions, there is this sense of alienation. First of all, I have to use a foreign language to explain the meaning of the constitution. And then I am getting the values from outside and I am pushing them down their throats. They don't feel a sense of duty-boundedness to practice [those values] because they are not coming from their own society.

These shifts, then, have crucially altered the relationship of citizens to public authority.

> Perhaps what has really happened in postcolonial Zambia is that we have created a façade that we call a state. It's a façade you can find in urban areas in the form of uniformed police carrying guns, uniformed military, and uniformed customs and excise people, uniformed immigration. [These officials]

> are trying ... not to keep law and order, but actually destabilizing law and order. It's a façade in the sense that the minute that you leave the capital city there is virtually nothing like that, and you find people are living in what one might call, using John Locke's argument, a state of nature.

This perspective mirrors the view of West Africanists Bierschenk and Olivier de Sardan (1997, 441), who see the postcolonial state as an enclave that ends '12 kilometers from the capital.' From this perspective, the power exercised by chiefs is qualitatively distinct from that of the state. In line with this chief, my interviewee views customary authority under colonialism as part of a division of labor within a unified grid of state power that was fractured after independence.

Postcolonial Zambia thus appears to be a land of two distinct and to some degree adversarial jurisdictions vying for the loyalty of overlapping sets of subjects. At the same time, core societal functions, such as the administration of land, continue to operate as if the customary authority were an integral aspect of a homogeneous grid of state power. The question that this hypothetical paradox conjures up refers back to the status of the landed citizenry, or *demos*, as a subject of statutory law. In practice, the dual normative setup functions relatively smoothly, and it is only in issues of great criminal or financial magnitude (murder, grand theft) that rural subjects have any dealings with statutory legal institutions.

The paradox, then, does not necessarily concern a plurality of jurisdictions, but the contradictory actions of a state which seeks to maintain transcendent legal authority over all citizens, but which keeps distinct groups of subjects on the margins of constitution-making. Juan Obarrio (2014, 231) has noted how state authority in Mozambique seeks to maintain a unified field reaffirming the authority of both 'formal' and 'informal' law. This involves persistent public efforts at shoring up the legitimacy of the state. In performing such state-making rituals, the state actively cultivates, in Obarrio's words, 'the spirit of the laws.' This spirit, he writes, "informs the performative practice and rhetoric of a state in search of renewed legitimacy, both at the 'central' level of executive and legislative powers and in a faraway rural customary/post-Socialist tribunal." Maintaining this image of a unified field of law perpetrates the politico-legal ethos of the colonial era. Above all, it marginalizes many institutional arrangements from the statutory realm by which the peoples indigenous to Zambia's territory have governed themselves and their relationships with one another for centuries.[17]

The Zambian constitution does not recognize any distinctions between the legal entitlements of different groups of citizens. The constitution's primary political purpose, in Zambia (as in Mozambique), is to reaffirm the project of national state formation for all citizens. Constitution-making comprises a crucial set of state-making performances, the most notable (and costly) of which have been the two major constitutional reviews carried out during the Third Republic (see Chapter 6). Both commissions, comprising several dozen commissioners, visited each of Zambia's

17 On the status of contemporary Zambian chiefs, see Baldwin (2016) and Gould (2010).

150 electoral constituencies and received, without reward or coercion, untold thousands of submissions on the substance of constitutional law. This administrative anecdote may seem banal, even trivial, but it speaks clearly to the fact that statutory law has a palpable authority for citizens all over Zambia, and not only for those within 12 kilometers of Lusaka. The vast number of submissions to both constitutional commissions suggest (to anticipate a theoretical distinction elaborated in the Excursus) that while there may well be more than one kind of public authority, the form of power that governs the Zambian *demos* is 'less than two.'

These efforts of the peoples on the margins of the state to contribute to constitution-making are, as we will see, of little consequence. The substantial provisions of constitutional reform are not determined by the will of the people, but by the machinations of privileged actors within the politico-legal domain. This fact is not simply an expression of political duplicity. The *demos* does not have one voice; it is a plurality. Zambia's peoples exist in diverse linguistic, economic and cultural configurations. This diversity makes it difficult to reduce the desires of the peoples to a singular will. Consequently, as I will argue (Chapter 4), grounding the constitution, and thus legality itself, in a political singularity – 'the will of the people' – is a problematic political sleight of hand that conceals, in equal measures, an imperial legacy and postcolonial political expediency.

## The ends of law

George Karekwaivanane (2017) has provided a compelling account of how law has participated in the constitution of state power in one African jurisdiction. Karekwaivanane focuses on the instrumental uses of law, and argues that it has had a dual character – law in Rhodesia (Zimbabwe) was used not only as a means of coercion by the colonial state, but also as a popular resource for challenges to colonial authority. In Karekwaivanane's (ibid., 11) account:

> Thinking about the role of law in the constitution of state power in colonial Africa raises a number of questions about African responses. Could law be used by Africans in pursuit of their own interests? What room, if any, existed for resistance within the legal arena?

The possible 'emancipatory potential of the law' (Santos 2002) is an important concern, and I return to it in the final chapter. In this respect, however, colonial Zambia and Zimbabwe seem to have quite different legal histories.[18] While Rhodesian anticolonial militants found myriad ways to use the court system to

18 The 'received' law in Zambia and Zimbabwe is based on different models. Where Zambia's statutory legal system is founded on English law, Zimbabwe (like Botswana, Lesotho, Namibia, Swaziland and South Africa) follows a hybrid version of the 'Roman-Dutch' system that Dutch settlers brought to South Africa in the 17th century (see Pain 1978). There are, of course, other crucial differences of colonial history between the two jurisdictions.

express resistance to the apartheid regime, there is little evidence of anticolonial legal activism in Zambia. Law was, without doubt, a pervasive tool of colonial repression, but its utility for struggles against colonial domination has not been documented. This lack of bottom-up legal pressure reflects, no doubt, the fact that there were virtually no Black lawyers in colonial Northern Rhodesia, itself a consequence of the systematic denial by the colonial government of educational opportunities for the indigenous population (Thomas 1971, 10). That said, Zambians hold legal skills in high esteem and, as we will see, the indigenous appropriation of the law 'in pursuit of [indigenous] interests' was given high priority after independence.

Already at the dawn of the independence era, law and lawyers loomed large in the social imagination of African leaders. Inaugurating the new Ghana School of Law building in 1962, six years after Ghana's independence, President Kwame Nkrumah (1962, 107) had this to say:

> The lawyers needed in a developing state are, in the first place, those trained to assist the ordinary man and woman in his everyday legal problems and particularly in the new problems likely to arise through industrialization ... Secondly, and perhaps most important of all, we need lawyers in the service of the state, to deal with treaties and commercial agreements and with questions of private and public international law.

Eight years later, in 1970, six years after Zambia's independence, President Kenneth Kaunda echoed Nkrumah's sentiments at a dinner address to the Law Society of Zambia. According to Kaunda (cited in Thomas 1971, 4),

> the lawyer, through his training and experience, is perhaps better fitted than anyone else to work out solutions to the social and economic problems of society. ... [I]t [hence] becomes the duty of all these who were more fortunate to use their knowledge and skills not just for the benefit of their clients, but for the advancement of the whole society.

Heeding clarion calls such as these, young citizens of young African nations enrolled in newly established law programs across the continent, contributing to a rapidly growing corps of legal professionals born, bred and trained in Africa. In Ghana, home-grown juridical expertise was not a new phenomenon; there were Black lawyers in Accra already in the mid-19th century. In Zambia, on the other hand, well into the first decade of independence the legal profession was almost exclusively White.

In the first decades of independence, African lawyers found the most secure job opportunities within Nkrumah's second category, as stewards of state interests. However, by the austere years of structural adjustment in the 1980s, the vision of the lawyer as the defender of the common man had all but evaporated. Writing at the time, Kenyan legal scholar Yash Ghai (1987, 774) was moved to complain that "Law has played little role in political and economic development.

Nor have lawyers been the central actors in promoting and mediating change; they are peripheral to the system of political and economic power." These were also quiet years for the Zambian legal profession. The economy was strapped for cash, and after several prominent lawyers participated in an aborted coup attempt against the Kaunda government in 1980 (Chapter 5), the profession kept a very low political profile.

The change in the regulatory system that engulfed dozens of African states in the early 1990s, as 'socialism' gave way to a 'neoliberal' policy regime, was a godsend for legal fraternities. In Zambia, privatization campaigns dismantled parastatal economies and created deregulated markets for the assets and properties of former state enterprises. The removal of currency regulations and tariff barriers unleashed tidal waves of foreign speculation, trade and investment, and burgeoning land and real estate markets emerged in the wake of fundamental economic and fiscal reforms (see Szeftel 2000, Rakner 2003, Mutesa 2005).

As a group, the dismantling of the parastatal economy provided private lawyers with unprecedented opportunities to ply their craft for lucrative gain. Lawyers already had a jealously guarded monopoly, protected by colonial-era legislation, that reserved many profitable opportunities for them alone, enabling ambitious practitioners to exploit the new opportunities aggressively. The newly achieved material security and, hence, autonomy of the legal profession had immediate political consequences. Lawyers who acquired means independently of state commissions and employment were now free to take on cases that challenged established political privileges. This is not to suggest that successful private lawyers in a market economy would be intrinsically predisposed to champion liberal ideals; financially independent lawyers can also ignore public succor and unfavorable media attention by using their newly consolidated leeway to service socially irresponsible clients (Trubek 1991, Ashar 2007). Somewhat surprisingly, perhaps, Kaunda's views (cited above) concerning the social responsibility of the legal profession found renewed resonance among an emerging corps of activist lawyers in the wake of UNIP's political demise. Indeed, Kaunda's ideals echo clearly in the documents justifying the participation of the Law Association in the Oasis Forum.

Against this backdrop, the rich literature on public interest lawyering offers a promising source of analytical concepts for thinking about LAZ's participation in the Oasis Forum. Indeed, public interest lawyers in rich capitalist economies have seen themselves, and have been assessed by others, as a kind of moral compass for the legal community. Public interest lawyers are, by definition, activists within the legal profession. Through their professional practices, they pursue ethical ends beyond the conventional objective of winning one's client's case. Mwale (2004, 9) has noted the lack of public interest law in Zambia. Elsewhere on the continent, however, the resurgence of constitutional politics has been accompanied by a growing interest in legal activism. To take one example, the non-partisan coalition Kenyans for Peace with Truth and Justice (2014) published a *Guide to Public Interest Litigation* [PIL] *in Kenya* which argues (iv) that

> [h]istory shows that PIL has been a particularly critical tool for testing, clarifying and shaping law, policy and practice in societies across the globe. PIL will make an important contribution to the lives of many Kenyans if it succeeds in influencing and reshaping the discussion on the issues of democracy, human rights and open governance.

Activist lawyers within the Oasis Forum shared such sentiments. There are indeed similarities between the LAZ lawyers and the public interest lawyers described in the academic literature. These include a purposive orientation to the law, a commitment to constitutionalism and to deploying law for the 'greater good.' There are also significant differences. The Forum's legal activists had no clients, or rather, their client was an abstraction – 'the people.' Further, unlike classical public interest lawyers, the legal activism of the Oasis Forum was not first and foremost that of lawyers in the courtroom. Rather they acted through LAZ, a statutory organization engaged directly with the state on matters of ostensible constitutional significance. Another difference concerns the business dimension of Zambian legal activism. LAZ's participation in the Oasis Forum's campaigns was not market mediated; if and when lawyers made money in Oasis Forum campaigns, it was through expert fees, honoraria and allowances – not as their firms' billable hours.

The waves of post–Cold War political change that lifted the champions of neoliberal deregulation to power had many unintended consequences, culminating in a legitimation crisis. The deregulationist reforms which were implemented from 1991 by President Chiluba's Movement for Multiparty Democracy (MMD) failed, in the short term, to turn the economy around. On the contrary, the 1990s was a decade of severe deprivation for the majority of the population, coming on the heels of two long decades of grueling economic deterioration. Public discontent was further fueled by vocal claims about the government's abuse of power from dissidents within the ruling MMD itself. Unravelling economic and political horizons contributed to the resurfacing of a deep disillusionment in politics, in politicians and in the land's political institutions that had been temporarily expelled by the ousting of UNIP in 1991. As mechanisms of *political* legitimation began to collapse, law began to take on an aura of moral authority capable of salvaging the national project upon which sovereign Zambia was originally predicated. By the end of the decade, an ideology of legalism (Shklar 1964) had taken the political stage as a compelling social imaginary, enabling well-intentioned professional elites to organize broadly based social resistance to allegedly illiberal politics. Chapter 4 attempts to convey a sense of the ideas and values that drove this upsurge of elite resistance.

# 4 Between the decision and the *demos*: Activist lawyers and constituent power

The political mythology of liberal constitutionalism puts the 'will of the people' at the center of constitution-making. In practice, as we have seen, Zambia's postcolonial constitutions have been framed and crafted by members of a thin stratum of political and professional elites, under the strict oversight of the executive. Since the 1991 constitution that ushered in the Third Republic, lawyers – the epitome of an urban, professional elite class – have played a pivotal role in facilitating constitutional reform. The chairs of the last three constitutional review commissions (CRCs) – Patrick Mvunga, John Mwanakatwe and Wila Mung'omba – were lawyers (men, too, for that matter[1]). Through the Oasis Forum, the Law Association also weighed in heavily on debates around the procedure of constitution-making.

This chapter addresses the tensions that emerge in constitution-making at the interstices of popular legitimation and elite crafting. To this end, I recount the conversations I had with some of my key ethnographic informants concerning the process and substance of constitution-making as it unfolded over the course of my fieldwork. This chapter thus serves to illustrate and elaborate prevailing notions about law and legal agency sketched in Chapter 2 while also illustrating aspects of how I came to understand lawyerly agency.

Not all lawyers think the same, and this narrative draws on a variety of lawyerly views, reflecting a range of roles and positions in the constitution-making process. Veteran lawyer and constitutional draftsperson Eva Jhala observed that lawyers have two personae in constitution-making processes: as citizens and as experts. My observations suggest a broader range of intersectionality at work, with lawyers getting entangled with constitution-making processes in a number of different roles and capacities. Lawyers could be *craftspeople* with relevant and marketable skills, like legal research, drafting and committee chairing; *activists*, campaigning for specific provisions; as *entrepreneurs* attuned to the business dimension of their expertise; as members of an aloof and confident *elite class*, self-empowered to advise, guide and shepherd the *demos*; and/or, in some instances,

1 Tabeth Masengu (2015) has written comprehensively on the gender dimension of Zambia's constitution-making processes.

DOI: 10.4324/9780429198984-5

as *constitutional theorists*, with a tendency to view constitution-making as a series of actions and events in unfolding time, and to envision possible consequences for social relations in social, legal, political and economic registers. The boundaries between these roles were fluid, and any given individual was likely to embody a number of them at the same time.

Most of the informants I cite below were committed members of the Oasis Forum.[2] While they represented somewhat different social positions and backgrounds, Forum activists were committed to common principles that had been hammered out and polished over the preceding three to four years in numerous public panels, retreats and workshops. Some of the informants quoted here were individuals who, while deeply concerned with constitution-making and largely unhappy with the government's positions, had maintained a social and political distance from the Oasis Forum. That said, variations in basic *principles* were slight across the board; a greater range of views emerged around their approach to constitution-making *strategies*. When pushed, nuanced differences emerged among the views of the Forum's various constituencies – lawyers, clergy and lay activists – concerning the best, or most effective means of achieving their common goals. The same was true of those outside the alliance. At the same time, Forum members understood well that their primary strength was in unity, and that maintaining a united front in their campaign activities was a strategic consideration of top priority. In some respects, I will argue, sustaining unity within the alliance was the Forum's primary strategic concern as well as its foremost accomplishment.

The conversations I draw on here took place between 2003 and 2006 in Lusaka, home to the vast majority of Zambian lawyers. At the time, my ethnography was driven by a desire to understand the interaction of law and politics in long-term historical processes of postcolonial state formation. This ambition, I have come to realize, harbors an inherent contradiction. I was probing for historical continuities, while my informants were caught up in a particularly fraught political moment. This is not to say they were unaware of Zambia's – and more broadly, Southern Africa's – political and constitutional history, or of the historical significance of the particular conjuncture of legal and political authority in which they were involved. Rather the contrary is true, as is clear from our discussions.

In any event, our conversations revolved around my informants' immediate concerns, which is to say the possibility of achieving substantial constitutional, electoral and political reform before the approaching elections, scheduled to be held in late 2006. I addressed this tension between long-term processes and short-term interests by framing our discussions within a conceptual framework that problematizes the relationship between constitution-making elites and the constituent power of the people.

2 While most are lawyers, I also include in this composite account the analyses of one non-lawyer – a clergyman closely involved in the Oasis Forum's political strategizing. The inclusion of a non-lawyer provides a counterpoint to the jural discourse of the lawyers, while highlighting continuities between the lawyers' thinking and that of non-jural activists within the Forum.

This strategy allowed us to think together about the possible longer-term effects of ongoing events and confrontations. As a rule, these conversations were relaxed – 'collegial' may best capture the atmosphere of most encounters. Zambian lawyers are invariably graduates of the University of Zambia. A Zambian lawyer's educational track leads through an LL.B[3] at the University of Zambia School of Law, to a one-year course in preparation for the bar examination at the Zambian Institute for Advance Legal Education (ZIALE). This path typically begins with undergraduate studies in the School of Humanities and Social Sciences. Many informants commented on how discussions with a social scientist reminded them of their undergraduate studies (!).

The central themes of my study – the Oasis Forum, the Chiluba corruption trials and the ongoing constitution-making process – were extremely topical, and the incumbent legal issues were very much on my informants' minds. The aim of this account is to provide access to the analyses that these reflective professionals were undertaking in political real time. That said, their views are organized here around an analytical scaffolding of my own device, guided by insights arising from the conceptual work carried out in Chapter 2 and the Excursus (in Section III). I hope this framework allows for the gist of my informants' thinking to be heard clearly, while not overplaying subtle distinctions between them.

## Perspectives on postcolonial constitutionalism

During the period in question, the Oasis Forum had an ongoing campaign to establish a constituent assembly for the purposes of drafting a new Zambian constitution. As will be discussed in some detail in Chapter 6, the Oasis Forum resisted the establishment of the Mung'omba Constitutional Review Commission and advised its member organizations to refuse appointments as commissioners. The Forum felt that a new CRC was superfluous, given the immense amount of material collected ten years earlier by the CRC chaired by veteran lawyer John Mwanakatwe, which also produced a draft constitution, the bulk of which had never been enacted. Many representatives of Forum member organizations declined appointments. Some who did agree to serve as commissioners were censured by the Forum (see below). Only at the very end of the Mung'omba CRC tenure, did Forum members engage formally with the commission's proposals. This, in brief, was the political context in which my conversations with activist lawyers and others about constitution-making strategy, recounted here, took place.

### *The time and place for legal expertise*

Constitutional draftsperson Eva Jhala[4] does not problematize the substance of legal expertise, and sees it as relatively technical and uniform among legal practi-

3 LL.B, or Bachelor of Laws (from the Latin *Legum Baccalaureus*).

4 Eva Jhala is a senior lawyer who has worked in both the public and private sectors. She was employed by the Mung'omba CRC and later, by the National Constitutional Conference, as

tioners. Differences in emphasis in legal thought arise, in her view, largely from individual differences in personality. Discussing her work with the Mung'omba CRC, Ms Jhala noted,

**EJ***:* You would go on debating, debating, debating issues which at the end of the day, really there's not much departure from what's happening in [some] other country. And [such debating] only comes about if you've got two groups of legal practitioners who have to prove to themselves that they know what is supposed to be the Constitution. It's like a fight between two elephants – they want to prove who's the strongest, but they have the same strength.

**JG (me)***:* Other than taking extra time, does this affect the substance of the principles?

**EJ***:* No. On the substance, at the end of the day, you're going to agree. Let me tell you, lawyers they know quite a lot. Being the legal fraternity, they involve themselves widely with the law, with political science and things like that. So, they'll dominate the debate at the expense of the other groupings in society.[5]

In contrast, one senior legal practitioner and constitutional theorist found substantial qualitative differences in the competence of legal experts. In his view, many lawyers are lazy, politically pliable and complicit with power for selfish, career-driven reasons:

> Even lawyers don't read the law. We act first and then read the law later. Once we have acted, we will find out what we have done is not consistent with the law, then we start playing around with the truth, so that it can fit within the four corners of the law. Unfortunately, it doesn't work.

In spite of this, law remains a powerful tool to be respected:

'I always tell my [law] students, the law is meant to protect us. Stick to the law and you'll never be faulted.'

Lawyers rely on the stability of legal statute to shield them from adversaries and disgruntled clients. But they also do their best to bend the law to their interests. Indeed, I sensed a tension among my informants between a foundationalist view of law as above social conflicts – an autonomous (if potentially malleable) force – and the realist notion of law's embeddedness (Cotterrell 2013) in social and political processes. Seeing law as an autonomous social force implies that the

a draftsperson, a technical role entrusted with translating the principles agreed upon by commissioners into constitutional text.

5 Indented citations like this one, and others in quotes, have been transcribed from tape. Some minimal editing of the text has been done to enhance readability, with great care to preserve the speakers' original intent.

proper position for legal expertise is above the political fray. Patrick Matibini[6] gives expression to this view:

**PM***:* Quite often you have critical legal issues that confront society, and unless you have people from the legal fraternity available to articulate these issues, the chances are that you may not have a clear direction. So some of the moral issues and arguments can only be discerned and comprehended once you understand the core legal issue at stake.

He notes further that

> 'As a profession, we owe certain moral and perhaps even legal duties to society, to ensure that in critical moments, we will provide appropriate guidance to the Zambian society.'

This particular notion of legitimate legal authority presumes a certain understanding of the law – one which is at once non-partisan, yet grounded in a 'purposive' jurisprudence.[7] Purposive legality implies a commitment to using the law to promote, in Dr Matibini's words, 'rule of law, constitutionalism, integrity in public office, supporting the campaign against corruption, promoting constitutional reforms and general legislative reforms so that we have an enabling legal environment which would forestall an emerging dictatorship.' For Dr Matibini, law has an obligation to cultivate democratic culture.

This is not a technical issue, solely internal to the judicial system; rather, purposive jurisprudence can have far-reaching social implications. Dr Matibini's avid participation in the Oasis Forum was a reflection of this view. On the basis of his experiences as a prominent Oasis Forum adviser, he distinguished between two generational blocks within activists and politicians. Dr Matibini sees Zambia divided between a group of old school, conservative, defenders of the status quo, on the one hand, and a new breed of activists, aligned with purposive and democratic values, on the other. For him, the political task driving legal activism is to catalyze

6 At the time of our conversations, Dr. Patrick Matibini was a law lecturer, legal academic and consultant running a one-man office in Lusaka, specializing in media law. He was a key contributor to Oasis Forum strategy discussions. Dr Matibini was subsequently involved in the National Constitutional Conference (see Chapter 6) and was granted the title of State Counsel by president Rupiah Banda in 2010. After a brief stint as a High Court judge, President Michael Sata appointed Dr Matibini as Speaker of the National Assembly in 2011, a position he held until 2021 when he was replaced by Nelly Mutti.

7 This understanding of legal purposiveness resonates with that of David Trubek (1972, 5) for whom the 'core conception of legal purposiveness is… highly instrumental: It assumes that social life can be shaped by some social will, for example a modernizing elite, which brings about development through legal enactment and enforcement.' The notion of purposive reasoning reappears in a more substantive role in Chapter 9 when discussing the Constitutional Court's emerging jurisprudence.

the transit from the old to the new crop of politicians. Politicians approach politics from different perspectives. For most, politics has been approached simply as a career as opposed to service. You need people who recognize the huge potential that the country has and the need to exploit that potential, people who'll be able to view participation in the political system as an opportunity to bequeath a certain legacy to the nation.

This sense of patriotic duty was not unusual among Forum activists. It felt genuine and went a long way to explain the substantial investments of time, energy and creativity members of the alliance expended over many years of confrontation with the president over constitution-making.

## *Ethics and legal expertise*

In Western jurisdictions, the legitimacy of the law is not supposed to depend on individual integrity. It is, rather, attributed to 'strong institutions.' American columnist David Brooks, for example, argued in the *New York Times* (21 February 2019) that American democracy can withstand Donald Trump's excessive use of discretionary powers because the nation's 'legal institutions instill codes of excellence that are strong enough to take the heat.' This view may yet prove overly optimistic as regards American democracy; it is certainly questionable in Zambia's case where, as we shall see, the judiciary seldom rises to contradict presidential prerogative.

Law may fare poorly when competing with the executive, but the perceived legitimacy of legal authority can be oppressive in its own right. Constitutional draftsperson Eva Jhala was keenly attentive to the ethical dimension of legal expertise. Her position was unusual in this context by virtue of her emphasis on the *limits* of legal expertise relative to the role of constituent power as the basis of law:

EJ: The constitution is not really a legal document, it's a political document. And the role of the legal practitioner should be more that of downstream expert input, and not at the initial stages, like sitting on the Commission. You may have two or three [Commissioners] for particular inputs and clarifications as they go along. Normally they like to turn to a lawyer and say, What does this mean? How will this work? How does this relate to another piece of legislation? Or, How might the legislation have to be changed to harmonize it with the current thinking of the people? I do not see the necessity of having, say, twenty lawyers on the [Constitutional] Review Commission that is gathering submissions from the people. Seeing the Constitution as a political document means it's within the polity. The people are coming up with a document that is meant to govern them.

An overemphasis on legal expertise, then, can undermine the democratic character of the constitution-making, and Ms Jhala was concerned that lawyers may have overpowered lay perspectives in their constitutional debates:

**EJ***:* The only group [other than lawyers] that would come out with a strong voice is from the media. So you have two dominant groups – the legal profession and the media. The rest are very quiet voices out there. They're not saying much, whereas, to me, it's supposed to be the other way round. The lawyers should be advising, and not dominating the debate, because the issues already come from the experts, from outside, into the Commission. So the people who are supposed to be in this commission are supposed to be ordinary people from civil society.

This is why, Ms Jhala explained, '[y]ou want the constitution to be very much balanced between legal norms and principles, and societal values and aspirations.'

Father Joseph Komakoma[8] is not a lawyer but a self-declared 'champion priest.' Fr Komakoma says he 'likes the law,' and sees clear affinities between the Catholic clergy and the legal profession who, he feels, share a 'similar background.' Like lawyers, he points out, 'Catholics also have a canon law which guides them.' True enough, both professions are strongly oriented toward text and precedent. Both callings, he noted, tend to produce progressive advocates at specific times that challenge the limits of established doctrine. In Zambia, the early 2000s was such a juncture, when the emergence of a reformist element in the Catholic Church's Zambian Episcopal Conference coincided with a similar trend in the Law Association. At that time, Fr Komakoma recalls, the progressives in both camps adopted a social agenda in defense of the 'greater good' against a 'narrow' understanding of legality:

**JK***:* Somebody who's an atheistic lawyer may be strongly motivated by the understanding of law as an instrument of building society, and will believe in that very strongly. He may not have any religious notions but, said simply, sees law as a critical element in building society because it weighs one's rights against the rights of others. It limits government, and it limits individuals. As a priest, I would walk quite a distance with such a person.

That said, Fr Komakoma was skeptical about the extent of lawyers' political commitments:

> Lawyers, aren't going to throw stones and whatnot; they would rather talk. They are not going to jump in the streets shouting 'We want a [people's]

8 Father Joseph Komakoma, an ordained Catholic priest, was an influential Oasis Forum strategist. As a columnist for the *Worker's Challenge*, a Church-sponsored newspaper on the Copperbelt in the 1980s, Fr Komakoma was an outspoken critique of the UNIP government at a time when few dared to call the state to account. He sustained his critical voice during the Chiluba years as a columnist for other Church publications, before becoming a regular contributor to *The Post* newspaper in 1999 (see Hinfelaar 2008, iv–v).

At the time of our conversations, Fr Komakoma led the Catholic Commission for Peace and Justice in Lusaka. He subsequently moved on to international duties as secretary-general of the Symposium of Episcopal Conferences of Africa and Madagascar (SECAM).

constitution!' They would prefer to go to a conference in a Provincial centre or District and speak to people from a podium.

Despite their limitations, Fr Komakoma appreciated working with the Law Association of Zambia (LAZ) lawyers in the Forum because they 'realize that law without legitimacy is bad law.' Fr Komakoma saw President Mwanawasa, the Forum's chief nemesis in their constitution-making campaign, as a prime illustration of the illegitimate application of law:

**JK**: President Mwanawasa sees himself as a lawyer, and he has to win every argument, more or less in the way that you do in court … What matters is not what is right. What matters is not a moral position. What matters is to win the argument. And if you are clever, and you are defending somebody regardless of whether that person is guilty or not, if your argument is stronger than the prosecution's, then you have won the case. End of the story.

In this regard, Fr Komakoma paints a predatory picture of legal expertise. He implies that law and its professional practitioners work with little regard for morality or justice. This view suggests a fundamental dilemma for the purposive approach prevalent among Oasis Forum lawyers: How can legal expertise provide the moral guidance that activist lawyers see as their social duty, when it is not in law's basic nature to pursue moral ends? More fundamentally still is the question of how, given law's apparent indifference to justice, might it achieve legitimacy?

The simple response might be to say that while law is morally neutral, lawyers need not be. As one lawyer noted, however, a culture of individual integrity 'may not be that deeply embedded in our society.' Personal integrity is especially at risk, the lawyer observed, because even ostensibly successful lawyers can be 'largely insecure' from a financial point of view. Personal integrity is 'flexible' when monetary and career considerations enter the picture; indeed, there is 'always a business angle' to lawyers' actions. Given the vagaries of Zambia's economy, and of the political fortunes of individual actors, even high-profile lawyers can experience their future as financially precarious, and consequently put their own interests above those of the greater good (and professional ethics).

Unsurprisingly, clergyman Fr Komakoma is uncomfortable with a view of political activism which brackets individual integrity. Fr Komakoma considers himself a 'principled pragmatist,' focused on results, but only within a clear ethical framework. By coincidence, perhaps, one well-known lawyer I spoke with characterized himself in precisely the same terms. When I called Fr Komakoma's attention to this convergence of terms, he drew a sharp distinction between himself and the lawyer in question. While a clergyman and a lawyer may both consider themselves 'principled pragmatists,' he said, their value systems may be quite different:

**JK**: [The lawyer] is building his future, building a career, [and] is motivated by profit – which in itself is not bad. But that's him, and here I am. [As a priest,] I have no career to build ... But to be a champion priest, you [also] want to excel, you want to be noted. So you have to admit that to a certain extent whatever we do, we build our status. But, it is not a career move for me. The profit thing is out of the question. There's no benefit [from political activism], apart from the satisfaction that you've done something for humanity ... So, what I meant by value system, is that you are driven by different aims.

All of the lawyers cited here were in private business for themselves. Some received financial benefits from their involvement with constitution-making.[9] Others earned consultancy fees from foreign donor agencies for commissioned projects related to legal reform. All of the activist lawyers I met seemed to live quite comfortably – they dressed sharply, drove nice cars and worked out of stylishly furnished, well-equipped and air-conditioned offices. None of them, however, indicated that money would have been a decisive factor driving their legal activism.

Patrick Matibini, for example, explained that

**PM***:* We're going through a very interesting transition, and whatever is done now will have a lot of bearing for the future. As a nation, we must be clear about these issues ... and maybe at [such] moments, business considerations should not be the primary issue. More important is the implication of our work for the development of the society in general.

On the other hand, endemic financial insecurity does affect activist strategies. The founder of one of Zambia's few pro bono agencies had gradually given up the unpaid work he and his partner had engaged in fresh out of law school. As he explained,

One of the things that one has to bear in mind is that yes, you can engage yourself in activism, but at some point you have to apply brakes and ask yourself, what are the results? First of all, education is very expensive. So whatever path you take must be justifiable. We have basically given up on *pro bono* work now because of the fact that the number of cases that have been successful, is very, very, very low. Very low.

There is hardly a consensus, then, as to whether the moral integrity of lawyers can be relied upon as a safeguard against abuses of the law by the state. Within

9 Generous donor support for the Oasis Forum allowed for workshop facilitators to draw sitting allowances for workshops, and per diems when travelling around the country on Oasis Forum business. This was and is standard practice in the non-governmental organization (NGO) domain. Members of the National Constitutional Conference would also receive generous sitting allowances, these too covered by donor support.

the Oasis Forum, the personal agendas of individual lawyers were not seen as a threat to the coalition's aims, since LAZ had committed itself to speaking alongside the civic organizations and the churches with one voice. Breaking with a long tradition of neutrality and autonomy, the Forum's activist-lawyers agreed to hold themselves ethically accountable in accordance with the high standards of the Church. This counterintuitive flourishing of a moral commitment to the common good was not something lawyers and their allies were inclined to take for granted. That it persisted over many years of common struggle may be attributable to the ways membership in the Oasis Forum enhanced the social credibility of the legal profession and advanced the belief that law could offer a defense against abuses of power.

## The prerogativist perspective

A prerogativist presidency was an unmitigated virtue in the 'one-party participatory democracy' of President Kaunda's Second Republic, and this legacy has not entirely disappeared. Indeed, claims activist clergyman Komakoma,

**JK***:* The problem we have, basically, is that the executive has an overbearance over all government institutions and all governance systems in Zambia. And that's why I'm saying we are still in the one-party structure, despite the rhetoric of 'We are a multi-party state, building a democracy.' So it's that mode we have to dismantle. And it can only be dismantled by radical changes to the structure of government.

The legacy of a legal system in the service of the state lives on, and not everyone was thrilled by LAZ's merger with an activist movement, and especially not with the association's submission to the Forum's doctrine of collective responsibility. A senior state lawyer in Kaunda's Second Republic felt that Oasis Forum lawyers were abrogating their responsibility:

> As a member of LAZ, I don't agree with the position the leadership of LAZ has taken. We as lawyers must come out distinctly, with a lawyers' position. It might coincide with the Oasis Forum, fine. But to tell us that we have to talk the Oasis language – that, to me, is unacceptable. I mean, we must appear to be independent, because in a time of crisis people look to us for guidance. We must be able to give that guidance.

This lawyer's career embodies the legal trajectory of the one-party state, having served in several high-profile positions in the United National Independence Party (UNIP) government. In the Second Republic, he insists

> 'the President had an upper hand in terms of appointments …, and that was quite influential. I mean if you feel that the President has appointed you, there must be some … quiet allegiance within yourself.'

My interviewee acknowledges that under UNIP, power was very centralized, and feels, in retrospect, that 'government had too much power.' At the same time, during the Second Republic,

> There was the rule of law, no doubt about it. I mean if you go into the *Zambia Law Reports* you will see for yourself, particularly in the area of human rights, detentions in particular. Courts were quite assertive protecting these rights, and the government obliged.

This description of a hybrid system whereby presidential prerogativism coexists with a bench that embraced liberal human rights is an attractive one for many lawyers, but sits uneasily with orthodox political liberalism. Via explicit constitutional provisions, and a culture of political legality, prerogativism survived the transition from the single-party state to the return of a multiparty dispensation in 1991, and it is interesting to consider how prerogativist practices adapted to the new neoliberal context of President Chiluba's Third Republic. My interviewee had these observations:

> You see, there had always been some casual intimacy between the executive, the President in particular, and the Judiciary. That would have been there even in the Second Republic, where the Chief Justice would go to see the President off at the airport, receive him when he comes back. There were social interactions, and I'm sure telephone calls and conversations. That would have been there, in both the Second and the Third Republics.

This lawyer had an important position in UNIP and expressed no reservations about his role in safeguarding Kaunda's centralized rule. He was adamant, however, in his condemnation of Chiluba's deployment of the same constitutional powers Kaunda had enjoyed:

> There's one thing about a being a politician and a lawyer that made me resent the Third Republic. I think it was too corrupt. Chiluba and his compatriots often did not remind themselves what the rule of law means. Now, how can you have a situation where Cabinet Ministers and Members of Parliament initiate a privatisation programme and then end up being the beneficiaries – buying shops and companies? It never happened anywhere like that.

At the time of our conversation, information had recently been made public indicating that President Chiluba had secretly given the chief justice a considerable amount of money. This took place right after the Supreme Court had dismissed the opposition's attempt to overturn Chiluba's victory in the 1996 elections. In reference to this, my interviewee remarked that in 'the Third Republic, the President must have had an edge over the bench. The very sad situation is how any Chief Justice was found in such an embarrassing situation.' Chiluba's gift to the Chief Justice drew on funds kept in a secret intelligence account that had originally been set up by President Kenneth Kaunda (see Chapter 7). Despite using mechanisms created and deployed by Kaunda, this lawyer felt that Chiluba had stepped over a line that his predecessor had respected:

> Now, if the President is going to be dishing out money to the Chief Justice … I think that goes beyond intimacy. If that is anything to go by it means really that the President has penetrated inside the [legal] establishment. In other words, he was in a position to get what he wanted, although, we couldn't exactly see how that was being done. But of course, in the Second Republic too, the President had a big say in judicial appointments. Certainly you could not be appointed Judge if the President disapproved.

A lawyer, then, can be comfortable with prerogativist powers, but object to their abuse. What was not clear, however, is where the boundary lies between the legitimate and abusive use of prerogativist power. Wherein reside the standards that both uphold and provide protection against political legality?

At the time of our conversation, my interviewee considered that Mwanawasa was toeing this elusive line, and objected to the disrespect shown the president by the Oasis Forum. In his view the Forum, in its criticisms of the incumbent president, overstepped the boundaries of political propriety. Non-state actors like the Oasis Forum go too far, he said,

> when you begin doing parallel programmes. The President appointed this one – No, this appointment is wrong. The President next fires the Vice-President – No, he should not have done it that way. The President calls for an *indaba*[10] – No, he should have consulted us. Do you think when a government anywhere on Earth is elected into office, it is the business of that government to get an approval for each and every item on their agenda?

*JG: One can ask, though, what is the strength of the current administration's mandate?*

It might be shaky, but that's no reason. Ok, we know it's a minority government, but that does not entitle the Oasis Forum to act like a substitute government. They can expose the shortcomings, they can suggest alternatives, but they can't go to Government and say 'This is the programme and you can't change it.'

*JG: But did not the minority government's weak mandate create the space that the Oasis Forum has come to occupy?*

That may well be so, but it should not be a precedent. You see, the role of the Church is well-known, the role of civil society is well-known, the role of trade unions is well-known, the role of Government is well-known, the

10 A public political consultation modelled after village democracy.

role of the opposition is well-known. There's a division of labour. We can't all be doing the same things. We should perform as best as we can, within the scope of our roles.

Situated here among the views of Oasis Forum activists, a senior UNIP lawyer's acquiescence to a prerogativist ethos may appear exceptional. I suspect, though, that his position reflected the mainstream view among the legal profession as a whole. Prerogativist powers are not a problem; but their arbitrary abuse is. The model for this form of power is a reconstituted version of the 'benevolent monarch' of imperial history, and its iconic embodiment in the Zambian context is that of Kenneth Kaunda's 'enlightened despot.' I think it is fair to say that Kaunda continues to be Zambia's most revered and respected leader, but there is a fundamental lack of clarity about how to reconcile the pillars of Kaunda's powers with the rhetoric of liberal constitutionalism.

## The will of the people

Able to rely on neither individual integrity nor institutional resilience, my informants accepted that the legitimacy of the constitution, of the law, of the state and indeed of the Oasis Forum itself must derive from the will of the people, a stock phrase invoked often and in diverse contexts. Clearly, something so ubiquitous and as politically consequential as constituent power was open to diverse interpretations. Even within the Forum, activists expressed divergent notions of how the people's constituent power should best be tapped in constitution-making. From the government's perspective, the constitutional review commissions represented the premier mechanism for popular legitimation. In contrast, CRCs – established through executive fiat – were seen by activists and scholars alike as flawed instruments for defining the law of the land. The primary criticism leveled against them was their subordination to presidential whim under the Inquiries Act.[11]

Not everyone saw things in such black and white terms. A senior constitutional scholar-lawyer told me he had initially felt that the Chiluba-era Mwanakatwe Commission should not have produced a draft constitution. This was, in his view, because 'the making of a constitution cannot be a responsibility of a small clique.' He ultimately changed his mind, however, when the Mwanakatwe CRC recommended that its draft constitution be subjected to the deliberations of a constituent assembly and a referendum. For him, 'that was the best they could have done. … At least, I cannot think of any other popular way of arriving at a constitution, other than going through that process.'

In a similar twist, the Forum activists initially boycotted the Mwanawasa-appointed Mung'omba CRC, but eventually vindicated its work and provided

11 The Inquiries Act (Cap 41 of the Laws of Zambia, §2) is a political tool that empowers the president 'to inquire into any matter in which an inquiry would, in the opinion of the President, be for the public welfare.'

their own submissions. Despite the Forum's initial skepticism, lawyer-activist Patrick Matibini felt that the Mung'omba CRC had produced a 'bankable' proposal for a new constitution. In Dr Matibini's view, Mr Mung'omba personally facilitated 'a people-driven process, and most of the recommendations, at least the progressive ones, have ... originated from the people.' Despite their hope that the Mung'omba Commission's 'progressive' formulations would frame subsequent debates, Forum activists remained concerned that a popularly endorsed constitution was likely to remain beyond reach.

Forum informants gave considerable thought to the practicalities of incorporating the will of the people in constitution-making. One part of the question concerned the institutional mechanisms through which the people's will could be known. The Forum's firm and unwavering line was to use a constituent assembly to allow the people's representatives to participate directly in drafting and adopting constitutional provisions. A parallel concern, less clearly articulated, was about how to deal with an ill-informed citizenry. Some were clearly worried about what they considered to be politically reactionary sentiments among the population.[12]

Lawyer-activist Patrick Matibini felt that

**PM***:* One way forward would be simply through giving [the Constituent Assembly] the power to adopt. And for me that is the easiest and most legally plausible option. By that arrangement we'd ensure that all members of Parliament are actually members of the Constituent Assembly. Then we would have this broad-based group to simply *adopt* the constitution and then let the National Assembly to *enact.*[13]

**JG***:* Certainly that would presume a very high level of political commitment on the government's part, and deep collaboration among all the players.

**PM***:* And also, literacy. I think people should be able to understand what is really happening in the process.

The problem of an uninformed *demos* is often evoked by critics of popular adoption by a constituent assembly. It was also implicitly present in the lawyers' belief in the need for their expert guidance. Despite these reservations, activist-priest Joseph Komakoma was unhappy with the way that Mwanawasa's government sought to undercut popular input in constitution-making:

**JK***:* And now Government is indicating that the people who submitted about the Constituent Assembly were misguided. Because they claim it can't work. But that's not the issue. The issue is how can we make the Constituent Assembly

12 The death penalty and the declaration of Zambia as a 'Christian nation' were considered to be contentious issues by the Oasis Forum despite popular support for these provisions (about the latter, see I. Phiri 2003, Gordon 2012).

13 To 'adopt' a constitution means to have its text approved by vote or comparable mechanism. Prevailing law required that a new constitution be 'enacted' into law by the national assembly.

work? Are the numbers of representatives adequate? Are they too high? Is there need to reduce the time, perhaps, to say if there is no resolution within one month, the Constituent Assembly ceases, and another avenue is proposed? Those are the kinds of issues we are supposed to be discussing now ... The question is how can we make it work, because this is what the people have decided.

Oasis Forum activists, lawyers included, saw that their struggle with the government hinged on fundamental questions of political legitimacy. They universally derided the government's claims to represent the will of the people. In lawyer-activist Patrick Matibini's view, the immaturity of Zambian democracy creates a demand for watchdog groups like the Oasis Forum to exercise vigilance on behalf of the population:

**PM***:* The people have been consistent. The people have been resolute. The people have been resilient. But what has been lacking, seriously and dismally so, is appropriate political leadership that can carry through these aspirations boldly, without feeling in any way threatened.

The Forum's activists were unconvinced by the government's claim to a democratic mandate. They pointed to the Mwanawasa administration's minority status (a small share of a low electoral turnout), and its razor-thin electoral margin, well below half of the votes. They also had little trust in the capacity of the electoral commission to ensure a fair poll. In Dr Matibini's words, 'as long as you have a flawed electoral system, you can never be too sure that the eventual leadership that emerges reflects the will of the people.'

In its struggle with government, the Oasis Forum felt it had several advantages. First was the unassailable quality of its bona fides as an impartial, non-partisan and professional alliance. Fr Komakoma provides a concise summary (emphasis added):

**JK***:* We didn't design it that way, but the three parties [to the Oasis Forum] had three distinct, complementary strengths: LAZ brought in ***legal authority***. This was essential because the Oasis Forum was purely motivated by a concern with constitutional issues. The point was to stop Chiluba's manipulation of the constitution and to safeguard Chiluba's individual interests. Revisions to the constitution should not be just for now, but for years to come. The Church ensured ***moral authority*** – a safeguard against 'narrow' legalism on behalf of morally just laws. The NGOCC provided a ***direct link to the people***, they had the capacity to mobilize popular support, which they did very effectively, e.g., via the green ribbon campaign.[14]

14 On the Green Ribbon campaign, see Chapter 6.

Patrick Matibini went further in grounding the Oasis Forum's democratic mandate. In his view, the legitimacy of the OF resides in the way its activities

> cut across a number of issues and disciplines to the extent that it embodies the will of the people. I think it transcends the legality that is associated with the Constitution ... [In this work,] lawyers certainly have a critical role to play in this development, but [constitutional reform] is not an exclusively legal issue.

The breadth and depth of the stakes involved in constitution-making is why Dr Matibini considered it vital that the *demos* participate directly in the adoption of the new constitution:

**PM***:* If we allow the Constitution to be enacted exclusively by the National Assembly, we risk the danger of one having most of the progressive recommendations thrown overboard. And also we risk the possibility of emerging with a largely partisan document .... If the enactment of the constitution was left to Parliamentarians exclusively, it's likely to be determined on partisan lines, and the danger in that respect would be that voting will be according to the whims, literally, of the President.

This, then, was a major challenge: How to embody a countervailing social force capable of outmaneuvering the president, who is armed with the resources and apparatus of the state, as well as with a bottomless repertoire of exceptional powers. To prevail against prerogativist whim it was necessary to harness the constituent powers of the *demos.* But how? In terms of lifestyle, residence, education and personal assets, the Oasis Forum activists were worlds apart from the statistically average Zambian citizen. When I asked how the Oasis Forum, a middle-class alliance of relatively well-to-do professionals, can claim to speak on behalf of the people, Fr Komakoma retorted:

**JK***:* How can we validate our claims to represent the people? The [Mung'omba] CRC itself validated our claims because they went to the remotest place of Zambia and collected views, and the sum total of those views coincides with what we are saying – We, the elite, Lusaka based, non-governmental civil society activists! So in a way, they justify what we've been saying, that we are representing the people's views, because there is no contradiction really ... We all agreed that this Commission, if anything, even went further than Mwanakatwe because they went to every constituency in Zambia.

**JG***:* So are you saying that a convergence of views is the same as representation?

**JK***:* It's only because they don't have a medium of expressing themselves, the people in the rural areas. So the only medium they use is the CRC. To pour water now on what they said to the CRC – that's the bigger injustice you can do to the people, because they have expressed themselves.

## *On 'going to the people'*

Fr Joseph Komakoma's view expresses principled pragmatism in an exemplary and reasonable fashion, but the question remains of why the Oasis Forum invoked the dubious mediation of a presidentially appointed commission to verify the people's will? Speaking in 2005, Fr Komakoma regretted that the forum had spent so much time and energy trying to negotiate with Levy Mwanawasa over the establishment of a constituent assembly.

**JK***:* If we had known right from the beginning that Mwanawasa is only concerned with winning, we would have changed our tactics, but we realized too late.
**JG***:* How would you have changed your tactics?
**JK***:* We would have ignored him and gone to the people only. We would have been working with the people right up to now, but we thought we could make progress with the President.

Were the Forum activists naïve, or did the lawyers in the alliance feel overconfident of their capacity to find common ground with Mr Mwanawasa, their professional colleague? It is here, perhaps, that the non-partisan activists' lack of political experience is most evident. Be that as it may, the Forum's disillusionment with President Mwanawasa's alleged 'filibustering' led them to boycott the Mung'omba CRC. This was a difficult decision for the LAZ in particular, where many members felt that their legal expertise was vital to the crafting of a coherent constitution. Indeed, not everyone toed the line.

One LAZ activist had to step down as chair of an influential civic organization when she accepted a seat on the Mung'omba CRC. This was her own act of principled pragmatism, which she ultimately justified by the need for a people-driven constitution. She felt it was her responsibility to bring her legal expertise to the CRC, but expressed a complementary commitment to honoring the demands of the *demos*:

> As a Constitutional Review Commissioner, I visited between 115 and 120 constituencies. People were very clear. The people know how they want to be governed .... If government isn't willing to conform to the will of the people, i.e., the Constituent Assembly, we should proceed to apply pressure. Pressure should mount!

The leadership of the Oasis Forum eventually acknowledged the importance of the Mung'omba commissioners' engagement with grassroots communities. The activist in question was adamant about the way her direct interactions with rank-and-file citizens validated her legal expertise, in much the same way that activist-priest Komakoma cited the commissioners' recommendations as a validation of the Forum's legitimacy as a voice of the people. But invoking the will of the people can be unpredictable, and volatile. On the one hand, Fr Komakoma was concerned that voters in the 2006 elections would vindicate Mwanawasa's prevarications over electoral reform.

**JK***:* We've done our bit. We've raised all the concerns, we've issued the warnings. So I would rather say well, okay, fine ... and if people simply re-elect Mwanawasa despite his filibustering over the Constitution, I will be very disappointed. Sorry to say. It would then mean that the people of Zambia don't want any progress at all.

Fr Komakoma also had a parallel concern. This was that the government's refusal to deliver a majoritarian ('50 + 1%') electoral provision before the next elections could lead to civil unrest:

**JK***:* We are fearing what could happen, because it does happen sometimes. Because now, Zambia is not what it used to be. The whole Southern Province is not with Mwanawasa, and that's a potential trouble area .... In the next few weeks there could be a strong proposition from the [opposition] United Party for National Development to say we are tired of your 'peace-making' and trying to negotiate with Mwanawasa. The elections are coming and we can't wait any longer. Sorry .... we have nothing to lose, so therefore we are going to cause confusion. And they can. And that's something we've tried to avoid, and we hope it won't happen. But it's always possible and it's a potential thing, the closer it gets to the elections ... Because the dynamics have changed, we have to proceed more carefully.

As it turned out, the Oasis Forum's cautious strategy did not bear the fruit it sought. Mwanawasa deflected demands for a constituent assembly until after the 2006 elections, in which he was re-elected with a 10% higher margin than in 2001. It was only after his re-election, in his second term, that he took concrete steps to have the Mung'omba Commission's draft constitution enacted. Mwanawasa rejected the vocabulary of a constituent assembly, but ultimately established a comparable body – albeit one stuffed with the Movement for Multiparty Democracy (MMD) loyalists – under the rubric of a national constitutional convention (NCC). Mwanawasa died before the NCC completed its work, and the NCC's constitutional proposal was rejected by parliament under the reign of his successor, Rupiah Banda. After Banda and the MMD suffered a resounding defeat in 2011, the victorious Patriotic Front under President Michael Sata restarted the process which eventually led to the enactment of the 2016 Constitutional Amendment Act (see Chapter 6).

## Reflections

### *Legal activism and constitutionalism*

My informants were astute and well-tempered professionals. Most of them had been frontline champions in struggles for core liberal virtues – rule of law, accountability, a majoritarian political order and popular participation in constitution-making. Their participation in the Oasis Forum signaled a significant historical precedent in the evolution of Zambia's political system. 'We have moved [forward],' as Fr Joseph Komakoma rightly notes. Despite deepening hardships for a large proportion of the population, the Zambian electorate, since 1991, has brought about three peaceful regime changes, enacted two substantial constitutional amendments and openly scrutinized the government's successes and failures in upholding the law of the land. While the Forum is better seen as an indicator rather than an instigator of social change, its story is worth carefully assessing. This is because the political challenges they confronted, rooted in the prevailing form of power, have changed little in the ensuing two decades. Ultimately, the Oasis Forum's campaign to democratize the process of constitution-making did not strengthen the capacity of the *demos* to hold government to account. It did, however, establish the possibility of non-partisan activism in the domain of state-making. It also galvanized the popular perception of lawyers as stewards of the national project. Allow me to pause and reflect on these two effects, beginning with the consequences of the Oasis Forum's constitutional activism for legal authority and its political deployment.

No group is more invested in the state-national project than lawyers. The authority of lawyers, and their livelihoods, devolves from the republican constitution, the foundation of the state-nation. Their everyday work is that of sustaining state authority in ritual and non-ritual contexts. Lawyers are instinctively obliged to defend the state order and to invest in state repair. In this respect, activist lawyers must walk a fine line – invoking statutory legal authority and expertise in order to challenge the legitimacy of the state apparatus upon which legality itself depends.

Lawyers understand that their professional credibility is contingent on how legitimate the law itself is perceived. My informants were also concerned with their socio-political legitimacy – how they are viewed by society – and this concern conjoins with an instinctive patriotic ethos to fuel their activism. A sense of legitimacy of the state and its legal apparatus is created, among other things, by public allusions to the will of the people by the political leadership, as well as by groups like the Oasis Forum. Legal actors reproduce this imagery recurrently and creatively. At the same time, the prerogativist form of power that frames empirical legality marginalizes popular inputs into state-making and obstructs political efforts to tighten the binds of accountability.

Lawyers are caught up in this field – obliged to defend their professional legitimacy by invoking the convergence of their views with those of the people, while at the same time navigating a politico-legal terrain within which legality is both bracketed and weaponized by the president. This paradoxical duality is, like the prerogativist form of power itself, more than one but less than two. It is more than one, because the prerogativist sovereign and the *demos* cohabitate a socio-political domain predicated on the colonial premise of embattled government. Even though the powers of the sovereign are thought to derive from the constituent power vested in the *demos*, the link between the sovereign and this constituent power is mediated by a flawed system of political representation, and by opaque political practices. The bond between the decision and the *demos* is less than two, however, because neither can exist without the other. The sovereign exists to ensure the integrity of the nation – and to contain the volatility of its constituent power – while the authority of the *demos* is recognized only insofar as it reaffirms sovereign authority. This dynamic explains, I think, the instability and opportunism of the legal profession, which is obliged to facilitate the imaginary of national unity (through uniform and universal law) that lies at the heart of the constitutional order.

There are, then, power effects, ideological divides and unreflected class dispositions affecting how lawyers understand their roles, and the consequences of their agency. Lawyers view their expertise as providing necessary guidance to the people, especially in times of crisis. Legal authority can be overbearing, however, crowding out popular political deliberation and action. And indeed, lawyerly authority is at times 'allowed' to overpower popular politics because it serves the interest of the powerful. Finding a balance between personal ideals, economic ambitions, professional norms and political opportunities is tricky. The heightened uncertainties of the political atmosphere surrounding constitution-making during the Mwanawasa administration were particularly challenging in this respect, if only because there was no clear precedent for this kind of politics. These caveats aside, it is evident that for all their learnedness and confidence, despite their suits, cars and substantial fees, lawyers are a subsidiary class, destined to facilitate a form of power they are beholden to, but don't necessarily respect.

## *The paradox of non-partisan politics*

The end of the Cold War presented Zambians with an opportunity, or perhaps an imperative, to re-imagine the state. Constitutionalism and constitution-making became key instruments of state-making and, at the same time, the main arena where elite Zambians have negotiated the parameters of public authority, largely among themselves, but ostensibly on behalf of the people. Many aspects of public contestation have changed over the past three decades, but despite heated struggles around the content and procedure of constitution-making, the form of power undergirding the state is essentially the same in 2020 as it was in 1991. This is not simply because of the tenacity of colonial residues in the constitutional order. These remnants are important, as I have tried to show, but their resilience also depends on the convenience of the prevailing form of power for Zambia's thin upper crust.

The prevailing constitutional order has overseen the entrenchment of a particular political economy, and of a distributional logic according to which national wealth is channeled into maintaining, and enhancing, the lifestyle of elite groups. Only after this primary target is met does the *demos* get its share. As one influential lawyer-politician (Kabimba 2016; *Lusaka Times* blog, 14 January 2016) put it, the 2016 constitutional amendments reflect a class struggle 'between those who wield state power and have always used it for self-interest and self-preservation, against the poor and under-privileged.' While this observation underplays the dramatic process of middle-class formation over the past three decades, the persistent gap between an urban, professional elite and a rural underclass is indisputable. By definition, elites benefit from this pattern of distribution and are thus predisposed to defend the status quo, even as particular factions within elite strata jockey for more influence or a bigger piece of the cake. Financial, social and political insecurity is undeniably a significant factor shaping individual experience, even among the better-off. But it is also true that the dynamics of elite formation – the mechanisms by which one accedes to wealth and power – have been relatively stable for a long time: urban residence; education; professional status; family connections to successful businesses, and to powerful politicians are markers that virtually all members of Zambia's elites have in common. The stability of elite formation contributes to why Zambia's best and brightest are drawn to the incrementalist project of constitution-making, and to related state-affirmative ventures, rather than to more radical political strategies.

Material considerations are important, but I believe the Oasis Forum activists when they claim that democratic values are for them more important incentives than monetary reward. Liberal constitutionalism is the language of civic virtue and individual integrity in a national public arena that is frequently despoiled by greed and deceit. The paradox, as I have argued, is that in its empirical manifestation, postcolonial liberalism is equally conducive to the recognition of rights and claims as to their derogation. Elites are consistently better positioned to defend their entitlements than those less well endowed; at the same time, they also tend to see only the emancipatory side of liberalism. This, perhaps, is simply the way the world works, and it may be naïve to believe that things could be otherwise. Still, the emancipatory instinct that postcolonial liberalism claims to honor also begs the question: Is it possible to imagine a mode of liberal politics that does *not* empower the elite to deny the less advantaged members of the *demos* of its 'just share' (see Ferguson 2015), while claiming to represent them?

This paradox is one of anthropologist Harri Englund's concerns. Englund's innovative study *Prisoners of Freedom* (2006) documented how the legalist language of human rights worked to obstruct the claims of marginalized Malawians for justice. In his subsequent analysis of call-in radio broadcasts, Englund (2011) revisits the effects of liberal discourse and asserts that as a register of beliefs and sentiments, liberalism comprises 'an internally diverse moral outlook.' If one scrutinizes the discourse produced by individual citizens – as Englund has so carefully done – 'multiple orientations within [Zambian] liberalism' are indeed evident. In its focus on the varieties of individual morality, however, I feel that Englund misses a cogent fact about liberalism's imperial legacy. This legacy has a structural, historical heft that is not the simple aggregate of individual creeds. It is encoded in constitutional provisions, in the culture of political legality and in the 'transcendental' form of embodied power that each president is obliged to occupy. The officeholder is, in reality, held by the office, albeit willingly so. In the face of this historical encumbrance, individual expressions of liberal morality can sustain belief in the possibility of a more just future, but their claims on the state are toothless without the force of collective political will.

Tensions within and among individual creeds, and between individual expectations and the empirical actions of their leaders tether citizens and leaders to one another, and to the state. The liberalism of the constitution, of the legal apparatus and of the public media provides a platform and a vocabulary for citizens to engage with their leaders, and with the contours of the national project. The Oasis Forum recognized the political benefits of controlling this platform, but overestimated its flexibility. President Levy Mwanawasa sought to appropriate the deliberative space of liberalism through his National Constitutional Conference, but seemingly had no further-reaching aim beyond reclaiming the political initiative from the Oasis Forum. Expressions of liberalism shape the public imagination of what is politically possible more than the diverse moral outlooks of the citizenry shape the constitution. This, in any event, seems to be the lesson of constitution-making in Zambia's Third Republic.

Presidents can and do personalize the form of power they inherit, despite its historical obstinacy. They inevitably seek to shape the contours of prerogativism to their individual ends, but as yet, none have succeeded in transcending it. The role of the constitution in sustaining the national project, the legitimacy of the state and thus of the presidency itself, is a powerful constraint on making a radical break with prevailing constitutional provisions. This may be, as I argue, because Zambian elites have not felt the necessity for a radical reform of the form of power. The postcolonial liberalism of the constitution's explicit and implicit provisions allows for multiple orientations and opportunities, both liberal and illiberal. Elite watchdogs can and do challenge ostensibly 'excessive' efforts to bend the law to the president's personal aims. Such principled public challenges cast some sections of the elites in the role of the people's representatives, and have allowed them to consolidate a kind of political agency unbridled by the compromises incumbent on political party affiliation. But Zambia's liberal, non-partisan elites appear, ultimately, unable to risk their established entitlements by aligning themselves with a revolutionary rupture. They may acknowledge the necessity of a radical break to achieve genuine justice for the majority, but in accordance with their professional socialization and their class positions, their pragmatic strategies have been limited to procedural maneuvers. At the level of moral values, or of strategic vision, elite actors can espouse a variety of positions; they are not cut from a single cloth. It can confidently be said, however, that elite lawyers are the most risk-averse faction among the professional avant-garde. This may be because as private entrepreneurs in an unpredictable market economy, they have much to lose.

II

# A genealogy of postcolonial power

# 5 Imperial constitutionalism 1924–1996

## Introduction

In 1969, Chief Justice James Skinner, a naturalized White citizen of Zambia, came under harsh attack by the nation's president, Dr Kenneth Kaunda. Under Skinner's watch, High Court Justice Ifor Evans, also White, had quashed charges against two Portuguese soldiers arrested for crossing over Angola's northwestern border with Zambia.[1] According to contemporary accounts, the two colonial militia had responded to an invitation by Zambian border guards to share a cigarette. Justice Evans noted that the arrest of the soldiers 'did not redound to the credit of the Zambian authorities,' calling the incident 'trivial, a mere technical breach.'[2] Kaunda took personal umbrage at Justice Evans' criticism since, in the president's view, he himself represented the 'sole authority in Zambia' (Phiri 2006, 137–8).

Kaunda considered Evans' comments to be 'politically motivated to discredit the government' (ibid.) and demanded an explanation from the Chief Justice.[3] In response, Skinner affirmed that he was

> satisfied that Justice Evans has acted on the principles of Justice. It is one of the functions of the judiciary to criticize the action of the executive or its individual servants whenever the need arises. If that right is denied then the courts would no longer effectively carry out their duties.[4]

1 The case was *Silva & Fritas v The People* (1969 ZR 121). Angola was a Portuguese colony at the time.

2 'Justice on Trial' *Time*, 15 August 1969: www.time.com/time/magazine/article/0,9171,901234,00.html.

3 According to veteran politician and one-time minister of defense, Alexander Grey Zulu (2007, 367), Zambia experienced 444 'border violations by racist regimes' between 1965 and 1972, suggesting that President Kaunda's reaction to the incursion was not unwarranted.

4 'In honor of Zambia's first Minister of Justice', *Lusaka Times*, 24 November 2008: www.lusakatimes.com/?p=5793. The Irish-born Skinner (1923–2008) was UNIP's legal counsel in the run up to independence and was instrumental in drafting Zambia's first constitution. A long-time UNIP member and supporter, Skinner served Zambia as minister of justice (October 1964–January 1965), Attorney General (January 1965–March 1969), minister of legal

DOI: 10.4324/9780429198984-7

Skinner's refusal to apologize to the president 'led the executive to unleash riotous political party cadres to invade the court premises' and Chief Justice Skinner was subsequently forced to leave the country for good (Malila 2020, 400).

Contemporary analyst Andrew Roberts observed that this collision between legal and political authority reflected 'a deep-seated problem in Zambian politics: the widespread confusion about where ultimate authority resides, as to the relationship between the law and the executive, and between the executive and the ruling party' (Roberts 1969, cited in Phiri, op. cit., 139). Robert's assessment has proved prescient. A good half-century on, as we shall see, this deep-seated problem, rooted in systemic ambiguities in the constitution itself, has yet to be resolved. In what follows, I recount in some detail the politics of Zambia's constitution-making history with specific attention to ways in which presidential powers have (not) evolved in the postcolonial era. Woven into this narrative is an account of the evolution of public reaction to prerogativist government. This brief chronicle does not attempt to be a history of popular resistance to autocratic tendencies in Zambia's politico-legal order. Rather, my aim is to flesh out the background of the specific social elements and sentiments that would eventually emerge, in 2001, as the Oasis Forum – a popular movement for a more democratic constitutional order.

## From Northern Rhodesia to Zambia's First Republic

As noted earlier, the powers of the presidency that Zambia's first president Kenneth Kaunda assumed in 1964 were virtually identical to those of the colonial governor of Northern Rhodesia (Sipalo 1978, 136).[5] Indeed,

> section eighteen of the Zambia Independence Order 1964 provided: "Where under any law in force in Northern Rhodesia immediately before the commencement of this Order any prerogative or privileges are vested in Her Majesty those prerogatives or privileges shall, from the commencement of this Order, vest in the President." (Craig 1973, 139)

The authority of the governor, along with the other fundamentals of colonial rule, was delineated in a series of documents, termed *orders-in-council*, approved by the British Parliament on behalf of the Crown. Orders-in-council evolved from very rudimentary legislative instruments, first introduced while Northern Rhodesia was governed as a protectorate on behalf of the British Crown by the British

---

affairs (January 1967–December 1968) before appointment to the judiciary as Chief Justice (March 1969–September 1969). He resigned from the Zambian judiciary as a result of this incident, but went on to serve as Chief Justice in Malawi for 15 years.

5 Ngenda Sipalo (1978) has written an excellent survey, based on meticulous archival work, of constitutional development in Northern Rhodesia/Zambia from the territory's earliest days until the introduction of one-party rule in 1973. Since his thesis is available online (see bibliography), it is not necessary to reproduce his detailed findings here.

South Africa Company (BSAC), into a full-blown republican constitution, which became the basis for Zambia's independence.[6] The penultimate order-in-council of 1963 was very close in structure and content to the Zambia Independence Order of 1964, which formed the basis for the Zambia Independence Act of 1964 (still a piece of British legislation), and, finally, for Zambia's first republican constitution of 1964.

Northern Rhodesia's governor was the British Crown's mandated representative in the colony. The scope of the governor's sovereign power as defined in the 1924 order-in-council was substantial, albeit subject to oversight in certain matters by the high commissioner of South Africa, the colonial secretary in London and, ultimately, the British monarchy. Over time, the powers of the governor took on greater scope and autonomy, although the colonial government was always, until the end, exercised at the 'pleasure' of the Crown.

When Northern Rhodesia/Zambia acceded from the BSAC administration to official colonial rule in 1924, 4,182 'Europeans' (1,919 men and 1,016 women) lived in the territory. The 'native' population numbered 'rather more than 1,100,000' (Northern Rhodesia 1926, 5). This translates to around 265 Africans for every colonial settler.

Given their numerical minority, the protection of the White men and women occupying the territory was a primary concern of the colonial government. The first *Colonial Report for Northern Rhodesia* noted with relief the 'tranquility of the native population' (ibid., 13) and yet, the problem of maintaining 'order' weighed heavily on the administration. Its primary strategy was to co-opt local power structures and the colonial administration portrayed itself as governing through local norms. From the outset, however, local law (and the interests of

6 Until 1899, much of the current territory of Zambia was 'administered' (as against 'governed') on the basis of loose agreements broached between agents of the British South Africa Company and King Lewanika of the Lozi (Barotse) peoples. The core concerns in these agreements were mineral rights, and compensation for their exploitation to Lewanika, who actively sought the protection of the Crown against hostile neighbors and Portuguese expansion from the east (Roberts 1976, 167, Sipalo 1978). In 1899/1900, these arrangements were formalized under orders-in-council, which established, for administrative purposes, two separate blocks of land – Barotse-North-Western Rhodesia (1899) and North-Eastern Rhodesia (1900), respectively. These two territories were 'amalgamated' as Northern Rhodesia in 1911, under a new order-in-council. This British imperial document marks the birth of the boundaries of contemporary Zambia.

In 1924, the British Crown took over direct control of Northern Rhodesia from the BSAC. The British Parliament enacted a new order-in-council, which vested power in a governor and a commander in chief, while acknowledging and protecting the mineral rights of the BSAC (Clough 1924). The first governor, Sir Herbert James Stanley (1872–1955), was also the new British protectorate's commander in chief.

While these early Northern Rhodesian orders-in-council can justifiably be seen as charting the contours of a national Grundnorm, such legislation only began to take on more recognizably constitutional characteristics after World War II (NR Legco 1945), and even more so as the anticolonial struggle heated up toward the end of the 1950s (NR Legco 1958, 1959, 1962, 1963).

the 'native' population more generally) was firmly subordinated to that of the imperial usurpers. As summarized by one contemporary commentator (Clough 1924, 280; emphasis added):

> With regard to natives the [1924] Order in Council provides that all Ordinances passed by the Legislative Council shall respect any native law or custom by which the civil relations of any native chiefs, tribes or populations under His Majesty's protection are now regulated, *except* so far as the same may be incompatible with the due exercise of His Majesty's power and jurisdiction

This simple conjunction – *except* – expresses a powerful force in the trajectory of Zambia's political order. This exception generated space for the emergence of a paradoxical duality of power which persists to the present day. On the one hand, colonial government espoused a rhetoric of liberal tolerance, in this case for 'Native law and custom.' On the other hand, the 'exception' signals the possibility of recourse to extra-legal violence and coercion in defense of the security of the governing class. Obviously, this duality does not originate with the 1924 order-in-council, but has much deeper roots, which I will attempt to make visible over the course of this chapter.

The colonial governor was, for all intents, the physical embodiment of 'His Majesty's power and jurisdiction.' This principle was spelled out in the Northern Rhodesia order-in-council of 1924 thus:

> The Governor presided over both the Executive and Legislative Councils. Executive power was concentrated in his hands. He was Commander-in-Chief of the Armed Forces. His assent was necessary for all legislation and he could subdivide the territory into Provinces. He represented the King for Ceremonial purposes. In his social and administrative functions he was assisted by the Executive Council of Senior Civil Servants to whom all instructions from the Secretary of State for the Colonies had to be communicated but he was not compelled to follow its advice though he had to inform the Secretary of State for the Colonies of his reasons... (Sipalo 1978, 46–47).

The seat of imperial power in London was, then, a distant if formidable eminence, and governors were apt to act first and seek approval later. The exercise of disciplinary measures over local populations was fueled by pressures from a rowdy and insecure settler constituency close at hand, and by the demand for cheap and obedient labor for the rising copper mining sector. Disciplinary discretion was tempered largely by the governor's sense of political expediency. The Colonial Office may have espoused a rhetoric of the 'paramountcy of Native interests' but, in most cases, governors' sense of expediency revolved not around service to indigenous communities but were rather targeted at future career options, i.e., approval from upstream authorities. Governors were in civil service rotation, and were rarely posted to Northern Rhodesia for more than three years. Those not yet ready to retire were acutely aware of their dependence upon a favorable assessment by the Colonial Office for a promotion to a more prestigious or lucrative station (Williams 2011).

Over the 40 years of British imperial 'protection,' the contours of governmental power hardly changed. The expansion of the membership in the various advisory bodies provided for in orders-in-council (i.e., the executive and legislative councils)[7] did little to undercut the autocratic nature of the governor's sovereign power. Resemblance to the scope of contemporary presidential powers is striking. The Zambian presidency, as established in the independence constitution of 1964, was a colonial artefact in the most concrete sense of the term imaginable.

## *Independence constitution*

The formulation of the independence constitution of 1964 was overseen by Britain, Zambia's colonial overlord. The foundational act of constitution-making took place without, as Melvin Mbao (2010, 90) reminds us, the 'direct and active involvement of the public.' Achieving Zambian independence was a protracted and complicated process, punctuated by the Cha Cha Cha uprising, a 'civil disobedience campaign that led to serious disorder' (Phiri 2006, 107), instigated by Kaunda's United National Independence Party (UNIP), between July and October 1961, and the general elections of October 1962, which allowed, for the first time, non-White suffrage. Following the elections, a multi-racial cabinet was installed in December 1962, comprising four Black and two White ministers. UNIP swept the subsequent elections of January 1964, and a new government took office with Kaunda as prime minister, presiding over a cabinet of 14 all-UNIP ministers (Phiri 2005, Mulford 1967). Kaunda's government immediately demanded constitutional negotiations aimed at full independence from colonial rule and in May 1964, leaders of UNIP, together with the opposition African National Congress, led by Harry Nkumbula, and the White settlers' National Progress Party agreed on the details of the independence constitution during talks in London.

The prolonged struggles and negotiations during this period revolved around two inter-related questions – race and federation.[8] Britain, White settlers and certain Black liberals favored a 'multi-racial' government based on a 'complicated formula' (Phiri 2005, loc. cit.) that would inflate the electoral mandate of the

7 For example, the introduction of 'unofficial members' to the legislative council in 1926 and to the executive council in 1939; or the appointment of a White settler, Colonel Stewart Gore-Browne (1883–1967), to represent African interests on the legislative council from 1938 to 1951 (Rotberg 1977).

8 From 1953 until 1963, Northern Rhodesia belonged to the Central African Federation along with Nyasaland (now Malawi) and Southern Rhodesia (now Zimbabwe), with its capital in Salisbury (now Harare), the capital of Southern Rhodesia. African nationalists were adamantly opposed to the federation which they justifiably saw as an effort to consolidate racist apartheid government in the three British colonies.

settler constituency. Arriving at a solution based on universal suffrage took several years of struggle and led to the dissolution of the Central African Federation. Constitutional negotiations, then, focused on the racial parameters of the electoral roll, not on the form of power encoded in the legal foundations of the emerging state. After independence, the powers of the executive enshrined in colonial-era orders-in-council remained in place, and the maintenance of extraordinary powers under an endemic 'state of emergency' further amplified executive discretion (Chanda 1986).[9]

There were, then, deep substantive continuities between the colonial and the independence constitutions. While it is true that the imperial form of power survived the transition to independence, one must not trivialize the significance of the changes brought about by decolonization. Zambia's independence meant the defeat of racism, the reaffirmation of Black humanity. This liberation was tied up inextricably with a constitution that, while not of the people's making, did create the People as a unity, a political singularity. The fact that independence was not so much 'wrested' as 'handed down' (CSAC 1996, 40), through an act of the British Parliament, does not negate the fact that the new constitution imparted freedom from racial oppression to all Black Zambians. This was a powerful accomplishment of the nationalist movement, and the new constitution conferred this freedom indiscriminately to a 'unified' citizenry i.e., the People. The new constitution did not so much 'express' the constituent power of the people as conjure it into existence. Thus, as Martin Loughlin (2017, 167) notes: 'constituent power not only involves the exercise of power by a people: It simultaneously constitutes a people. Constituent power expresses the fact that unity is created from disunity, inclusion from exclusion.'

Upon assuming the presidency in October 1964, Kenneth Kaunda embraced and embodied the powers of his imperial predecessor. He soon found, though, that even these extensive legal entitlements were insufficient to accomplish his vision of establishing a Humanist society, dedicated to equality, development, the promotion of Pan-Africanism and the liberation of Southern Africa from colonialism and apartheid (Hall 1969).

The independence constitution codified Zambia's republican status as a unitary state, and a (modified) executive presidency (Tordoff 1974, 12). According to the 1964 constitution:

> a bill to amend the Constitution required the votes of not less than two-thirds of all the members of the National Assembly. Further, insofar as it altered any part of the Constitution relating to fundamental rights, such a

9 A state of emergency was actually introduced some months before Zambia's independence by then Northern Rhodesian Prime Minister Kenneth Kaunda, to allow for military action against the millennialist Lumpa Church of the prophetess Alice Lenshina, whose followers refused to pledge authority to the new republic (Hinfelaar 1991, Mulenga 1998, Hudson 1999). It remained in force for 27 years until Kaunda's exit from power in 1991.

bill could not come into force until submitted to a national referendum and approved thereby.

This clause was eliminated through a 1969 amendment and referendum billed as the 'referendum to end all referenda' (Ndulo & Kent 1996, 264). The justification for this move was to make it difficult to alter provisions protecting the rights of individuals. As Ndulo and Kent (1998, 11) note, however, '[t]he removal of the referendum clause was later to facilitate the adoption of a one-party system of government.' This it did by removing 'the need for a referendum to do so and left the entire Constitution subject to amendment of those in control possessed a majority of two-thirds in Parliament.'

Zambia experienced growing political tension between 1967 and 1972, and occasional violence between UNIP and the young democracy's main opposition parties. The formation of the United Progressive Party (UPP) in 1971 under the leadership of former UNIP and Republican Vice President Simon Kapwepwe – Kaunda's childhood friend and long-time political ally – evoked a 'hysterical' reaction (Tordoff 1974, 33). Kapwepwe's UPP was banned and Kaunda instigated the preparation of a single-party constitution. The National Commission for the Establishment of a One-Party Participatory Democracy (generally known as the Chona Commission, after its chair, Vice President Mainza Chona) was set up with the specific mandate of recommending what form a one-party participatory democracy should take. In December 1972, legislation was passed establishing the one-party state. Presaging political tactics that President Chiluba would employ in 1996, Kaunda's 'government indicated that it would depart in many respects from the recommendations of the Chona Commission' (Tordoff 1974, 35).[10]

## *One-party constitution*

On 25 August 1973, the 1964 constitutional arrangement was annulled by UNIP and replaced with a one-party state constitution, enacted by parliament, establishing the institutions of the Second Republic (Ndulo & Kent 1998, 13). The new constitution outlawed opposition parties and granted UNIP constitutional supremacy over the civil service and the state apparatus at all levels. Kaunda had long made explicit his preference for a one-party state, but had promised not to force such a regime on the nation. Growing challenges to his rule, accompanied by sporadic political violence, led Kaunda to renege on his earlier promise. The political opposition challenged Kaunda's move as unconstitutional, but the courts condoned UNIP's maneuver.[11]

10 The Chona Commission formulated a number of liberal recommendations – such as placing limits on detention without trial, restricting the president to serve only two five-year terms and sharing the president's executive powers with a prime minister – but these were not included in the 1973 constitution (see Ndulo & Kent 1996, 264, Phiri 2006, 150).

11 *Nkumbula v The Attorney-General* (1972 ZR 206).

The new constitution gave Kaunda a monopoly on power.[12] While the explicit break with the pluralist tradition appears to be a revolutionary move, constitutional historian Ngenda Sipalo (1978, 174) notes that the 1973 one-party constitution

> did not ... represent an effective break with the past. The truth of the matter is that the 1973 Constitution simply represented an embodiment of the rules, regulations, laws and procedures which has marked the Constitutional development for the past fifty years or more.[13]

The 1973 constitution removed the political opposition from parliament. The subsequent legislation this enabled bolstered the president's discretion in many ways. Executive power continued to be vested in the president, who was entitled to act with absolute impunity:

> [I]n the exercise of these power the President shall act in his own deliberative judgment and shall, subject to the provisions of the constitution, not be obliged to follow advice tendered by any other person or authority. He is the Commander in Chief of the Armed Forces. He is also the Head of State. The President is immune against criminal proceedings in respect of anything done or omitted to be done by him either in his official capacity or in his private capacity and no civil proceedings shall be instituted [sic] in respect of which relief is claimed against him in respect of anything done in his private capacity. (§§51(2), 54, 37, 47; cited in Sipalo 1978, 206)[14]

No political competition of any kind was tolerated. The Chief's Act of 1965 had already empowered the president to recognize or withdraw recognition from any traditional leader in Zambia. The Local Government Bill repealed the Barotse Native Authority Ordinance, removing any pretensions to countervailing authority from Zambia's most powerful traditional leader, the Litunga of the Lozi peoples. The new constitution empowered the president to appoint up to ten nominated members to parliament, ensuring that Kaunda could draw on his

12 The process by which Zambia's Second Republic ushered in a 'one party participatory democracy' in 1973 has been extensively documented elsewhere (e.g., Tordoff 1974, Sipalo 1978, Gertzel et al. 1984, Mwanakatwe 1994) and does not need repeating here.

13 Carlson Anyangwe (1997, 6) extends the thread of legal continuity to subsequent constitutions as well:

> The 1964 independence Constitution, the 1973 one-party Constitution, and the 1991 multi-party Constitution (including the amendments effected in 1996) are basically the same (except that Zambia is no longer a one-party state) and deviate only on matters which may be considered as *de minimis.*

14 The distinction in Article 47 between the incumbent president's private and official capacities is significant. I return to this in Chapter 7.

most loyal sycophants for ministerial positions.[15] By 1978, all but one ministry (Finance) was in the hands of a nominated member of parliament.

President Kaunda also reserved extensive rights to appoint and dismiss anyone with significant governmental responsibilities. These included the Chief Justice and all Supreme Court judges. The president, not the prime minister, chaired cabinet. No bill passed by parliament could become law without the president's assent. Should push come to shove, the president had the power to dissolve parliament.

Kaunda was also the president of the ruling party, UNIP, now the only legal political organization in Zambia. Via the UNIP constitution, Kaunda exercised full control of 'the Party and its Government.' He chaired the UNIP central committee, chosen by the party's general assembly, which he also controlled. According to the UNIP constitution (§12(1)(c); cited in Sipalo 1978, 200), the central committee exercised 'complete control over all officials.' The UNIP general assembly was also the body that selected UNIP's presidential aspirant, the only candidate entitled to stand in presidential elections.

The one-party state persevered more on the crest of Kaunda's political capital as 'Father of the Nation' than on its capacity to deliver the 'peace and development' promised by UNIP. The Second Republic immediately faced serious economic challenges. The early 1970s saw the double whammy of a crash in the value of copper, Zambia's main source of hard currency revenues, compounded by a sharp rise in the price of oil. As a land-locked country, most energy, consumables and capital goods had to be transported long distances from ports in South Africa and Tanzania. Copper mining and smelting are very energy intensive. Add to this the growing threat of military confrontation with the apartheid regime in Rhodesia (Zimbabwe), and it is not hard to understand why the Zambian economy went into a tailspin. Kaunda's dream of a humanist society receded into the future.

The UNIP government guarded its authority jealously, and the government's massive intelligence apparatus labored vigilantly to identify potential dissidents. This practice led to numerous, often arbitrary, detentions of citizens. In many instances, courts found these detentions illegal and obliged government to release the victims of arbitrary arrest, while also awarding significant damages. As it turns out, the government's fears of dissidence were not unfounded, as some citizens felt the constraints of one-party participatory democracy to be too rigid. In 1980, a number of lawyers decided to vent their frustrations with the illiberal order and attempted to take the law into their own hands. A crew including Mundia Sikatana (who would hold ministerial posts after the 1991 change of regime), South African attorney Pierce Annfield, and rising legal star Edward Shamwana plotted to overthrow the UNIP government by hijacking the president's airplane. The coup never got off the runway, literally, and the perpetrators were apprehended. The subsequent treason trial (1981–82), in which Shamwana was

15 Ministers were required to be Members of Parliament. Following Zambian convention, the terms Parliament and National Assembly are used here synonymously.

found guilty and sentenced to death had, no doubt, a sobering effect on liberal passions within the legal profession.[16]

By the late 1980s, the Zambian economy was in desperate straits. The politically volatile urban population was plagued by shortages of basic foodstuffs like sugar, salt, bread and cooking oil. When available, rampant inflation had made basic commodities all but unaffordable for the average wage earner. Zambia's experiment with an economic order dominated by parastatal monopolies had reduced the economy to shambles. Kaunda's refusal to accept structural adjustment policies led to a messy falling out with the International Monetary Fund (IMF). Despite the country's immense natural wealth, the average citizen – especially in the populous urban centers – was living from hand to mouth. At the same time, the apartheid government in South Africa targeted Zambia with repeated attacks and related destabilization efforts (Zulu 2007). After a decade of consistently negative growth, inflation and unemployment were overwhelming. The UNIP government's continued support for liberation struggles across the region, its economic policies and the nation's unmanageable national debt[17] had driven Western creditors away. It was obvious to all but its most die-hard loyalists that by 1990, UNIP had run out of options.

With opposition political organizations banned, there was little room for organized activism. Toward the end of the Second Republic, some were nonetheless prepared to challenge UNIP's monopoly on power in public.[18] In an early essay, law professor Alfred Chanda (1986, 29), who would come to personify Zambian legal activism in the Third Republic, found that 'the exercise of emergency powers in Zambia by the executive, particularly the power of preventive detention, derogates fundamentally from the rule of law.'

During the last week of June 1990, three days of rioting rocked the capital Lusaka and other urban centers. The spark igniting the spontaneous violence was the government's intention to double the price of mealie-meal, the maize flour from which Zambians prepare their staple *nshima*; 27 people died (Rakner 2003, 63). While rioting crowds in 1986 had vented their anger against the IMF, the 1990 food riots 'focussed on the political system itself' (Bates & Collier 1993, 429). Only days later, on 30 June 1990, a 30-year-old army lieutenant, Mwamba Luchembe, occupied the public broadcasting center in Lusaka and announced

16 According to court archives (*People v Shamwana* 1981), on his apprehension by the police Shamwana blurted out: 'I was stupid to be involved in this thing because I am to be appointed Chief Justice next week.' Kaunda commuted Shamwana's sentence to life and released him in 1990 in connection with a general amnesty for political prisoners. Shamwana went on to defend a group of senior UNIP officials against trumped-up treason charges brought by the Chiluba government (the so-called Black Mamba affair) in the run up to the 1996 elections.

17 The national debt had reach USD7.3 billion by 1991, representing 180% of GDP and 560% of Zambia's dwindling exports (Andersson & Ndulo 1994, 24; cited in Rakner 2003, 136).

18 The 1980s also saw the rise of gender activism in the bar (with the Zambian Association for Research and Development in the forefront), with academic lawyers, in particular, challenging government policy from a feminist perspective; see Munalula (1989).

that the army had assumed control of the country. The initial reaction of the population was one of 'enthusiasm and jubilation' (Mwanakatwe 1994, 148; also van Donge 1995, 197). Military officers loyal to the government, however, quickly quelled the coup.

UNIP was still in nominal control of the country, but its demise was imminent. From the late 1980s, a loose coalition of dissident forces had begun to organize clandestinely in preparation for regime change. Following the tumultuous events of June, the dissidents went public. On 20 and 21 July 1990, they convened a 'National Conference on Multiparty Option' at the Garden Motel in Lusaka, which was attended by an assortment of politicians, intellectuals, business people, farmers, church leaders and union activists. This conference gave birth to the Movement for Multiparty Democracy (MMD) (Mbikusita-Lewanika & Chitala 1990, Rikalainen 2006, 34–35).

Conventional civil society, associated with independent non-governmental organizations (NGOs) and the private media, was virtually non-existent during the Second Republic. NGOs would proliferate in the liberalized dispensation of the Third Republic, fueled by foreign funding, but during the crucial transition period from the Second to the Third Republics, the Catholic Church and the trade union movement were the only independent voices with significant leverage against the government. A potential source of critique, the statutory Law Association of Zambia (LAZ) tended to eschew commenting on issues which could be deemed political. During the period before the transition, the *National Mirror* (a weekly newspaper owned jointly by the Catholic and Protestant umbrella bodies), the important Catholic Bemba-language *Icengelo*, and the *Workers' Challenge*, a monthly publication published on the Copperbelt, provided the labor movement with a platform to criticize government policies (Hinfelaar 2004, 395, Rikalainen 2006). The editor of *Icengelo*, Franciscan Fr Umberto Davoli, played a key public role exposing abuses of power within the UNIP administration, and provided Zambian Congress of Trade Unions (ZCTU) leader Frederick Chiluba with column space to write about the need for a referendum on multiparty politics. In addition, Archbishop Adrian Mung'andu of the Lusaka archdiocese gave the MMD permission to hold a pivotal political rally in Lusaka (Cheyeka 2003, 6). Kaunda, a devout United Church of Zambia Protestant, reacted strongly, condemning the Catholics' intervention in politics (ibid., 4–5, Rikalainen 2006, 35).

In the tense days following the urban riots in June, the Catholic bishops issued a pastoral letter titled 'Politics, Economics and Justice.' The bishops spoke out 'on behalf of the poor and in particular for the cause of justice' (ibid., 34), attacked the regime for corruption and inefficiency and called for a referendum on the reintroduction of a multiparty political system (Phiri 1999, 337; Bartlett 2000, 432–3). The bishops' statement was published as a full-page advertisement in the government-controlled *Times of Zambia* on 31 July 1990, further fueling the growing momentum of the MMD.

Under intense political pressure, Kaunda initially acquiesced to the popular demands for a multiparty referendum, but subsequently changed his mind about its necessity. In September 1990, the government unilaterally announced its intention to amend the constitution, and on 8 October 1990, Kaunda appointed Dr Patrick Mvunga, the UNIP government's last solicitor-general, to head a commission to review the constitution. The mandate of the Mvunga Constitutional Review Commission (CRC) was, *inter alia*, to

> examine and determine a system of political pluralism that would ensure a government which would be strong enough to rule the Zambian Nation and ensure the personal liberties of the people, but without prejudice to the generality of this power ... and ... to examine and determine a system of Government that would ensure the separation of powers of the Legislature, the Executive and the Judiciary so as to enhance the roles of these organs. (Republic of Zambia 1991a, 2–4; see also Mwanakatwe 1994, 210, Ndulo & Kent 1998, 16–17)

The Mvunga Commission organized 11 public consultations in provincial centers across the country and received nearly 1,000 submissions from individual and institutional petitioners. These formed the basis of a report and draft constitution which it submitted to the president in April 1991. Meanwhile, in December 1990, parliament removed the constitutional provision, dating from 1973, that ensured UNIP's political monopoly. By March 1991, the MMD (along with at least six other groups) had officially registered themselves as political parties (Phiri 2006, 182). The MMD held its first party convention in February 1991, electing Zambian Congress of Trade Union leader Frederick Chiluba as its president with overwhelming support (ibid.).

The MMD harbored fundamental distrust of Kaunda's intentions and boycotted the Mvunga Commission.[19] When the commission's draft proposal for a new constitution was revealed in April 1991, the MMD rejected it vehemently (Mwanakatwe 1994, 217), invoking the movement's commitment to

> institute the ideals of democracy, namely, basic human rights, i.e., free and fair elections, freedom of assembly and association, freedom of expression, the right against discrimination and above all, the accountability of the government to the people as a whole.

In retrospect, the recommendations of the Mvunga Commission appear to have covered most of these bases, and represented a radical departure from the conventions of the Second Republic. The commission proposed many dramatic restrictions on the powers of the executive – e.g., requiring parliamentary ratification for key appointments, and for triggering emergency powers – while

19 MMD Interim Committee President Arthur Wina and Secretary Akashambatwa Mbikusita-Lewanika were appointed to the commission, but declined to take up their appointments (Republic of Zambia 1991a, 2).

upholding other fundamental liberal principles, such as respect for basic human rights and the autonomy and independence of the judiciary. The proposed constitutional draft did, however, retain some clearly controversial provisions, such as the prerogative of the president to 'dissolve the National Assembly if the latter makes it unmanageable for him to govern' (Republic of Zambia 1991a, 18).

The MMD leadership's reaction to the Mvunga draft and to the UNIP government's White Paper in response to it (ibid.) was driven more by political anxiety than by principled liberalism. According to the MMD position statement, Kaunda had '[f]rom the very beginning... pre-empted the [Constitutional Review] process by announcing in advance the type of constitution he wanted and prescribing the terms of reference designed to serve only the interests of his Party' (Mwanakatwe 1994, 217). In truth, it is hard to see how creating the legal foundations for political pluralism served UNIP's interests.

### *Constitutional deadlock*

In mid-1991, UNIP still held all seats in the National Assembly, and Kaunda was arguably in a position to enact whichever constitutional amendments he pleased. Yet, the president seemed, not unreasonably in light of the recent riots, to be concerned with the likelihood of social unrest and violence should the MMD not sign on to his constitutional reform. In order to reach a consensus, Kaunda offered to hold talks over the new constitution with the MMD and other political parties at State House. Anglican Bishop Stephen Mumba chaired the decisive meeting on 23 July 1991 at the Anglican Cathedral in Lusaka.[20] At the end of the day, Kaunda acceded to virtually all of MMD's demands for revising the constitution (Sangwa 2000, 492). The new constitution was enacted by parliament on 2 August, and approved by the president on 29 August 1991, restoring a multiparty electoral system. The 1991 constitution also entrenched the Bill of Rights (Section III) with the inclusion of Article 79(3),[21] thus reinstating the institution of national referendum which Kaunda tried to eliminate in 1969 (Republic of Zambia 1991b, Ndulo & Kent 1998, 28). At the same time, unintentionally perhaps, the entrenchment of Article 79 made repeal of the constitution as a whole virtually impossible (see Annex A). As we will see, this will seriously complicate later efforts at constitutional reform.

Multiparty elections were held on 31 October 1991. Despite a low turnout and administrative problems with the voters' roll, the outcome was generally judged to be free and fair (Rakner & Svåsand 2005, 91). Predictably, the MMD won an

20 Mwanakatwe (1994, 219–22) provides the best account of this historic event.

21 Article 79(3): 'A bill for the alteration of Part III of this Constitution or of this Article shall not be passed unless before the first reading of the bill in the National Assembly it has been put to a National referendum with or without amendment by not less than fifty per cent of persons *entitled* to be registered as voters for the purposes of Presidential and parliamentary elections' (Republic of Zambia 1991b; emphasis added); see Annex A.

overwhelming victory. MMD candidates captured 125 of 150 parliamentary seats and more than three-quarters of the presidential vote. Zambia had moved peacefully from a *de jure* one-party state to a *de facto* single-party rule.

Understandably, the hastily assembled 1991 constitution left many Zambians dissatisfied. In the words of disgruntled MMD founding member Akashambatwa Mbikusita-Lewanika, the new constitution was merely 'an unsatisfactory compromise patched up under pressure to facilitate multiparty elections.'[22] Despite the MMD's election-trail promises to instigate thorough constitutional reform immediately upon assuming power, no action was taken during Chiluba's first two years in office. Under mounting pressure in 1993, the MMD government finally appointed a constitutional review commission headed by veteran lawyer John Mwanakatwe[23] to collect views from the general public and propose a draft constitution.[24]

As had been the case in 1991, many were skeptical about the government's intentions. Mbikusita-Lewanika, who had resigned from Chiluba's cabinet in protest over alleged corruption, thought the Mwanakatwe CRC was instituted 'for self-preservation and the pleasure of the Western donors' (cited in Sangwa 2000, 494). Mbikusita-Lewanika felt the whole exercise was doomed to be about 'a personalised executive using vulnerable persons and propaganda to short-cut and stage-manage constitutional reform' (ibid.). Nonetheless, departing from earlier constitution-making processes in Zambia, the Mwanakatwe CRC had serious pretensions to popular legitimacy. Only 5 of 24 commissioners were selected by the president; 7 were nominated by NGOs, 5 by opposition parties, 2 by church bodies, 4 by academic and professional organizations and 1 by the ruling party (Sangwa 2000, 494). The coverage of the Mwanakatwe CRC was also extensive. The commission organized 46 open hearings in all nine provinces, and collected a total of 996 oral affidavits, plus an additional 519 written submissions (Republic of Zambia 1995, Gould 2002, 306).

The Mwanakatwe Commission's composition was diverse and its terms of reference were progressive. Encouraged by this, a mushrooming corps of civil society activists were hopeful that, this time round, there would be a chance to create a constitution that would 'stand the test of time.' Popular expectations were largely vindicated. Among its many recommendations, the commission advocated for 'the strengthening and expansion of human rights protection,' including 'rights related to residence, human dignity and reputation, culture,

22 Akashambatwa M. Lewanika (1993). 'Let the people determine a democratic constitution,' *Weekly Post*, 17 December 1993, 6 (cited in Sangwa 2000, 492).

23 Mr Mwanakatwe was, in his own account (Mwanakatwe 2003), the first Northern Rhodesian African to receive a university degree (a BA from the University of South Africa in 1950). He was called to the English bar in 1964, and became Zambia's minister of education in Kaunda's first cabinet, responsible for the successful implementation of Zambia's wildly ambitious educational program in the 1960s, and the establishment of the University of Zambia. Chiluba appointed him chancellor of UNZA in 1992.

24 Statutory Instrument No. 151 of 22 November 1993.

marriage; a clean environment and equal pay for equal work.' The commission's proposals sought to enshrine academic and intellectual freedom, as well as the right to strike in the constitution. It also proposed 'a drastic increase in the protection of women's rights and the prohibition of laws, customary practices and stereotypes that undermined the dignity of women' (Matibini 2008, 10).

On the contentious issue of restricting the powers of the executive, however, the commission's proposals were 'rather timorous' (Hansungule 2003, 28). Instead of introducing stronger checks on executive discretion, the commission proposed a tightening of the citizenship rules for presidential eligibility. Where the 1991 constitution stipulated merely that the president be a Zambian citizen, the Mwanakatwe report required that a president's parents be 'Zambians born in Zambia of Zambian citizens.'[25] This particular clause was to have harsh political repercussions.

The proposal of the Mwanakatwe Commission that would prove the most controversial concerned the way a constitution was enacted into law. The commission's terms of reference required that it 'recommend on whether the Constitution should be adopted by the National Assembly or by a Constituent Assembly, by a National Referendum or by any other method' (Statutory Instrument 151 of 23 November 1993).[26] Zambia had no experience with, or legislative provisions for, a constituent assembly (CA), yet the commission reported that

> petitioners were overwhelmingly agreed that the constitution should be adopted through the constituent assembly and a national referendum. Adoption by the current legislature was the least favoured because of the dangers of one-party dominance and a repetition of the past experiences in formulation of the constitution. (Republic of Zambia 1995)

25 This provision was reworked in the government's Constitution Amendment Act to read 'both his [sic] parents must be Zambians by birth' (Republic of Zambia 1996, Article 34).

26 I haven't been able to identify how the notion of a constituent assembly entered Zambian political discourse. Historically, revolutionary France's *Assemblée Nationale Constituante* (1789–91) provided the moniker, if not the explicit model that was subsequently appropriated for constitution-making in dozens of countries around the world, from Denmark (1849) and post-revolutionary Russia (1917) to (post-)colonial India (1946) and beyond.

It is likely that the proposal for a CA, first alluded to, but rejected by the Mvunga Commission (Republic of Zambia 1991a, 43), and subsequently endorsed by the Mwanakatwe CRC in 1995, took its immediate inspiration from neighboring Namibia, where a constituent assembly drafted Namibia's independence constitution between 1989 and 1991. South Africa's constitutional assembly was also a likely precursor. The Namibian and South Africa examples were based on elected representatives from established political parties. The Mwanakatwe Commission also provided for political party representation by including all members of parliament, but proposed expanding the composition of the CA to include 'one representative from each District in Zambia; representatives from political parties not represented in Parliament; CSOs, academia, civil and professional associations; traditional rulers; women's organisations; churches and other religious organisations' (cited in Motsamai 2014, 4).

The commission proceeded to outline in great detail a possible lineup for the constituent assembly and a procedural process by which, in accordance with existing legislation, a constitution adopted through a constituent assembly might be enacted into law.

According to many contemporary accounts, the MMD government rejected 'most of the progressive recommendations' of the Mwanakatwe CRC (e.g., Ndulo & Kent 1996, 274). It refused to revisit the Bill of Rights (Section III) as both an unnecessary (since the current constitution purportedly ensured the adequate provision of rights) and excessively expensive measure (as this would require a national referendum by virtue of Article 79; see Ohtonen 2005). The Constitutional Amendment Bill that government tabled before parliament also diverged from the Mwanakatwe proposal by repealing the 50 + 1% majority provision for presidential elections.[27] According to the new constitution, a simple majority of votes (the 'first-past-the-post' rule) would be sufficient to elect a president. Furthermore, President Chiluba rejected the adoption of the constitution through a constituent assembly, and proposed to enact the new constitution (as had been the case with all previous constitutions) by the legislature. The government's White Paper (Republic of Zambia, Government Paper No. 1 of 1996) justified its position on the basis that

> a constituent assembly is a transitional measure to be used where a parliament is not universally constituted by the majority of citizens such as was the case in Namibia and South Africa. The issue of a constituent assembly does not therefore arise in the Zambian situation where a parliament is constituted through universal adult suffrage.

Constitutional scholar John Sangwa explains the government's rejection of Mwanakatwe's proposals in terms of the MMD's narrow political self-interest. In his view (Sangwa 2000, 497), Kaunda's recent return to politics and his presidential candidacy in the 1996 elections radically changed the political landscape, driving the MMD government to hedge its position by all means possible: 'Four years of structural adjustment programs had created serious despondency among the people.' The MMD's survival in the 1996 elections could only be 'guaranteed until there was a serious contender' (ibid.). In this view, UNIP under Kaunda posed the only viable threat to MMD hegemony, and Chiluba needed to block Kaunda from the running. Putting constitutional reform in the hands of a popular body, like the proposed constituent assembly, was likely to weaken the MMD's chances at the polls in 1996. The 50 + 1% majority vote clause, in particular, was unpalatable to the ruling party. Only by maintaining total control over the constitutional reform process could Chiluba ensure his re-election.

27 The '50 + 1%' provision means that a victorious presidential candidate must receive at least one vote more than half of the votes cast. This implied the likelihood of at least one run-off election and potentially weakened the chances of the incumbent party prolonging its tenure.

Mr Sangwa's view is credible in light of the amendments Chiluba introduced to the 1996 Constitutional Amendment Bill. For safe measure, Kaunda was disqualified on two counts – his parents were Malawian and he had already held seven terms of office. Not to leave anything to chance, Chiluba's constitution amendments also disqualified Kaunda's vice-president, Inyambo Yeta, who would have had to abdicate his Lozi chieftaincy in order to contest the presidency. Abdication by a chief was unthinkable in customary terms. Chiluba's machinations produced the desired result. Kaunda and UNIP boycotted the elections and Chiluba was re-elected with 70% of a meagre 40% voter turnout. The MMD maintained its absolute parliamentary majority despite mounting popular dissatisfaction (Gould 2002, Phiri 2003, 412).

## *Reactions to the 1996 constitution*

Chiluba's constitutional mischief generated substantial political fallout, both immediately and in the longer term. Public response took two forms: legal and civic. On the legal front, Derrick Chitala, then secretary-general of the opposition Zambian Democratic Congress (Zadeco), twice attempted to instigate a judicial review of the legality of the 1996 Constitutional Amendment Bill.[28] In the first instance, Chitala asked the court to quash Chiluba's decision to have the new constitution enacted by parliament. He further asked the court to oblige government, through a writ of *mandamus*, to establish a constituent assembly in order to adopt the constitution. Chitala's application for a judicial review was rejected in the High Court and, on appeal, also by the Supreme Court.

In the second instance, Chitala sought a judicial review to challenge the validity of the new constitution itself. Chitala argued that the constitution defined by the Constitutional Amendment Bill before parliament was essentially a new piece of legislation, and could not be enacted through the mere amendment of the 1991 Constitution Act. Such a move, it was argued, would be *ultra vires* (in contradiction) of Article 79 of the constitution. This motion was also dismissed by both appellate courts. These incidents affirm what will be seen in Chapter 6 in connection with the Zero Option and Black Mamba treason trials, and in the court's response to the 1996 Presidential Petition: While the judiciary was prepared to reprimand the government on blatant rights violations, neither of the upper benches was willing to entertain motions which would challenge the president's discretionary authority, even when the sanctity and integrity of the constitution was at stake. By the end of his first term, in the eyes of many urban elite groups, Chiluba had transformed himself from a democratic liberator into a feared and ruthless autocrat. Nonetheless, the public reaction to the

28 This account of the legal process is based on Sangwa (2000). Chitala was a key player in the founding of the MMD in 1991, but had a falling out with Chiluba. He left the MMD in 1995 and formed a new party, Zambia Democratic Congress (Zadeco) with Dean Mung'omba (Rakner 2003).

constitutional reform of 1996 laid the foundations, for the first time in Zambian political history, for the emergence of a non-partisan political force with the will and the means to mount an organized challenge to the government's betrayal of its declared liberal principles.

## *Popular constitutional politics*

The response of civil society to the 1996 constitutional reforms involved a range of players, but was spearheaded by the Catholic Commission for Justice and Peace (CCJP) headed by Fr Joseph Komakoma.[29] At the CCJP's instigation, 27 non-governmental organizations formed the Civil Society Action Committee (CSAC) to contest the government's constitutional policy. For the CCJP leadership, and their allies in the CSAC, the key issue was the constitution's mode of adoption. The CCJP was adamant about the need for a 'people-driven' constitution drafted and adopted by a constituent assembly, as recommended by the Mwanakatwe Commission.[30] The CSAC's common purpose was to prevent the new Zambian constitution from being like the previous three, i.e., merely 'passed by different Governments to serve their own ends' (CSAC 1996, 1, Rikalainen 2006, 41).

The CCJP's main partner in the CSAC was the Non-Governmental Organizations Coordination Committee (NGOCC). This loose conglomeration of women's organizations comprised militant groups like the Zambian Civic Education Association (ZCEA, led by UNIP lawyer Lucy Sichone), the Zambia Association for Research and Development (chaired by feminist author Sara Longwe) and Women for Change (under activist Emily Sikazwe), as well as more conservative rural associations devoted to nutrition, livelihoods and family planning.

The alliance between the Church and the women's organizations built on several layers of existing ties. The NGOCC had initially emerged from the Young Women's Christian Association (YWCA) in the 1980s (Ohtonen 2005, 35–36) and, during the final years of the Second Republic, the Catholic Church, trade unions and emerging independent women's organizations[31] were among the only channels through which views critical of the government could find

29 Fr Joseph Komakoma (interview, 8.7.2004): 'In 1995-96, we had a Citizens' Convention. That originated from the promptings of the CCJP. It is the CCJP which called upon other NGOs and organisations. In order to make an impression. [we said] "Let's come together and form a coalition." And that was the first coalition of the NGOs on an issue. Later on there were other coalitions, but the very first one was instigated by the CCJP.'

30 The CSAC and subsequent constitutionalist movements recognize the legal requirement that the National Assembly *enact* the constitution, but demanded that the text of the constitution be drafted and *adopted* by a popular body. The distinction between popular adoption and legal enactment has caused endless confusion in debates about constitutional reform in Zambia to this day.

31 In addition to the older Catholic Women's League and the YWCA, these included a number of proto-NGOs (the Zambia Alliance for Women, the Zambia Association for Research and Development, the Women's Development Network) that emerged in the wake of the

public expression. The NGOCC strongly supported the CCJP's demand for a constituent assembly, but also sought to focus attention on the need for radical reform of the Bill of Rights, which they saw as limited and discriminatory. One NGOCC representative on the Mwanakatwe Constitutional Review Commission, Hilary Mulenga Fyfe (quoted in Siame et al. 1998, 35), expressed the disappointment prevalent among women activists over the government's response to the commission's report:

> How was I to know that the Government's White Paper would say "not accepted, not accepted" to every right that we were given by God. How very contradictory of the Government, when they confirm that 'in Zambia power belongs to the people, who should exercise that power through appropriate democratic notions.' This is contradicted by a refusal for a Constituent Assembly.

The Civil Society Action Committee consolidated attempts to mobilize popular support for a constituent assembly. On 10 October 1995, a self-appointed steering committee (comprising the CCJP and the ZCEA, among others) organized a mass rally at Freedom Statue in Lusaka. The police initially granted the groups permission to demonstrate, but withdrew it at the last minute and proceeded to violently disperse the demonstrators. The police arrested four members of the steering committee, including Fr Komakoma from the CCJP and lawyer Lucy Sichone of the ZCEA (*Post*, 17 October 1995).

In November 1995, the CSAC convened a 'National conference on the mode of adoption of the draft constitution.' The conference agreed on the need for an all-inclusive convention to discuss the draft constitution. This took place during the first ten days of March 1996, when the CSAC convened a 'Citizen's Convention on the Draft Constitution' in Lusaka. The invitation to the conference asserted that a 'broad consensus has not yet been reached regarding some key issues in the Draft Constitution.' Contentious issues included qualifications for the presidency, the separation of powers and the mode of adoption of the constitution, but the main thrust of the deliberations, which highlighted women's and children's rights, was an impassioned critique of Zambia's patriarchal order (CSAC 1996). At this point, representatives of the legal 'fraternity' were largely bystanders to a nascent movement with clear political aims: wresting the constitution-making process away from the ruling party of the day, and subordinating deliberations about the allocation of power and the rights and freedoms all citizens should enjoy to a popular body.

In effect, the CSAC rehearsed how a constituent assembly might function. Over the ten days of the conference, 281 registered participants assessed the provisions of the draft constitution produced by the Mwanakatwe CRC, article

Nairobi conference crowning the UN Decade for Women (1985) and the African preparatory meeting in Arusha, Tanzania, in 1984 (Ohtonen 2005, 35).

by article. The CSAC produced a detailed report of convention deliberations as well as a 'Citizens' Green Paper' summarizing the convention's position on each article of the Mwanakatwe draft.[32] While the Citizen's Convention assembled at the Mulungushi Conference Center for its first session, the Chiluba government was submitting its controversial Constitution Amendment Bill to parliament next door. Even as the deliberations were in process, it was evident that the citizens' campaign would not meet its primary aim of blocking the bill. The fact that hundreds of citizens nevertheless persisted in their commitment to the discussion indicates that they saw their actions in a broader political context: Chiluba would most probably prevail during this round (as indeed he did), but the Citizen's Convention affirmed their long-term commitment to popular and accountable government.

The Citizen's Convention attracted the elite of Zambia's budding civil society. Leading intellectuals, clergy and activists rubbed shoulders with key opposition politicians including Kenneth Kaunda, Grey Zulu, Inyambo Yeta and Dean Mung'omba. Lawyers also turned out in large numbers: Lucy Sichone, of course (but not coup-plotter Edward Shamwana, now pardoned by Chiluba), and the cream of legal academia; Professors Patrick Mvunga and Michelo Hansungule, as well as Drs Rodgers Chongwe, Tukiya Kankasa and Alfred Chanda all took part. With such fundamental legal issues at stake, it is not surprising that legal actors showed a keen interest in the proceedings. It is noteworthy, however, that the legal profession failed to make a collective response to the government's manipulation of the constitution. I have found no record of an official statement by the Law Association on the Constitutional Amendment Bill; nor did LAZ take a stand on the procedure by which it was prepared and passed. The controversial provisions of the 1996 Constitutional Amendment Bill were clearly aimed at disqualifying Kaunda from contesting the presidency, and a partisan issue such as this did not move LAZ to action. Individual members could, and did, participate in public debates and protests, but at this point, LAZ remained on the sidelines. Within four years, as Chapter 6 shows, this would change – with dramatic political consequences.

32 Summary of the Resolutions by the Citizens' Convention on the Draft Constitution, Mulungushi International Conference Centre, 1–10 March 1996.

# 6 The Oasis Forum and the emergence of liberal constitutionalism

## Chiluba loses his grip

On the morning of 28 October 1997, Lusaka residents awoke to hear a previously unknown military officer who called himself Captain Solo speaking over public radio. Captain Solo (whose real name was Lieutenant Stephen Lungu) announced that the hitherto unknown National Redemption Council had ousted the Movement for Multiparty Democracy (MMD) government headed by President Chiluba for its 'corruption and criminality.' Solo's assumed moniker was ironically apt – the coup was the work of a few disgruntled junior officers – and was quashed by loyal Zambian military officers within hours (Rakner 2003, Phiri 2006). The public's reaction was subdued, with most Lusaka residents remaining home from work, tuned to the radio.

Zambians' lack of enthusiasm for Captain Solo's political project probably had less to do with their love of President Chiluba than with their distrust of military saviors. Chiluba, a trade union leader from the once-affluent Copperbelt (Ferguson 1999), had originally risen to power on a massive wave of popular support for 'change' and 'democracy.' By 1997, however, the public's romance with the MMD had turned decidedly sour. Chiluba was now widely seen as an arrogant autocrat, who had few qualms about abusing his high office to promote self-enrichment. The MMD's alleged decline into kleptocracy has been recounted in greater detail elsewhere (van Donge 2009, Rakner 2003), and it will suffice here to note the cogent features of the Chiluba administration's problems with legality and his (ultimately unsuccessful) recourse to judicial harassment as a political strategy.

Chiluba struck out forcefully at perceived political threats. It is widely believed, but never substantiated, that government agents were behind the deaths of confrontational politicians Baldwin Nkumbula (the son of ex-President Kaunda's erstwhile political nemesis), Cuthbert Ng'uni, Major Wezi Kaunda (the ex-president's son) and Paul Tembo. In 1997, ex-President Kenneth Kaunda was fired upon by a police officer at a political rally in Kabwe. Kaunda escaped injury but outspoken lawyer Rodger Chongwe was wounded in the neck. Another controversial lawyer, Richard Ngenda, also died under suspicious circumstances during Chiluba's reign. Many believe that MMD members, Finance Minister Ronald

DOI: 10.4324/9780429198984-8

Penza and lawyer Edward Shamwana (introduced in Chapter 5) were assassinated to protect corrupt MMD ministers. No charges were brought in any of these incidents, but the extended list of alleged victims and the widespread public perception that the government was involved in illegal political violence, speaks volumes about the deteriorating relationship between the president and his public.

While these intimations of political assassination are mere conjecture, there is ample evidence of Chiluba's schemes to use the legal system to harass and hamper political competitors. The first indication of Chiluba's willingness to use the courts to intimidate his opponents occurred in 1993. In February of that year, the government-controlled *Times of Zambia* published a document titled the 'Zero Option plan' which the newspaper claimed linked the main opposition party, the United National Independence Party (UNIP), to a plot to overthrow the MMD regime. In response to the alleged Zero Option plot, Chiluba declared a state of emergency on 4 March 1993, and a total of 26 persons, including many senior UNIP officials, were detained (Human Rights Watch 1996, 6).[1] While the Supreme Court ruled against the validity of the state of emergency in May, UNIP members of parliament (MPs) Wezi Kaunda, Cuthbert Ng'uni and five others were charged with offenses against the security of the state. None were convicted, but Mr Ng'uni died in detention (Ihonvbere 1995, Kaunda et al. 1994).

The Zero Option debacle incensed the recently liberalized private media. The independent *Post* newspaper, in particular, openly accused the government of political harassment and victimization. Meanwhile, a steady flow of founding MMD members left the party and/or resigned their ministerial posts, citing rampant corruption among MMD leadership. The president also sacked a number of senior party members for insubordination and lack of loyalty. This political in-fighting was played out visibly in the pages of the *Post* and other independent media.

Chiluba responded with aggressive attacks against the *Post*. According to the American watchdog organization Human Rights Watch, the *Post* was subjected to more than 100 legal writs between 1991 and 1996. The *Post*'s owner and editor Fred M'membe and staff were repeatedly charged with defamation and sedition and, among other things, for possessing and printing classified documents. M'membe and his co-editor Bright Mwape, along with lawyer-columnist Lucy Sichone (see note 5) received the unusual distinction of being sentenced to prison *in absentia* 'for an indefinite period' by an MMD-controlled parliamentary standing orders committee.[2] The court's efforts to block the political harassment of the private media did not dissuade the government from further legal attacks against its political opponents.

1 The state of emergency was lifted after three months.

2 High Court Judge Kabazo Chanda found that the three journalists had been illegally sentenced. He also ruled that 'indefinite jail terms are incompatible with our legal system and [that] unorthodox disciplinary procedures cannot be allowed.' See *M'membe v The Speaker* (1996/HCJ/X).

The so-called Black Mamba treason trial signaled not only a new level of government aggression, but also the dawn of modern legal activism in Zambia. It is a story replete with unresolved ambiguities, but its main points merit a brief summary. In 1996, Chiluba's first term was expiring and new elections were due to be held later in the year. After a brief retirement from politics, Kenneth Kaunda resumed the presidency of UNIP and was preparing to challenge Chiluba at the polls.

Amid growing civic and political opposition to the Constitutional Amendment Bill, the government fast-tracked the bill through the MMD-controlled parliament in May 1996, essentially disqualifying Kaunda's candidacy. Justifiably upset, Kaunda issued an incautious statement predicting civil unrest in response to his victimization. In June, a series of explosions at various sites rocked Lusaka. Bombs went off at the international airport and the upmarket Intercontinental Hotel, killing one and injuring one other. According to police sources, an anonymous caller identifying his group as the Black Mamba claimed responsibility for the bombings.[3] The government ordered the arrest of eight UNIP officials including the party's vice-president, Senior Chief Inyambo Yeta. The detainees were charged with treason and murder, and were committed to the High Court for trial. No credible evidence linking the UNIP members to the bombings emerged in the course of the trial and the High Court acquitted all defendants in November. Unsubstantiated testimony suggested that state security forces may have been involved in the explosions.

For this inquiry into the interstices of law and politics, what is perhaps most significant about the Black Mamba trial is the concerted response by a legal team, composed largely of lawyers with UNIP sympathies, who contributed their expertise in defense of the accused on a *pro bono* basis (interview, 2003). The team of defense counsel, led by former coup conspirator Edward Shamwana (pardoned in 1990 by President Kaunda), included former Law Association of Zambia (LAZ) chairperson Sakwiba Sikota and outspoken civil activist Lucy Sichone.[4] For the first time in Zambia's history, senior lawyers banded together to challenge political maneuvers by the executive.

The Black Mamba trial coincided with the run-up to the 1996 general elections, a time of heightened political tension and media attention. The *Post*,

3 Coincidentally, perhaps, ex-President Kaunda had once been likened to a black mamba by British methodist missionary Merfyn Temple (see Pettman 1974, 38).

4 Lucy Sichone, who passed away in 1998 at the age of 44, can be justifiably termed the mother of Zambian legal activism. She was a UNZA graduate, a Rhodes scholar and former member of the UNIP Central Committee. Disillusioned with party politics, Sichone left UNIP in 1994 to form the confrontational Zambia Civic Education Association which pioneered non-partisan grassroots political education in Zambia. On her passing, *Post* editor M'membe called her an 'outstanding intellectual' and a 'great heroine'; UNIP's Wezi Kaunda said she was 'more brave than some of the Zambian men'; and Edward Shamwana testified that 'as a human being, she touched many people at different levels' (quotations from *Post* obituary by Goodson Machona, 25 August 1998).

already at loggerheads with the Chiluba government, devoted page upon page of newsprint to verbatim transcripts of the treason trial proceedings.[5] These transcripts revealed the defense counsel as fearless, articulate and witty crusaders against a legally sloppy and duplicitous executive branch. Defense counsel had no qualms about openly taunting prosecution witnesses as 'state plants' and 'liars.' Through these widely circulated accounts – often summarized with editorial analysis elsewhere in the paper – an urban, literate and politically enlightened readership could begin to glean the subversive potential of a legal profession which had, until then, generally been seen as complacent, self-serving and opportunistic.

The Black Mamba trial was aborted when the state prosecution failed to produce evidence connecting the accused with the Lusaka bombings. This did not dissuade the Chiluba government from attempting once again to hobble its opponents through litigation and exceptional measures. After the aborted Captain Solo coup, Chiluba again declared a state of emergency, his second in six years, and fast-tracked emergency legislation through parliament giving the executive extensive powers of detention, seizure of property and the suspension of other constitutional rights. Along with dozens of military personnel suspected of complicity in the coup, police detained former President Kaunda, key opposition figure Dean Mung'omba and MMD lawmaker Nakatindi Wina.[6] Kaunda was soon released, but Mung'omba and Wina languished in prison without charges for more than a year. Of the 109 witnesses called by state prosecution, none was able to link Mung'omba or Wina to the coup in any way. After a year during which the state failed to raise charges, the High Court mandated the release of the political detainees and entered a *nolle prosequi*. Emboldened by the state's earlier failure to secure a Black Mamba conviction, High Court Judge Japhet Banda declared that '[T]he court will not be an accomplice to the unfortunate and unreasonable delay in the trial of accused persons' (New People African Feature Service 1999). It would seem, in retrospect, that the Chiluba administration's repeated efforts to enlist the judiciary in its political witch hunts galvanized commitment to political activism within the legal profession. It was not the state's attempted manipulation of the courts which unleashed full-blown legal activism in Zambia, however. This only occurred when Chiluba overstepped a hitherto invisible line in his attempts to manipulate the constitution in order to stay in power.

5 This was the first instance of an unusual journalistic practice which editor M'membe would deploy repeatedly in subsequent legal clashes with government.

6 Dean Mung'omba had an international banking background, and was among the founding members of MMD in 1991. After falling out with Chiluba in 1995, he formed the Zambian Democratic Congress (Zadeco); with fellow dissident Derrick Chitala, Mung'omba contested the republican presidency in 1996, but drew less than 15% of the poll; he died in April 2005. Princess Nakatindi Wina, a member of the Barotse Royal Establishment, was an MP in the Western Province Lozi stronghold of Sesheke, and wife of MMD national secretary, Sikota Wina.

### *Lawyers step up*

Supreme Court Justice Mumba Malila (2020, 400) recently remarked how, '[i]n the whole time that Dr. Kenneth Kaunda was President, Zambian courts showed unmitigated timidity, if not a complete absence of judicial activism, to espouse human rights causes.' President Chiluba's alleged desire to hang on to presidential power as his second term neared its end appears to have dislodged the legal profession's 'unhealthy sense of judicial restraint' (ibid., 392) and spawned an unprecedented wave of commitment to democratic governance within the legal complex.

President Chiluba introduced a two-term limitation on presidential tenure in the 1996 constitutional amendment. This measure, aimed at sidelining ex-President Kaunda's candidacy, now proved to be Chiluba's undoing. As the end of Chiluba's increasingly controversial second term approached, the president began having second thoughts about his future as a civilian. From as early as 1998, Chiluba conducted a silent campaign for amendments to the MMD and republican constitutions that would allow him to contest the 2001 elections.[7] This is what finally induced the legal profession, increasingly concerned with the integrity of the constitution, to raise its collective voice (Gould 2006). In early 2001, the Law Association of Zambia forged an alliance with Zambia's three Christian church bodies (the Catholic, Protestant and Evangelical umbrella organs), and the women activists' Non-Governmental Organisations Co-ordinating Committee (NGOCC) to mobilize mass action against Chiluba's alleged third-term bid.[8] This emphatically non-partisan coalition called itself the Oasis Forum.

The experience of the Oasis Forum's anti-third-term campaign constitutes a unique chapter in the story of Zambian political activism. Popular opposition to Chiluba's third term and to his attempt to manipulate the constitution to political ends was rife. Even within the MMD leadership, a large contingent felt Chiluba had become a liability and was eager to see him step down. The Oasis Forum harnessed these popular sentiments to mobilize nationwide protests under the banner of No Third Term. Chiluba's failure to secure a third term cannot be solely attributed to the Oasis Forum, however. Like Kaunda's upset in 1991, Chiluba's demise was, in the end, the result of complex political tactics and processes, in which legal rules, moral principles and popular sentiments meshed with the narrow aims of individual political actors. That said, the political significance of the Oasis Forum was immeasurable. It catalyzed, organized and gave focus to a popular movement challenging the abuse of presidential powers. Even beyond this specific achievement, Oasis came to embody and symbolize a new political

7 Chiluba's main weapons in this campaign were the district administrators, a new position of his creation. DAs were nominally members of the civil service, but were direct presidential appointees. Chiluba apparently intended for the DAs to mobilize 'popular demand' for his continuation in office.

8 For a more detailed account of the Oasis Forum's No Third Term campaign, see Gould (2006).

phenomenon – a mode of political agency that was driven neither by a will to partisan power nor by narrow sectarian interests, but by a 'moral and legal authority' (Komakoma, interview 2003).

The Oasis Forum was the direct heir to the Civil Society Action Committee which, as seen in Chapter 5, was convened in 1995 by activists in the Catholic Church and the women's movement. Faith-based and feminist bodies continued to have crucial roles in the Forum, but the participation of the Law Association altered the nature of the alliance and its political strategies in crucial ways. The Forum was not initially conceived by lawyers. By most accounts, the groundwork for its assemblage was carried out by Mark Chona, the younger brother of Mainza Chona, a key facilitator of the 1973 single-party constitution.[9]

Meanwhile, LAZ Chairperson Christopher Mundia was similarly appalled at the possibility of a third Chiluba administration. For Mundia, the decisive impetus to action came from public statements by district administrators (DAs) in the Eastern Province and the permanent secretary of Lusaka Province demanding changes in the MMD and republican constitutions to allow for a third term. In January 2001, Mundia contacted LAZ Vice-Chair Patrick Matibini and Secretary George Kunda; together they convened an emergency meeting of the LAZ Council.

The council agreed that they had a duty to prevent Chiluba from again toying with the constitution. Under these exceptional circumstances, the legislative statute governing the Law Association was seen to allow for purposive action to this end.[10] On 19 January 2001, Chairperson Mundia held a press conference in which he called upon the Attorney General for guidance concerning the legality of amending the constitution:

> 'LAZ is concerned and is carrying out consultations with its members and will soon make its views known,' Mundia noted and continued: 'The constitution is clear on the fact that the current president does not qualify for re-election ... The constitution being the supreme law of the land should ensure the sustainability of the rule of law and any changes must be done with caution.' (*Post*, 22 January 2001)

Nevertheless, LAZ remained uncertain about the appropriate and effective means to achieve this. Then, Mr Mundia received a call from Mark Chona, who informed

9 Mr Chona was appointed chairman of the controversial Task Force against Corruption, established to investigate Chiluba-era corruption cases, a position he lost in 2005 (for more on this, see Chapter 7). He is well known to be close to the Catholic bishopry. It is widely believed that he acted as President Kaunda's emissary to Southern African governments and resistance movements during the Angolan, Mozambican, Zimbabwean and Namibian liberation struggles. For Mr Chona's account of the founding of the Oasis Forum, see Gould (2012, 438–40).

10 Law Association of Zambia Act (Cap 31, Laws of Zambia), Section 4 stipulates that the association should identify itself with society and its institutions.

him that the churches and the non-governmental organizations (NGOs) wanted to join the Law Association.

Initially, the fresh coalition planned to hold their convention at the Mulungushi International Conference Centre, the site of the 1996 CSAC Citizens' Convention. Government, however, intervened to block this plan, so the organizers moved the venue across the street to the Oasis restaurant where, according to one account.

> It was a wonderful day because the Bishops were there, and the Chairman of the Christian Council of Zambia, and the Evangelical Fellowship, they were all there. And thankfully, we got very good speakers and they made excellent speeches. The atmosphere was electric! You felt there is a revolution! People refused to break for tea, they refused to break for lunch; there was heavy rain, but they all fitted, they just crowded in. Members of Parliament took time away from Parliament and joined us ... The chiefs from different areas came and the trade unions joined and it was fantastic! The diplomatic community was there and thankfully, [they] assisted a lot in helping to finance that program.

### *The legalization of the Oasis Forum*

The meeting at the Oasis restaurant culminated in a joint resolution, the Oasis Declaration. At the time, the Oasis Declaration was held up as the quintessential articulation of how progressive Zambians understood a genuinely modern form of government. The following excerpts convey a sense of the language:

> The Law Association of Zambia in conjunction with the Church ... and the Non-Governmental Organisations Co-ordinating Committee (NGOCC) and the People gathered here, having deemed it necessary, expedient, imperative and desirable to promote and conduct a debate in relation to the intimation by the ruling party, the Movement for Multi-Party Democracy (MMD) to amend the Republican Constitution to provide a third term of office in order to facilitate the eligibility of the incumbent President FTJ Chiluba in the forthcoming Presidential and Parliamentary Elections ... [And whereas] ...the Constitution of Zambia as amended in 1996 declares that 'Not withstanding anything to the contrary contained in this Constitution or any other Law, no person who has twice been elected as President shall be eligible for re-election to that office.' Now this Forum declares as follows: ...that the Forum calls upon the incumbent Republican President to exercise statesmanship by unambiguously pledging to Uphold, protect and defend the Constitution of Zambia and not contest the 2001 Presidential Elections.

It should be immediately evident that the declaration was drafted by lawyers. LAZ took an active voice and assumed a stance of organizational, moral and political leadership in the face of impending crisis. In its language and its substantive intent, the Oasis Declaration expresses a specifically legalist imagining of political authority and morality. Note, however, that this lawyerly declaration was not meant as a guide to legal action – it is not a meditation on the legal procedure or on substantive constitutional issues. Rather, it is an expression, both in form and content, of a kind of politics in which the authority of the law transcends, and arbitrates between, the self-serving interests of social and political forces. It is, above all, meant to guide popular civic action, as evidenced in its §14, which calls upon

> the women, men and the youth of this country to close ranks and resist ever again from being used and abused in any political process for selfish political ends that may threaten our nation's peace and security (ibid.).

The Zambian people did, indeed, answer the call. For the next several months, countless Zambians wore a green No Third Term ribbon on their breast, distributed by the NGOCC. Every Friday afternoon at 17:00, Lusaka and Copperbelt city streets resounded with a cacophony of car horns in the thousands honking in solidarity with the No Third Term campaign. Mass meetings organized by the Forum in every provincial capital attracted the participation of broad cross sections of civil and political society.

The political tension around the third-term issue quickly polarized the nation and raised the specter of popular violence. All over the country, traditional chiefs, Catholic clergy, NGO activists and urban professionals publicized their stand on Chiluba's third term, as did the leaders of civil servant, worker and student unions. The MMD was itself increasingly divided. At the end of March, 14 members of the MMD National Executive Council signed a joint statement against the third term (*Post*, 28 March 2001). Then, on 12 April, a prayer meeting for members of parliament at the Cathedral of the Holy Cross in Lusaka issued a statement which was 'categorically ... opposed to any attempts to confer a third term of office' on Chiluba. Among the 59 signatories, 40 were MMD lawmakers.

Despite the mounting pressure, on 30 April 2001, an extraordinary MMD convention amended the party constitution allowing Chiluba to contest the party presidency. According to the party constitution, if re-elected to lead the MMD, Chiluba would have automatically become the MMD candidate in the republican presidential elections (*Post*, 30 April 2001). Anti-third-term delegates, including a number of powerful National Executive Committee members, were blocked from entering the convention, and police confiscated 92 pistols from participants. This confrontation signaled the de facto split of the MMD into two warring factions as the pro-Chiluba group announced the expulsion of 22 MPs opposed to Chiluba's third term; among the expelled politicians were the republican and party vice-presidents (Phiri 2006, 204).

After the MMD convention, the anti-third-term campaign shifted gears. Fr Komakoma of the Catholic Commission for Justice & Peace declared 'political war' against Chiluba (*Post*, 3 May 2001), and a group of parliamentarians instigated a motion to have Chiluba impeached (*Post*, 4 May 2001). Meanwhile, High Court Judge Tamula Kakusa granted an injunction blocking the expulsion of the renegade MPs, and the Speaker of the House Amuusa Mwanawamba refused to declare the expelled MMD MPs' seats vacant (*Post*, 7 May 2001). Then, in its Monday 7 May 2001 edition, the *Post* reported that on the previous Friday, Chiluba had 'bowed to pressure from several sections of the Zambian public and finally announced that he would be leaving office after his term ends this year.' Despite the apparent finality of Chiluba's announcement, rumors continued to fly about Chiluba's secret plans to retain the presidency until finally, in August, the MMD National Executive Committee selected lawyer-politician Levy Mwanawasa as the MMD's presidential candidate (Rakner 2003, 114).

The visibility of the Oasis Forum's participation in blocking Chiluba's third-term bid catalyzed the political ascendancy of the legal profession in ways that few could have predicted. It also furthered the politicization of constitutional issues to a new level of public awareness. One important, if contingent, factor was the election of a lawyer, Levy Mwanawasa, as Chiluba's successor.[11] Mwanawasa entered the presidency as a relatively unknown, but far from popular politician, after grabbing a heatedly contested poll by the slimmest of margins. Anointed by the now-despised Chiluba, Mwanawasa received less than 30% of the vote and defeated his main opponent, Anderson Mazoka (1943–2006) of the United Party for National Development (UPND), by under 2% of the ballot.

Only months after his election, however, the new incumbent turned the tables on his mentor. In an inspired political move that temporarily reversed his fortunes, President Mwanawasa went before parliament requesting the lifting of Chiluba's immunity in order to allow for a full investigation of alleged irregularities under the former president's regime. Having extracted approval from a stunned parliament, Mwanawasa proceeded to set up an ad hoc Task Force against Corruption, chaired by Mark Chona, the man whose role in assembling the Oasis Forum was indirectly responsible for Mwanawasa's presidency. Meanwhile, opposition leader Mazoka and a number of other also-rans petitioned the Supreme Court to review the legality of Mwanawasa's election. (The story of Chiluba's subsequent indictment, and his parallel trials, in Lusaka and London, is the focus of Chapter 7.)

Almost overnight, it seemed, the political guardianship of the country had been thrust into the hands of the legal guild. The Law Association had earned a

11 Levy Mwanawasa (1948–2008) was a Copperbelt lawyer with strong political ambitions. He was among the first intake at the UNZA School of Law in 1970, graduating with an LL.B in 1973. He was admitted to the bar in 1975 and practiced in Ndola. During the Kaunda era, Mwanawasa was LAZ' vice-president in 1985–6 and also served as Solicitor General. Mwanawasa was among the team that successfully defended Lieutenant General Christon Tembo in a 1989 coup attempt against Kaunda. A founding member of the MMD, Mwanawasa chaired the National Interim Committee's legal subcommittee (1990–1), and was elected MMD vice-president in 1991. In 1994, Mwanawasa resigned from the vice-presidency in protest over Chiluba's protection of MMD Minister Michael Sata, whom Mwanawasa accused of corruption.

reputation as a formidable opponent of political impropriety, while the legacy of the previous regime and the legitimacy of the new incumbent rested in the hands of the courts. A new age of legalism was born. Lawyers seized upon their new-found political agency with enthusiasm. The Law Association, for one, maintained an assertive role in the Oasis Forum, and entered into a protracted war of nerves with the Mwanawasa regime over constitutional reform, demanding a 'people's constitution' that would 'stand the test of time.'

The new breed of legal activists, many of whom had strong links to the university's School of Law, acknowledged that the constitution had serious shortcomings. Failure to effect far-reaching liberal reforms in 1991 and 1996 attested, among other things, to the overblown powers of the president. Many lawyers agreed with Professor Alfred Chanda (1996, 137) that there were no legislative means available to oblige the incumbent president to restrict the established powers of his office. Indeed (ibid.), 'Parliament is still subordinate to the President and dances to his tune.'

Despite an apparent popular desire to make break with the authoritarian framework of the Second Republic, the 1991 constitution and its amendment in 1996 did virtually nothing to restructure the form of sovereign power. The nominal independence of parliament and the judicial system was incrementally expanded, but all of the president's fallback controls over legislation, appointments and expenditure remained in place. To wit: the president retained the imperial legacy of the prerogative to control the government apparatus seemingly at whim.

## The Mwanawasa years and beyond

The Oasis Forum's cohesion and public credibility were based on its shared commitment to defending the integrity of the constitution. By 2003, the Forum found itself embroiled in a feud with President Mwanawasa over the latest round of constitutional reforms. Like his predecessor, Mwanawasa assured the nation that he would initiate a thorough constitutional review in the early days of his administration. Under heavy pressure from the Forum to take action on constitutional reform in April 2003, two years into his tenure, Mwanawasa appointed a new constitutional review commission (CRC), chaired by Mr Wila Mung'omba, a UK-trained lawyer with significant administrative experience. Like the previous Mwanakatwe CRC, the Mung'omba Commission toured the country, evoking oral and written submissions from the general citizenry. On the basis of these submissions, the Mung'omba CRC prepared a draft for a new constitution which it submitted to the government in December 2005.

The Forum had objected vehemently to a new CRC and had demanded the immediate establishment of a constituent assembly (CA) to draft and adopt a constitution based on the Mwanakatwe Commission's recommendation from 1995. Government resisted this demand on two grounds: Adopting the constitution by a CA would, one, 'usurp the legislative powers of Parliament' and two, 'contravene Article 79 of the prevailing constitution' (Republic of Zambia 2010,

29).[12] The Mung'omba Commission encountered numerous obstacles, despite the commissioners' genuine desire to produce a strong and compelling document and much hard work.[13] Foremost among these hurdles was the Forum's staunch resistance to the use of the Inquiries Act[14] as a framework for constitutional reform. In this, the Forum found an ally in the political opposition, whose primary goal was to have a new constitution in place before the next elections (scheduled for late 2006), with the old majoritarian provision restored requiring a 50 + 1% share of the poll in the presidential contest. Opposition parties saw this as critical to dislodging the MMD from power. While struggling to maintain its non-partisan profile, the Forum was in open conflict with the president over the constitution's mode of adoption (by constituent assembly or by parliament) and gave its full support to the opposition's demand for a new constitution before the 2006 elections. Mr Mwanawasa, who had come to power in 2001 with less than 30% of the popular vote, was in no rush to remove the 'first-past-the-post' clause in the existing constitution. It was clearly within the realm of possibility that Mwanawasa would lose to the UPND's Anderson Mazoka in a run-off ballot.

This brief summary of the political barriers to the enactment of the 2005 draft constitution hardly does justice to Zambia's inflamed political atmosphere in the mid-2000s. The political arena was highly polarized by the confrontational relationship between the president, on the one hand, and the major opposition parties, as well as the Oasis Forum, on the other. Unsurprisingly, legal experts outside the government – including the Law Association – criticized the government's position on constitutional reform. Eventually, the opposing factions accepted a compromise of sorts: There would be no constituent assembly, but the finalization of the new constitutional text was to be relegated to a National Constitutional Conference (NCC), to be appointed by the president. Mwanawasa's administration acknowledged the resistance to the Inquiries Act as a framework for constitutional reform and enacted specialized legislation to

12 Informants within the Forum considered these arguments to be spurious. They acknowledged that only parliament could *enact* a new constitution, but there were no constitutional barriers to having a popular body like a constituent assembly *adopt* a constitutional text for submission to parliament.

13 'The Mung'omba Commission … gathered through collecting submissions from 12,569 individuals across Zambia's 150 constituencies and visiting nine other countries to study successful constitutional review processes' (Holder 2011).

14 All of Zambia's constitutional review commissions have been established under the Inquiries Act (Cap 41 of the Laws of Zambia), bringing them under direct executive control in all of their functions. The Act empowers the president to appoint a commission (§2(1)) 'to inquire into any matter in which an inquiry would, in the opinion of the President, be for the public welfare.' It also, among other things, allows the president to decide (§2(2)) 'whether or not the proceedings [of the Commission] shall, in whole or in part, be held in public.' Commissioners are obliged (§5) 'to make a full, faithful and impartial inquiry in accordance with the terms of the commission concerned and to report the result of the inquiry to the President,' who can decide whether or not to make the commission's report public.

govern the NCC.[15] In Mr Mwanawasa's view (2007, 11), this legislation ensured that the president would 'play very little role in [the] process of adopting the new constitutional text.'

The National Constitutional Conference was eventually instated in August 2007. It incorporated representatives from a wide and varied number of Zambian governmental and civic bodies although more than half of the 495 NCC delegates were politicians. In protest at the heavy involvement of partisan actors, the NGOCC and the Catholic Church both declined to send delegates to the NCC.

In his speech to the opening session of the NCC, Mr Mwanawasa (Republic of Zambia 2007) rebutted the controversies surrounding the conference. He was particularly scathing in his assessment of the view that a political process like constitution-making 'must be legitimized by the instruments of civil society organizations (the church and some political leaders) for it to be acceptable.' This, he exclaimed (10), 'is a negation of democracy!' He also warned dissenting voices that his decision to relinquish overall control of the process should not be taken for granted (4):

> There is a chorus in the Lenje language which says '*nakasha kolya koinuka* …' which is a warning to a duiker or an impala that she should not always graze looking down but she should graze and stoop from time to time! Our people should not be complacent that they will always have a government such as ours, which allows them such freedoms!

Politically, Mr Mwanawasa (1948–2008) came of age in the final years of the Second Republic. He was a founding member of the MMD and served as Chiluba's first vice-president. Like Chiluba, he grew up in the shadow of Kenneth Kaunda and may have sought to recapture the ethos of UNIP's golden age, when trust in Kaunda and his vision were strong among the Zambian citizenry. In the same speech cited above (7–8), Mr Mwanawasa intoned:

> We must understand that politics is about leadership. When leaders drive people's emotions positively, towards the range of enthusiasm, performance in society rises. If people are driven by leaders towards animosity and anxiety, the country would be thrown off stride. The job of leadership in politics is to help every Zambian bring out the best.

15 "The National Constitutional Conference (NCC) was established under the National Constitutional Conference (NCC) Act No. 19 of 2007 (amended in 2010). The Act stipulates the composition, functions, powers and above all the procedure on how the functions of the Conference shall be conducted.

According to Part II Clause 3 of the NCC Act, the NCC is a forum for the examination, debate and adoption of proposals to alter the Constitution as contained in the Draft Constitution submitted by Mung'omba Constitutional Review Commission" (NCC website: www.ncczambia.org).

Mwanawasa had resigned from his vice-presidency in Chiluba's administration over perceived corruption in Chiluba's cabinet. This suggests that, at heart, Mr Mwanawasa believed in accountable government. The acceptability of a government was, in Mwanawasa's view (Republic of Zambia 2007, 6), ensured through periodic elections as 'a litmus test as to its suitability.' He also defended the view, however, that between elections, an elected government should be relatively autonomous from popular oversight.

> While it must seek to incorporate as much as is *reasonably* possible [popular] views, a government is empowered in exercising its mandate to make such judgements [sic] or decisions as it considers *reasonably* justifiable and in the interest of the nation and reject those which would be injurious to national interests. It is healthy to criticize the decisions of government but dissent must be *reasonable* and should at all times avoid to be malicious. (ibid., 5–6; emphasis added)

Given his juridical background, it is understandable that 'reasonableness' would be the president's key operational term for assessing accountable government.[16] It is also clear, on the other hand, that Mr Mwanawasa felt that the president alone is the ultimate judge on what is reasonable. While Mr Mwanawasa's concessions to civil society demands went further than those of other Zambian presidents, in his thoughts and political strategies he remained a vehicle of the prerogativist form of power he embodied.

The NCC sat for three years, outliving its initiator. President Mwanawasa passed away of a stroke mid-term, in August 2008, in a Parisian hospital. The NCC delivered its final report and draft constitution under the watch of Mwanawasa's successor, Rupiah Banda, in August 2010.[17] The conference's final narrative report reached 1,140 pages, plus annexes. Like the CRCs whose work it drew upon, the NCC was a very expensive endeavor. For the duration of its deliberations, commissioners collectively drew more than $65,000 in allowances for each *day* the CRC was in session.[18]

16 In the jurisprudence governing the judicial review of official actions, the notion of (un)reasonableness is a key criteria for determining the justifiability of an official act or decision. In a seminal ruling (*Council of Civil Service Unions v Minister for Civil Service*), Lord Diplock defined unreasonableness to characterize an act '[s]o outrageous in its defiance of logic or accepted moral standards that no sensible person who had applied his mind to the question to be decided could have arrived at it.'

17 Fourth republican president, Rupiah Banda (1937-2022) served as Levy Mwanawasa's vice-president from October 2006 to November 2008, as acting president (upon Mwanawasa's death) from June to November 2008, and as elected president from November 2008 until September 2011.

18 The NCC comprised 495 members – all of whom drew sitting allowances ranging between $130 and $260 a day for countless sessions over more than three years (Holder 2011). The executive committee of the NCC alone had 47 members, its 7-member secretariat notwith-

In the detail of its provisions, the draft constitution proposed by the NCC represented a radical departure from its predecessors. The 113 articles of the 1991 constitution had expanded to 139 articles via the 1996 amendments; the NCC draft, in turn, comprised 352 articles.[19] This unwieldy explosion in constitutional substance reflected, to some extent, a pent-up desire to produce a 'people-driven' constitution. Through their public consultations, both the Mwanakatwe and the Mung'omba CRCs had expressly catered to civil society demands. According to one prominent commissioner, 'We were not producing what we wanted, but what the people submitted.' Nevertheless, the critical question of the president's discretionary powers was not addressed in the NCC's proposals. While both the Mwanakatwe and Mung'omba CRCs had received submissions highly critical of the scope of executive discretion, none of the drafts submitted for enactment contained significant reformulations of executive prerogatives.[20]

### *The 2016 Amendment Act*

When President Banda tabled a draft constitution based on the NCC's deliberations before parliament, in early 2011, 'the Oasis Forum embarked on nationwide campaign against the draft constitution, staging public rallies and lobbying opposition lawmakers to kill the proposed MMD-sponsored Constitution of Zambia bill' (Sishuwa 2020, 24). The draft constitution lacked the support of the main opposition parties, Hakainde Hichilema's UPND and Michael Sata's Patriotic Front (PF), and failed to pass.

Michael Sata of the Patriotic Front defeated Rupiah Banda at the polls in September of that year[21] and within weeks, the new president appointed a

standing. The primary (material) beneficiaries of this exercise were politicians, civil servants and representatives of urban professional groups.

19 The Mung'omba CRC's 2005 draft constitution, upon which the NCC's draft was nominally based, comprised 378 articles. The current constitution, as finally enacted in January 2016, has 276 articles.

20 The 'Executive (Sub-)Committee' of the NCC, which considered draft articles related to the presidency, recorded the following deliberations on Article 122: Office of the President (Republic of Zambia 2009, §3.1.1–3.1.2):

'In the discussion that ensued on this Article, members observed that Zambia has always had an Executive President whose power was drawn from the Constitution. In view of this and considering that the country enjoyed peace under the current hybrid system, some members were of the view that the system should be retained as proposed under the Mung'omba Draft Constitution. It was justified that Zambia needed a strong President who would inspire confidence and sense of security whenever problems beset the nation.

The other members had a contrary view. They were concerned about the President having too much powers [sic] and therefore, advocated for the reduction of the Presidential powers. They suggested that the Presidential system be defined on the basis of the Ghanaian and South African Constitutions. The opposing views were not upheld by the Committee, as most of the members supported the adoption of the provisions as provided by the Draft Constitution.'

21 Sata lost the 2008 by-election to Rupiah Banda following Mwanawasa's death. The Sata presidency is discussed in Chapters 8 and 9.

20-member Technical Committee on Drafting the Zambian Constitution (Republic of Zambia 2011). In its terms of reference, as well as in its composition, the TCDZC was designed to assuage critics of Mr Mwanawasa's constitution-making strategy. Chaired by former Chief Justice Annel Silungwe, the TCDZC incorporated members from the Law Association, the (Protestant) Council of Churches and the Catholic Church – all Oasis Forum member organizations. The Citizen's Forum and Transparency International Zambia, prominent pro-democracy bodies close to the Oasis Forum, were also represented, as were the surviving chairs of previous CRCs (Patrick Mvunga and Wila Mung'omba). It was, overall, a very liberal panel. Political liberalism also characterized the technical committee's mandate. The committee was asked to review all previous efforts at constitution-making, back to and including the 1991 Mvunga Commission, and to draft a constitution based on 'constitutional democracy and a culture of constitutionalism' (TCZDC 2011, 4). Among the many specific instructions guiding the work of the technical committee, two are particularly relevant to the culture of prerogativism. According to these provisions (ibid., 5), the TCDZC must

> (e) draft a National Constitution that ensures the separation of powers amongst the various State organs including the Executive, the Legislature and the Judiciary so as to create checks and balances between them and to ensure accountability of the State and its officers to the people of Zambia; [and]
>
> (f) draft a National Constitution that will ensure that excessive and unfettered powers are not given to any particular organ of the State, Commission or constitutional functionary[.]

This latter proviso must be reasonably understood to also apply to the president.

President Sata instructed the committee to submit its draft to the president directly. According to Mulela Margaret Munalula[22] (2016), the committee's draft 'was ideally supposed to be presented to the President and simultaneously released to the public in preparation for a national referendum and subsequent enactment by Parliament; yet this did not happen … the process stalled for over a year.' The delay in action over the new draft may have been due to President Sata's deteriorating health, rather than any political misgivings the government might have had. In October 2014, after less than three years in office, President Sata passed away in London without having submitted the TCDZC draft to parliament for enactment. Sata's successor, Edgar Lungu, elected to the presidency

22 Professor Munalula is an experienced legal practitioner and legal academic, with an LL.B. from the University of Zambia and a PhD from Notre Dame. A UNZA law professor and a member of the TCDZC, she was appointed to the Constitutional Court in March 2016 (see Chapter 10 for an extended discussion of her judicial activism), and elevated to ConCourt Deputy President in 2022.

via a by-election in January 2015, restarted the enactment process and submitted the TCDZC draft to parliament later that year. Renamed the *Constitution Amendment Bill of 2015*, the bill was approved, with some last-minute revisions (see Munalula 2016, for details) and signed into law by President Lungu in January 2016.

The 2016 constitution is a storied mishmash of elements. At its base is the Mvunga Commission's revisions of the 1973 one-party constitution, enacted in 1991 under political duress by a one-party parliament. Mounted in a rush, the then-opposition Movement for Multiparty Democracy had boycotted Mvunga's Commission. A new Bill of Rights and its entrenchment via Article 79 (see Annex A) are persistent residues of the 1991 document. Ultimately, the immense energy and money invested in updating the Bill of Rights by the TCDZC, the NCC and the two previous CRCs proved futile. Government organized a referendum on the TCDZC's draft Bill of Rights (and on the proposed repeal of Article 79), in connection with the general election of August 2016. The constitutional referendum failed to muster the required support of 50% of all eligible voters.[23] Despite the alleged desire of the Zambian people for a new, people-driven constitution, the long-drawn-out and elite-driven reform process evidently failed to mobilize the *demos.*

This may well have been a consequence of the legacy of top-down constitution-making. The TCDZC made a valiant effort to redress the impression of an elite-driven process. From a procedural perspective, '[n]ot even the NCC constitution-making process was as broad based and widespread in terms of citizen participation as has been the TCDZC's constitution-making process' (Lungwangwa 2015, 86). Citizen reactions to the committee's first draft constitution were elicited from a wide array of forums and conventions at the community, district and provincial levels. Expert testimony was evoked through ten three-day sector group conventions. A national convention of approximately 500 delegates 'representing twenty identified sectors of the Zambian society' (ibid., 81) culminated in the feedback process which led to the formulation of the TCDCZ's second and final draft. These consultations were a logistically impressive and, once again, exceedingly expensive mode of eliciting the will of the people. Like all of the earlier consultations on constitutional drafts, the TCDCZ's feedback arrangements were plagued by what might be termed a 'stakeholder' approach to constitution-making. This approach has prevailed in all of the constitution-making bodies, from the recommendations for constituent assemblies by the Mwanakatwe and the Mung'omba CRCs, to the composition of the NCC. An identical approach

23 In the national referendum in 2016, Zambians were asked to answer Yes or No to the following proposition "Do you agree to the amendment to the Constitution to enhance the Bill of Rights contained in Part III of the Constitution of Zambia and to repeal and replace Article 79 of the Constitution of Zambia?" The referendum mobilized only 44% of eligible voters. Of those who did vote, 71% cast votes in support of the amendment, implying that only 24% of eligible voters favored fundamental constitutional reform (for a discussion, see Maingaila 2016).

informed the decisive national convention of the TCDCZ. There have been minor differences in the composition of the consultative bodies, but all have been based on the selection or invitation of representatives of 'identified sectors' of society. The 'will of the people,' as measured through these stakeholder consultations, represents an always already institutionalized *demos*, entrapped in institutionalized relationships to state power, defined and overseen through the Societies Act (Cap. 119). Such stakeholder organizations, with few exceptions, are confined and constrained by their subsidiary relationship to the state. That said, a stakeholder approach to constitution-making is certainly more democratic than the top-down imposition of a constitutional text, but it allows no space for unbridled and spontaneous constituent power to find expression.

Without gaining approval via a public referendum, parliament was obliged, once again, to simply amend the 1991 constitution as it had done in 1996. The Bill of Rights (Part III) of the 1991 constitution, untouched by the amendments of 1996, was left intact while Parts I, II and IV were repealed and replaced with new articles.[24]

The failure to achieve a fundamentally new constitution in 1996, and again in 2016, thus hinged on Article 79.[25] This meant that the human rights provisions of the 1991 constitution (scarcely different from those codified in the [post]colonial 1964 document) could not be expanded to encompass new thinking about gender, childhood, citizenship, indigeneity and so forth. The failure of the referendum also made it impossible to seriously delimit the scope of presidential discretion, provisions for which were buried in the Bill of Rights. Indeed, contrary to the TCDZC's mandate, the 2016 constitution failed to bring the branches of government into a judicious balance with one another. Instead, it sustained Zambia's prevailing prerogativist jurisprudence.

Cornell-based Zambian law professor Muna Ndulo (2019) affirms this perception:

> The 2016 Zambian Constitution, [even] more than the 1991 Constitution that it replaced ... gives enormous powers to the executive without any checks, thereby promoting authoritarianism. It allows the President limitless

24 The new Part I of the 2016 Amendment Act comprises §§1–7 of the 1991 constitution; the new Part II reproduces §§8–10; the new Part IV is §§33–60. The remaining amendments substitute new articles based on recommendations of the Technical Committee on Drafting the Zambian Constitution appointed by President Michael Sata in 2013. The 'entrenched' Bill of Rights and Article 79 were, of legal necessity, left intact (Munalula 2016).

25 It is perhaps a tribute to the enduring ethos of constitutionalism in Zambia that there have been no serious proposals concerning the bypassing of Article 79. The unamendability of core constitutional principles has not led to a situation in which the Zambian people would have 'become frustrated and resort[ed] to extra-legal behavior' (Katz 1995, 254). Under the auspices of Zambia's conservative legal ethos, a stalemate in the incessant tug-of-war between constitutionalism and popular will sees quasi-liberal legalism prevailing over democratic aspirations.

powers without any restraint whatsoever including making appointment to all important positions in the three spheres of government.[26]

The fact that the lion's share of the president's prerogative powers is entrenched in the 'unamendable' Bill of Rights makes it difficult to determine the extent to which prerogativism reflects the current will of the Zambian people. In one respect, however, the 2016 constitution realizes a key Oasis Forum demand *circa* 2003–6: Article 47(1) stipulates that "[e]lections to the office of President shall be conducted directly, under a majoritarian electoral system, where the winning candidate must receive more than fifty percent of the valid votes cast."

## *Constitutional closure: The death of Bill 10*

This majoritarian reform soon came under assault. In 2019, the Patriotic Front government of President Edgar Lungu established a national dialogue forum (NDF) to 'reform the law on the electoral process, public order and regulation of political parties based on submissions from various stakeholders' (National Dialogue [Constitution, Electoral Process, Public Order and Political Parties] Bill 2019). After hurried consultations, the NDF drafted a new Constitution of Zambia (Amendment) Bill (No. 10 of 2019) for consideration by parliament. Parts of Bill 10 sought to revise clumsy formulations in the text of the 2016 constitution. The bill's more controversial elements, however, lay elsewhere. If passed, Article 30 of the draft bill would have significantly watered down the majoritarian provision of the 2016 constitution. This would occur by allowing 'a presidential candidate [who] does not receive more than fifty percent of the valid votes cast' to 'negotiate and form a coalition government with a presidential candidate that participated in the initial ballot,' providing that the two candidates together accrued more than half of the votes cast. There is, of course, no shortage of splinter parties willing to 'top up' a minority party's mandate and thus share, however modestly, in the spoils of government.

The main opposition party, the United Party for National Development, boycotted the NDF, as did church and civil society groups, including the Oasis Forum. University of Zambia (UNZA) law professor Cephas Lumina (2020) claimed that '[t]he ruling party dominated the National Dialogue and participation was coerced.' The 'defective process' he felt, 'inevitably produced controversial amendments favouring the ruling party.' Professor Muna Ndulo (2020), for his part, pronounced that Bill 10 was 'designed to remove parliamentary oversight

26 Constitutional scholar John Sangwa appears to differ with this view. In a letter to the online *NewsDiggers* newspaper (22 May 2020), Sangwa says he was 'elated on 5th January 2016, when President Lungu signed the Constitution (Amendment) Bill into law. I never thought there would be a day, in my lifetime, when a sitting President would reduce his own powers and grant the Judiciary, the National Assembly and the people oversight over the office of President.' Professor Munalula (2016, 1131) has also extolled the 'landmark' provisions of the 2016 constitution. We return to this issue in Chapter 10.

over the presidency and thereby install a constitutional dictatorship.' These concerns were echoed by the Commonwealth Lawyers' Association (Kalunga 2019), which complained that '[t]he Bill proposes to concentrate power in the President by removing Parliamentary oversight over some important executive functions.'

A number of NGOs, including the NGOCC beseeched the government not exploit its incumbency to 'walk a path this nation has walked before which leads only to wastage of resources and a flawed constitution requiring amendment as soon as it is adopted' (Phiri 2019). LAZ also petitioned the Constitutional Court to block the enactment of Bill 10, but its plea failed – not surprisingly, perhaps, given that the bill had not yet been approved by parliament.

When Bill 10 did come to a vote in late October 2020, it fell short of the necessary 111 votes (two-thirds of parliament) needed for ratification, by 6. The death of the bill, in effect, ended a 17-year cycle of constitutional reform that began when President Mwanawasa appointed the Mung'omba CRC in 2003. Parliament's rejection of the government's initiative was not, it would seem, a reflection of the 'will of the people,' which was never seriously canvassed. Rather, Bill 10 failed simply because it was seen as a PF ploy to bias the political playing field ahead of the 2021 elections. One could say then, that little has been learned since the passing of Chiluba's Amendment Bill in 1996. Chiluba's Amendment Act succeeded because his party, the MMD, had the votes. President Lungu's gambit failed because the Patriotic Front did not. In neither case did the most controversial reforms – Mr Chiluba's presidential parentage clause, Mr Lungu's coalition government, and the weakening of parliamentary oversight on the executive – respond to clear popular demands. The difference, of course, is that in 1996, parliament acquiesced to using constitutional reform as a means to short-term political ends; by 2021, parliamentarians had lost appetite for such a strategy. Be that as it may, it is unlikely that the 2016 constitution will be the target of significant political designs in the coming years. There may well be a legitimate need to update the Bill of Rights, but even if there is a change of power in the 2021 general election, parliament will probably have little passion to further fiddle with the constitution. This implies that the cornerstones of prerogativism lodged in the entrenched Bill of Rights are likely to 'stand the test of time.'

# III

# Law, politics and unfettered power

# Excursus: Redescribing postcolonial power

Building on efforts to 'unthink' the (post)colonial state in Chapter 2, this theoretical excursus seeks to flesh out the historical and intellectual foundations of prerogativist power. As was argued in that earlier chapter, the either/or dispositions of political liberalism have held analyses of postcolonial power in inflexible restraints. In the interests of destabilizing these entrenched habits of thought, I propose an alternative perspective. My proposal involves three theoretical moves: The first seeks to situate contemporary prerogativism as a historical residue of colonial government. The second grapples with the ambiguities of sovereign personhood, leading to an image of the postcolonial form of power as dually embodied, encompassing public vs private personae with very different relationships to legality. My aim is to show that the postcolonial form of power reflects a dialectical 'both/and' logic of assembly for which, to borrow a phrase from Donna Haraway (1991, 180; cited in de la Cadena 2015, 31) 'one is too few, but two are too many.' The third move is to trace the genealogy of postcolonial sovereignty from early modern absolutism to the imperial form of power in which prerogativism is grounded. These maneuvers are motivated by a desire to engage with the powers, ambivalences and vulnerabilities of presidentialist rule outside of the liberal box.

While the discussion in this chapter is cast in abstract terms, its ultimate aim is practical. I sense a political need materializing: A need to confront liberalism with its foundational hypocrisy – the necessity of sustaining a *narrative of embattlement* to deny certain groups the hallowed liberal privileges of dignity, autonomy and liberty. The urgent tenor of this liberal narrative is such that it necessitates the availability of unfettered power. In order for this illiberal requirement to coalesce seamlessly with liberalism's democratic facet, recourse to violence is embodied in an elected official – the president (by whatever title).

This emerging political demand arises from acute and deepening disparities of wealth and power that prevail between Them and Us. It arises from the evident failure of liberal dispensations to effectively address calamities like COVID-19 and the accelerating climate emergency. Its aim is to make transparent the ways in which regimes rooted in the rhetoric of political liberalism at certain locations induce exclusion, inequality and division elsewhere. In a positive sense, the growing need to reassess liberalism emerges from growing awareness at myriad

DOI: 10.4324/9780429198984-10

locations across the planet that another world, another form of power, *must* be possible if we are not to squander entire ecosystems and the irreplaceable information and wisdom they comprise.

This detailed examination of law and politics in one post-colony, Zambia, seeks to inspire Zambians to reflect in new ways on their politics and their history. At the same time, this focused case analysis reveals structural properties of the postcolonial form of power that one might reasonably expect to find, in some variation, in many former British African colonies. It is the purpose of this chapter to begin sketching out a vocabulary to discuss these properties, and to reflect on their sources, mechanisms and effects.

## Colonial emergency and postcolonial jurisprudence

My first move draws on Nasser Hussain's (2003) seminal theorization of the *Jurisprudence of Emergency*. Hussain lays out key methodological foundations for an investigation of the paradoxical form of postcolonial sovereignty. His main empirical focus is on British India in the 18th and 19th centuries, but the crux of the narrative is broader, revolving around the transmutations of English law over the course of Britain's long colonial era, and the implications of this for state formation in Britain's colonial empire and in England herself. Hussain argues that the understanding of legality at the core of Britain's colonial law emerged in response to an ideological construct, central to Enlightenment philosophy. This was that of the 'Oriental despot,' which framed the ways East India Company administrators portrayed the rulers and political structures they encountered in India. The labelling of indigenous government as despotic served the dual task of defining colonial power as an order based on law and justice, while legitimizing India's imperial subordination in the name of civilization. All of this is familiar from Edward Saïd's classical work on *Orientalism* (1978) and the substantial literature it generated.

Where Hussain's historiography breaks new ground is in its unearthing of recurrent discourses within British colonial administration which *identified with* this ideological construct of despotism, and saw it as a legitimate and inevitable means to social order in the Indian colonial context (op cit., 52–55). Already at its moment of conception, the political structures that would eventually evolve into the modern Indian state were constituted around a tension between constitutional legality and a form of exceptional rule that was impervious to liberal norms – or between, as Hussain frames it, legal 'rationality' vs sovereign 'will.'

Hussain insists that the 'rule of law' in colonial India was not a mere façade. The need of the colonial ruling class to maintain a semblance of legality led, in certain instances, to political outcomes which did 'from time to time go against its interests' (ibid., 11, *pace* Guha 1997, 64; cf. Benton 2002, 255). At the same time, colonial rule *also* emulated the 'despotism' it claimed to supersede. The colonial governor could and did exercise 'exceptional' powers that, in effect, bracketed any legal constraints on his discretion. Such exceptional acts extended from the routine suspension of *habeas corpus*, to the military massacre of civilians under conditions of a perceived political emergency.

Here, the simultaneous cultivation of law and exception was a structural response to the configuration of colonial social relations. Under imperial government, liberal legality was essential to the legitimation of racial domination. Liberal principles could not, however, be extended beyond precisely defined boundaries of race and class without undermining the hegemony of colonial rule. Were the Queen's darker subjects allowed access to the full measure of the law, the colonial state and its White minions would have been denied many racialized privileges, as well as routine access to emergency powers. Without routine recourse to real or threatened violence and coercion, the ultimate means of colonial domination would unravel. Hussain's analysis pauses at the threshold of independence. Yet, as he suggests (ibid., 137ff), the conceptualization of colonial state formation as an indivisible combination of legality and exception opens up robust avenues of inquiry into the relationship of postcolonial jurisprudence to the government of the politically excluded sections of the population, begging the question of how the 'will of the people' legitimizes state violence against the *demos*.

Adom Getachew (2020, 386) has recently reminded us, 'Even as Nkrumah and others celebrated the emergence of independence as the culmination of the people's collective power and insisted on the continued need for mass mobilisation, the people as political agent were subject to the state's disciplinary formation.' This is true, of course, of any modern state. But postcolonial variants entail certain modulations of this basic principle. After independence from imperial rule, the postcolonial subjects of an independent state were embedded – entrapped may be a better word – in a hegemonic politico-legal epistemology of government. Within this epistemic and political cage, their citizenship was imbued with both a positive and a negative charge. The positive role of 'the people' and their will was reduced to the validation of elite rule – a notional recipe for the eventual and inevitable politics of the party and its government, enacted with the Zambian constitution of 1973. Far more expansive in this epistemic formation was the negative identification of the *demos* with unpredictability, indiscipline, volatility, unruliness, subversiveness – in short, an always already lurking threat to the security of governing elites.

Independence elicited the positive *dispositif* of the people-as-validation, but merely tacked it onto the pre-existing and persistent colonial ethos of embattled government. This casting of the *demos*-as-threat is, of course, the foundational premise upon which the 'exceptional' legality characteristic of imperial liberalism – the jurisprudence of emergency – rests. Generations of Zambians have grown to expect little more from politics than systemic exclusion from the statutory domain and, on occasion, an election-season *chitenge*, baseball cap or T-shirt.

The point is that Hossain's apt theorization of imperial liberal legality should not be taken too narrowly. Alleged colonial emergencies were indeed invoked to trigger 'disciplinary' measures against native populations. These measures took many forms, marked by gradations of violence that were legally illegitimate. This implied that the embattled (post)colonial state needed to maintain a political and material military *readiness* to respond to perceived threats and that this readiness implied an established disciplinary presence that fenced the *demos* into spaces of surveillance and control. These 'fences' found expression in pass laws and poll taxes, in curfews and checkpoints – in all manner of policy and practice that aimed at managing and curtailing the mobility of native populations beyond their role as non- or under-remunerated labor. Independence cancelled many of the administrative emblems of racialized and spatialized repression, but the logic of these documents has lived on in the draconian sanctions and arbitrary privileges associated with possessing (or not possessing) a party membership card, or even something as banal as a notarized birth certificate. All of this, I argue, stems from the epistemic dynamics of imperial liberalism.

Few postcolonial African states have been spared recurrent 'states of emergency.' On occasion (under conditions of military coup, for example), a state of emergency can suspend the fragile vestiges of liberal legality enshrined in postcolonial constitutions. More typically, however, a declared state of emergency co-exists with normal judicial routines (Chanda 1986). But more importantly, even without a declared state of emergency, African presidents systematically enjoy a wide range of exceptional powers linked to ever-present threats to security, domestic and foreign. Even under the most overtly liberal postcolonial regimes, 'sovereign will' is often sufficient to suspend freedom of speech, assembly or movement for select parts of the population. The analytical challenge that Hussain's jurisprudence of emergency poses is that of conceptualizing a system of public law that is constituted around a liberal notion of rule of law, on the one hand, but which, on the other, comprises within itself the means to override this very legality.[1] Hussain's recognition of the internal paradoxality of imperial law allows for a deeper interrogation of the dialectical nature of the form of power it facilitates.

The next move, then, is to show how this paradoxical form of legality, and the broad scope of discretionary power it implies, is embodied in the paradox of presidential personhood. To these ends, the next section outlines how the characteristics of sovereign power which administered colonial Zambia devolved directly from the absolutism of the English monarchy. This genealogical argument is not purely metaphorical. My contention is that in key respects, the unbridled authority of postcolonial presidents migrated, via a colonial constitution based on imperial liberalism, from early modern Europe to postcolonial Africa. The primary vehicle transporting this migrant has been modern legal canon, and colonial constitutions crafted by imperial lawyers. This argument reflects the findings outlined in Chapters 5 and 6, which trace the historical trajectory of postcolonial prerogativism from colonial to postcolonial constitutions.

## The president's two bodies

In the 2001 elections, Zambia's second president, Frederick Chiluba, was succeeded by a lawyer, Levy Patrick Mwanawasa. Mwanawasa needed to establish

1 This issue has received extensive attention in two contemporary literatures: one, on 'post-conflict' reconstruction (e.g., De Brabandere 2010) – with special reference to the restoration of sovereignty after civil war; and another on the precedence of states of emergency in liberal democracies (especially after 9/11 – see Campbell 2008, Lazar 2009).

his independence from the wildly unpopular Chiluba and asked parliament to lift his predecessor's juridical immunity, allowing for Chiluba to be indicted for corruption.[2] As recounted in Chapter 7, Chiluba was tried twice – once through civil proceedings in London and again on criminal charges (abuse of office) in Lusaka. Chiluba boycotted the London hearings but prepared an elaborate defense that he presented in 2009 to a Lusaka magistrate. Around that time, a pamphlet (Chiluba n.d.) was circulated, which reproduces this testimony. In this text, the former president described his politico-legal status as president as embodying two legally distinct persons. One was his official manifestation as head of state; the other was his private embodiment as the leader of a political party, the Movement for Multiparty Democracy (MMD). In Chiluba's view, the charges against him were misguided because they conflated these two personae. The allegedly corrupt actions he was accused of were not carried out as head of state, he claimed, but in his private capacity as MMD president, and did not involve public funds, but monies he had received from 'friends in the region' in support of his political projects as a private citizen.

It is an unusual legal defense and it took some time to make sense of it in analytical terms. My Zambian informants were largely of the opinion that Chiluba's creation of two parallel yet distinct personalities was a legally unsustainable ploy to divert attention away from his blatantly illegal actions. These interpretations are reasonable, but they failed to explain some of the messy facts of the case. Why, for example, was Chiluba acquitted by a Zambian magistrate in a Lusaka court? And why did the Zambian Attorney General refuse to domesticate the guilty verdict that had been handed down by the London court? Why not render it legally enforceable in Zambia, when it was the Zambian state and the Attorney General in particular who had instigated the London proceedings in the first place? Was there something in Chiluba's habitus, frail and broken after seven years of house arrest and legal harassment, which prevented the state from delivering the seemingly inevitable *coup de grâce* on the former president? And if this was the case, did this imply that presidential suffering necessitated a legal response couched in mercy and forgiveness? What became of the ethos of outrage and vengeance that had propelled Chiluba's initial investigation, indictment and prosecution? How, if at all, did Chiluba's unconventional 'two-body' defense contribute to his eventual vindication? It wasn't until I read the pioneering study by German historian Ernest Kantorowicz (1957), *The King's Two Bodies. A Study in Mediaeval Political Theology*, that I began to grasp the theoretical significance of Chiluba's self-portrayal as legally bi-polar. Kantorowicz' image of the president's legal duality opened the door to grasping the link between the postcolonial form of power and early modern absolutism.

2 The extended legal and extralegal processes that followed from these political maneuvers are elaborated and contextualized in Chapter 7.

## The monarch's colonial regent

In his inquiry into the foundations of the legitimacy of Northern Rhodesia's colonial state, historian Terrence Ranger (1980) argues for the importance of scrutinizing African 'acquiescence' to colonial rule. As already noted, violence and direct coercion played a constitutive role in the establishment of the colony, but in terms of manpower and ammunition, the colonial government was, as noted earlier, too 'thinly spread' (Killingray 1986, 413) on the ground to maintain its control on the basis of force alone. 'Colonial rule in Northern Rhodesia,' claims Ranger (1980, 350), 'required a shared system of ideology which linked rulers and ruled.' After the territory's annexation from the British South Africa Company under direct Crown government in 1924, 'the Northern Rhodesian government sought to create such an ideology around the idea of Imperial Monarchy.'[3]

Ranger's suggestion that African subjects were somehow complicit in their own oppression requires some qualification. While in principle, all non-White colonial subjects suffered in equal measure from the indignities of racial disenfranchisement and discrimination, some Northern Rhodesians were 'more equal than others,' to borrow Orwell's (1945) famous phrase, with traditional leaders enjoying rights and privileges not available to commoners under the doctrine of indirect rule (Chanock 1985). This does not invalidate Ranger's claim, inasmuch as Zambia's influential traditional leaders may well have been the most receptive to a monarchist ideology. It is also so that the alleged complicity of colonial subjects in their own domination does not contradict the parallel fact of African hatred of, and courageous resistance to colonial subjectification. In any event, the 'shared ideology' of imperial monarchism failed to sustain colonial hegemony, and Africans' will to self-rule eventually prevailed. In the meantime, however, colonial government assembled a politico-juridical apparatus which in significant respects survived the transition to independence. For my purposes here, the nature and persistent effects of this apparatus reward critical scrutiny.

In colonial Northern Rhodesia, the legal embodiment of the British Crown[4] was the governor. In terms of the allocation of power, or chain of command, the monarch held ultimate responsibility for all governmental decisions and actions affecting the colony. In practice, this responsibility was delegated to a secretary of state for the colonies, based in London, who proposed candidates to the Crown for appointment to an available governorship. Responsibility, and power, for the day-to-day running of a colonial territory resided with the governor.

3 Kenyan historian Ali Mazrui (1967) made a similar contention when he argued that postcolonial African presidents were drawn to a monarchical legacy when inhabiting their newly found positions of power.

4 Northern Rhodesia was ruled under two queens (Victoria, until 1901; Elizabeth II, from 1952 until independence in 1964), and four Kings (Edward VII and VIII, and George V and VI).

Governors were civil servants, not partisan agents. The governor, as legally empowered in the colonial order-in-council (see Chapter 5), was nominally an apolitical actor, the agent of the monarch's 'pleasure.' The governor typically had no temporal political entanglements, beyond the everyday politics of what Williams (2011) renders as 'running the show.'[5] The duration of a governor's appointment was thus not contingent on fickle electoral outcomes. A change in government in England would inevitably entail a change in the secretary of state, but this was an externality to be dealt with pragmatically, not a game-changing event. Success in colonial government might lead to a more comfortable posting, possibly with a better salary, but governors must inevitably retire. To evoke Kantorowicz's terms, their eternal 'Body politic' and the powers incumbent on it would then pass on to the next governor, leaving only a temporal 'Body natural' of mortal (if often aristocratic) means.[6]

In practice, there were few areas of government in which the governor did not exercise undiluted discretion. Colonial rule was, for all intents and purposes, an absolutist mode of government, and the governor's powers were despotic in the literal sense of the term. Note, however, that the liberal constitutionalism of the colonial order found expression in a very limited form of representative government, the monopoly of the White settler population. Behind official rhetoric of 'fairness' in the treatment of colonial subjects, 'natives' were subject to restrictions and obligations under colonial rule not applied to 'persons of European descent,' including certain taxes, access to many public spaces, education, government jobs and legislated justice.

The absolutism characteristic of colonial rule was not the simple extension of the routine practices of the British government to its overseas territories. With the 'Glorious' Revolution of 1688, and the 1689 Bill of Rights that followed, the English monarchy lost its primacy over parliament, and in the Victorian era (the latter two-thirds of the 19th century), the English journalist Walter Bagehot could famously quip, 'The Queen reigns, but she does not rule.' The absolutism appropriated for the imperial government was, then, a pragmatic re-creation, a reconstituted template from a bygone era. The colonial government was not the first site where this form of power was deployed. Perry Anderson (1974, 24 *et seq*) notes how absolutism in early modern Europe re-appropriated an idealized version of 'the jurisprudence of antiquity,' i.e., ancient Roman law, in its struggle to discipline the feudal vassals. In a very similar maneuver, British imperialism re-appropriated early modern absolutism in order to shore up colonial domination.

5 Colonial administrator turned historian Anthony Kirk-Greene (1979, 1980, 1991, 1999, 2000) contributed substantially to our understanding of the nuts and bolts of colonial administration. For an assessment, see Jackson (2004).

6 An upper-class background was an unwritten requirement for governorship. Many governors were obliged to partially finance their family's travel, their personal furnishings and other accoutrements of the post (Williams 2011). Virtually all governors had to generate the bulk of their office's operational costs through local taxation.

In both instances, it was 'the threat of peasant unrest' that was 'unspokenly constitutive of the Absolutist state' (ibid., 23).

Despite the absolutism at the core of its authority, imperial government was a nominally liberal legal order (Pitts 2005, Hussain 2003). Its capacity for illiberal and discretionary violence was sanctioned by the prevailing ethos of embattled government but was seldom spelled out in explicit terms. The encoding of absolutist prerogative in the governmental arrangements of the colony implied the creation of a dual personality for the governor. He [sic!] was at once publicly accessible, obliged to account for and justify sovereign acts against the backdrop of the constitutional order's nominal liberalism. At the same time, the governor was an opaque embodiment, beyond public, even legal scrutiny or sanction. It is this bundle of paradoxes – of race, law and personhood – that lies at the core of the imperial form of power and of the politico-legal apparatus that constituted colonial government. Since substantial elements of this imperial form of power are reproduced as postcolonial sovereignty, it will be useful to unpack this paradoxical assemblage further.

## A profile of imperial power

The first feature of the imperial form of power, to state the obvious, is its centralized and unbridled scope. A second defining feature of imperial power is the sacred (or 'transcendental') basis of the sovereign's presumed legitimacy. The sacred, as Giorgio Agamben (1991, 105; cited in Fitzpatrick 2005, 53) has noted, 'is necessarily an ambiguous and circular concept' – necessarily, because the sacred cannot be made directly visible. The legitimation of power through reference to its sacred roots commonly relies on supplementary secular support in the form of military might or legal script.

Monarchist English philosopher John Locke (2005[1690], §205) had this to say about the properties of the sovereign's 'transcendental' legitimacy in the early modern era:

> [I]n some countries, the person of the prince by the law is sacred; and so, whatever he commands or does, his person is still free from all question or violence, not liable to force, or any judicial censure or condemnation. ...[T]here cannot be a wiser constitution: for ... the inconveniency of some particular mischiefs, that may happen sometimes, when a heady prince comes to the throne, are well recompensed by the peace of the public, and security of the government, in the person of the chief magistrate, thus set out of the reach of danger: it being safer for the body, that some few private men should be sometimes in danger to suffer, than that the head of the republic should be easily, and upon slight occasions, exposed.

In other words, a prerogativist form of power blessed with sacred impunity is justified by the peace and stability that unquestioned authority ensures. Early modern absolutism was legitimized by its apologists, most notably King James I,[7] via a doctrine known as the 'divine right of Kings' (Figgis 1922 [1896], Engster 2001; see also Hadfield 1949). The sacred source of monarchical legitimacy lifted the king above competing, countervailing (and incessantly inter-warring) local authorities in the early stages of European state formation. In retrospect, it was a successful strategy. The 'divine' kings who prevailed in the early modern era spearheaded the consolidation of unified proto-states in England and France. These kingdoms then provided the model for the European system of mutual interstate recognition codified in the accords of Westphalen in 1648.

Academic literature on kingship underscores the sacred aspect of early modern sovereignty (Engster 2001, Graeber & Sahlins 2016). Sacred sovereignty appears widely (in Schmitt, Kantorowicz and Agamben, for example) as a condition of possibility for the gradual consolidation of the early modern state. These authors argue that in order for a state to subsume fragmented and divisive principalities and political communities under its authority, a transcendental form of legitimacy was required (see also Corrigan & Sayer 1985). Early modern sovereigns were kings and princes, hereditary titles for the most part, who competed with one another and for the military and fiduciary control of previously fragmented territories. As Engster (2001) demonstrates, no temporal leadership qualities were sufficient to achieve the sort of cohesion that early modern state formation instantiated; it was primarily through co-opting some degree of God's will, or divine provenance, previously monopolized by the Church, that the successful early modern kings and princes shored up their temporal legitimacy.

It is not coincidental, then, that Zambia's early presidents – Kaunda and Chiluba in particular – also labored to establish a divine basis for their powers. Through his doctrine of humanism, Kenneth Kaunda (1973, 70–71; cited in Dillon-Malone 1989, 39, 42) promoted the idea that 'in the institution of the State, Man is confronted with power in the most absolute sense that can be known on earth … the State is not the source of power, it merely mediates power derived from God.' Kaunda, echoing James I, thus sought to portray himself as the human embodiment of the divine state. Chiluba, for his part, sought to spiritually bolster his political legitimacy through the declaration of Zambia as a Christian nation, under his benevolent stewardship.[8] Through these maneuvers,

7 James I (1616; cited in Burgess 1992, 837): 'THE State of MONARCHIE is the supremest thing upon earth: For Kings are not onely GODS Lieutenants upon earth, and sit upon GODS throne, but even by GOD himselfe they are called Gods.'

8 Chiluba's declaration of Zambia as a Christian nation was initially enunciated in his private capacity, but later introduced as a presidential amendment to the 1996 republican constitution. Upon his election in 1991, Chiluba invited leaders of Zambia's dynamic evangelical churches to carry out cleansing rituals to drive out evil spirits at State House, the president's official residence, before taking residence. Similarly, an 'anointing service' was conducted by the Council of Churches in Zambia, the Evangelical Fellowship of Zambia and the Episcopal Conference of Zambia, Zambia's three main Christian organizations (I.O. Phiri 2003, 405–6). See also David Gordon's (2012, 192–8) critical discussion of the effects of Chiluba's political evangelism.

presidents Kaunda and Chiluba evoked a version of the divine right of kings, originally intended to undergird the British monarchy, in support of their presidential authority.

The third feature of the imperial form of power derives directly from its transcendental character. This is where Kantorowicz's thesis about the two-body problem of the monarch comes to bear on the argument. Kantorowicz (1957) shows how lawyers in the early modern period belabored the apparent contradiction between the mundane and divine embodiments of the monarch. Contemporary texts – Kantorowicz cites sources ranging from medieval legal scholars to Shakespeare's *Richard III* – portrayed the early modern kings of Britain as possessing two distinct bodies – a mortal, 'temporal' manifestation, as well as an immortal persona, which survived the death of the human form and persisted in the eternal sovereignty of the state. Kantorowicz's thesis hinges on the testimony of 16th-century legal theorist Edmund Plowden (1816, 212a; cited in Kantorowicz 1957, 7), who proposed that

> the King has in him two Bodies, *viz.*, a Body natural, and a Body politic. His Body natural (if it can be considered in itself) is a Body mortal, subject to all infirmities that come by Nature or Accident, to the Imbecility of Infancy or old Age, and to the Defects that happen to the natural Bodies of other People. But his Body politic is a Body that cannot be seen or handled, consisting of the Policy and Government, and constituted for the Direction of the People, and the Management of the public weal, and this Body is utterly void of Infancy and old Age, and other natural Defects and Imbecilities, which the Body natural is subject to, and for this Cause, what the King does in his Body politic, cannot be invalidated or frustrated by any Disability in his natural Body.[9]

While Plowden does not directly invoke the divinity of the king's body politic, this passage is clearly a legalist expression of political theology.[10] The affinity of the English monarch and God (*Rex Angliae Dei gratia*), an ideological pivot of early modern government, thrived under colonial rule, as Ranger suggests. It has, indeed, persisted in ritual canon to the present day.[11]

9 The generality of this paradox is evident in Quinta Jurecic's (2017) somewhat whimsical argument about Donald Trump's tweeting behavior. Jurecic channels Kantorowicz when she claim that 'the distinction between @POTUS and @realDonaldTrump is the distinction between the office and the person who fills it, what we might call the President's "Twitter politic" and his "Twitter natural."'

10 According to Schmitt (1922), all key concepts of the modern doctrine of the state are secularized theological concepts (see Vinx 2019). For his part, Kantorowicz (1957, 8) notes how the etymology of the body politic is rooted in the concept of the king's *character angelicus*: 'The body politic of kingship appears as a likeness of the "holy sprites and angels" because it represents, like the angels, the Immutable within Time.'

11 For example, the title (or 'style') of the late British monarch was 'Elizabeth the Second, by the Grace of God, of the United Kingdom of Great Britain and Northern Ireland and of

The *fourth* and summary characteristic of the imperial form of power is its penchant for decisionism. This follows logically from the transcendental nature of sovereign authority and its dual embodiment. It is the sovereign, as Carl Schmitt (2005 [1922], 1) asserted, who 'decides on the exception.' This was enunciated succinctly by Locke (ibid., §160), who proclaimed that '[t]his power to act according to discretion, for the public good, without the prescription of the law, and sometimes even against it, is that which is called prerogative.' The capacity to suspend the prevailing legal order, and to exercise discretionary power at will, was the prerogative of imperial monarchs, their colonial governors and, now, of postcolonial presidents. As contemporary affairs are again making clear, the status of decisionist powers within nominally democratic government is a systemic and unresolved paradox (e.g., Scheuerman 2008).[12]

These then are the core elements of the imperial form of power, which framed colonial constitution-making in many British colonial territories. The question remains, however, of how this paradoxical bundle of early modern principles and beliefs was smuggled across space and time to inform constitutional provisions for the colonial governor's authority, and ultimately for postcolonial presidentialism. On the one hand, we can identify colonial constitutional provisions that enable prerogativism; on the other hand, prerogativism relies on 'pre-textual' conventions of imperial liberalism. To understand this latter form of continuity, I turn to Russian literary theorist Mikhail Bakhtin's notion of the chronotope, as recently revived for use in socio-legal analysis by Canadian legal anthropologist Mariana Valverde.

## Adventures of prerogativism in space/time

In devising his notion of chronotope, Russian scholar Mikhail Bakhtin was interested in the genealogy of literary elements – plot, setting, characterization and so on – in European literature.[13] He worked out an analytic for describing the genesis of the modern novel through the identification of aesthetic elements in earlier forms of literature. In Bakhtin's (1981, 250) usage, chronotopes are space/time assemblages, the 'organizing centers for the fundamental narrative events of the novel.' At its most basic, a chronotope can be a particular site (the road, the castle, the salon) where literary action takes place. Bakhtin insists, however, that any such site is inextricably intertwined with the specific forms of time through which action is portrayed. The time of the road is encapsulated in specific kinds of transient encounters; an encounter in a salon has a biographical character and

Her other Realms and Territories Queen, Head of the Commonwealth, Defender of the Faith.' Her royal coat of arms includes the phrase 'Dieu et mon droit' (God and my right), a residual of the early modern monarchy (first adopted by Henry V [1386–1422]).

12 On the distinction between decisionism and prerogativism, see Chapter 2.

13 Bakhtin's (1981) influential essay 'Forms of time and of the chronotope in the novel' was originally composed in the 1930s but not published (in Russian) until 1975 (Bemong et al. 2010), the year of his death.

so on. A chronotope, then, depicts a particular narrative device characterized by a specific unity of time and space, of sites and occurrences.

Bakhtin allowed that the term 'chronotope' has usefulness beyond the realm of literature. He noted (1981, 84) that he used the term 'almost as a metaphor (almost but not entirely).' He also had this to say about the historicity of chronotopes (1981, 249n; emphasis added):

> Cultural and literary traditions (including the most ancient) are preserved and continue to live not in the individual subjective memory of a single individual and not in some kind of collective "psyche," but rather *in the objective forms that culture itself assumes* (including the forms of language and spoken speech), and in this sense they are inter-subjective and inter-individual (and consequently social).

It is not, then, unreasonable to apply Bakhtin's notion of the chronotope to the juridical realm. Since law is, if anything, an 'objective cultural form,' it would seem quite natural to substitute 'the juridical' for the 'literary' in Bakhtin's observations about the chronotope. This, in effect, is precisely what Mariana Valverde (2015) has done. In her discussion on the adjudication of indigenous territorial rights in Canada, Valverde uses the chronotope to depict the role that the 'Honour of the Crown' plays in juridical contestations between the Canadian state and indigenous First Nations.

Valverde employs Bakhtin's concept to illuminate the imperial legalities at play in struggles over indigenous land rights in Canada. I will take a brief detour into Valverde's use of the chronotope, as it has proved useful for understanding two crucial points. One is the way that a governmental practice embodies social relations rooted in a particular spatiotemporal configuration. The second is the way that a chronotope, such as that of early modern absolutism, can migrate from one place and time to another. It was by following Valverde's lead, that it seemed plausible that the chronotope of absolutist sovereignty might replant itself from early modern England to (post)colonial Zambia. I thus take her example a step further and attempt to disinter the chronotope of early modern absolutism from (post)colonial constitutional canon.

Valverde's argument focuses on empirical details that are specific to postcolonial Canada, where the 'received' common law of the former colonial metropolis has been 'domesticated' alongside (but with a legal status superior to) indigenous forms of legality. Her account revolves around the 'bizarre' (180) notion of the mystical spatiotemporality of the Crown and thus has general relevance for thinking about the relationship between imperial liberalism and postcolonial legality. Valverde's essay demonstrates how a 'neo-medieval' (147) chronotope, the 'Honour of the Crown,' born in and of the early modern English state, has insinuated itself into 21st-century Canadian jurisprudence. She finds this chronotope at work in juridical efforts to resolve territorial conflicts in Canada between the Canadian state and indigenous First Nations.

In the disputes scrutinized by Valverde, the state has come to recognize the legitimacy of indigenous claims, while nonetheless refusing to acknowledge the genuine sovereignty of native Canadian peoples. The justification for withholding genuine sovereignty is a 'transcendental' one: to allow First Nations to rescind their allegiance to the Canadian state would be an affront to the 'Crown's Honour.' That said, 'it is precisely the mystical spatiotemporal logic of the Crown's virtues ... that enabled aboriginal people to begin holding provincial governments to account' (142).

Valverde's analysis shows that ('non-modern') legal chronotopes can and do migrate from context to context, across temporal and spatial distances, and that such migrations can have paradoxical politico-legal effects. This substantiates the hypothesis that the chronotope of early modern absolutism, appropriated in the first place for the assembly of an imperial form of power, can and does exercise active agency in the constitution of postcolonial power in Zambia. Valverde's example has another useful lesson as well. Even within the allegedly hyper-rational domain of liberal legality, there reside mystical vestiges of a bygone ontology that evade direct scrutiny. The 'Honour of the Crown,' like presidential prerogativism, is not available for analytical dissection in a court of law. Despite the rhetoric of juridico-bureaucratic reasonableness that undergirds common law jurisprudence, some sacred cows graze where they please.

The paradoxical features of the imperial form of power passed on to Zambia's presidents via the jurisdiction's postcolonial constitutions. One evident illustration of this paradox, as we will see in Chapter 7, is the case of Mr Chiluba who claimed to have two bodies: one official, visible and eternal; and another private one, opaque and temporal. Mr Chiluba, like any other human being, has only one body; how then do we reconcile the paradox? In line with my efforts to undermine the either/or juxtaposition of liberal theory, I propose viewing postcolonial power through a both/and optic. In other words, Mr Chiluba's two bodies are best understood not in mutually exclusive opposition to one another but, invoking Donna Haraway (1991, 180), as a complex interiority that is 'more than one but less than two.' Chapter 7 demonstrates ways in which the postcolonial president's two bodies have a different relationship to the enabling and constraining provisions of constitutional legality. It would appear – paradoxically – that the president's private, mortal corpus can operate more freely below the moral radar of the juridical system. At the same time, Mr Chiluba's license to suspend or at least stand outside the law was contingent upon his occupation of the immortal body of a constitutionally sanctified presidency. The two bodies are empirically inextricable, yet analytically discrete.

The aim of this redescription of presidential power is to 'disrupt the analytical dualisms that ha[ve] ... become part of ... proposals for emancipation via political and theoretical unification' (de la Cadena 2015, 31). The proposals I seek to disrupt are those which chart the path toward the 'emancipation' of postcolonial politics through unification under the banner of 'political liberalism.' More precisely, I argue against a political strategy that seeks to repair postcolonial government via the exorcism of the president's (inherently corrupt) temporal body. I do so not out of any affection for corruption, or for authoritarian rule; far from it. I submit, nevertheless, that efforts to separate the president's two bodies from one another, as political liberalism prescribes, will either fail or result in irreparable damage to the body politick, i.e., the possibilities of genuinely popular government. There is, of course, ample evidence of both outcomes.

# 7 'Lawfully illegal'[1]

## Part I: A tale of two trials

Zambia's second president, Frederick Jacob Titus Chiluba,[2] has the paradoxical distinction of being the first Anglophone African president to come to power (in 1991) via a peaceful transition from single- to multiparty politics, while also being the first African president to face trial on charges of corruption in his official capacity (Rakner 2003, Lewis 2009). This chapter examines the litigation against Chiluba initiated by the Zambian state between 2003 and 2009. There were, in fact, two separate trials: Civil proceedings in the High Court of England and Wales in London and a criminal trial in a Lusaka magistrate's court. Chiluba was acquitted in Lusaka but found liable for the misuse of public funds in London. Using trial materials and first-hand ethnographic data, I consider the basis of Chiluba's claim that his alleged abuse of public office was, in the former president's own words, 'lawfully illegal.' By virtue of the uncommon body of evidence that came to light in the course of the investigations into Chiluba's actions – including bank records of a Zambian intelligence service account – the events around these trials provide a unique opportunity to think about the roots, nature and limits of executive power in the postcolonial world.

The narrative of this chapter begins with Zambia's 'war on corruption,' a concerted and ultimately unsuccessful campaign initiated by Chiluba's successor, President Levy Mwanawasa, to hold President Chiluba to account for the alleged theft of considerable sums of public money. Mwanawasa's war on corruption has many unique features but is, in many respects, representative of a wider front of similar campaigns, often supported financially by Western governments to promote 'good governance' (or discipline inimical leaders) in poor, aid-dependent postcolonies (Abrahamsen 2000; Seidman et al. 2007). As I hope to show, a close look at this campaign and its consequences brings to light complex issues concerning postcolonial intersections of law and politics, disputes around

1 This is a quote from President Chiluba (n.d., 19), referring to his presidential powers.

2 Chiluba (1943–2011) often referred to as FTJ, was a chairperson of the Zambia Congress of Trade Unions and a founding member of the Movement for Multiparty Democracy. He served as Zambia's president for two terms (1991–1996, 1996–2001).

DOI: 10.4324/9780429198984-11

constitutionalism and the paradoxical manifestations of the postcolonial form of power that I term political legality.

## *The specter of presidentialism*

The end of the Cold War precipitated the demise of de jure single-party rule in most of Africa. While some of the new pluralist constitutions limited presidential terms in office, courts, legislatures and constituent assemblies across the continent have tended to preserve the core elements of executive discretion. In 1996, the Zambian parliament for example enacted a two-term limit on presidential incumbency but preserved far-reaching derogation clauses (cf. Hatchard 1995, Beyani 1998).[3] As already noted, the Zambian head of state's powers is today as extensive and arbitrary as those of the last colonial governor of Northern Rhodesia.[4]

Zambia's war on corruption lies within this juridico-political context. It was instigated in 2002 by Zambia's third president, Levy Mwanawasa (1948–2008).[5] The story is rich in incidents and ironies. As in most stories of political intrigue, the devil is in the details. Although the narrative is intricate, involving many turns and personalities, it must be rendered in full for its paradoxical logic to emerge. The transcripts of the two completed[6] Chiluba trials reveal in rich and subtle detail the extent to which Zambian presidents have recourse to a wide range of powers and resources beyond judicial and legislative oversight. These are grounded in, but not limited to, the state's security apparatus and especially the intelligence services. Republican presidents are conventionally also the leaders of the ruling party, and their ability to conceal significant actions and transactions from all but a few chosen confidents renders both 'law' and 'politics' as unreliable paths to public accountability. It also calls into question the efficacy of liberal legality in the face of presidential prerogative. Given the persistent failure of well-organized efforts to undermine prerogativism in favor of political liberalism,

3 A derogation clause allows for the suspension or breach of constitutional or other statutory rights under exceptional circumstances, such as war, catastrophe or public emergency (Higgins 1976/77, 281).

4 Compare, for example, Zambia's Public Order Act (which grants the executive virtually unlimited powers of derogation) from the late colonial era of the 1950s, through the first independence constitution of 1964, with the constitutional provisions of 1996. Literally nothing has changed (see Ruedisili 1996). See Chanda (1997) for a similar appraisal of the State Security Act. Interestingly, it was only the interim constitution of 1963 (which oversaw the period of limbo during which executive authority passed from the colonial governor to an independent president) that explicitly delimited the emergency powers of the head of state.

5 Mwanawasa, a lawyer by training and profession, was Zambia's third president. He had been vice-president under Frederick Chiluba from 1991 to 1994, and occupied the presidency from early 2002 until his untimely mid-term death in August 2008.

6 Hearings on Mr Chiluba's abuse of office in Lusaka aborted twice due to prosecutorial mismanagement, before eventually going to term.

this example also evokes questions about liberalism as an empirical standard for evaluating postcolonial government.

At the core of the Chiluba saga is a complex and highly politicized legal process. The indictment against President Chiluba involved numerous counts of theft and was pursued in two jurisdictions. The process begins with a dramatic political maneuver – the National Assembly's lifting of Chiluba's immunity to criminal investigation and prosecution in 2002. Seven years later, in August 2009, a lower court judge acquitted Chiluba of all charges, including that of stealing $500,000 in public money. Two years earlier in London, a High Court judge had found Chiluba liable for defrauding the Zambian people to the tune of roughly $46 million.

There is compelling evidence, discussed below, to the effect that during Mr Chiluba's two terms in office (1991–2001), he diverted a considerable amount of money from the public coffers for his own personal ends. Estimates of the extent of Mr Chiluba's purported mischief vary from hundreds of thousands to hundreds of millions of dollars. What constitutes 'public' funds, however, proved controversial in the course of the trials. At no point did Chiluba admit to any wrongdoing. Deeply rooted loopholes in Zambia's postcolonial legal order permitted the president to appropriate public funds in ways that are, arguably, immune to judicial sanction. It was widely believed both within and beyond Zambia's borders, that Mr Chiluba contravened established liberal conventions. And yet, demonstrating his *legal* culpability under Zambia's ostensibly liberal constitution proved difficult. It should be noted at this point that Chiluba's prosecution over seven years of court proceedings was, if not orchestrated, clearly bankrolled by Western governments, with Zambia's former colonial overlord, the United Kingdom, in the role of the leading protagonist.[7] This may be largely incidental. It is pertinent, however, to underscore how British involvement in addressing Chiluba's behavior represented yet another residual element of imperial power at work in Zambia's political domain.

## *The spoils of security*

Chiluba's defense hinged to a large degree upon his allegedly inscrutable role as the primary protector of national security. It is useful, then, to briefly review what this might mean in practice. The sovereign power of the Zambian state had been under external assault since its birth in October 1964. The apartheid regimes of South Africa and (Southern) Rhodesia (now Zimbabwe) waged covert war against Zambia for decades in retribution for her support to national liberation movements in Angola, Mozambique, Namibia, Zimbabwe and South Africa. Heavily indebted single-party regimes, like Zambia under President Kenneth

7 Ryder (2011) notes that 'the UK Department for International Development (DfID) took the unusual step of working closely with enforcement agencies, investigators, and others in London to secure assistance for the Zambians.'

Kaunda and his United National Independence Party (UNIP), also came under intense pressure from international financial institutions via the harsh policy conditions associated with structural adjustment loans of the 1980s (Simutanyi 1996). Harnessing harsh International Monetary Fund (IMF) conditionalities, alongside 'softer' development modalities (e.g., 'democracy support'), Ronald Reagan and Margaret Thatcher, among others, waged an aggressive campaign for regime change against Kaunda throughout the 1980s (see Chapter 3). The economic inefficiencies of the UNIP administration, exacerbated by donor-imposed austerity measures, help explain UNIP's dwindling popular support and the smooth and rapid fashion in which Kaunda was deposed in 1991 in the immediate aftermath of the Cold War (Mwanakatwe 1994). There were, it is safe to say, tangible national security concerns on the president's plate.

UNIP's successor administration, headed by President Frederick Chiluba and his Movement for Multiparty Democracy (MMD), were devout disciples of deregulated market-driven development (i.e., neoliberalism, or what was at the time termed the Washington Consensus). Immediately upon acceding to office, Chiluba embarked on dismantling the sprawling parastatal economy, including the core extractive sector. MMD politicians and their cronies went in for the quick kill, selling off the marketable pieces of former state companies. Unfortunately for the economy, the dismantled bits and pieces of the industrial stock were generally not redeployed in ways that would have provided employment for redundant workers or tax revenues for cash-strapped public services. Privatization had a dynamic effect on the national economy in the longer term, but its immediate human costs were dire (e.g., Pletcher 2000).

By the mid-1990s, Zambia's political elite had consumed the windfalls of privatization and was looking eagerly for other sources of rent. The civil war in the Democratic Republic of the Congo, rich in natural resources, raged just across Zambia's northern border and was of keen interest to Chiluba's circle. Chiluba's efforts to access the spoils of the Congolese civil war were not particularly successful, however. Chiluba was crowded out by more experienced and better-connected ex-freedom fighters like presidents Kagame (Rwanda), Mugabe (Zimbabwe), Museveni (Uganda) and Nujoma (Namibia). Not to be completely left behind, Chiluba created a niche for himself as a Southern African Development Community (SADC) mediator in the Great Lakes Region peace process (BBC 1999).[8] This role, at last, provided a means for Chiluba to insert himself and his covert intelligence apparatus into the high-stakes political business that fed off the war engulfing the eastern Congo.

Opaque dealings with foreign politicians were a key factor in the widespread suspicions concerning Mr Chiluba's efforts at self-enrichment during the early years of economic liberalization. His increasingly authoritarian style of

8 SADC is an intergovernmental body consisting of Angola, Botswana, the Democratic Republic of Congo, Lesotho, Madagascar, Malawi, Mauritius, Mozambique, Namibia, Seychelles, South Africa, Swaziland, United Republic of Tanzania, Zambia and Zimbabwe.

government also contributed to public animus toward the president, eventually enabling President Mwanawasa to have him indicted for abuse of office. This apparent gesture toward the principles of liberal legality had several unintended consequences. One of these involved a senior government lawyer, Mr Mukelabai Mukelabai, the Director of Public Prosecutions (DPP). After parliament lifted Chiluba's immunity to investigation, Mr Mukelabai became the first coordinator of the ad hoc Task Force against Corruption that Mwanawasa established to investigate and prosecute Mr Chiluba. Mr Mwanawasa's Task Force is as clearly an expression of presidential prerogativism as are Mr Chiluba's 'lawful illegalities,' and its story bears recounting in detail.

## Act 1: Deposing the DPP

Mr Mukelabai Mukelabai had had an earlier legal encounter with Mr Chiluba. In 1989, as a radical trade unionist championing the still clandestine Movement for Multiparty Democracy, Chiluba was arrested and charged by the UNIP government for illegal assembly in the town of Monze, in Zambia's Southern Province. The state advocate assigned to this politically volatile case was Mukelabai Mukelabai, a young prosecutor just out of law school. Mr Mukelabai was the son of a policeman, also a state prosecutor. From his father, Mr Mukelabai absorbed a deep respect for the law and an equally profound skepticism toward politics. Mukelabai lost the Monze case against Chiluba, who went on to win the republican presidency in the 1991 multiparty elections. Mr Mukelabai eventually graduated up the ranks to the Lusaka headquarters of the state prosecution apparatus under Chiluba's administration. In this capacity, he obediently prosecuted a number of controversial cases against Chiluba's political enemies who had been indicted on trumped-up treason charges, harassed and eventually acquitted (see Chapter 5). In 1998, Chiluba appointed Mr Mukelabai – by then one of the country's most experienced prosecutors – to the powerful office of the Director of Public Prosecutions.[9] This was a major recognition for Mr Mukelabai; the DPP is one of a handful of public officials whose immunity from outside interference is explicitly protected by the constitution.

According to his co-workers interviewed for this study, Mr Mukelabai ran the DPP's office under the Chiluba administration with a firm hand and uncompromising professionalism. The independent press, however, published evidence of the MMD's corrupt dealings on a daily basis, and Mukelabai recalls the deep professional frustrations of this period with a sigh and a shake of his head. Professionalism, he insisted, demanded that he remain aloof from politics. When the Oasis Forum launched a spirited campaign to block Chiluba's unconstitutional bid for a third term in office in the 2001 elections (Gould 2006; see Chapter 5), Mr Mukelabai remained true to his father's legacy and kept to

9 This section draws on interviews I conducted with Mr Mukelebai in Cape Town, in September 2005.

the sidelines.[10] But when President Levy Mwanawasa asked parliament to lift Chiluba's immunity in 2002, Mr Mukelabai felt that the opportunity had come to 'nail' Chiluba for his corrupt dealings. Convinced that Mwanawasa was serious about attacking corruption and restoring rule of law to Zambia's beleaguered government, Mr Mukelabai approached the president in his role as chief state prosecutor and proposed a plan for a coordinated campaign to bring the primary culprits, and especially Mr Chiluba, to justice.

## *Politics of governance*

President Mwanawasa's announcement in 2002 that he was instigating a war on corruption received a lukewarm response from Zambia's liberal elite. Mwanawasa had yet to assuage the skepticism that Mr Chiluba's anointment had cast over his integrity. In contrast, Mwanawasa's move was applauded loudly among Zambia's international creditors. In the late 1990s, controversies around human rights and governance abuses under President Chiluba led a number of Zambia's so-called 'development partners,' spearheaded by the Scandinavian block, to cut back radically on their funding commitments. The Danish Ambassador to Zambia, for example, noted in 1999 that his government 'has placed emphasis on good governance and human rights' as a condition for continuing with direct budget support (Human Rights Watch 1999). By the 2001 elections, much of the donor community was convinced that poor governance, and especially corruption, was the main obstacle to development in Zambia. Mr Mwanawasa's distaste for corruption was genuine enough. In 1994, he had resigned from his post as republican vice-president allegedly (he made no public statement about his motives) in protest over Chiluba's protection of Michael Sata, a controversial cabinet minister. (Mr Sata would be elected president in 2011.) At the same time, Mwanawasa was also aware that his success in office was contingent on securing debt relief from the donor community under the World Bank's Heavily Indebted Poor Countries (HIPC) initiative.[11] From the donor perspective, corruption was inimical to liberal progress; meeting the donors half-way on improving Zambia's governance record was a necessary condition for debt relief.

Against this backdrop, President Mwanawasa was understandably receptive to Mr Mukelabai's proposal for an anti-corruption campaign, and work on this endeavor started in 2002. The idea was to set up an inter-agency task force against corruption to bring together the state's main investigative bodies and

10 The establishment of the Oasis Forum was brokered by Mark Chona, an ex-adjutant of former President Kaunda with close ties to the intelligence community. Mr Chona will reappear in this narrative shortly.

11 The aim of HIPC was to restructure or forgive unmanageable debt to donor institutions for countries that met specific conditions (such as stabilizing their economies and privatizing public assets). Toward the end of Chiluba's reign, the total debt in 1998 was more than two times gross domestic product and almost seven times exports (Andersson et al. 2000, 45).

coordinate their work with the public prosecutor's office.[12] The aim, according to Mr Mukelabai, was to pool resources for an intense investigation, bring a few of the main culprits to trial and get some quick, high-profile convictions to show that it was possible to bring down previously untouchable political players. Mr Chiluba and his head of intelligence, Xavier Chungu, were the main targets. With Messrs Chiluba and Chungu behind bars, DPP Mukelabai thought, the Task Force could be dissolved and subsequent investigations and prosecutions would revert back to the relevant specialized agencies.

Initially, Mr Mukelabai ran the Task Force from the DPP's office, an unprecedented administrative challenge for any public authority in Zambia. As the complexity of the cases became apparent, he realized that his office lacked the capacity to adequately build the prosecution cases. Mark Chona, already familiar from his role in organizing the Oasis Forum (Chapter 5), was called in to take over the management of the Task Force. Over the three years he headed the Task Force, Mr Chona mobilized large amounts of donor support for legal actions against Chiluba.[13] Invoking the lack of competent expertise in the DPP's office for investigating and prosecuting complicated corruption cases, Chona suggested that the Task Force hire private lawyers to beef up the team. Two brothers, Mutembo and Nchima Nchito, a pair of young, up-and-coming Lusaka lawyers, were brought on board, despite having no previous investigative credentials. It is worth noting that none of the arrangements associated with Mr Mwanawasa's anti-corruption campaign, from the establishment of the Task Force itself, by presidential decree, to the employment of private prosecutors, had any grounding in Zambian administrative law (see Ntomba 2016, 96–100). There is no legislation or statutory instrument on record defining the powers or limitations of these organs and individuals. Indeed, in some important respects this alleged exercise in good governance was run much the way that covert security forces function – on an ad hoc basis and in a gray zone of legality.

Mukelabai Mukelabai's original vision of an intensive six to eight-month campaign fell apart as the Task Force became embroiled in internal politics. As two initial indictments against Chiluba collapsed through prosecutorial mismanagement, the Task Force team began to quarrel about the chain of command, about prosecution strategy and, tellingly, about money. Mark Chona and the Nchitos were private agents, on lucrative donor-scale contracts, while Mukelabai and his team of state prosecutors were drawing modest civil servant salaries. As their differences escalated, Mukelabai tried to have the Nchito brothers removed from the prosecution. Mark Chona and the Nchitos approached President Mwanawasa, accusing Mukelabai of sabotaging Task Force operations. The private actors Chona and Nchito appear to

12 The main agencies involved in the TFAC were the Zambia Police, the Drug Enforcement Commission, the Office of the President and the Anti-Corruption Commission.

13 The Task Force's primary cooperating partners were Denmark, Ireland, the Netherlands, Norway, Sweden, the United Kingdom, as well as the United States. Donors 'provided three-quarters of the funding needed' (Ryder 2011, 5).

have convinced Mwanawasa that Mukelabai had become an obstacle to the war on corruption and together they conspired to have him removed from the operation. Perhaps the fact that Mr Mukelabai had initially been appointed to the DPP post by President Chiluba contributed to their animus. There was no legal way, in any event, that the head of the governmental prosecution apparatus could be involuntarily sidelined from the state's biggest case. The constitution was unequivocal – the Director of Public Prosecutions shall not be 'subject to direction or control by any other authority.' The only way to get rid of Mukelabai was to have a presidentially appointed tribunal of three High Court judges find him guilty of 'misconduct.'

President Mwanawasa pressured Mukelabai to resign and offered him the carrot of a 'study leave' in India and an eventual position on the High Court (interview, 12 September 2005). Mukelabai initially acquiesced, but on reflection (and the advice of his attorney) decided to reject the deal, invoking the DPP's constitutional protection. In an unusual act of defiance, Minister of Justice George Kunda also challenged Mr Mwanawasa's efforts and issued a statement in support of Mr Mukelabai on 7 January 2004. On 12 January 2004, Mwanawasa held an ad hoc press conference at which he disclosed that he had received two 'anonymous letters from the public' alleging that Mukelabai had held secret eight-hour meetings over the Christmas holidays with spy master Xavier Chungu in the southern tourist town of Livingstone. The implication was that Mukelabai was conniving with Chiluba, through Chungu, to sabotage the prosecution case against the former president.

On 15 January, President Mwanawasa appointed a tribunal to investigate the charges against Mr Mukelabai. The tribunal sat for three months in early 2004 and found no evidence of misconduct. Despite the fact that Chungu was under heavy surveillance, the government could not produce a single witness placing Mukelabai and Chungu in a meeting together. Ironically, there would have been no obstacle to the DPP interrogating Chungu or negotiating with him at any time in the privacy of his own office. This was fully within his mandate as DPP.

Despite finding no misconduct, the tribunal recommended that Mukelabai be 'retired in the public interest.' President Mwanawasa put the recommendation into immediate effect, which amounted to the unconstitutional termination of the DPP's appointment (Ntomba 2016, 123). The consensus among the many legal experts I interviewed in the wake of Mukelabai's dismissal was that Mwanawasa and Mukelabai had both erred. President Mwanawasa clearly overstepped his legal mandate, but Mr Mukelabai had left himself open to executive interference. The fact that Mr Mukelabai had allegedly accepted a meeting with the vice-president to discuss prosecutorial strategy, thereby acquiescing to 'direction' by State House, was seen as the fundamental compromise that weakened his immunity. In any event, depressed and disillusioned, Mukelabai opted not to contest the president's action and quietly left the country to take a job in South Africa, heading a research program on organized crime and corruption in the SADC region.[14]

14 A tragic epilogue: I interviewed Mr Mukelabai in Cape Town on 12 September 2005. On 29 September, he was found dead in his Cape Town apartment at the age of 44. According to

## Act 2: Trials of a president

After Mr Mukelabai's departure, the Task Force team continued its work of compiling evidence and building a prosecution case against Chiluba. By September 2004, the Task Force felt it had amassed sufficient evidence to indict the former president. Chiluba was arrested and charged with six counts of 'Theft by a Public Servant contrary to sections 272 and 277 of the Penal Code' (Cap. 87 of the Laws of Zambia).[15] According to Counts 1 and 2, Chiluba, together with Messrs Aaron Chungu and Faustin Kabwe of Access Finance Services, Limited, allegedly stole money in the form of government cheques totaling $175,000. In the remaining charges (Counts 3, 7, 8 and 9), Chiluba is accused, together with Aaron Chungu, Kabwe and/or 'other persons unknown,' of stealing cash belonging to the Zambian government totaling roughly $333,000 (J5–J11).[16] The stolen assets at stake thus amounted to a little more than $500,000. This is significantly less than the sums noted in connection with his earlier arrests,[17] not to mention the $46 million that Chiluba was found to have stolen in a parallel civil suit in a London court (see below).

### *The matrix of plunder*

Behind the legalese lurked a complicated 'matrix of plunder,' as it was coined in the independent *Post* newspaper (25 June 2002; see also Lewis 2009, 136, van Donge 2009). According to Task Force sources 'more than 450 companies, 270 fixed assets, and 170 individuals across the world were estimated to be involved in fraudulent activities linked to Chiluba's administration' (Lewis 2009, 142). The evidence tabled before trial judges in Lusaka and London is significantly more modest in scope. In any case, the indictment charges Chiluba and his co-accused of moving substantial sums of money between multiple banks and companies in several countries, including the United Kingdom, the United States, Belgium and Switzerland.

The prosecution's primary evidence was based on an analysis of Zambia National Commercial Bank (ZNCB) records subpoenaed in the pivotal 'Chiluba

---

the autopsy report, Mr Mukelabai died of internal hemorrhaging, most likely the result of a ruptured intestinal ulcer. There was no indication of anything suspicious related to his death.

15 Charges against Chiluba are duplicated in parallel counts against his co-accused Faustin Kabwe and Aaron Chungu of Access Finance Limited. The reason for the separate counts is that Chiluba is charged in his capacity as a public servant, while the others are accused as private persons. Otherwise, as Magistrate Court Judge Jones Chinyama notes, 'it seems to be the case for the prosecution that the three accused persons acted jointly and together to steal the sums of money alleged' (J6; see note 23).

16 References in this form (i.e., J5) refer to the page (i.e., in this instance, to page 5) of the court judgment of Justice Jones Chinyama as published.

17 Mr Chiluba had been twice arrested after leaving office. Once in February 2003, he was charged with the theft of some $4 million and again, in August 2003 with the theft of $40 million. Both of these cases collapsed due to prosecutorial errors (Lewis 2009, 138–9).

is a thief' defamation proceedings.[18] This evidence showed that the alleged laundering of government funds followed a repetitive pattern.[19] The money originated in the Ministry of Finance from where it was wired to a special Zambia Special Intelligence Service (ZSIS) dollar account (code-named Zamtrop) at the London branch of the Zambia National Commercial Bank. From the Zamtrop account, money was routinely transferred to accounts held by Access Financial Services Limited (AFSL), a Zambian company, or to the London-based law firm of Meer, Care and Desai.[20] A significant amount of the Zamtrop money reflected in the subpoenaed ZNCB records was paid to two American companies (Wilbain Technology, Inc. of Delaware, and Systems Innovations, Inc. of Virginia) in lieu of payments on contracts between these companies and ZSIS (on behalf of the Zambian government). Zamtrop monies held by Meer, Care and Desai found their way into the hands of a Geneva-based haberdashery (for tailor-made shoes and clothing for Mr Chiluba), the Chief Justice of the Zambian Supreme Court, Chiluba's children and so on. Zamtrop monies were also used to buy houses for the two lawyers who defended Chiluba in the 1997 presidential petition case.[21] Prosecution evidence was straightforward and often very detailed. Chiluba was implicated in much of the action but took care to cover his tracks. Sworn testimony had him handing over the keys for the Zamtrop-financed houses to his erstwhile lawyers, and yet not a scrap of paper connecting him directly to the transfer of funds or to the purchasing of the properties was produced in court.

18 On 17 August 2001, the independent *Post* newspaper in Lusaka published an editorial headlined 'A thief for President,' which claimed, among other things, that incumbent President Chiluba had 'diverted money from legitimate purposes to his own personal use.' *Post* editor Fred M'membe and three others were subsequently arrested and indicted for defamation under Section 69 of the Zambian Penal Code, which makes it an offence 'to publish anything, in any form, deemed as tending to bring the office and person of the president into hatred, ridicule or contempt.'

Mr M'membe hired Mutembo Nchito to defend him. On hearing of M'membe's indictment, in January 2002, Nchito expressed his satisfaction because 'it will enable the public to know what Chiluba and his friends were doing while he was in government' (IFEX 2002). To these ends, Nchito obtained a court order in May 2002 to subpoena the bank records of a Zambia intelligence services account at the Zambia National Commercial Bank's London branch. These bank transcripts allowed investigators to reconstruct Chiluba's alleged 'matrix of plunder' (see Lewis 2009, 135–6).

19 The intricacies of the case elude brief description and need not be rehearsed here. For a succinct summary see van Donge (2009) and the original *Post* 'Matrix of Plunder' article of 25 June 2002. Details can also be read from the Chinyama (*The People v Chiluba*) and Smith (*Zambia v Meer*) judgments. The latter maps the 'matrix' in much detail.

20 Meer, Desai and Care were defendants in the London civil case, in connection with which the trial judge found that senior partner Iqbal Meer 'had provided dishonest assistance to the Zambian officials and conspired to misappropriate monies from the Zambian government.' Mr Meer had earlier represented Nelson Mandela in England, and Mandela had given him a character reference. See www.lawsociety.org.uk/newsandevents/news/view=newsarticle.law?NEWSID =340538.

21 This was a case where opposition candidates petitioned the Zambian Supreme Court to rule on the validity of Chiluba's re-election in the 1996 presidential poll.

## *One crime, two verdicts*

This, in brief, was the evidence available to the two courts, one in London and the other in Lusaka, that tried Mr Chiluba on abuse of office. As already noted, one, based on civil hearings in the High Court of England and Wales, Judge Peter Smith found Chiluba guilty. The other, based on criminal charges in Lusaka's magistrate's court with Chief Magistrate Jones Chinyama[22] presiding, resulted in an acquittal. In considering the reasons for this discrepancy, it is instructive to read side by side the findings of the two trials. Civil and criminal trials, of course, work under different regimes of proof. In order to convict defendants in the criminal case, Senior Resident Magistrate Jones Chinyama needed to satisfy himself that the evidence demonstrated guilt 'beyond a reasonable doubt.' In the civil proceedings, in contrast, Judge Smith had greater discretionary leeway to decide whether he could hold Chiluba & co liable for damages. He merely had to weigh the 'balance of probabilities' (§90)[23] and conclude whether it was likely that the defendants had committed fraudulent or dishonest acts.

Because of these differences of process, jurisdiction, legal context and outcome, a systematic comparison of these two actions is complicated, and various credible interpretations of the processes and their outcomes are possible. However, from the point of view of how the legacy of postcolonial legality has contributed to the respective outcomes, these cases are a unique and fertile source of data for scrutinizing the legal foundations of the postcolonial form of power. How were standards of legality constituted in these two cases? How was the constitutionally established exceptional authority of the executive reflected in these proceedings? While doctrinal analysts will be better placed to weigh in on the technical competences of the two judgments, for my purposes it is interesting to scrutinize the divergent ways that the two trial judges labor to make sense of the evidence before them and to justify their respective judgments.

Differences in the standards of proof in the two trials are obviously important to take into account, but they cannot, I believe, fully explain the diametrically opposed outcomes handed down by the two trial judges. This side-by-side reading provides a rare opportunity to examine different approaches to executive discretion and impunity and reveals very different attitudes to the contextual parameters of legality. What is most striking, however, is the ways that both judges, in their fashion, obscure the nature and limits of postcolonial executive prerogative.

### *The People v Chiluba*

It would be hard to overestimate the pressures weighing on Lusaka magistrate justice Jones Chinyama as he formulated his judgment in *The People v Chiluba*

22 Justice Chinyama was elevated to the Supreme Court in 2016.

23 Citations like this (i.e., §90) refer to numbered paragraphs in the Smith judgment.

*and Others* (SSP/124/2004). The case in itself was unprecedented; according to one analyst (Lewis 2009, 130), Chiluba was 'the first African former head of state ever to be tried for serious crimes in a free and fair domestic court process.' Public passions against Chiluba had been systematically stoked by the popular *Post* newspaper since the 1990s. Twice earlier, the Zambian state's case against Chiluba had imploded, and twice Chiluba was re-arrested and fresh charges brought against him. The state was clearly not indifferent to the outcome. While still alive, President Mwanawasa had himself issued a number of statements which could reasonably be considered prejudicial to the case against Chiluba and his co-accused.[24] This was one of the most discussed and politicized cases in the history of the Zambian judiciary.

These pressures are manifest in Chinyama's judgment in several ways. He is, first of all, concerned that his court not be considered inefficient. The case dragged on for nearly five years (from 11 October 2004 to 17 August 2009). He insists, however, that the trial was prolonged for reasons beyond his control and that, in fact, 'the court [only] sat for 135 days denoting a period of about five and a half months' (J2).[25] Against the backdrop of the trial's intense politicization, he belabors the issue of fairness. Alluding to defense concerns that the accused have 'not only been tried in this court but also in the media,' he quips that 'one might add, in the court of public opinion' (J19). Despite these pressures, Chinyama avers resolutely, if improbably, that 'the negative publicity championed by the executive and the press are not factors' in his deliberations, insisting that such pressures 'have no place in deciding the innocence or guilt of the accused persons' (J26).

Justice Chinyama also has a technical problem of law that he needs to dispose of – the question of whether or not President Chiluba was a 'public servant.' It's a tricky question and no doubt the source of considerable reflection. If Chiluba is *not* a public service (as the defense claims), he has been mischarged under the 'Theft by a Public Servant' section of the penal code. This would cast a shadow on the competence of Chinyama's court (since he had allowed the action to proceed) and could possibly lead to the collapse of yet a third, and exceedingly lengthy, attempt to prosecute the former president. If Mr Chiluba, on the other hand, *is* found to be a public servant, this sets the uneasy example of bringing the presidency under the jurisdiction of some rather vague and unpredictable bits of law. This would comprise a quite shaky precedent, and no responsible judge would want his reputation stained by such a crude tactical error.

Much hinges on Judge Chinyama's interpretation of what constitutes public servitude; unfortunately, the law itself gives him little to go by. It is both imprecise and splintered, with bits and pieces appearing in different acts. There is also – and

24 Mwanawasa allegedly announced publicly that Chiluba would be pardoned if he returned 75% of the money he stole from government (Lewis 2009).

25 References to the Chinyama ruling on the Chiluba case (*The People v Chiluba*) take this form, where J ('Judgment') is followed by the page of the report.

tellingly – no solid body of precedent articulating the nuances of presidential accountability. Chinyama finds himself in judicial no-man's-land with a rather illegible map. Existing legislation gives no generic definition of what defines a public servant, but several sections of the constitution and secondary legislation provide unsystematic, but detailed lists of positions both included in and falling outside this category. The presidency is not mentioned in either regard. Despite this general inconclusiveness, Chinyama asserts confidently that 'it is clear from the law that [the President] is not' a public servant. You can almost hear the hearts of the prosecuting attorneys skip a beat when they hear this: Chiluba has been mischarged and will again evade conviction!

Perhaps Chinyama was merely toying with the prosecution. He had good reason to be annoyed, if not with Mutembo Nchito, the Task Force's lead private prosecutor, then at least with Mr Nchito's close ally and business partner, Fred M'membe, whose *Post* newspaper had consistently given Chinyama heat over the long duration of the trial. On the other hand, perhaps the judge was simply perpetrating the dense legal buffer around the head of state, thus feeding the legacy of prerogativist immunity (while also covering his own back). In any event, the prosecution's despondency is short-lived: Chinyama quickly executed a *coup de grâce*. According to a 1973 precedent, he announced, if a

> person is charged with the offence of Theft by Public Servant and he is found not to be a public servant, it is competent to enter a conviction for the offence of Theft contrary to section 272 of the Penal Code. (J278)

Chinyama adjusted the charges to reflect this new reality, returning Chiluba to the sweatbox. Yet, no sooner has Chinyama revised Chiluba's charges, making the former president eligible for conviction, than he declares (abiding by Chiluba's own unsworn testimony) that the monies Chiluba has allegedly stolen may not, *beyond reasonable doubt*, be government property. Thus, (for Count 1),

> the money has not been traced to the Zamtrop account and … even if it were, there is the possibility … that the money could be attributed not only to the Government money in the account but also to the private money that went into the account and whose expenditure has not been accounted for. The ingredients of theft have not been proved. (J279)

The prosecution is not having a good day. The case they had felt was watertight has failed.

## THE PRESIDENT'S GOOD WORD

One of the most unusual gestures in Judge Chinyama's ruling in *The People v Chiluba* is the way he signaled his deference to presidential prerogative by allowing Mr Chiluba to enter *unsworn* testimony into the official transcript. Chiluba's speech (reproduced in Chiluba n.d.) is a carefully rehearsed performance intended to set out the key arguments of his case. Conventionally, unsworn testimony is not legally admissible in court. In an exceptional act of judicial discretion, Chinyama both allowed it and subsequently cited Chiluba's main points in his judgment. Chinyama felt no need to justify his leniency:

> In defence [Chiluba] made an unsworn statement. In law such a statement is not regarded as evidence as it is not given on oath and is not subject to being tested in cross examination. However, I will take it into account in arriving at my decision in this judgment. (J54)

Chiluba's defense involved three main arguments:

1. The money he had allegedly stolen were his personal assets, representing gifts and donations from private sponsors, i.e., 'brothers in the region' (Chiluba n.d., 54) for his individual political projects.
2. The money was kept in a secret ZSIS account, beyond the reach of conventional oversight mechanisms, to protect the anonymity of the donors.
3. Intelligence chief Xavier Chungu alone managed the deployment of these funds on Chiluba's instructions. Chiluba did not get involved in the details of these payments and transfers.

The crux of Chiluba's defense is this: While exercising his responsibilities as head of state, Mr Chiluba was at the same time a private politician heading a political party, i.e., the leader of the Movement for Multiparty Democracy. The charges against him, he claims, are untenable because they conflate these two distinct roles and the financial resources available to him in these discrete embodiments. The image, then, that Chiluba conveys is of a president with dual personhood. On the one hand, he is a public official, on the other, a private individual with a personal agenda cordoned off from the dictates (and constraints) of his public office. As a public official, the president oversees government, its operations, the formulation of policies and their implementation. Thus speaks the constitution. The national budget is the executive's main tool for public government business. Chiluba also portrays his political agenda as one of commitment to the liberation of Africa from imperialist schemes. The emancipatory potential of the state budget, however, is compromised by the fact that it comprises a large amount of resources contributed by 'former colonial masters' obsessed with regaining control of Zambia via 'what neo-colonialists call donor help, tied with a lot of strings' (ibid., 35). Donor conditionalities constrain genuine sovereignty, claims the former president. The head of state cannot pursue all of the goals he should in the interests of the country and the region without the threat of donor sanctions. Hence the need for a source of resources outside the budget frame, uncontrolled by neo-colonial interests.

It is in this spirit of anti-imperialist patriotism that Chiluba conjures up his private alter ego, the 'extra-legal' president, who can – and indeed must – operate outside strict judicial scrutiny. The extra-legal president is not his creation, of course. Its pedigree can be traced to imperial jurisprudence, when the embattled colonial state was surrounded by hostile natives. Chiluba's situation thus mirrors that of the imperial monarch's representative, the colonial governor, who needed the authority to suspend legal constraints in order to ensure the security of British settler subjects. The president's extra-legal body also descends directly from Chiluba's predecessor, founding President Kenneth Kaunda, under whose reign Zambia lived in an endemic state of emergency for 27 years (Chanda 1986). The existence of the ZSIS Zamtrop account, according to Chiluba's testimony, dates from the days when Zambia, under Kaunda, provided support to the national liberation movements in Southern Africa. Such support could not have been given openly, since the Western countries that controlled the World Bank and the IMF were 'opposed to the liberation of Africa.' Kaunda's own pan-African mission necessitated the establishment of a secret ZSIS account, outside normal regulatory mechanisms governing the oversight of public assets. In order to guarantee a semblance of accountability in the use of secret public funds, the ZSIS account fell under a convention known as the 1970 Financial Charter which stipulated that 'no one but the Auditor General in person' could audit such sensitive accounts, thus blocking 'attempts by the Western countries to foil and thwart the liberation wars' (Chiluba, n.d., 19).

The scope of Mr Chiluba's exceptional operations depended on the material and organizational resources of the covert security apparatus; hence the critical importance of the ZSIS Zamtrop account to his defense of national security. According to Chiluba's testimony, ZSIS funds were used to 'sort out' matters as diverse as rape of a secretary by a UNIP-era member of the central committee and urgent medical care for former First Lady Betty Kaunda (p. 19). Chiluba claimed to have also drawn on the ZSIS funds to enable his diplomatic functions in the Angola peace process, in the Great Lakes Region negotiations following the Rwanda genocide and in the Sudan (p. 20). Chiluba terms such sensitive, but necessary, expenditures 'lawfully illegal' (p. 19). Carl Schmitt himself could not have said it better (see Chapter 2).

In Chiluba's telling, the Zamtrop intelligence account held two kinds of money. The bulk of the Zamtrop balance was normal government funds allocated to ZSIS via the national budget, approved by parliament and transferred to Zamtrop from the Ministry of Finance. In addition, a temporary 'suspense account' within Zamtrop allegedly held the president's private funds – i.e., donations from private supporters. Chiluba indicates that he drew on personal funds kept in the Zamtrop account to help his anointed successor, MMD candidate Levy Mwanawasa, in his campaign for the presidency in 2001. These funds, 600 million kwacha (~$200,000), plus three vehicles, represented contributions to Chiluba from private donors for his various personal projects provided under the golden rule of anonymity (p. 22).

Chiluba observes that this practice of anonymous private donation is 'universal.' Such donations do not undermine executive sovereignty since private contributors do not stipulate how the funds are to be used: 'They are made aware that the party President has personal needs as distinct from general party activities' (p. 14). Such private donations are not pure charity, however, but are based on a universal understanding of *quid pro quo* 'between parties and the people that help them' (p. 14).

Chiluba claims to have received a substantial amount of money from anonymous 'well-wishers who had been satisfied with our economic policies' (p. 14). In his unsworn testimony, Chiluba itemizes roughly $4.3 million in such donations between March 1997 and December 1999 alone (p. 54). These donations, Chiluba claims, were for him 'personally and for party projects and activities ... which would cater for the nation and the region' (pp. 14–15). One such project was the FTJ Chiluba Institute for Democracy and Industrial Relations (ibid.).

As head of state, Chiluba claimed not to know the source of these contributions (which, one imagines, would render the *quid pro quo* principle hard to adhere to), or how his instructions were carried out. 'As the Head of State, you are rarely concerned about details, the President is interested to know if it has been done and that it has been done correctly. I never got to know the details' (p. 53). All of the practical details were the responsibility of Chief of Intelligence Xavier Chungu. It was ostensibly Chungu who advised Chiluba to channel all of his private project money through the ZSIS Zamtrop account in the interests of 'accountability and responsibility' (p. 15). Not only did Chiluba operate in a liminal zone of executive exception, but he also claimed not to be directly culpable for the acts of lawful illegality of which he was accused.

## AN EPITOME OF EXCEPTION

On 17 August 2009, Chiluba was acquitted by Principle Resident Magistrate Jones Chinyama of all six counts of theft lodged against him. The judgment was reached in a Magistrate's Court, the lowest rung of Zambia's three-tiered statutory legal system. Chiluba's acquittal was met with shock, scorn and disbelief by the independent *Post* newspaper and numerous liberal-minded organizations. A number of Lusaka-based diplomats voiced 'concern' and 'surprise' over the ruling. Many observers, Zambian and foreign alike, vented their suspicion that President Rupiah Banda's government had somehow meddled in the subordinate court's decision.[26]

Reasons for this skepticism are not hard to find. General distrust in judicial independence notwithstanding, Chinyama's acquittal seemed to contradict two recent court findings. First, Chiluba had already been found liable in 2007 for fraudulent conversion of public goods in a civil case initiated by the Zambian government in a London court. The London judgment ordered Chiluba to repay $46 million he had taken from the Zambian people (more on this below). Second, in early March 2009, Magistrate Court Justice Charles Kafunda had found

26 The late Rupiah Banda (1937-2022) was serving as vice-president under Levy Mwanawasa at the time of the latter's mid-term death in 2008, one year before Chinyama delivered his judgment. Banda acceded to the presidency as stipulated by the constitution and secured the presidency by his own right in the subsequent by-election in October 2008.

Chiluba's wife Regina guilty of receiving stolen goods from her husband and sentenced her to three and a half years in prison (Mail & Guardian 2009). What's more, in May 2008 the government announced that it had recovered nearly $60 million in cash and assets allegedly stolen during Chiluba's presidency.[27]

The government's anxious response to the public furor tended to fuel, rather than assuage, suspicion of political meddling. Immediately upon hearing Chinyama's ruling, Maxwell Nkole, Mark Chona's successor as chairman of the anti-corruption Task Force, lodged an appeal with the High Court challenging the judgment of the subordinate body. In a surprise move, DPP Chalwe Mchenga, the officer with the clearest constitutional mandate to pursue the matter, announced that the state would *not* appeal Chiluba's acquittal as there was no 'likelihood of it succeeding.'[28] The government withdrew the Task Force's appeal and Mr Nkole, its chairman, was subsequently relieved of his position by President Rupiah Banda for 'indiscipline.'

As public outbursts rose in pitch and volume, Works and Supplies Minister Michael Mulongoti declared in a radio interview that

> We consider the general harmony in the country. Even courts are sensitive to the political situation in the country. You cannot just say, jail everyone. No, there is forgiveness, there is reconciliation. Everything is there. So Chiluba, whether we like it or not, he was president of Zambia. Not everyone hates Chiluba. There are wrong things he did, there are also good things he did.[29]

Meanwhile, Stephen Lungu, president of the Law Association of Zambia (LAZ), a founding member of the Oasis Forum, proclaimed that '[g]oing through the judgment, we tend to believe that there was quite good grounds [for an appeal].'[30] Hard on the heels of LAZ's announcement, republican Vice-President and Minister of Justice George Kunda[31] announced:

> 'On Chiluba, it would be unprofessional, in fact, professional misconduct for the Director of Public Prosecutions to appeal knowing well that the case is frivolous and of no merit whatsoever for him to go ahead and lodge an appeal.'[32]

27 Ryder (2011, 8) notes that an itemization of the recovered assets was not made public.

28 'Why state won't appeal,' *Times of Zambia*, 28 August 2009.

29 *Post*, 21 August 2009. Mulongoti's statement, and this passage in particular, were subsequently widely cited by critics of the government as an 'admission' of executive interference in the judicial proceedings.

30 "DPP should have appealed Chiluba's acquittal – LAZ," *Post* 21 September 2009.

31 Minister of Justice and Republican Vice-President George Kunda was a one-time chairperson of the LAZ. As LAZ chairman, he had a reputation as a staunch critique of Chiluba's abuses of the constitution. In his capacity as Attorney General, Kunda was responsible for initiating the civil action in the UK High Court that led to Chiluba's 2007 conviction in London.

32 Janet Chileshe, 'Gov't won't appeal acquittal – Kunda,' *Post*, 23 August 2009.

LAZ's opinion fell on deaf ears. In the five years following the late President Mwanawasa and DPP Mukelabai hatched their campaign to 'nail' Chiluba and his accomplices, the Zambian state had come to embrace a different understanding of the necessity of holding a former president to account.

Before reflecting on how and why Chinyama reached his counterintuitive conclusion, it is worth considering the judicial work exercised by his English counterpart, Mr Justice Peter Smith of the High Court of England and Wales, in the parallel civil action against Mr Chiluba in London.

### *Zambia v Meer*

The civil case tried in London from 31 October 2006 to 27 February 2007 was significantly broader in scope than the Lusaka criminal action. The three defendants charged in Lusaka (Frederick Chiluba, Aaron Chungu and Faustin Kabwe) were also defendants in London. In London, the Attorney General (AG) also submitted claims against 15 other individuals and companies including ZSIS Director General Xavier Chungu, Ministry of Finance Permanent Secretary Stella Chibanda and Zambia's former ambassador to the United States, Atan Shansonga.

The trial was presided over by English High Court Justice Peter Smith. Justice Smith is a judge of some controversy.[33] One cannot, of course, know whether the turmoil surrounding some of his other recent cases affected Justice Smith's reasoning in *Zambia v Meer, Desai & Care and Others* ([2007] EWHC 952 (Ch)). It is, nonetheless, evident from the latter ruling that Smith was engaged with tangible concerns in at least three areas: jurisdiction, fairness and – most germane – in his overall comprehension of the actions of the Zambian parties to the action.

**Jurisdiction**. There are many reasons why holding this trial in an English court was problematic. As the Law Society of England and Wales (LSEW 2007) queried with respect to the Chiluba trial, 'When is the UK the appropriate venue to hear a civil application to recover government funds taken from another sovereign nation?' More specifically, the issue arises of whether the jurisdiction of an English court extends to alleged acts of fraud perpetrated by Zambians in Zambia? Are Zambians legally obliged to deliver remedies as directed by an English judge?

33 In April 2008, Justice Smith was reprimanded by the independent Office for Judicial Complaints for misconduct over an alleged conflict of interest complaint by a plaintiff in his court. This was an incident where Smith found against a plaintiff who was represented by a law firm that had just rejected Smith's job application.

In 2006, Smith attained some public notoriety for having inserted a 'secret code' in his ruling on a copyright infringement case against *Da Vinci Code* author Dan Brown. While his ruling was upheld on appeal, the appellate court judge expressed his displeasure by commenting that 'it might have been preferable for him to have allowed himself more time for the preparation, checking and revision of the judgment.'

See http://en.wikipedia.org/wiki/Peter_Smith_(judge); www.stevencarrigan.com/blog/2008/04/da-vinci-judge-mr-justice-peter-smith.html.

The particulars of this action make things especially complicated. A cogent concern is the tension between the ongoing criminal case in Lusaka and the civil proceedings in London (involving the same plaintiff, many of the same defendants, and concerning overlapping issues). Due to the criminal proceedings in Lusaka, many of the Zambian defendants had forfeited their passports and could not travel to London for hearings against them.

To aggravate things, the Zambia-based defendants challenged the legality of the London proceedings. After Smith rejected their application to terminate the action (this ruling was upheld on appeal), Chiluba and five other Zambian co-defendants withdrew from the process. They refused to submit further testimony and ignored the transcripts, etc., prepared for them. In Smith's own rendition, this refusal to cooperate in the trial suggested that

> in some way the proceedings before me and my sitting as a Special Examiner in Zambia are unconstitutional as regards Zambia, an infringement of Zambia's sovereign rights and an attempt by the former colonial power to impose its will on Zambia. (§24)

Smith rejected this suggestion in no uncertain terms as 'one of many instances of [the Zambian defendants] misleading the public for their own purposes' (§27). Still, the 'discontinued participation' (§28) of Chiluba et al., which Smith had no means to sanction, clearly undermined his court's aura of fairness. As the LSEW (op cit.) inquired, 'How do you proceed with a civil case where one party refuses to participate without resulting in a miscarriage of justice?' The question is not rhetorical, and yet Justice Smith's response was simply to discount the credibility of the defendants' claims, and soldier on.

Against this background, it is interesting how little information is provided in the ruling about the background to the action itself. We are told that the action was instigated by the Zambian AG, and that it was he who decided on London for the venue.[34] What is not mentioned is the touchy issue of how the Zambian government covered its expenses?[35]

**Fairness**. Challenged directly by Chiluba and the other Zambian defendants, Smith went to considerable lengths to salvage a semblance of judiciousness in the proceedings. By his own account, he bent over backward to ensure that the absent defendants were provided with all possible information and that their integrity vis-à-vis the Lusaka criminal proceedings was not compromised. Smith claimed to be 'quite satisfied that [the Zambia-based defendants] have had the

34 The trial took 51 days between 31 October 2006 and 27 February 2007. From 29 November to 14 December 2006, Smith Peter J heard evidence at the High Court Lusaka.

35 According to a widely circulated (but unverified) anonymous article, Mark Chona, the Task Force chairperson, secured Mr Blair's services for $5 million. Former UK Prime Minister Tony Blair's brother led the prosecution team, which may have something to do with the British government's leading involvement. I have not found a reliable source on the overall sum, or a breakdown of individual contributions.

fullest opportunity to present a case against the claims brought against them, but they have chosen for their own reasons not to do so' (§31). In Smith's own words (§69), the reason Chiluba discontinued his participation was the lack of an honest defense for his 'shameful' behavior.

**Comprehension.** Smith is confident that he can see through Chiluba's deceit to his premeditated conspiratorial intent. He recognizes that the Zambian government may have a legitimate need for covert intelligence operations, but he sees no evidence of genuine intelligence work in what he terms the 'Zamtrop conspiracy.'

> I accept that it is theoretically possible for the operation ... to have had an innocent explanation namely the desire to cloak genuine ZSIS operations in secrecy. However my firm conclusion is that in reality this whole operation was created to be used as an engine of fraud at the expense of the Republic. (§150)

Indeed, on the basis of the prosecution's evidence, Smith is 'satisfied that the Zamtrop account was set up primarily to steal Government money. It is not,' in his estimation, 'that the Zamtrop account was set up legitimately and then used partially for illegitimate purposes' (§82). All in all, Smith seems surprisingly secure in his understanding of the needs and aims of the Zambian Secret Service. Concerning the purchase of properties in the names of Chiluba's lawyers, Smith declares that 'there can be no ZSIS purpose to justify this purchase' (§455).

Paradoxically, it is the behavior of the plaintiff, the Zambian AG that gives Smith the greatest pause. His main bewilderment relates to the 1970 Financial Charter that purportedly governed the Zamtrop account (see above), and he fails to 'understand the reluctance of AGZ to produce the document' (§140). Eventually, after much prevarication on the part of the AGZ, Smith obtained a copy of the charter, a classified Zambian government document that 'governs the financing of ZSIS' (§142). Despite the obviously sensitive nature of this information there was, in his view,

> nothing in the Finance Charter that justified [the AGZ's] reluctance and none was seriously put forward ... The only explanation that seemed to me to have any kind of credibility was the ***"traditional"*** view of secret service organisations that everything they do (down to the ordering of the light bulbs) is a secret. (§140; emphasis in original)

This issue seems to be Smith's greatest source of concern: Why would the prosecution withhold evidence that supports its case? Smith is convinced, correctly no doubt, that a great many people in government were aware of the diversion of public funds to the Zamtrop account. He is puzzled that no whistleblowers came forth. He is especially befuddled by the failure of the Auditor General (who can be assumed to have known about the Zamtrop business, but was apparently not a major beneficiary to the theft) to challenge the conspiracy. In the end, he settles on a simple explanation:

> a substantial body of evidence ... shows there is a climate of fear operating in the [Zambian] public service. It is difficult in a western world to perceive how intimidatory those in power can be in a country like Zambia. The threat of losing one's job in the public service is a strong deterrent against questioning matters. There is no residual backup system of a welfare state approaching anything like that in western countries. To lose one's job is to force one's family into starvation and potential homelessness. Thus that is a powerful weapon without any need to issue threats of violence. It is quite clear from the evidence that those in power and those associated with those in power were not questioned. What they said went unchallenged because of the fear. (§44)

## A COVERT STATE

Smith's assessment that Chiluba and Chungu were feared is not inaccurate. The Special Branch (aka the 'Office of the President') has a notorious (if, for obvious reasons, largely unsubstantiated) reputation for implementing the political violence of the state. The mid-1990s, in particular, was a time of unusual unrest in Zambia's urban centers, with unprecedented incidents of hold-ups, breaking and entering and car-jacking, perpetrated by a new breed of criminal unknown in the Second Republic. Links between semi-organized criminal gangs and shady characters purportedly under Chiluba's patronage were the subject of widespread conjecture.[36]

But even without the threat of violence, Zambian civil servants are not wont to challenge their superiors. Smith's hypothesis about fear as the principal factor motivating a great cover-up is only a partial truth, at best. It does not account for the fact that, at the same time, in other areas of political life, Zambians were assertively challenging Chiluba's style of government. Prominent lawyers and politicians had consistently resisted Chiluba's efforts to have opposition leaders removed from politics over the course of two trumped-up treason trials (see Chapter 6). Some Zambians may have feared Chiluba, but the nation did not cower in dumb submission in the face of his increasingly autocratic style of government. Clearly, there were more fundamental obstacles to exposing the workings of the covert state.

Smith senses but cannot articulate the fact that the action in his court has overstepped an important border. Deeply rooted Zambian patriotism (if this is the proper term) cannot condone the disclosure of the inner workings of the

36 Several suspicious events, above all the apparent assassination of recently sacked Finance Minister Ronald Penza in a car-jacking at his home gate in November 1998, lent credibility to such speculation. After Penza's murder, *Post* editor Fred M'membe was quoted as claiming that 'Most people now strongly believe Ronald was executed by state agents and everything police are doing is cover-up.' www.independent.co.uk/news/killing-of-minister-alarms-zambia-1185872.html.

security services to outsiders, and especially not to former colonial authorities. Smith acknowledges the Zambian 'obsession' with secrecy surrounding ZSIS but dismisses it as a kind of superstitious paranoia. For many of the Zambians I have discussed this with, however, the intelligence services represent a form of nationalist agency of such potency that the disclosure of its operational secrets to foreigners would border on treason.

This reluctance has strong historical roots that are firmly entwined with the legacy of prerogativism. The Special Branch and the ZSIS lie at the core of national sovereignty, safeguarding the body of the head of state. The Special Branch is both feared and respected. It has been the last bastion against internal treachery and the malice of Zambia's foreign, racist enemies (above all, apartheid Rhodesia and South Africa, and the Portuguese colonial forces in Angola and Mozambique). These external struggles are largely past, but they had a formative impact on nationalist sensibilities.[37] Few Zambians believe that they live in a world free of foreign threats. Many foreign countries and their nationals, as well as the IMF are all viewed with various degrees of suspicion. One can imagine the soul-searching the AG must have endured before eventually handing the Financial Charter over to Smith.

Smith is probably correct in assuming that the 'non-participating Zambian defendants' would have had nothing to say that would have changed his mind about their guilt. Under no circumstances could Smith assign any credibility to Chiluba's insinuations that (a) Zamtrop, as an instrument of the president's intelligence service, fell under his discretionary authority and needed no accounting for; or that (b) the funds in Zamtrop that Chiluba used for his personal ends were private gifts from foreign admirers.

Smith's remarks on Chiluba's sources of private funds are indicative of his triteness in the face of executive exception:

> 'Insofar as the payments can be identified as from 3rd party sources the receipt of such monies is and the failure to declare them is plainly a breach of the duties [Chiluba] owed to the Republic of Zambia.'

Chiluba was understandably disinclined to provide empirical details about the identities of his foreign supporters, yet this is somewhat beside the point. Chiluba's fundamental and defensible claim was that, under Zambian law, whether the Zamtrop money was private or public was nobody's business, most certainly not the concern of an English court. Indeed, Chiluba would eventually call Smith's conviction both 'racist' and 'obscene.' A president's decisions in security-related matters cannot be constitutionally challenged, or even scrutinized. Chiluba's

37 Indeed, Mark Chona's role as an intelligence liaison between Kaunda and the liberation movements against colonialism and apartheid is the key source of his authority; Chona's instigation of an action that demands the disclosure of such sovereign secrets is not, it would seem, without a certain irony.

third caveat was that the president does not get involved in the nuts and bolts of day-to-day intelligence operations. Accordingly, if there was mischief it was Xavier Chungu's responsibility. In light of the evidence, Chiluba's assertion that he did not know what his director of intelligence was up to is disingenuous, not to say disloyal. In this respect, one can concur with Smith that Chiluba's claim of ignorance is not only a ploy to deflect judicial scrutiny, but also a rebuke to the inappropriateness of the English judge's encroachment on 'sacred' ground.

In his judgment, delivered on 5 May 2007, Justice Smith declares himself convinced that Chiluba and friends have perpetrated a string of premeditated conspiracies to defraud the Zambian government and people.

> The conspiracy was effected because of the intimidation of government employees by [Stella Chibanda, Permanent Secretary at the Ministry of Finance] and maintaining that there should be no challenge to what was going on because it was all "secret operations" of the Government Security Arm ZSIS. None of this was true; the Zamtrop Account was set up as part of the conspiracy to steal. It was operated under the Financial Charter 1970 to hide what was going on and to inhibit legitimate queries. (Summary, §32)

Former President Chiluba and his Director of Intelligence Xavier Chungu were found to be liable for damages to the Zambian people totaling roughly $46 million.[38]

### *Justice Chinyama's judgment*

A good two years later, after looking at much of the same evidence, Lusaka Magistrate Jones Chinyama came to a different conclusion. Access Finance operatives Faustin Kabwe and Aaron Chungu were found guilty of three counts of theft, but President Chiluba was acquitted on all six counts against him. In justifying his ruling, Chinyama invokes an earlier Supreme Court precedent (*Mutale v The People*), which held that

> where two or more inferences are possible it has always been a cardinal principle of the criminal law that the Court will adopt the one which is more favourable to an accused if there is nothing in the case to exclude such inference.

38 In 2007, the Zambian Attorney General sought to register Judge Smith's fresh ruling in Zambia, thus allowing for the Zambian judicial system to commence actions to recover the stolen funds enumerated in the London judgment. This effort failed and Smith's ruling proved to be unenforceable (Mbao 2011, 267).

Zambian High Court Judge Evans Hamaundu ruled in August 2010 (2007/HP/FJ/004) that the London ruling against Chiluba et al. could not be registered in Zambia since judgments of British superior courts do not comply with the provisions of the Foreign Judgments (Reciprocal Enforcement) Act (Cap. 76 of the Laws of Zambia). This reasoning implies that the entire London episode was misconceived. The state did not appeal the Zambian High Court's ruling.

Chinyama thus concludes that

> In all the nine counts above, the possibility of at least two inferences is there. I have adopted the inference that the monies were paid from the private funds in the Zamtrop account whose expenditure has not been explained. I find nothing to exclude the inference. (J281)

Chinyama's reasoning, given his basic premise, is coherent, but it sidesteps a troublesome legal issue: Is it possible to keep 'private' money in a government account? This point was central to the Task Force's aborted appeal. The testimony of Auditor General Anna Chifungula (DW [Defence Witness] 7) is clear: It is 'not permissible to put private money in a Government account and where this is found to have taken place the money is confiscated and becomes public funds' (J255). On the other hand, the same Auditor General describes a 'document of trust' explaining and accounting for the existence of private assets in the ZSIS. A former intelligence officer (DW6) suggests the distinction between a 'government account' and a 'service account.' Zamtrop would not, in this understanding, be subject to regulations governing governmental accounts. Chiluba also argues that Zamtrop should not be considered a 'government account' in the first place. These conflicting technicalities remain intrinsically unresolvable due to the opaqueness (or non-existence) of relevant norms.

The prosecution's key witness, a Mr Hamunjele from the Bank of Zambia (P[rosecution]W[itness] 31) states unequivocally that 'Financial Regulations prohibit the depositing of private funds in Government Accounts' (J194). Another witness, Trevor Nyoni of the Anti-Corruption Commission, found that while it was 'wrong to keep private funds in a Government account … about US$8.5 million of private funds went into the account from as early as 22nd January 1997 until 26th March 2001' (J201). Was this legal, illegal or lawfully illegal? In his unsworn testimony, Chiluba himself insisted that the president can 'comingle' (J268) his personal assets with government assets and maintain his proprietary rights to them. This was done, he noted, by keeping his private funds within a separate suspense account within Zamtrop (Chiluba, p. 47). Chinyama's judgment supports Chiluba's unsworn testimony to the effect that the Zamtrop money Chiluba used for his personal needs was indeed 'private' (J239). The credibility of this view is obscured by the secrecy in which regulations governing the intelligence services is shrouded. At the end of the day, one can only give the executive the benefit of the doubt, which is what Judge Jones Chinyama quite clearly has decided to do.

### *The scope of exception*

The question that Justice Chinyama doesn't consider, and which neither the prosecution nor the defense give voice to, is this: What were the Access Finance functionaries, Faustin Kabwe and Aaron Chungu up to, other than just moving money around from account to account? The explicit understanding offered by

Mr Chiluba (p. 45) is that his co-accused were 'friends of the service,' involved in fronting intelligence activities. Where Justice Smith resolutely denied the possibility that the defendants might have been involved in legitimate intelligence activities, Chinyama never addresses this central issue (and indeed convicts Kabwe and Chungu). By implication, then, his judgment allows that the monies paid to American contractors or channeled through the English law firm of Meer, Desai and Care could have been used to pay off agents or informants, fund surveillance operations, procure and equip safe houses and so on. Such activities are routine for any modern intelligence agency. From this angle, the elaborate financial arrangements coordinated by Access Finance would not have been engineered so much to hide them from the Zambian people, as from the nation's imagined adversaries – individuals identified by the state to be spied on, recruited or eliminated in the service of national security. But why then convict Kabwe and Chungu?

Chiluba's 'friends of the service' may or may not have been facilitating important security work. The outcome of the case is premised on one's initial assumption. Either Chiluba is an unscrupulous con-man or an executive statesman, carrying out the demanding duties of his office. Many of those who defend the president's exceptional powers allow that Chiluba may have succumbed to minor temptations along the way but that these are the occupational hazards of the presidency, not purely criminal acts. Indeed, in an interview with one of Chiluba's lawyers (perhaps not the most impartial of sources), I was told: 'I can assure you, Chiluba did not steal. He may have pocketed a bit, but not in the manner they are suggesting.' Irrespective of the scope of Mr Chiluba's abuse of public funds, there remained significant support for the idea that he was above scrutiny for the things he did while president. 'An African president should not have to steal to secure a proper education for his children!' was a recurrent argument. Chiluba himself (p. 59) felt that in a situation where people had 'a bit of African culture where one respects leaders more' his actions would not be subjected to judicial sanction. For committed liberals like Justice Smith, any (African) president with his hand in the till is an unqualified scoundrel. Neither of these views engages fully with the constitutional groundings of presidential prerogativism nor with its legal implications.

The thrust of Chiluba's defense is that the activities documented in the Zamtrop transcripts were the legitimate work of the executive defending national security. The president is under no legal obligation to disclose any of the details of security operations to anyone but the Auditor General. Even the courts are not allowed to know – or, apparently, even to ask – whether the operations that were being funded via the Zamtrop account by government (and by the president's foreign friends) have anything to do with national security.

What are legitimate intelligence expenditures, anyway? To what ends is an African president entitled to employ the state's security apparatus in order to guarantee the safety of its citizens? Is it valid to invest in networks and properties that intelligence estimates suggest may be useful at a later date? Where should the authority reside to define limits on security spending? In a domestic or a foreign court? In an expert tribunal? In parliament? At the ballot box? Zambian law has virtually nothing to say about this. The president's powers derive largely (but not entirely) from implicit privileges grounded in a prerogativist constitution and in an implicit culture of political legality, but never formally tested. These conventions then allow for the institutionalization of discretionary powers beyond the letter of the law, both reflecting and constituting the prevailing form of postcolonial sovereign power. The 1970 Financial Charter, governing the Zamtrop account, is a unique (albeit opaque) convention. According to these constitutional provisions and cultural dispositions, the only legitimate oversight of covert intelligence operations is by the president himself. It is worth underscoring that Chiluba's defense team never denied the movements of money demonstrated by the prosecution. They simply asserted that Chiluba was exercising the executive discretion conferred upon him via law and cultural convention.

## Part II: The paradoxical sovereignty of the postcolony

The distinction between what is 'law' and what is 'politics' is unusually hard to draw when examining the Chiluba trials. Chiluba's prosecution was certainly as much a political spectacle as a legal process. In some respects, the trial courts were placed in the unenviable position of passing judgment on the moral integrity of the first ten tumultuous years of Zambia's Third Republic, a time of profound socioeconomic transformation. This is especially so for Justice Chinyama's courtroom in Lusaka, scrutinized by the media for years with rapt attention. Throughout the Chiluba prosecution, Zambia's international status as a 'developing' democracy was also on trial, and there is truth in Paul Lewis' (2009) claim that the Chiluba case evolved rapidly from a national political concern to a donor-driven crusade, reflecting postcolonial and geopolitical interests. The legitimacy of domestic legal institutions was not enhanced as external actors assumed responsibility for exacting a verdict and subsequent punishment. This may contribute, to some degree, to the Zambian state's brusque dismissal of Justice Smith's judgment.

Zambia was not the only testing ground of post–Cold War liberal triumphalism. Sixty-six ex-presidents around the world were indicted between 1990 and 2008 for crimes committed while they were in office (Lutz & Reiger 2009).[39] For some (e.g., Sikkink 2011), this swell of prosecutions expressed a wind-change in the parameters of executive sovereignty and associated notions of impunity. Of these 66 indicted executives, however, only one (Italy's Silvio Berlusconi) was from a so-called advanced market democracy. The vast majority of the indicted leaders presided over governments in the South (45) or in former communist

39 Lutz and Reiger's list includes 67 ex-presidents, but Kenneth Kaunda's inclusion seems inaccurate since he was never formally indicted.

regimes of Eastern Europe (9). It is hard to avoid the impression that immunity from the ongoing judicial assault on sovereign impunity has clear geographical boundaries and that these correspond roughly to those of Cold War capitalism. Criminal culpability, on the other hand, resides rather neatly in precisely those regions of the world that were directly subjected to the harshest measures of market liberalization in the wake of the Cold War. In light of the fallout from the global financial crisis, and especially the money-laundering revelations of the Panama Papers (Obermayer & Obermeier 2016), it would surely be naïve to assume that the boundaries of accountable and responsible government were identical to those of capital's empire.

## *Innocence and guilt*

The reasoning of the two judges assigned to try Chiluba and his co-defendants is framed by the imperative of reaching an unambiguous conclusion. 'A court,' as Martti Koskenniemi (2002, 34) reminds us, 'rules – and must rule – over individual guilt and innocence and in so doing must strive for neutrality and transparency.' Chinyama and Smith must rule, despite the untested and slippery character of the juridical frameworks within which they are obliged to operate. In doing so, they inevitably became involved not only in determining innocence or culpability but also in repairing the fissures that the Chiluba trials rent in liberal premises concerning the legitimacy of the prevailing form of power.

Mr Smith's judgment allows the reader intimate access to the epistemic efforts he has carried out to shore up his initial premise of Zambia as a (flawed) liberal jurisdiction. He disavows the constitutional foundations of executive discretion in Zambian jurisprudence. He similarly overrides Chiluba's unusual but not unreasonable claim of his dual (public/private) personhood. The thrust of his analysis is to reduce the ethics of presidential rule to a vague notion of 'public servant accountability,' which stubbornly ignores the exceptional role that presidents occupy in a postcolonial – or indeed any nominally democratic – dispensation. Justice Smith also refuses to recognize, at least in this particular instance, that issues of 'national security' have any bearing on considerations of presidential accountability. Despite faux-anguished references to Britain's legacy as Zambia's former colonial master, his ruminations reveal an understanding of neither the imperial groundings of Zambia's postcolonial government, nor of the structural illiberality it encompasses. While 'culture' plays no formative role in his assessment of Chiluba's behavior, Justice Smith does invoke the social affect of 'fear' (but not, for example, of 'deference' or 'patriotism') to explain civil servant complicity. This conflation of pathos with ethos, of emotion with moral judgment, has no legitimate role in juridical reasoning; its decisive role in allowing Justice Smith to find Chiluba guilty signals the presence of a special sort of juridical sensibility which is *both* a paragon of liberal sentiment *and* heavily in debt to the epistemic habits of empire.

The intricacies of Judge Chinyama's reasoning are less explicitly displayed. In common with Judge Smith, Jones Chinyama ignores the distinction between Mr Chiluba's private and public bodies, choosing to focus only on the president's official persona. This allows him to bypass the sticky issue of whether Mr Chiluba might be found guilty of 'theft of public funds' under *any* circumstances. Chinyama further resisted intervening in the jurisprudence of presidential discretion by withdrawing behind a tried and true technicality – Mr Chiluba was not, in the court's assessment, guilty 'beyond a reasonable doubt.' However, Judge Chinyama did not elaborate on why his uncertainty concerning Mr Chiluba's guilt should be considered reasonable. Indeed, Judge Chinyama relied heavily (one is tempted to say exclusively) on the former president's own unsworn testimony to generate doubt about his guilt. The accused's own word, then, was sufficient grounds for doubt about his guilt. In the realm of liberal legality, such a concession is highly unconventional, and only makes sense in light of the fact that the accused was not just any Body, but a presidential one. Mr Chinyama's ruling clearly signals the court's tacit intent not to meddle with the foundational jurisprudence around presidential prerogativism, and thus represents a paragon of political legality.

Did the courts that tried Mr Chiluba achieve genuine neutrality and transparency? One can have reasonable doubt. The major obstacle to delivering well-reasoned justice, however, as the evidence suggests, was not so much a compromised bench – as the neopatrimonial model predicts – as the difficulties that the courts had in coming to terms with the form of sovereign power that Mr Chiluba embodied. That said, the former president's acquittal and the Zambian state's refusal to lodge an appeal rekindle entrenched suspicions concerning how the intimate relationship between the executive and judiciary branches of government might have enabled judicial complicity in the presidential abuse of power. A great many Zambians (as well as non-Zambians) embraced the possibility of a compromised judiciary as an explanation for Chinyama's ruling. A problem with this interpretation is, of course, that lacking a confession or comparable smoking gun, external interference in the court's judgment is impossible to prove beyond a reasonable doubt. One can still ask, however, what conclusions are reasonable, based on the preponderance of the available evidence?

### *The case for executive interference*

Distinguished members of the Zambian law fraternity, headed by ex-Law Association president and reigning Minister of Legal Affairs George Kunda, as well as the extant Director of Public Prosecutions Mchenga Chalwe publicly insisted on the legal validity of Chinyama's ruling. These views emanated from the state apparatus, however, and were widely read by Chinyama's critics as channeling the will of the incumbent president, Rupiah Banda.[40] Banda, it was

40 After losing to the Patriotic Front's Michael Sata in 2011, parliament lifted Mr Banda's immunity in March 2013 at the behest of then Minister of Legal Affairs Wynter Kabimba. This was in connection with allegations of, inter alia, appropriating $2.5 million from the Treasury in a 2008 oil deal (Reuters 2013). After President Sata's untimely passing in 2014, Mr Kabimba lost his job (see Chapter 9). The High Court restored Banda's immunity in

thought, was not eager to see the precedent of a conviction established in an executive abuse-of-office hearing due to his own allegedly corrupt practices. Was Chinyama, then, acting under President Banda's influence?

At a general level, many Zambians claim to know of incidences where a sum of money slipped to a judge, court clerk or bailiff has secured a desired juridical outcome. In a 2004 interview, a senior law professor and UNIP-era Solicitor General, however, underplayed the likelihood of direct executive interference in court proceedings:

> As a matter of principle, it's not easy for the executive to fish out the decision they like from the Zambian bench … In fact, during the period 1991-2001, I defended a lot of UNIP cases and I don't remember one instance when anyone of them was sent to prison. This is at Magistrate level. So it is quite difficult, really, to tamper with the Judiciary. It is an institution that has been established in such a manner that if it is to die or wear out, it will take a long time, because of its structure and because of the training that the personnel has received.

In another field interview, a foremost constitutional lawyer offered a less flattering view of the independence of the bench. Discussing his failed attempt to have the High Court overturn Chiluba's 1996 Constitutional Amendment Act, my interviewee felt that the main reason that the bench did not 'rise to the occasion' was that

> the Executive branch of government is still very, very powerful … The last thing that anybody wants is to find himself in a confrontation with Government, because at the end of the day you end up losing anyway … So, [for] most of the judges it's like making a choice: Who can I offend and get away with it? It is much easier for a judge to rule against me, because I'll go and complain [about] this and that and it ends there. But when they rule against the Executive, there are ramifications. Most of the judges lack the stamina.

This account suggests that the executive does not exert pressure on the judiciary directly, but rather through the threat of possible 'ramifications.' Drawing on his own experiences as a former DPP and a High Court judge, one justice explained in some detail how this might work. In this account, there are three main ways that government can influence the work of judicial officers. These are

1. Through the use of 'administrative manipulation' to undermine judges – by demoting their office accommodations, and subjecting them to budgetary

---

2016, thus stopping legal procedures against him. President Banda passed away in March 2022.

cuts for transport allowances, vehicles, fuel, paper, ink, photocopies, etc., making efficient work difficult.

2. By creating 'compromised loyalty' through promotions, especially when a more junior judge bypasses another, more competent candidate.
3. By setting an example for other judges through the 'scandalizing' of a fellow judge.

Another lawyer provided a graphic illustration of this third form of pressure. Under Chiluba's administration, Chief Justice Matthew Ngulube, known for his 'brilliant legal mind,' quashed Section 54 of the Public Order Act in an appeal to the Supreme Court. This was the section that required a discretionary police permit for any public assembly. Chiluba considered Justice Ngulube's ruling to be a particularly hostile gesture, since it weakened the government's powers to restrict opposition demonstrations. In reference to this action, my interviewee asked me,

> Do you know what happened to Ngulube? A few months [after his ruling], there was a story published about him having raped a woman … A plot was conceived at State House, using Chiluba's Press Assistant who went to some rag called *The Confidential*, and concocted this story. I know this first hand, because I acted for the Chief Justice with two other lawyers. The whole idea was to force him out of the office. [Government lawyers] said, "These allegations must be investigated, but they cannot be investigated whilst he's still holding the office, [so] he should resign." We told [Justice Ngulube], "Don't resign," and he stayed on. But although he did not resign, he went through a very stressful situation. Once you are in that environment, you are basically alone … and no person would like to find himself on one side, and the state machinery on the other side. It's not a good experience. And that sent a clear message to the other judges: If you don't play ball you create problems for yourself.[41]

Aside, perhaps, from the vagueness of the justifications provided in his ruling, there is no direct evidence that Justice Chinyama's ruling complied with any other authority other than that of the law. The fact that eight years after his ruling on *The People v Chiluba*, Chinyama rose from the bottom tier of the judiciary to the Supreme Court (on 8 August 2016) may seem to suggest otherwise. This

41 The story, sadly, does not end there. Justice Ngulube's name appears in the subpoenaed Zamtrop records (see above) as a recipient of $168,000. This was widely understood as comprising a reward for his rejection of the political opposition's petition to nullify Chiluba's 1996 presidential victory. When this payment came to light, the Chief Justice stepped down pending retirement. While there is no testimony establishing that Ngulube's ruling on the presidential petition case was predicated on the promise of a bribe, this example affirms that the 'ramifications' of judicial actions involving a president are real, and can be both positive and negative.

hypothesis is complicated, however, by the fact that the president who is assumed to have interfered in Chinyama's ruling had been out of office for five years by the time of his promotion. If Judge Chinyama's accession to the Supreme Court was a prize for his loyalty, it was not to any sitting president but an expression of institutionalized deference to the postcolonial form of power itself.

## The president's (not quite) two bodies revisited

The conformity of a leader to the constraints of law is only likely to reflect liberal virtues when enforceable rules genuinely guide political behavior toward these ends. This is not the case where a prerogativist form of sovereignty frames the constitutional order. Quite the contrary: The prevailing constitutional order, and the structure of incentives it invokes, encourages the blurring of a distinction between personalized agency and the pursuit of a greater, national good. What is fascinating about the Chiluba saga is the *absolute* conflation of legality and exception. Numerous incidents of political importance to the Chiluba administration involved the security apparatus, despite the absence of any imminent threat to the nation.[42] Personal interests and predilections doubtless contribute to a president's style of rule, but of equal importance are the *structural* groundings of executive comportment – that which I have termed the prerogativist form of power. As I have tried to show, postcolonial jurisprudence is far more than formal rules. It encompasses the constitutional groundings of presidential powers, as well as political and judicial cultures deeply in debt to the state's imperial past, and above all to a deep-rooted legacy of deference to the executive. Mr Chiluba's legal episodes clearly show that at the core of Zambia's politico-legal order is the organic union of legality and exception.

In Chiluba's reign, individual agency and institutional structure were not at odds with one another in any systemic sense. Individual greed was not in conflict with constitutional constraints. Rather, the parameters of postcolonial sovereignty provided a flexible platform for Chiluba to launch his personal, partisan and allegedly patriotic projects. Zambia's presidentialism cannot, thus, be productively theorized as a kind of 'perverted' or 'anti-'liberalism, nor as a teleological contest between 'rule of law' and 'rule by man.' The truth is much messier than these neat labels, and the ways that postcolonial states are theorized should better reflect this complexity. The constitutive schitzolegality of the Zambia state (as in much of the postcolonial world) encompasses at once both the liberal and the exceptional.

The premise of institutionalized schitzolegality might be used, as I am well aware, to exonerate all manner of official mischief. To be clear: there is little

42 These include the so-called Soriano arms scam (involving Congolese businessman Raphael Soriano, aka Katebe Katoto, the elder brother of Kinshasa Governor Moïse Katumbi), the Carlington maize scandal, a large volume of missing cobalt, alleged kick-backs from transport and telecommunication investments and so on (see Mbao 2011, 263–4; Gould 2023, 725).

intrinsic value – for Zambia as a nation or for the Zambian *demos* – in Mr Chiluba's Zamtrop maneuvers. This is true regardless of whether Chiluba's actions were lawfully illegal or simply criminal, as Justice Smith's liberal common sense would have it. This is where things get tricky, and I must exercise care and caution to ensure that my critique of imperial liberalism (and its residual effects in postcolonial constitutionalism) are not seen as a rejection, *tout court*, of the normative case for executive accountability. The thrust of this analysis is that Mr Chiluba's actions were – as Judge Chinyama, and the state legal apparatus as a whole eventually upheld – not empirically illegal. The legacy of imperial liberalism, and its predicative assumption of embattled sovereignty, bequeaths absolute discretion to the president in any matter which can be construed as affecting national security, while grants the president the prerogative of defining what constitutes a matter of national security. As is well known, and as the trial evidence irrefutably revealed, the state contains, in its opaque heart, an apparatus dedicated to enabling absolute discretionary actions by the executive – including the appropriation of public funds – in such instances. This is precisely the position that the Zambian legal apparatus upheld in *The People v F.T.J. Chiluba and two others.* As we have also seen, recurrent, extensively belabored and disproportionately expensive deliberations around constitution-making in Zambia have done literally nothing to dislodge the president's prerogativist privileges.

The executive, then, has access to an extra-legal domain of opaque agency, epitomized by the various strands of the intelligence services, to pursue whatever discretionary ends the executive deems important at any given time. All Zambian presidents, thus, from founding father Kenneth Kaunda to the incumbent Edgar Lungu, have been able to 'move with impunity between appeals to the form of law and forms of extrajudicial practice that are clearly construed as lying outside or prior to the state' (Das & Poole 2004, 14). Earlier chapters have documented how, in their time, presidents Kaunda, Chiluba and Mwanawasa had all exploited extra-legal powers to self-serving political ends. There are ample indications that presidents Banda, Sata and Lungu have behaved similarly. The ends may justify the means, but the evidence also reveals ways in which the tendency of postcolonial presidents to invoke extrajudicial prerogative allows the authority of the constitution, the juridical order and the presidency itself to occlude popular demands for genuine reciprocity and consultation between the governors and the governed.

The point, then, is not whether, or in what sense, Mr Chiluba's discretionary use of public funds was lawfully illegal. This is not, I suggest, what is controversial about Mr Chiluba's legal travails. What invites further discussion, however, is what this realization tells us about the postcolonial form of power and about whether a retheorization of the postcolonial state and the form of power around which it is constituted might indicate ways to establish and sustain genuine mechanisms of responsiveness to popular will and popular needs.

The starting point for this discussion, I suggest, is the president's 'not quite' dual embodiment and what it reveals about the politico-legal dynamics of postcolonial sovereignty. As noted (Chapter 3, Excursus), Zambia's politico-legal culture confers two bodies upon the executive – an official, publicly visible, nominally accountable manifestation, as well as a private, opaque, profane and altogether mortal embodiment, rooted in the party and largely beyond public scrutiny. The 'official' body of the president is, in effect, 'eternal.' This need not be glossed as mysticism, and can rather be framed simply as a legal convention: A constitution is in effect 'for the time being.' This implies that the powers it confers have no expiration date and that the objects it conjures into existence reside outside secular time. Ironically, the president's temporal body is more complex than his eternal one. The abstract essence of the president's transcendental embodiment is 'miraculous,' but also simple. In comparison with the messiness of the president's profane personhood, the eternal body is one-dimensional. It provides personhood to the state and empirical form to the *telos* of state formation – the aspirations of the nation embodied. It also, of course, enables the lawfully illegal gestures of the temporal sovereign. The mortal body is, of course, prone to death, illness and decay, and to sin. The office itself waxes eternal, but its mortal occupants inevitably become entangled in the mundane economics of property ownership, commerce and intra-party intrigues.

Chiluba equated his temporal being with his political self: a man of the party. It is a partisan personage and in his rendition, a patriotic one. He justified his actions (and implicitly his various excesses) via reference to the nation, the will of which he believed to coalesce in the ruling party, which was voted into power in 1991 and 1996 with substantial popular mandates. This move to identify himself as the humble embodiment of the *demos* channels the transcendental spin of Kaunda's humanism. Both Kaunda and Chiluba sought to invest their private beings with the semblance of divinity, blurring the distinction between their temporal and eternal selves as well as, perhaps, legitimizing the merging of their private and public interests. On the one hand, Chiluba sought to cordon off his private self from the constitutional strictures on public office while, on the other hand, anointing his private, partisan, patriotic, road-building, cell-phone championing and regional resource-mobilizing self with divine, Christian purpose. Kaunda, with his tears and unsullied white handkerchief, as well as his bodily disciplines – his Eastern guru and his vegetarianism – provided the template for this super-mortal incarnation. Kaunda sought to project a selfless essence, one that transcended the sectarian interests of tribe and congregation. Chiluba, in contrast, embraced ethnic, congregational and class interests but in doing so, portrayed himself as the more genuine, pragmatic and human leader.

*Summa summarum*: Like any human being, presidents inhabit one physiological corpus. From the vantage point of the power invested in them, however, presidents have two personalities, but not quite. The president's private body can hide in the murky shadows of state secrecy, but cannot detach itself from its public embodiment. The eternal office, in other words, is the prerogativist politician's condition of possibility. It is in this sense, as described in the Excursus, that the president's body is 'more than one but less than two.'

This caveat is important, I feel, because thinking of the president's body as a plurality risks reproducing the hierarchical, repressive and analytically paralyzing dualisms encoded in the epistemic habits of empire. These are the epistemic moves, which routinely – and unreflexively – distinguish between the modern and the traditional, the savage and the civilized, the loyal and the insurgent, the Christian and the pagan, the White and the non-White; and which superimpose this last dualism as *the* normative framework that orders all the others in hierarchical asymmetry. For the imperial governor, 'race' was the operational category undergirding government's ethos of embattlement; for the postcolonial president, absolute fealty (or its lack) is the biopolitical operator most often deployed to make the subjects of his government legible.

It is not helpful to fall back on these colonial habits; rather, they should be exorcised. Only by emancipating public discourse from inflexible hierarchies based on hate and fear can critical analysis discover new paths of analysis and imagination. To juxtapose the president's two bodies as distinct entities – one public and liberal, and one private and corrupt – introduces a false, and intellectually numbing opposition, and suspends analysis in the realm of the liberal moralism of the imperial era, rather than stimulating a deeper understanding of the contours of empirical sovereignties. To break free of the epistemic conventions of empire requires at least two conceptual moves: One is to give up the presumption of politico-legal coherence, of a unity of the state's purpose or effect. The other is to abandon the disposition to juxtapose the two opposing traits of legality and its exception as the thesis and antithesis of a dialectical teleology. The postcolonial form of sovereign power is paradoxical, but its contradictions demonstrate an innate 'intention' toward neither a grand liberal nor an absolutely despotic synthesis. To coin a term from analytical philosophy, the postcolonial form of power is 'paraconsistent,' comprising logically exclusive truths (see e.g., Priest 2002).

Such a conceptualization makes the empirical experience of postcolonial discretion accessible in newly nuanced ways. Rather than paralyzing analysis over consternation at the hypocrisy or duplicity of some specific acts of executive agency, such paraconsistent paradoxes, when seen from the perspective of the 'less than' dually embodied form of sovereign power, demand further investigation, the un-thinking of complacent models. Mr Chiluba's account of his behavior as lawfully illegal alerts us to the constitutional continuities between the imperial monarchy and a prerogativist form of power. This, however, is not the end-point of analysis, but its beginning. One need not uncritically endorse Mr Chiluba's distinction between his 'private' and 'public' embodiments – neither as rationale for, nor as obfuscation of his official mischief. Instead, Chiluba's distinction poses the analytical task of understanding how this paradox resonates across the polity as a whole. What are its effects for how prerogativism extends its logic from State House (the geographical seat of presidential authority) into the various sites where state authority is exercised and the legitimacy of rule is contested? What work (procedural, ideological, reciprocal, coercive) is required for postcolonial power to accomplish stability and continuity? What skills are required for containing the tensions and fissures inherent in such a paradoxical form of power and how are they refined? Where do these capacities reside? What is, actually, empirically accomplished and by whom, through what practices? And, finally, what is the role of legality in subjecting prerogativist rule to popular accountability? These are the questions which the ensuing case studies (Chapters 8 and 9) of two of Lusaka's most controversial lawyers seek to illuminate.

# 8 In the shadows of prerogativism

Previous chapters have illuminated the workings of prerogativist power through the various juridical institutions and practices entrusted with shoring up the legitimacy of the state – trials and tribunals, an ad hoc task force, constitution-making pageantry. This final case study shifts perspective to look directly at how political legality is manifested in the everyday work of governing a plurality of peoples with divergent interests. At stake in this analysis is the status of political legality in contemporary Zambia. Does anyone, as political commentator Reginal Ntomba (2016, 33) asks, care 'about what the law says when political survival is desperately at stake?' Is it so, as Ntomba claims, that in Zambian politics, 'it's not always that the law prevails; many times expedience carries the day.'

The vignette sketched in this chapter highlights the dramatic rise and fall of one lawyer-politician and seeks to add two things to the analysis thus far. One, it shows explicitly how an ambiguous regulatory framework surrounding political party institutions serves to blur the boundary between the legal and the political in the executive operations of the state. Two, it makes tangible the ways in which prerogativist powers are bound to the physical persona of the president, enhancing the volatility of government grounded in a prerogativist form of power, while also confining the scope of its productivity. This chapter also provides further elaboration of a motif that emerged in the excursus regarding the dynamics of prerogativist power largely freed from the constraints of countervailing civic and media contestation.

## Managing the migration of power

As we saw in Chapter 7, President Chiluba ascribed his 'lawfully illegal' acts to his persona as a politician, that is, to his position as head of the Movement for Multiparty Democracy (MMD). Chapter 7 argued accordingly that it is presidents' 'not-quite' duality – their coterminous embodiment of an 'eternal' constitutional office, as well as that of a mortal private politician – that enables the powers of prerogativism. Even without recourse to the prerogativist powers of the republican presidency, the leader of the ruling party enjoys far-flung political privileges. Zambia has not seen coalition governments; in the words of former President Edgar Lungu (Mfula/Reuters 6 July 2017), 'We follow a system

DOI: 10.4324/9780429198984-12

of winner takes all.' The ruling party, inasmuch as it maintains a parliamentary majority, has unbridled leeway to determine state policy and legislation. The legacy of the Second Republic, in which ruling party leadership determined government policy, has persisted. Members of the president's cabinet, composed of fellow ruling-party comrades, partake in this power in the pursuit of their sectoral and personal agendas. A minister, while a vital cog in the executive machinery of the state, is not the president, however, and ministerial powers are exercised at the president's pleasure. Indeed, presidential power is indivisible, even when shared or delegated. But what if the president is weakened – distracted by ill-health or embroiled in legal assaults on his legitimacy?

Such conditions can create ambivalence surrounding the seat of authority. A ruler's illness or absence can catalyze a struggle over succession within the ruling party. This is what happened in 2014 when fifth republican president, Michael Sata, fell terminally ill. An examination of the inner workings of his administration thus provides a unique opportunity to examine the volatility of political outcomes associated with a prerogativist form of power. What happens to absolute power when it can no longer be wielded single-handedly? More cogently, what does the process by which presidential power migrates, wholly or in part, from one body to another reveal about the nature of that power and the tenor of its embodiment? How does the prerogative persevere in a state of liminality eventuated by the demise of the president's mortal body?

## *A slippery baton*

In 1991, Zambia experienced its first transfer of postcolonial power – from the United National Independence Party's (UNIP) Kenneth Kaunda to the MMD's Frederick Chiluba. The 1991 change of president also implied a new ruling party and sweeping changes in the government's policy regime, entailing a profound restructuring and repopulation of the state apparatus. As a result, and against the backdrop of the mass mobilization of Zambian society that brought the MMD to power, it appeared to some (e.g., Joseph 1992) that the nature of power itself had undergone a qualitative transformation, from authoritarian rule to liberal constitutionalism. This impression did not last long (Wunsch et al. 1992, Mwiinga 1994), but the dramatic nature of the political transition obscured the 'miraculous' sleight of hand that had transpired. The miracle in question was the migration of the president's 'transcendental' powers from one mortal body to another.

In 2001, 2008 and again in 2014, similar passages of presidential authority took place, but in these later instances the migration of power occurred within the ruling party. First Chiluba passed the baton to Levy Mwanawasa; then, seven years later, the late Mr Mwanawasa's powers devolved to his vice-president, Rupiah Banda. After the mid-term death of the Patriotic Front's (PF) Michael Sata, in 2014, his minister of justice, Edgar Lungu, acceded to the presidency. These conveyances of power, from Chiluba to Mwanawasa, and from Sata to Lungu, especially, were marked by a brief hiatus during which the actual locus of power appeared difficult to pin down. It seems that such transitions are especially fertile moments to observe the dynamics of political legality, the fleeting yet consequential fusion of the political and the legal. Examining such miraculous, yet routine migrations of power, allows us to see its volatility, and to observe how this volatility resonates throughout the state apparatus. As a prelude to a more detailed examination of these dynamics during, and immediately after, the Sata presidency, let us look at the transmission of power from Frederick Chiluba to his successor, Levy Mwanawasa.[1]

The transition from the Chiluba presidency to Levy Mwanawasa's first term in office in 2001 taxed the paradoxical and fragile continuity between the president's 'immortal' embodiments. Mr Chiluba, as we have seen, was reluctant to relinquish the reins of power. Given the popular animosity toward his person – epitomized, and catalyzed, by daily attacks in the *Post* newspaper – the question of his successor was key to his post-presidential security. As the clock was running out on designating the MMD's candidate for the 2001 elections, Mr Chiluba finally indicated his endorsement of former Vice-President[2] Levy Mwanawasa as the MMD's candidate. In doing so, he bypassed his most loyal lieutenants.[3]

In the absence of Chiluba's own memoirs, the justification for his endorsement of Mwanawasa remains unclear: On the one hand, Ntomba (2016, 31) suggests that Chiluba saw Mwanawasa as his 'puppet.' Support for this premise rests on the fact that Mwanawasa ostensibly suffered brain damage after a serious automobile accident in 1991 (Larmer & Fraser 2007, 630), possibly leading Chiluba to consider him weak and pliable. Another hypothesis has Chiluba responding to the MMD's fragile political situation. In this scenario, Chiluba considered Mwanawasa to be the safest candidate to challenge robust opposition forces by virtue of his distance from the Chiluba faction. Thus, according to Ryder

1 In his analysis of Levy Mwanawasa's death and funeral ceremony, historian Walima Kalusa (2017) provides a sublime illustration of the transcendental character of the president's body. In Kalusa's account (ibid., 1147; citing the *Sunday Post* of 12 September 2008), the embalmer commissioned by the Ministry of Health injected the president's corpse with fluids intended to bring about the 'permanent preservation of the body' and ensure that Mr Mwanawasa "would, for the next 50 years, 'look the way he used to look when he was alive.'" Kalusa portrays the pomp and ritual of Mr Mwanawasa's funeral as a ploy by the ruling MMD, caught up in an internal power struggle following the president's untimely demise, to instill faith in the party and its unity. This is no doubt accurate, but beyond this, we can see in Mr Mwanawasa's state funeral a concerted effort to sustain popular faith in the immortal character of the presidency itself. This aim was underscored by the testimony of no less an authority than founding President Kenneth Kaunda himself who, in Kalusa's account (ibid., 1150) "insisted that, even in death, Mwanawasa would continue to 'ask God to take care of Zambia.'"

2 Mr Mwanawasa resigned from the vice-presidency in 1994 'publicly accusing the government of corruption and economic irresponsibility. Chiluba allegedly allowed public officials to embezzle assets from the ministries they controlled and rewarded key supporters with old-style paper bags filled with cash' (Ryder 2011, 4). Former MMD minister and future PF Vice-President Guy Scott (2019, 99) provides an insider account of this incident.

3 According to one account (Ntomba 2016, 31), these included MMD politicians Enoch Kavindele, Emmanuel Kasonde, Miles Sampa, future President Michael Sata, as well as Eric Silwamba, who was also the MMD's legal counsel and Chiluba's close advisor.

(2011, 2), 'Chiluba's decision appears to have been based on his conviction that Mwanawasa's personal integrity would reflect well on the party and on his own legacy.' A third hypothesis, also noted by Ntomba (op. cit., 32), is that Chiluba wanted someone who could transcend tribal loyalties (Mwanawasa represents a small ethnolinguistic minority, while Chiluba comes from the populous ciBemba-speaking majority), and would thus be better positioned to unite the country. These three premises are not mutually exclusive; each could have played a role in Chiluba's decision to back Mwanawasa in the 2001 elections.

Conventionally, a party's leader is automatically its presidential candidate. In an unprecedented arrangement, Chiluba sought to remain at the head of the MMD despite Mwanawasa's candidacy. Ultimately, Chiluba became 'frustrated by the bickering' (ibid., 33), and stepped down from the MMD presidency after a few months, whereupon Mwanawasa took over as acting president of the MMD. All in all, the conveyance of power from Chiluba to Mwanawasa was anything but straightforward. As Ntomba (ibid., 34) notes,

> In addition to the illegality of appointing Mwanawasa as acting party president, the National Executive Committee [of the MMD] allowed him to act for three years, instead of the three months stated in the party statutes, after which an extraordinary congress should have been called. Mwanawasa's tacticians were keen to have him gain control of the party, and they were seemingly only prepared to call for an election when they were sure he had become rooted. So determined were they that they did it at the expense of their own laws.

The MMD presidency was vital to Mr Mwanawasa's ability to govern Zambia, and his allies within the party were evidently prepared to bend their statutes to ensure that Mr Mwanawasa was in control. This bending of the party constitution mirrored Mr Mwanwasa's maneuvers to undermine any residual leverage Mr Chiluba might have had over him. The centerpiece of this strategy saw the new president ask parliament to lift Chiluba's legal immunity, thus allowing for the former president to be indicted for abuse of office, etc. (Chapter 7). These were all decisionist maneuvers in the Schmittian sense – unprecedented and discretionary acts of an exceptional sovereign that took place outside the normal framework of both party and statutory law. Mr Mwanawasa's Task Force against Corruption, in particular, established by presidential decree, 'did not possess the legal personality that an act of parliament would have conferred' (Ryder 2011, 4). Indeed, it had no legal grounding whatsoever, despite the fact that it represented the Mwanawasa presidency's most significant political and financial investment.

If the transition from Chiluba to Mwanawasa was fraught with irregularities, the transmission of power to Edgar Lungu after Michael Sata's premature death in 2014 was messier still; indeed, it had all the hallmarks of a palace coup. Unlike Chiluba's explicit endorsement of Mwanawasa, President Sata's choice of a successor was widely disputed, and many crucial decisions appear to have been made in a shroud of secrecy, muddled by rumors and complicated by Mr Sata's rapidly declining health (Scott 2019, 236–44). After Michael Sata's death,

Vice-President Guy Scott assumed the role of acting president, as per constitutional mandate, pending a by-election. The previous time a president, Levy Mwanawasa, had died mid-term, Vice-President Rupiah Banda had emerged as the party's candidate for the presidential by-election. For evident racial reasons, Mr Scott, a Zambian-born son of White English settlers had, in his own words (Scott 2019, 238), 'no realistic prospect of being either the candidate or indeed the winner of the next election.' The Patriotic Front was internally divided concerning who should stand against the United Party for National Development's (UPND) formidable Hakainde Hichilema; the party was nevertheless agreed, it seems, that their candidate could not be White.

Who, then, would carry on Michael Sata's legacy? From the PF's assent to power in the 2011 elections until early 2014, it increasingly seemed that the party's secretary-general (SG), Wynter Kabimba was, alongside Guy Scott, Sata's main lieutenant (Zimba 2012). Mr Kabimba's assertive role in building up the PF's grassroots organization and in enforcing party discipline among PF cadres strengthened this impression. His appointment as minister of justice alongside the secretary-general's post gave Mr Kabimba unprecedented power within both government and the party. As the president's condition weakened, Wynter Kabimba seemed a strong candidate to succeed Sata.[4]

In early 2014, Mr Sata disappeared from public view and fortunes shifted. In August 2014, Mr Kabimba was sacked from both his party and cabinet positions and a faction around Edgar Lungu wrested control of the PF apparatus. When Sata flew to London for medical treatment in late October, Lungu had been authorized to act as president. Upon Sata's death in London, Vice-President Scott assumed the interim presidency, temporarily wresting the presidential 'instruments of power' (Scott, loc. cit.) from Mr Lungu. The Scott faction (for want of a better term) attempted to regain control of the party and rallied behind Sata's nephew and Deputy Commerce Minister Miles Sampa. Sampa's candidacy was ultimately overturned in court, leaving Edgar Lungu to stand as the PF's candidate in the 2014 by-election. The practical details of this contested transfer of power have been dealt with amply elsewhere and need not engage us here.[5] In what follows, I explore the inner workings of the Sata administration in the run up to the dramatic events surrounding President Sata's inopportune departure.

## A tale of two tribunals

President Mwanawasa's adroit maneuvers against the little-loved Mr Chiluba, alongside his success in securing debt relief in his first term (2001–6), won him

4 The glossy monthly *Bulletin & Record* (Zimba 2012, 6) published a glowing profile of Mr Kabimba with this introduction: 'The Patriotic Front's secretary general … currently ranks as the third most important person in the ruling Patriotic Front and is seen by some as possibly a likely successor to party president Michael Sata.'

5 See, for example, Goldring and Wahman (2016) and Fraser (2017). See especially Guy Scott's (2019) compelling account.

considerable political breathing space. Mwanawasa was re-elected in 2006 with a substantially improved margin over his razor-thin majority in 2001 (Gould 2007).[6] Zambia's enduring poverty, Mwanawasa's abrasive personality and the president's endless bickering with the Oasis Forum took its toll, however. From 2001 to 2006, the opposition Patriotic Front, led by veteran politician Michael Sata, increased its parliamentary presence from 1 to 43 seats. In addition, the PF captured majority control of local government bodies in virtually all of Zambia's main towns, suggesting substantial support from urban populations (Larmer & Fraser 2007).

After Mwanawasa's untimely passing in August 2008, Rupiah Banda, his vice-president, stood as the MMD candidate in the presidential by-election. Banda squeaked through with 40% to Sata's 38% share of the poll, with an anemic 45% voter turnout (Cheeseman & Hinfelaar 2010). In preparation for the 2011 elections, Sata reorganized the PF's management. In 2009, outspoken Lusaka lawyer Wynter Kabimba was assigned the role of secretary-general (Hopkins 2010).

Mr Kabimba's relationship with Michael Sata went back to the late 1980s when Mr Kabimba was Lusaka's town clerk, and Sata was Lusaka's district governor. After retiring from the local government in 1995, Mr Kabimba launched his own successful private practice in Lusaka. Since the 1990s, Mr Kabimba had been a political floater, tenuously involved with a number of opposition splinter parties. After throwing in with his former boss, Michael Sata and his party, the Patriotic Front, Wynter Kabimba rapidly rose into the national political spotlight.

As the PF's secretary-general, Kabimba amplified the party's use of legal tactics to pursue political ends.[7] Mr Kabimba also managed the revamping of the PF's downstream party machinery, beefing up the PF's presence below the provincial level. Aware that the PF lost the 2008 by-election in rural constituencies, Secretary-General Kabimba sought to mobilize PF bodies at the provincial and district levels. Surprisingly, perhaps, the resulting organizational setup resembled the Leninist party model that had inspired Kaunda during the struggle against colonialism (cf. Hopkins 2010). Mr Kabimba also made his mark as a stout advocate of discipline on the Patriotic Front. Ostensibly supported by a strong mandate from the president, by his own account (ibid.), Mr Kabimba closely scrutinized the behavior of PF officials for indications of corruption or misdoing.

It may be a mere coincidence that a lawyer was called upon to consolidate the PF's political structures, but perhaps not. In any case, Wynter Kabimba's analysis of the PF's predicament in the wake of the 2008 elections reflected a strikingly lawyerly mode of strategizing. Mr Kabimba's legal knowledge and his practical

6 In 2006, Mwanawasa pulled in 43% of the vote with a 70% voter turnout, which translates roughly into support of 30% of the electorate. Michael Sata came in second with a little less than 30% of the raw vote.

7 This tendency is epitomized by the PF's frequent use of court petitions to overturn electoral results.

litigation experience prepared him well to instill obedience in the Patriotic Front's party constitution and manifesto. It is also likely that the autonomy he enjoyed by virtue of his lucrative private legal practice gave him the leeway to throw himself into this risk-laden political project. In many ways, Wynter Kabimba invested the juridical capital the legal profession had accumulated since 1991 into the political realm extremely effectively. While drawing on the same degrees of freedom offered by post–Cold War political and economic liberalization, Mr Kabimba's embodiment of political legality was a far cry from the ethos of non-partisan, liberal nationalism embraced by the Oasis Forum.

President Sata acknowledged his secretary-general's instrumental role in the PF's victory in the 2011 elections by appointing Wynter Kabimba as minister of justice in 2012. Mr Kabimba thus found himself occupying the position of secretary-general of the ruling Patriotic Front alongside that of minister in the republican cabinet. This dual appointment renders the paradoxical duality of sovereign power in the juridical realm uncommonly transparent. Merging these positions in a single incumbent, who simultaneously runs the ruling party and oversees the judicial system (including the ongoing constitutional review process), represents as tangible an embodiment of political legality as one might imagine. Mr Kabimba held onto these two positions for two years, until August 2014, when he was summarily sacked from both posts.[8] The ways that Wynter Kabimba sought to deploy prerogativist powers during those two years provide materials for an illuminating case study of political legality in the everyday workings of a postcolonial jurisdiction.

## *Disciplining the Patriotic Front*

According to the party constitution, the secretary-general of the Patriotic Front is a political appointment by the head of the party. The PF's SG is commonly described as the party's chief executive officer (CEO) – an employee answerable to party leadership, yet wielding a broad array of managerial powers. The party constitution stipulates a wide range of duties for the secretary-general. As SG, Mr Kabimba focused on a few priority areas, promoting the aims of the party manifesto in government programs, overseeing discipline within the party and consolidating the party's grassroots structures. The SG's work is nominally subordinate to the will and oversight of the party president, but in real life, the position can bequeath a great deal of discretionary power on the president's behalf, especially if the president is distracted or ailing.

8 Exactly two months before President Sata passed away in a London hospital, Wynter Kabimba was replaced in both his party and cabinet positions by Edgar Lungu. Mr Lungu is a lawyer with a military background, and was then an elected PF MP from Lusaka's Chawama constituency. President Sata proffered no reason for Mr Kabimba's dismissal and Kabimba gave no public statement. Concerning Sata's decision to appoint Edgar Lungu to replace Mr Kabimba, Vice-President Guy Scott (2019, 237) notes that 'personally I doubt [Sata] really knew what he was doing.'

A cabinet minister is also a political office, appointed by the republican president from among the members of parliament (MPs) and ratified by parliament. In Wynter Kabimba's case, his parliamentary seat was not an elected position but based rather on presidential prerogative to appoint up to ten non-elected parliamentarians (see Chapter 5). The minister of justice oversees the juridical apparatus, including efforts at constitutional reform. Such processes represent moments of heightened interaction between legal and political principles, conjunctures where politics can and does intervene directly in defining the contours of legality itself. The ongoing cycle of constitution-making inherited by the Sata administration had begun in 2003 and has been the focus of intense political dispute (Chapter 6).

In Zambia, a party's president is conventionally that party's presidential candidate in the national elections, normally held every five years. This implies that the president of the ruling party and that of the republic is the same person. Inasmuch as the ruling party's secretary-general is appointed to cabinet – as was the case with Wynter Kabimba – the norms of accountability regulating the behavior of the dual officeholder are ambiguous. Can it be assumed that the interests of the party are identical to those of the judiciary? There is no constitutional provision for such a duality of power, and the concomitant ambiguities of accountability (to the party or to the constitution) are masked by the indivisible executive mandate undergirding both positions.

Wynter Kabimba is not the first ruling party secretary to be appointed to cabinet. Mr Kabimba's mentor, Michael Sata, also served simultaneously as ruling party national secretary and as cabinet minister, although his position in Chiluba's MMD government as minister without portfolio distanced him from the day-to-day workings of the line ministries. Although Mr Kabimba is on record as having initially resisted a cabinet appointment, he eventually learned to appreciate the opportunities it gave him to provide political guidance, or 'coordination' as he put it, to his colleagues in cabinet. Minister Kabimba explicitly exploited his position in cabinet to promote the PF's manifesto among fellow cabinet ministers – with clear echoes of 'the Party and its Government' underlying his efforts.

Wynter Kabimba's time in government was not without controversy. He had been probed by the Anti-Corruption Commission in late 2012 over allegations of shady dealings with the controversial oil transport and storage giant Trafigura; sinister rumors had also circulated about alleged opaque financial dealings with hardnosed Zambian financier Rajan Mahtani, purportedly a major PF backer (Goodley & Hollingsworth 2012). No indictments emerged from these insinuations, however, and Mr Kabimba was seen to enjoy Mr Sata's unwavering endorsement. Of all the controversies surrounding Mr Kabimba's brief moment of power, the one that gained the greatest public visibility involved a tribunal investigation instigated by the Chief Justice (CJ) into Wynter Kabimba's conduct on the basis of a public complaint. While the tribunal, chaired by Supreme Court Justice Evan Hamaundu, disposed of the charges against Kabimba with little effort (see below), the proceedings of the investigation reveal the subtle contradictions rooted in the duality of Wynter Kabimba's powers.

In order to make sense of the Kabimba Tribunal and the light it sheds on political legality, one needs to go back a few years to an earlier tribunal, involving Ms Dora Siliya, an MMD minister who attracted a great deal of public scrutiny during Rupiah Banda's brief tenure as republican president. The Kabimba Tribunal would deal with the legitimacy of Mr Kabimba's powers to harness the legal system to undermine his party's political opponents; Dora Siliya was just such an opponent.

## *Legalism vs political contingency*

After winning a parliamentary seat on the MMD ticket in 2006, Dora Siliya was appointed deputy minister in President Levy Mwanawasa's second cabinet. She was soon elevated to the full ministerial portfolio at the Ministry of Communications and Transport. While at the Ministry of Communications and Transport, Ms Siliya became embroiled in a controversy revolving around the privatization of the public telecommunication utility, Zamtel. In preparation for selling off the utility, the ministry contracted with a Cayman Islands–based company, RP Capital, to assess Zamtel's worth. In awarding this contract, the value of which was pegged at $2 million, Ms Siliya bypassed mandatory procurement protocols and ignored the legal advice of the Attorney-General (AG) (Chama 2017). Indeed, based on the testimony which subsequently came to light, Minister Siliya managed the deal much as one would a personal business transaction. Stirred by public complaints, the Chief Justice established a tribunal of three judges, chaired by Deputy Chief Justice Dennis Chirwa, to investigate whether (among other, lesser charges) Dora Siliya had breached the parliamentary and ministerial code of conduct. Had this been the case, Ms Siliya would have been stripped of both her ministerial and parliamentary positions.

The Chirwa Tribunal documented all manner of impropriety in the way Dora Siliya was awarded the RP Capital contract but, somewhat inexplicably, absolved her of abusing the ministerial code of conduct. Not surprisingly, no evidence emerged proving that Ms Siliya would have received a kickback or any other financial benefit from RP Capital, an offshore financial broker specializing in 'unregulated collective investment schemes.' It was evident, however, that she gave RP Capital preferential treatment and used her privileged knowledge as minister to grant the company pecuniary benefit (a specific breach of the code). Instead of affirming this obvious misbehavior, the Chirwa Tribunal settled for recommending that the president consider whether Ms Siliya's failure to take the AG's advice into consideration was a breach of the constitution.

Both parties appealed to the High Court, where Justice Philip Musonda further absolved Dora Siliya of any allegations of unconstitutional behavior. Musonda reasoned that the law obliged a minister to consult with the AG, but not to comply with the advice given. According to Ms Siliya's lawyer, Eric Silwamba (2009), such advice was in any case merely "'legalistic' from the executive's point of view."[9] By this, Mr Silwamba meant that the AG's advice did not necessarily 'factor the social, political and economic conditions prevailing at the time, which elected officials representing the people must take into account.' On further appeal, the Supreme Court affirmed the High Court judgment, ruling that constitutional issues were beyond the tribunal's jurisdiction. These rulings suggest that representatives of the executive branch of government have exceptional capacities to stand outside juridical dictates if 'social, political and economic' contingencies so demand. By virtue of these exceptional provisions, Minister Siliya survived judicial scrutiny of her unconventional procedures without a scratch.

### *Dora Siliya's electoral blues*

As secretary-general of the Patriotic Front, Wynter Kabimba oversaw a spectacularly successful electoral campaign in the combined presidential, parliamentary and local government elections of 2011.[10] The PF captured the presidency and increased its presence in parliament by 17 new seats (an increase of nearly 30%). The fallout from the parliamentary polls generated a flood of litigation. In nearly half of the parliamentary contests, the losing candidate petitioned the court to overturn the electoral result. Quite a number of these petitions were successful, especially when the petitioner succeeded in demonstrating bribery, vote-buying or other corrupt practices on the part of the victor. Dora Siliya's re-election as an MMD member of parliament from the Petauke Central constituency in Eastern Province was among the petitioned results. By official count, Ms Siliya had defeated the PF's Leonard Banda by 14,561 votes to Banda's 5,759.[11]

Leonard Banda charged that Dora Siliya's electoral campaign was marred by 'widespread undue voter influence, electoral bribery, voter treating, abuse of government resources and all manner of illegal practices contrary to the Electoral Act and the Electoral Code of Conduct' (*Banda v Siliya* 2011). Justice Charles Kajimanga dismissed the petitioner's allegations, but his ruling was overturned on appeal to the Supreme Court. In June 2013, almost two years after the election, acting Chief Justice Lombe Chibesakunda concurred with Mr Banda's original charges and nullified Ms Siliya's election, leaving Petauke Central without a member of parliament pending a by-election.

Predictably, the CJ's ruling spawned an outcry among opposition politicians. Following the nullification of Dora Siliya's election, MMD President Nevers Mumba issued a press statement on 30 June 2013 stating that 'MMD may have a reason to believe that the PF agenda of depleting the opposition numbers of Parliament is now being aided by the Supreme Court bench.' Mr Mumba singled

9 Mr Silwamba was a member of the legal team that secured an acquittal in President Chiluba's abuse-of-office trial (see Chapter 7).

10 Guy Scott (2019) provides a detailed and colorful account.

11 When Edgar Lungu took over the Patriotic Front after Michael Sata's death, Dora Siliya shifted allegiance from the MMD to the PF while retaining her Petauke seat. She subsequently held several ministerial positions in President Lungu's cabinets.

out acting CJ Chibesakunda for siding with the PF in the nullification of several MMD elections, including that of Ms Siliya. For these insinuations of judicial prejudice, Mr Mumba was subsequently cited for contempt of court (about which more shortly).

It is worth pausing here to note that for the purpose of election petitions, Zambian courts have adopted a standard of proof which is 'somewhere between the civil standard, the balance of probabilities, and the criminal standard of beyond reasonable doubt' (Munshya 2013; citing *Lewanika and Others v Chiluba*). Hence, while in a technical sense Ms Siliya's alleged misbehavior had to be 'established to a fairly high degree of convincing clarity' (ibid.), it did not need to meet the criteria of a criminal offense for her election to be nullified. This distinction between 'civil' and 'criminal' corruption would prove critical in the ensuing fracas over Ms Siliya's right to re-contest the Petauke seat.

Although the Supreme Court ruling of June 2013 should have settled Dora Siliya's by-electoral ineligibility once and for all, her lawyer managed to re-open the issue by initiating a judicial review of the case in the High Court.[12] This action no longer cited the Chirwa Tribunal and its ruling. Instead, in August 2013, Ms Siliya's lawyers sought to reboot their client's political fortunes by asking the High Court to review the validity of the Electoral Commission of Zambia's (ECZ) decision to disqualify her from filing a nomination for the Petauke by-election. Ms Siliya's claim was based on the fact that while the Supreme Court affirmed her complicity in electoral corruption, it had not issued an 'official report' to the ECZ documenting her misbehavior, as stipulated in the Electoral Act (No. 12 of 2006).[13]

The Electoral Act does not anticipate a situation where the High Court's rejection of a petition would be overturned by the Supreme Court. The High Court could not have issued a report about Ms Siliya's corrupt practices, as required by the Act, because it didn't find any. The Supreme Court noted corrupt practices in Ms Siliya's campaign, but the Act doesn't assign the Supreme Court with

12 In Zambia, the State Proceedings Act (*Laws of Zambia*, Cap 71) blocks citizens from obtaining an injunction against the state. Such a motion would have been unthinkable under the party-state of the Second Republic, but from the mid-1990s on, judicial review has increasingly been used to challenge the discretionary powers of the executive branch. Judicial review can, in principle, only be invoked to scrutinize the *procedural* correctness of an act or decision of the state, not its substantial merits. The distinction is a fine one, however. A court can, for example, be asked to rule on whether a minister's decision was 'reasonable' but not whether it was legal (see p. 135, note 16 above). The inherent subtleties of this distinction have opened the floodgates for the adjudication of many kinds of executive action.

13 In August 2013, the Electoral Commission of Zambia announced that it would not accept Dora Siliya's nomination as a candidate for the Petauke position. On 3 September 2013, High Court Justice Ms Mungeni Siwale Mulenga ruled for the plaintiff (Siliya) and obliged the ECZ to accept her nomination.

Then Attorney General, Mumba Malila, appealed this ruling to the Supreme Court. Despite the AG's plea, the Supreme Court upheld the High Court decision, allowing Dora Siliya (and several others) to take part in subsequent by-elections.

an obligation to report to the ECZ pursuant to its nullification of an election. Less tritely, the Act does not stipulate what level of 'corruption' should trigger a report. Handing out free beer and T-shirts may be justifiably seen as an illicit electoral practice, sufficient, perhaps, to nullify a candidate's victory, but it is not a criminal offense. It is noteworthy that none of the allegations brought against Dora Siliya by Leonard Banda, her competitor from the Patriotic Front, involved any activity which is remotely criminal. The wording of the Act suggests that the court should issue a report in cases of misbehavior which are liable to prosecution, but is this the only instance where a report is required? Or is it so that only 'corrupt practices or illegal practices' that are legally criminal are sufficient to justify annulment? The legislation is unclear. Indeed, the Act fails to spell out what kind of 'report' the court should issue. Generally, court proceedings result in judgments. Did the drafters of the Electoral Act expect the court to prepare an additional document and, if so, who or what might legitimately author such a report? Again, this is unclear.

Just prior to the Supreme Court's ruling that reinstated Ms Siliya's eligibility, Attorney General Mumba Malila had complained (as reported by *Lusaka Voice*, 26 February 2014) that

> The State is unhappy with the way in which the learned High Court judge interpreted the law. The High Court judge failed to give a purposeful interpretation of Section 22 of the Electoral Act but preferred to rely on statutory interpretation.

In this uncommon criticism of a court judgment, the AG invokes the notion of 'purposive' interpretation, according to which statutory legislation should not be read with rigid literalism, but interpreted in light of the court's social and political context. Such an approach can be used, as critics of purposivism have argued, to render the constitution 'the plaything of willful judges' (Bork 2005), or inversely, to help the judiciary keep legislation relevant to the contingencies of the times, as argued by, among others, US Supreme Court Justice Stephen Breyer (Sunstein 2006). What, or whose purpose was High Court Justice Mulenga to have served? The state's premier lawyer suggests that some valid purpose existed which transcends the literal words of the Electoral Act, or perhaps that the statute in question can (or should, under certain circumstances) be read in more than one way. Note also the evident resonance between the AG's purposiveness and MMD attorney Silwamba's views (above) on the importance of social, political and economic conditions for judicial rulings. While the letter of the law would seem to demand a 'report' from the court stipulating Dora Siliya's guilt of corruption, Section 22 of the Act also clearly intends that corrupt politicians be prevented from re-contesting elections they have won unfairly. Perhaps it is not misplaced to suggest that the AG's invocation of purposiveness was an affirmation of the inevitability of political legality in such cases. In this case, however, he may have felt that it was a political legality of the wrong kind. In the end, the court sought security, as courts are prone to do, in the literal parameters of correct procedure.

Against this background, we can now return our attention to Wynter Kabimba and the paradoxical relationship between exception and legality in the ways he sought to embody a form of political power that is 'more than one less than two.'

## *In the name of exception: The Kabimba Tribunal*

After the PF's electoral victory in 2011, the judiciary came under assault. Soon after assuming office, President Sata instigated a tribunal under the Inquiries Act to investigate misbehavior by three senior judges in the High and Supreme Courts (for further details, see Chapter 9). It is difficult not to see these investigations as political inquisitions, aimed at causing disquiet and indecision on the senior bench. The three judges sought a judicial review to challenge the president's decision to have them investigated. The main grounds of their application were that the president had overstepped his powers when he bypassed the Judicial Service Commission, the body constitutionally empowered to investigate alleged misbehavior by members of the judiciary. The trio's application was struck down by the Supreme Court with the remarkably explicit prerogativist reasoning that the president could not have overstepped his powers since he is 'the overall authority on everything' (*Attorney General v Mutuna* 2012).

This is not the place to delve further into the convoluted case against the three judges;[14] I bring it up to highlight the contentious atmosphere surrounding the relationship between the judiciary and the executive as the Patriotic Front took over the reins of power. In historical terms, the Zambia judiciary has generally been deferential in its relationship toward executive discretion. Indeed, when the three judges mentioned above challenged the president's authority to have them investigated, the Supreme Court noted that 'the issues raised in this appeal [had] never been raised in any court of law' before this (ibid.)

To recap: Dora Siliya was exonerated twice in the Supreme Court; this was vexatious for the PF. With Ms Siliya back in the race, Petauke Central would no doubt continue to elude PF control. Beyond that, the Supreme Court ruling was particularly bothersome for Wynter Kabimba, due to the fact that Ms Siliya's acquittal highlighted his failure, despite concerted efforts, to block just such an outcome. Soon after his appointment as minister of justice, Mr Kabimba undertook a campaign to see that Section 22 of the Electoral Act (disqualifying corrupt politicians from re-contesting elections) was rigorously enforced. In this, he had the support of at least one stalwart champion of political liberalism, Transparency International Zambia (TIZ). On 23 July 2013, TIZ director Goodwell Lungu (cited in Hamaundu Tribunal report, 44) wrote to the Electoral Commission of Zambia expressing

14 Note, however, the irony in the fact that the three Supreme Court judges who came under scrutiny in 2012 were the same three justices who, in 2003, sat on the tribunal which led to the unconstitutional dismissal of Mukelebai Mukelebai, the Director of Public Prosecutions (Chapter 5).

> Transparency International Zambia's concerns regarding what [Goodwell Lungu] termed as the trend where the High Court and the Supreme Court were nullifying parliamentary seats on account of corruption but the same candidates who were being cited for corruption were allowed by the Electoral Commission to re-contest the nullified seats.

Mr Kabimba harbored similar concerns. The evident purpose of his efforts was to prevent discredited opposition MMD and UPND politicians from contesting their annulled seats in subsequent by-elections. Given her original electoral margin, Dora Siliya was likely to repeat her landslide victory against the PF candidate in a by-election. This was not in the PF's interests. In light of the fact that the PF had captured only 40% of the parliamentary seats in the 2011 poll, using Section 22 against opposition competitors was vital to the party's political fortunes. The PF petitioned 50 of the 68 contests it had lost and, through by-election victories, succeeded by May 2014 to narrow the margin to 70 of 141 occupied seats. With 22 parliamentary by-elections taking place in the first three years of the PF government, by-election strategy was of key importance to the PF and its ambitious secretary-general.

Mr Kabimba seems to have been particularly intent on preventing Dora Siliya from participating in the Petauke Central by-election. So much so, in fact, that he wrote to the Solicitor General asking for a legal opinion about Dora Siliya's eligibility to be on the ballot. It was this move that eventually led to his investigation by the judiciary, with the purpose of testing the limits of his authority as a minister of justice to promote PF party interests. What triggered the investigation was the fact that Mr Kabimba forwarded his query concerning Ms Siliya's eligibility to the acting Chief Justice. This was unusual. What made this move particularly contentious was the fact that his letter was written on Patriotic Front stationary. The formal substance of the complaints against Wynter Kabimba is that he used his ministerial post to exact material ('pecuniary') benefit for the PF by requesting a legal opinion from the Solicitor General and passing it onto the PF lawyers without charge. The underlying premise is that the opinion was (potentially) advantageous for the PF's political situation. Mr Kabimba was also accused of putting ministerial pressure on the Chief Justice in order to exact a judgment beneficial for his party.

## *Wynter Kabimba's stationary collision*

Establishing Mr Kabimba's abuse of power before the tribunal implied unbundling a complicated series of actions. In order to do so, the tribunal needed to demonstrate Mr Kabimba's disregard for legislative constraints. The tribunal's mandate and proceedings will be discussed below. Before that, it will be helpful to present an annotated summary of the relevant facts of the matter as recorded in the tribunal's report. In abridged form, these were as follows:

> *7. In his quest to contribute to what became public debate, Hon. Wynter Kabimba between 23rd July, 2013 and 1st August, 2013 sought an opinion from the*

> *Solicitor-General* [Musa Mwenye] *regarding the legal position of the candidates whose parliamentary seats had been nullified on account of corrupt practices.*
>
> *8. Between 23rd July, 2013 and 1st August, 2013, the Solicitor-General duly rendered the legal opinion to the Honourable Minister of Justice.*

Solicitor General Musa Mwenya's response was precisely what Wynter Kabimba had hoped for. According to the Solicitor General, the Electoral Act is clear on the point that politicians who have been found guilty of electoral corruption should not be allowed to stand for election for five years. The Solicitor General proceeds to consider how to enforce this rule. '[I]t is clear' he writes,

> that what triggers the disqualification of the candidate who is adjudged, in an election petition, to have been involved in corrupt practices is the report which the High Court is obliged to render to the Electoral Commission upon conclusion of the proceedings.

In light of this, Mr Mwenya suggests that the petitioners' lawyers be encouraged to pressure the High Court through the office of the registrar, to issue reports urgently about corrupt politicians.

> *9. On 1st August, 2013, the Honourable Minister of Justice sent to Messrs Ellis and Co the legal opinion rendered by the Solicitor-General under cover a letter on PF letter head as Secretary-General for PF.*

Ellis and Co. were the PF's legal team and it perhaps seemed natural for Wynter Kabimba to write to his party's lawyer on party stationary. While it may be irregular for a minister of justice to share in-house correspondence with a private law firm, the exchange would normally not have come under public scrutiny. But Mr Kabimba wanted to eliminate any shadow of a doubt about Dora Siliya's eligibility and saw to it that

> *10. Copies of the letter and the opinion were sent to His Excellency the President of Zambia and the Acting Chief Justice of Zambia.*

The incumbent president, Michael Sata, was also the president of the Patriotic Front. It was, again, irregular for the minister of justice to forward ministerial correspondence to the republican president on Patriotic Front stationary but, once again, this was not likely to be seen by anyone else but the president. The acting Chief Justice, on the other hand, is constitutionally cordoned off from all political pressure. The only reason for the secretary-general of the Patriotic Front to address a letter to the Chief Justice would be to petition for judicial action (to instigate a tribunal, for example). For Mr Kabimba to share ministerial correspondence with the Chief Justice as PF secretary-general was an evident breach of protocol. It is a source of some puzzlement why an experienced legal practitioner like Wynter Kabimba would commit such an error.

Accident or not, Mr Kabimba's maneuver appeared to have the desired effect. Hence,

> *11. On 8th August, 2013, the Judiciary issued a press statement explaining that where in an election petition, the finding of corrupt practices is made or confirmed by the Supreme Court, then the requirement that the High Court should render a report to the Electoral Commission of Zambia is overtaken by events. The press statement also explained that Supreme Court Judgments are binding on the public and all Institutions, including the Electoral Commission of Zambia.*
>
> *12. On 9th August, 2013, the Acting Registrar of the High Court sent the press statement to the Electoral Commission of Zambia.*

What is here termed the judiciary's press statement was drafted by public relations officer Teddy Musonda, a civil servant, but not a court justice.[15] Mr Musonda's press statement, which was subsequently forwarded to the ECZ, was possibly intended to function as the requisite 'report,' stipulated in Section 104(6) of the Electoral Act, which the Solicitor General advised Mr Kabimba to expedite. This maneuver also had the desired effect. Upon receiving Mr Musonda's press statement,

> *13. The Electoral Commission of Zambia issued a statement stating that in view of the press statement by the Judiciary, the Electoral Commission of Zambia would not accept applications for nomination in the forth-coming by-elections from candidates whose Parliamentary seats had been nullified in the Petauke Central, Malambo and Mulobezi Constituencies on account of corrupt practices.*

Wynter Kabimba's ploy appeared to be working, but the battle was not over yet. As already noted, the ECZ's decision was overruled through a judicial review in the High Court. The High Court ruling was then appealed to the Supreme Court where (as already noted), the ECZ's decision to disqualify Dora Siliya was again rejected.

This was bad news for Secretary-General Kabimba, but there was worse to come. In December 2013, as part of its consideration of Dora Siliya's application for a judicial review, the Supreme Court ruled on MMD President Nevers Mumba's alleged contempt of court.[16] In its ruling, the Supreme Court offered a

15 The irregularity of this move was noted by many. Law Association of Zambia President James Banda issued a statement on 9 August 2013 according to which 'LAZ is deeply concerned that the Judiciary has elected to interpret the law on such a serious national issue through a press release by a person other than a qualified Judicial Officer.'

16 This concerned the press release, noted earlier, in which Nevers Mumba accused Acting Chief Justice Chibeskunda of siding with the PF in the nullification of Siliya's election.

rare commentary on Justice Minister Kabimba's recent maneuvers. In their ruling of 23 December 2013, a panel of five Supreme Court judges, chaired by Deputy Acting Chief Justice Florence Mumba remarked that

> given the sequence of events, we are of the view that the statement issued by the Public Relations Officer and the subsequent Report to the Electoral Commission of Zambia; were influenced by the letter of 1st August, 2013 by the Patriotic Front. (*Banda v Siliya*, 453)

This, the court opined, lent credibility to Nevers Mumba's complaint about the Chief Justice's bias. As a result, the Supreme Court panel not only refused to fine or otherwise punish Mr Mumba, but also admitted to being 'uncomfortable and worried that the letter of 1st August, 2013 and the legal opinion attached thereto, was copied to the Hon. Acting Chief Justice.' Clearly, copying the solicitor general's legal opinion to the Chief Justice on ruling party stationary raised judicial dandruff at the highest level.

The next day, two concerned citizens, Mr Lucky Mulusa (an MMD politician whose electoral victory had also been nullified) and Mr Brebner Changala (a self-styled civil rights activist with links to the opposition UPND) wrote to the acting Chief Justice asking her to establish a tribunal to investigate whether Mr Kabimba had abused his ministerial position, breached his oath of secrecy and interfered with the judiciary.

Acting CJ Chibesakunda agreed with the petitioners, and a three-member tribunal led by acting Supreme Court Judge Evans Hamaundu began its inquiry into Mr Kabimba's actions on 7 January 2014. According to its report, the tribunal assigned itself the following tasks,

(a) *To investigate whether or not the Minister of Justice abused his Office when he used a Government legal opinion offered to him in his capacity as Minister of Justice by the Learned Solicitor-General to pursue a private agenda of the Patriotic Front Party and subsequently by a private litigant.*
(b) *To investigate whether or not the Minister of Justice breached his Oath of Secrecy when he released a classified Government legal opinion for use by the Patriotic Front and subsequently an individual litigant, Leonard Banda [the defeated PF politician who had petitioned Dora Siliya's election result].*
(c) *To investigate whether or not the letter copied to the Acting Chief Justice by Hon. Wynter Kabimba, on a Patriotic Front letter head, attaching thereto a legal opinion of the Solicitor-General, constituted an interference with the independence of the Judiciary as guaranteed by the Constitution.*

At the core of the allegations was the premise, conveyed in Lucky Mulusa's testimony (Hamaundu Tribunal report, 26) that

> there is a boundary between Secretary-General of the Patriotic Front and Minister of Justice. That the current political dispensation was not that of

'the Party and its Government.' That, therefore, the Party is separate from the Government.[17]

Given the sequence of events, it would seem that Messrs Mulusa and Changala read the Supreme Court's ruling in the Nevers Mumba contempt case as an invitation to inconvenience the PF secretary-general. In retrospect, the tribunal appears not to have shared the Supreme Court's anxiety as expressed in the Nevers Mumba contempt ruling. Quite the contrary, the Hamaundu Tribunal panel rejected all of the allegations against Wynter Kabimba. One is tempted to surmise that the tribunal was uncomfortable with investigating the doubly empowered Mr Kabimba and sought the easy way out. The tribunal heard testimony from only six witnesses and ended its hearings well ahead of schedule. Among the principals *not* called upon to testify was the acting Chief Justice, whose judicial independence was in question; the public relations officer, who drafted the press release/report to the ECZ; MMD President Mumba, whose contempt of court hearing sparked off the whole inquiry; Bonaventura Mutale, the PF attorney to whom Mr Kabimba addressed his original missive; and Dora Siliya herself, who was arguably the primary target of Secretary-General Kabimba's campaign.

Arguably, the tribunal declined the challenge of making a thorough legal assessment of the charges against Mr Kabimba. The panel most specifically did *not* engage with the issue of whether 'there is [or should be] a boundary between Secretary-General of the Patriotic Front and Minister of Justice.' In effect, the tribunal invoked a *forum non conveniens* caveat (Stein 1985) and slipped out of a jurisdictional back door. The panel dodged the allegations against Mr Kabimba by claiming that the legislation under which the tribunal was constituted (Section 13 of the Electoral Act) was only concerned with ministers and MPs exacting illicit monetary benefits by virtue of their positions.[18] Since none of the evidence indicated that Mr Kabimba, or anyone else, would have profited financially from his actions, the entire business 'conveniently' fell out of the tribunal's jurisdiction.

What proves to be controversial about the Kabimba Tribunal, then, is not its analysis, findings or legal reasoning, but the argumentation of the principal parties interviewed by the panel. Of especial interest is the testimony of Wynter Kabimba himself, and his legal colleague, Solicitor General Musa Mwenya. Given the fact that Messrs Mulusa and Changala based their petition on the incommensurability of Mr Kabimba's roles as cabinet minister and PF secretary-general, the question that begs attention is that of how the minister of justice and the Solicitor General defended the blurring of juridical and executive powers?

Wynter Kabimba's testimony can be summarized in three basic premises. First, he argues (§§367) that 'he discharges his duties not only as Minister of Justice

17 'The Party and its Government' was a standard maxim of the UNIP one-party era.

18 The relevant bit of legislation is Part II of the Parliamentary and Ministerial Code of Conduct Act.

but also as Secretary-General of the Patriotic Front,' and that there is, therefore, '[an element of] cross-cutting in the day-to-day performance of his duties in the two portfolios' (§30). Second, Mr Kabimba claims (§38) that 'the allocation of the dual roles to him has been done by the President in his prerogative. That, therefore, in practice the office of Secretary General of the Patriotic Front is part of Government.' Third, he insists (§34) that

> whether this issue is looked at from the perspective of him being a Minister of Justice or a Secretary General of the Patriotic Front, he obtained the Solicitor-General's opinion in the performance of his duties to serve the Zambian People.

There is, then, in Wynter Kabimba's view, no legal distinction between his tasks as minister of justice and as Patriotic Front secretary-general. In both roles, he performs the singular mandate of patriotic service to the Zambian people at the behest of the president. It is worth stressing that Mr Kabimba did not represent these views to a journalist, or a legal anthropologist, but to a panel of three of Zambia's most senior judges. He is, in other words, staking a claim at the apex of the juridical domain. It is also noteworthy that his interrogators felt no compunction to respond to or comment on this rare expression of unmitigated political legality.

Musa Mwenye, the Solicitor General, was not quite as adamant about the indivisibility of the party and its government. He noted, specifically, that

> if the Patriotic Front or any member of the Patriotic Front had asked for [the legal opinion solicited by Kabimba] he would not have given them because there were imminent proceedings, on the subject of the opinion, to which the Patriotic Front would have possibly been a party. (42)

That said, Mr Mwenye denied the need for a clearer statutory distinction between Kabimba's two roles. In his view, 'there was no need to have a law to allow Mr. Kabimba to perform the dual roles of Minister of Justice and Secretary-General of the Patriotic Front.' He gave as an example the hypothetical instance that 'even him as Solicitor-General he could be Chairperson of the Rotary Club without there being a necessity for a law to create his additional position of Rotary Club Chairperson' (ibid.). Could it be that the Solicitor General considered it possible that rotarians might have hegemonic designs regarding political domination in Zambia? The Patriotic Front clearly did, and had no qualms about it.

When Wynter Kabimba claims that there is no contradiction between his two roles, he is both stating a fact and delineating a prescription for the party-state order he is seeking to (re)instate. At that moment, the judiciary, including the Solicitor General, declined to disavow him of this project. It would be imprecise, however, to characterize Mr Kabimba's motives as based purely on an ideological commitment to party-state hegemony. His actions also expressed strategic considerations of a more pragmatic order – concerning the party's grip on power and his own position within the party organization. It was necessary to consolidate the party, and 'its' government, but within this project there was also plenty of room for tending to one's personal concerns. The recent Chiluba judgment had reaffirmed that this blending of personal interest and public service is not an inconsistency, but part of the legitimate game of postcolonial government.

### *The contours of postcolonial legality*

This account of Wynter Kabimba's rise and fall complements the story of Mutembo Nchito's career in Chapter 9, while also revealing significant contrasts. Taken together, these portraits map a range of intentionalities, practices and outcomes incumbent upon lawyers in the pursuit of political legality. These two cases, set against the backdrop of presidential maneuvers documented in the previous chapters – Mr Mwanawasa's disposal of his director of public prosecutions (DPP); Mr Chiluba's lawful illegalities – sketch a diverse tapestry of the ways mainstream Zambian constitutionalism is beholden to political legality. Of course, these specific incidents hardly exhaust the scope or diversity of the phenomenon. Similar portraits of, for example, members of Mr Chiluba's legal defense team, would no doubt bring additional depth to the picture.

Like Mutembo Nchito, Wynter Kabimba exercised his substantial legal skills to private political ends under the auspices of a prerogativist presidency. Mr Kabimba's story revealed ways that ambitious political lieutenants can appropriate, for a time at least, facets of executive power to promote their political ambitions. These case analyses also underline the central role that juridical bodies (courts and tribunals) play in both mediating and facilitating such gambits. These vignettes also offer quite stark contrasts to the Oasis Forum's liberal legalist challenges to Mr Mwanawasa's prerogativist maneuvers. By juxtaposing these distinct legal strategies, I want to provide an illustration, involving characters already familiar from earlier chapters, of how juridical actors work the politico-legal apparatus over time. By showing how political legality plays out in the real time of electoral cycles, on the one hand, and by underscoring the significance of the president's temporal embodiment on the other (three presidents die in the course of these vignettes), my intent is to highlight how the conceptualization of Zambia's constitutional order in terms of political legality reveals avenues of productive action that the liberal model cannot access.

As Nasser Hussain (2003) demonstrates, a clear distinction between liberal and exceptional standards of legitimacy is always elusive because the moment of overlap between them is shrouded by the 'national interest.' Issues of stability, peace, security and independence will invariably trump juridical principles of transparency and accountability – and not only under a declared state of emergency. And it is just such issues of the national interests that were allegedly the focus of the governmental work entrusted to Mr Kabimba and his compatriots and which, he claimed, the executive and his party carried out tirelessly in the service of the Zambian people. This is the core of prerogativism – the premise that the sovereign must be free of constraint, and scrutiny, to protect the people. Of course, it is hard to see how Ms Siliya's candidacy, for example, might have posed a danger to national security – unless, of course, the possibility of MMD's return to power is defined as just such a threat.

I am not competent to judge Mr Kabimba's actions. That said, it seems clear that he was attempting to exercise a form of power – one in which the legal and the political are seamlessly merged – which has been conventionally wielded by the president alone. His possible motives could be many. Perhaps he was acting in anticipation of eventual ascension to higher office. With or without the president's blessings, he may have sought to expand the scope of postcolonial prerogativism. In any case, he crossed a well-established line. Mr Kabimba may have felt that he had the president's support, and maybe he did. He was initially attacked by opposition figures, but ultimately, it was the Lungu faction within the PF that ousted him. Within months of his exoneration by the Hamaundu Tribunal, he lost his grasp on power.

How did he fall so decisively? As a nominated MP, Kabimba only had the president clearly in his corner. Normally that should be enough, as long as presidential favor persisted. But President Sata was ailing, and while Wynter Kabimba was busy with his many endeavors – state, party, commercial and domestic – others may have had cause and opportunity to turn the president against him. This seems to be a reasonable explanation. Mr Kabimba was a threat to other ambitious factions within the party, and when his position became vulnerable, he was taken down by players jealous of his power.

I submit, though, that this is at best a partial truth. As offensive to his adversaries as Mr Kabimba's ambition may have been, equally noxious was his attempt to usurp the strictly conscribed and sacred powers of the postcolonial sovereign. This small incident reveals the inscrutability of presidential prerogativism. The Chiluba acquittal demonstrates its irrefutability, but through Mr Kabimba's fall we see the intractability of its social location, of its material embodiment. Mr Kabimba's fate contrasts with that of President Chiluba, who was caught in a kindred conflation of party and state powers. The decisive difference between Messrs Kabimba and Chiluba, though, is that Chiluba was the president, ordained with a transcendental prerogative, while Wynter Kabimba was not. Elections in Zambia may not always be free and fair, and presidents are routinely elected with small margins and minority mandates. Yet, once elected the magic of the exception anoints them. In this sense, elections do indeed matter.[19]

In any event, it is evident that the case against Wynter Kabimba – like that against Chiluba – was poorly cast. Messrs Mulusa and Changala were confident that a moral wrong had occurred, but they failed to find the juridical means to prove the illegality of Mr Kabimba's actions. I think it is worth considering the likelihood that the interpenetration of the juridical and the exceptional is so deeply rooted in Zambia's postcolonial jurisprudence that no such means are available. What we have seen in the contestations around Dora Siliya's and

19 Mr Kabimba founded the Rainbow Party after his ouster from the PF. As its candidate in the 2016 presidential elections, he garnered 9,504 votes nationally.

Wynter Kabimba's actions is how certain forms of juridical contestation skirt the problems associated with the paraconsistency of the law, even when this is the obvious focus of the dispute. What this implies is a kind of depoliticization through proceduralism. The decisive form of juridical work required to accomplish radical precedents is not solely juridical but to a decisive degree managerial. It revolves around rigorously structured procedures – petitions, inquiries, tribunals, judicial reviews – that all have a firm statutory basis. As we have seen, the thick underbrush of procedural technicalities repeatedly ensures that purposive juridical projects tend to fall prey to deficiencies of terminology, jurisdiction or timing. It is through these technical loopholes that political legality perseveres. It is through such technical details, and not opaque conspiracy, that the postcolonial prerogative of executive exception prevails.

# 9 The allure of postcolonial legality

## Principled pragmatism revisited

This vignette highlights the career of Mutembo Nchito, a lawyer who seems to thrive at intersections where law and politics collide. Mr Nchito[1] became known as a crusader against the abuse of public authority, but upon accession to high office, fell from grace in the wake of accusations of his own misuse of power. It is tempting, then, to read this story as an illustration of Audre Lorde's (2018) much-cited axiom, '[t]he master's tools will never dismantle the master's house.' Mr Nchito is the younger of the two private lawyers employed to assist President Mwanawasa's Task Force against Corruption, as detailed in Chapter 7. Mr Nchito has had a whirlwind career, much of it spent in intimate proximity to prerogativist power. In his early 30s, he defended *Post* editor Fred M'membe in the pivotal 'Chiluba is a thief' case that exposed the president's 'matrix of plunder' (Chapter 7), and was subsequently employed by President Mwanawasa's Movement for Multiparty Democracy (MMD) administration to prosecute Mr Chiluba for abuse of office. Patriotic Front President Michael Sata appointed Mr Nchito Director of Public Prosecutions (DPP) in 2011.[2]

Alongside these accolades, Mutembo Nchito has also experienced some striking setbacks, including the bankruptcy of an airline company he and his brother owned jointly with *Post* publisher M'membe, leading to defaulting on a multi-million dollar loan from the parastatal Development Bank of Zambia (DBZ). Mr Nchito has been the object of numerous legal challenges, including a suit by the DBZ, culminating in an investigation by a presidential tribunal instigated by Patriotic Front President Edgar Lungu. I'm not in a position to say whether any of Mutembo Nchito's actions – as a private prosecutor, airline CEO or DPP – have been criminal or legally negligent. Journalists, academics and learned judges have expressed different views on Mr Nchito's legal culpability, and the materials

1 Unless otherwise specified, references to 'Mr Nchito' are to Mutembo and not his elder brother Nchima, Mutembo's business partner in the endeavors recounted here.

2 Mr Nchito thus provided legal services to two presidents who were bitter adversaries for many years.

DOI: 10.4324/9780429198984-13

available, while extensive, are full of contradictions and lacunae.[3] Be that as it may, Mutembo Nchito's tale, not unlike that of Wynter Kabimba recounted in Chapter 8, tells of a rapid ascent to the pinnacle of juridical power, and a dizzying fall from grace. It reveals the dangers of courting prerogativism and adds a page to the narrative I have been building throughout this study of the difficulties inherent in attempting to dismantle the foundations of that power with legal tools. My task here is not to condemn or exculpate Mutembo Nchito's actions, but rather to interrogate his politico-legal alignments and practices in order to deepen our understanding of the paradoxical nature and mechanisms of prerogativism.

Primary scrutiny is on Mutembo Nchito's period as director of public prosecutions under President Michael Sata, and on the legal battles (involving yet another tribunal) that ensued with Mr Nchito's removal from that position by President Lungu in 2015. As we will see, Mr Nchito has shown himself to be an exemplar of political legality, a style of politico-legal activism he did not create, but which he has deployed with considerable agility. And while the narrative reveals instances of questionable judgment, it is worth recalling that Mr Nchito, along with *Post* publisher Fred M'membe, made politico-legal history in 2001 by standing up in a principled and courageous fashion to President Chiluba, at a time when challenging the republican president was virtually unprecedented. Together, Messrs Nchito and M'membe took on Mr Chiluba in court at the end of a decade during which a number of the president's political opponents had been jailed, and several had died in mysterious circumstances. Harnessing the *Post*, which they were repeatedly forced to defend in court against political harassment, partners Nchito and M'membe galvanized the liberal consciousness of Lusaka's rising middle classes, arguably creating space for the emergence of the Oasis Forum (Chapter 6) and kindred reformist movements. At the end of the day, these are indelible facts that render Mutembo Nchito's subsequent efforts to weaponize the law in the defense of his personal standing all the more evocative. As the above axiom from wordsmith Audre Lorde suggests, the more general point of this chapter is to reflect on the limits of legal activism, and on the particular ways that progressive legal intent can be consumed by the promise of unfettered power.

## *A time to sow: The seeds of prerogativism*

Let us roll back a bit to recall the broader political context within which these events take place. In August 2008, President Levy Mwanawasa died in a Parisian hospital, midway through his second term, having seen the outcome of neither

3 I interviewed Mutembo Nchito in August 2004, when he was working for Mr Mwanawasa's Task Force against Corruption, and again in September 2012, early in his stint as DPP. The latter talk was off the record at Mr Nchito's insistence, and I have not included material from that talk in this account. The information informing this section comes from official court records.

his constitution-making project nor his prosecution of President Chiluba. As prescribed by the constitution, Mr Mwanawasa's vice-president, veteran United National Independence Party (UNIP) politician Rupiah Banda took over State House. In the statutory by-election to fill the presidency in October 2008, Mr Banda, running on the MMD ticket, narrowly defeated the Patriotic Front's Michael Sata, with Mr Banda accruing 40% of the ballot to Mr Sata's 38%.[4] In August 2009, a year after Mwanawasa's death, former President Chiluba was acquitted of corruption charges in a Lusaka magistrate's court. Mr Banda's administration, which did not share Mr Mwanawasa's obsession with burying Mr Chiluba's political career, did not appeal the acquittal. Mutembo Nchito, who had devoted the previous six years to the prosecution of his archnemesis, was understandably disappointed. Mr Banda's MMD government also walked away from registering Judge Peter Smith's London judgment against Chiluba into domestic law. Meanwhile, public disaffection with the MMD's style of government was festering. Political change was once again on the horizon.

Mutembo Nchito's career has included years of public service, but he is, above all, a businessperson, running a private legal firm together with his brother Nchima, alongside other enterprises. In the end, it seems, problems with his business ventures undermined his efforts to fight political abuse as a lawyer.

It all began with an airline. Around the turn of the millennium, Mutembo and Nchima Nchito went into business with Fred M'membe, the owner of the independent *Post* newspaper. Their respective companies, the Nchitos' JCN Holdings and Mr M'membe's *Post* Newspaper, jointly acquired a moribund regional airline company, Mine Air Services, which they renamed Zambian Airways.[5] A profile in the *Lusaka Times* (23 April 2009) describes how the three partners came to own the airline:

> Zambian Airways was a company originally owned by ZCCM [Zambia Consolidated Copper Mines, the national parastatal mining conglomerate] as Mines Air Services Ltd founded in 1948. During the [post-1991] privatisation process, ZCCM sold the small airline to its employees in a Management Buy-Out process. The lawyers for the process were the Nchitos and their [then] firm MNB. It is said that the airline was unfairly wrestled from the employees when the Nchitos turned a huge legal bill tendered into shareholding and took over ownership of the airline.

The *Lusaka Times* is not an infallible source and all of the details in this account of the airline's acquisition may not be fully accurate. That said, the airline proved to be a troublesome investment.[6] In 2007, the airline was deeply in debt from hangar

4 UPND's Hakainde Hichilema came in third with less than 20% of the poll.
5 The M'membe-Nchito airline is not to be confused with the defunct state-owned airline Zambia Airways that operated from before independence to 1994.
6 National airlines in Africa have had a high level of financial failure (see Kaswende 2012).

fees, fuel bills and overdue pension contributions. In an effort to keep the business afloat, the owners borrowed $3 million (part of a $5.5 million overall capitalization package) from the Development Bank of Zambia.[7] The express aim of the loan was to expand Zambian Airways by purchasing additional Boeing 727-244 jets.

Despite the influx of new capital, Zambian Airways continued to face liquidity problems and its owners, the Nchitos and Fred M'membe, reneged on their loan agreement with DBZ. In 2008, DBZ agreed to restructure the loan, and DBZ's credit was converted to common stock equity, making the bank a co-owner of the airline. With this increase in capital, Zambian Airways was in a position to access an additional loan of $3 million from the domestic Finance Bank Zambia (FBZ), owned by financier Rajan Mahtani.[8] Mahtani's FBZ granted Zambian Airways a loan, but the partners again failed to meet the conditions of the restructured DBZ debt. Instead, in January 2009, the owners suspended their airline's operations. The partners' last hope was that government would rescue their nominally 'national' airline, but on 21 January 2009, then minister of communications and transport, Dora Siliya (already familiar from Chapter 8), announced in parliament that the government would not bail out the company. According to Minister Siliya, the business was in debt at that time to the tune of $29 million. With the airline suspended, DBZ sued Messrs Nchito and M'membe to recover its capital.

Ever confident of his legal acumen, Mutembo Nchito took on the legal representation of his partners in court. DBZ's case initially came up before Justice Albert Wood. Midway through the examination of witnesses, however, the parties were informed that the case had been transferred to Justice Nigel Mutuna. In a hearing in April 2012 (*DBZ v JCN Holdings*), the defendants took issue with Judge Mutuna's jurisdiction in the matter and moved to adjourn the hearing. When Judge Mutuna denied the application to adjourn on a procedural point, the three defendants left the courtroom in protest. A later Supreme Court judgment (*JCN Holdings v DBZ*, 517-18; emphasis added) provides this account of the exchange:

> **Mutuna, J:**
> Mr. Nchito, may I stop you there. This is an application for an adjournment. The rules of this court stipulate that the application for an

7 DBZ is a Zambian parastatal agency that offers subsidized loans to Zambian businesses seen to be contributing to national development.

8 Rajan Lekhraj Mahtani is a Zambian-born businessman and banker whose father immigrated to Zambia in the 1930s. Throughout his career, Mr Mahtani has cultivated strategic relationships with high-profile Zambian politicians, incumbents and opposition alike. This tendency has incurred both benefits and risks. Mahtani curried the favor of Presidents Kaunda and Chiluba, yet both imprisoned him for political reasons. He maintained close relations with Chiluba's successor, Levy Mwanawasa, but fell out of favor with Mwanawasa's replacement, Rupiah Banda, over a mismanaged real estate deal. Finance Bank Zambia (FBZ) was a major player in the Zambian financial landscape. It oversaw Zambia's most extensive network of rural banking outlets, comprising 34 branches.

adjournment should be filed 10 days before the hearing. You have not complied with those rules so I cannot entertain that application.

**Mr Nchito, SC**:
My Lord maybe if you hear me then you can rule.

**Mutuna, J**:
Mr. Nchito, I cannot hear you in the absence of a formal application.

**Mr Nchito, SC**:
My Lord these very sittings are an abrogation of the rules of justice and we are saying we have raised very serious issues before this Court....

**Mutuna, J**:
Mr. Nchito I am making a ruling.

**Mr Nchito, SC**:
My Lord, you have not heard me.

**Mutuna, J**:
I can't hear you for the simple reason that you have made no formal application.

**Mr Nchito, SC**:
My Lord then I have no reason to sit in this Court. May I be excused? You can do what you want.

**Mutuna, J**:
*Please feel free.*

**Mr N[chima] Nchito**:
In the same vein my Lord we are seeking leave to leave the Court. This Court may proceed in the way that it deems appropriate.

**Mr F. M'membe**:
It applies to ourselves my Lord. We cannot render ourselves under the execution of an axe willingly. It will be reckless on our part. Thank you. (All three Counsel for the Defendant storm out of the courtroom).

Judge Mutuna proceeded with the hearing, noting that the three departed attorneys had an evident conflict of interest. They should not, the judge opined, 'have assumed the role of counsel because the companies in which they have vested interest in are the subject matter of this dispute.' Judge Mutuna also expressed his view that the three respondents, through their actions in court, 'clearly compromised the good repute of the legal profession.'[9] Judge Mutuna ruled in favor

9 This constitutes an explicit contravention of rule No. 29(1) of the Legal Practitioner's Act (Laws of Zambia, Cap 30).

of DBZ and ordered the defendants to repay 14 billion Zambian kwacha, with interest, to DBZ.[10]

The partners appealed Judge Mutuna's ruling to the Supreme Court. When their appeal was heard between July 2012 and December 2013, a panel of three judges, chaired by Acting Chief Justice (CJ) Irene Lombe Chibesakunda, found that the administrative judge-in-charge, Charles Kajimanga, had improperly transferred the High Court case from the original trial judge, Albert Wood, to Judge Mutuna. Mutuna had purportedly explained to the parties that Judge Wood had recused himself, but there was no note on record establishing that fact. Indeed, the dubious nature of case transfer from Justice Wood was the reason Mr Nchito had asked Judge Mutuna to adjourn the hearing that he and his partners had exited so dramatically, albeit – as the official transcript above clearly shows – with the court's express permission. Lacking documentation to justify the transfer, the Supreme Court found that Judge Mutuna had no jurisdiction to preside over the hearing.[11] The court thus ruled that 'the proceedings before Mutuna, J, were a nullity and that his ruling and judgment are *void ab initio*.' The case was ordered back to the High Court for retrial. As of this writing, that process has yet to be finally resolved.

The Chief Justice's ruling, in effect, vindicated Mutembo Nchito's claim that Judge Mutuna's court had been 'an abrogation of the rules of justice.' But the CJ also offered an unambiguous reprimand of Mutembo's defense team: 'Counsel should have found a better way of handling their displeasure, including by way of appeal to this Court. We hope we will not see this kind of *contemptible misconduct* again from members of the Bar' (ibid., J51; emphasis added). These were harsh words from the acting CJ to an incumbent DPP. Their punitive tone may reflect the bench's displeasure over the political fallout of Judge Mutuna's ruling; a month after Mutuna handed down his judgment against Mr Nchito and his partners, President Sata established a tribunal, chaired by Malawian High Court justice, Lovemore Chikopa, to investigate the possible impropriety of general judges Mutuna and Kajimanga, as well as that of Supreme Court Judge Philip Musonda in their handling of the DBZ case.[12] Was the president protecting his DPP, Mutembo Nchito? It certainly appeared so to the public media. Mr

10 At the average kwacha to dollar exchange rate for 2014, the penalty amounts to roughly \$5,425,000.

11 Judge Wood later testified to a tribunal investigating Judge Kajimanga's possible misconduct to the effect that Wood had been improperly sidelined from the case, thus fueling suspicions that Kajimanga and possibly Mutuna were biased against the defendants (ZANIS 2013).

12 Philip Musonda was the judge-in-charge responsible for allocating cases to different High Court justices; Kajimanga had transferred the DBZ case from Wood to Mutuna in a deputy capacity. Justice Musonda, who was of retirement age, resigned immediately, Kajimanga and Mutuna were suspended, but they challenged the appointment of the tribunal. The Supreme Court, in a split decision, upheld the legality of the Chikopa Tribunal but advised that it not continue its work (*Attorney General v Mutuna*). For a summary, see the Report of the International Commission of Jurists (ICJ 2012). Muna Ndulo (2018) offers a legal assessment, which finds the Supreme Court '[a]dopting the doctrine of Executive Supremacy.'

Nchito's rash outburst in Judge Mutuna's court would later come back to bite him, but this was not his most consequential misstep as DPP. That would happen when Mutembo Nchito sought to merge his persona as a public official with his private embodiment as the object of civil litigation.

## *Nolle* controversies

After the MMD's Rupiah Banda acceded to the presidency in 2008, Zambian Airlines creditor Rajan Mahtani ran into legal difficulties on two fronts. In October 2010, Mr Mahtani was arrested and charged with forging documents in an attempt to take over Zambezi Portland Cement, a local company in which Mahtani's bank, FBZ, had invested. Then, in December 2010, Mr Mahtani was accused of breaching banking laws by owning more than 25% of FBZ shares without the Bank of Zambia's statutory approval. Mahtani was also charged with illegally transferring FBZ assets to his holding company, Finsbury Investments, adding money laundering to the docket. Based on these charges, the Bank of Zambia seized FBZ, and in September 2011 sold it to the FirstRand Bank of South Africa for the surprisingly small sum of $5.4 million.[13] Subsequent events confirm the impression that political intrigues were behind Mr Mahtani's legal woes. Only weeks after Mr Mahtani's loss of FBZ, Michael Sata defeated Rupiah Banda for the presidency with 42% of the vote to Mr Banda's 35%. Within a month, President Sata cancelled the sale of FBZ to FirstRand and returned it to Mr Mahtani. As if to close the cycle of vengeance and retribution, in December 2011 the new president appointed Mutembo Nchito as his Director of Public Prosecutions.[14]

Despite his newly attained powers as the state's chief prosecutor, Mutembo Nchito's Zambian Airways headaches were far from over. In April 2012, having regained control of FBZ, Rajan Mahtani sued the Nchitos together with their partner Fred M'membe on charges of 'fraudulent misrepresentation' in acquiring a loan for Zambian Airways from his bank.[15] A month later, in his capacity as DPP, Mutembo Nchito discontinued a forgery case against Mr Mahtani and

13 In June 2016, Atlas Mara Zambia, a subsidiary of former Barclays bank executive Bob Diamond's African banking empire, bought out Rajan Mahtani's Finance Bank for $61 million + 3.3 million Atlas Mara shares.

14 Mutembo Nchito's nomination was overshadowed by his ongoing legal problems with Zambian Airways. On these grounds, the MMD opposition fiercely contested parliament's ratification of his appointment. Former MMD Vice-President and Minister of Justice George Kunda moved to reject the president's recommendation by virtue of the 'dark cloud over the character of the nominee.' Patriotic Front ally Sylvia Masebo, however, spoke for the majority when she claimed that 'there could never be someone better for the job than Mr Nchito.' Ms Masebo also said that 'the appointment of Mr Nchito shows how serious President Michael Sata is with the fight against corruption.' Mr Nchito's appointment was ratified by 86 votes to 50 (Daily Parliamentary Debates for the First Session of the Eleventh Assembly, Tuesday 20 December 2011).

15 'Fraudulent misrepresentation' in this connection implied that Fred M'membe and the Nchito brothers knew at the time that they could not repay the loan.

his lawyer, John Sangwa, by issuing a *nolle prosequi*.[16] Then, in late November 2012, Rajan Mahtani relinquished FBZ's claim for $4.2 million against Zambian Airways. In a story hardly bereft of irony, the agreement was signed by the firm of Chiluba's attorney and John Sangwa and sealed by Judge Nigel Mutuna. The press had a field day over Mutembo Nchito's apparent *quid pro quo*, but legally he was on solid ground. According to the constitution, it is the DPP's prerogative to discontinue any prosecution as he sees fit. Nonetheless, Mutembo Nchito's way of wielding the *nolle prosequi* would prove to be his undoing.

## *Unfettered discretion?*

After the president, the Director of Public Prosecutions occupies the second most legally protected position in Zambia's politico-legal domain. In the interests of shielding the office from external interference, political or otherwise, the 2016 constitution (Article 180(4)) extends the broadest possible legal discretion to the DPP.[17] In providing that 'the Director of Public Prosecutions shall not be subject to the direction or control of a person or an authority in the performance of the functions of that office,' the constitution (Article 180(7)) confers powers and protections that resonate with presidential prerogativism. This same Article, however, continues with a critical caveat:

> the Director of Public Prosecutions shall not be subject to the direction or control of a person or an authority ...*except* that the Director of Public Prosecutions shall have regard to the public interest, administration of justice, the integrity of the judicial system and the need to prevent and avoid abuse of the legal process.[18]

Among the most consequential and controversial of the DPP's powers is the ability to discontinue criminal proceedings against an accused party. This is generally

16 *Nolle prosequi* is Latin for 'will not prosecute.' A *nolle prosequi* is issued pursuant to Section 81 of the Criminal Procedure Code (CAP 88 of the Laws of Zambia). In Zambia (see Jere 2017, Chirwa 2020), a *nolle prosequi* is neither an acquittal nor a full dismissal of a case, which can, in principle, be reopened at a later date.

17 According to Article 180(4) of the 2016 constitution,

> The Director of Public Prosecutions may—
>
> (a) institute and undertake criminal proceedings against a person before a court, other than a court-martial, for an offence alleged to have been committed by that person;
> (b) take over and continue criminal proceedings instituted or undertaken by another person or authority; and
> (c) discontinue, at any stage before judgment is delivered, criminal proceedings instituted or undertaken by the Director of Public Prosecutions or another person or authority.

This Article is identical to the comparable provision (Article 56(3)) of the previous 1991 constitution (Republic of Zambia 1991b).

18 For a discussion of the legal implications of this caveat, a new addition to the 2016 constitution, see Justice Munalula's dissent in *Maambo* (1117).

done through the issue of a *nolle prosequi* to the court in question. While the language entrenching the DPP's powers has been relatively stable since colonial-era legislation, the discretionary character of the office's authority has recently drawn strong critique from liberal lawyers. Legal scholars Hamalengwa and Mwewa (2014), for example, portray the *nolle* as a 'colonial relic,' which has led to significant political abuse. When challenged, however, courts have deferred to the prerogativist cloak shielding the DPP from outside interference. Established law concerning the *nolle* was set by a 1977 Supreme Court ruling (*DPP v Augustino*) affirming that DPPs have 'unfettered' powers to deploy a *nolle prosequi* at their sole discretion.[19] As with the dismissal of Messrs Mahtani's and Sangwa's forgery charges (above), DPP Nchito made ample use of the *nolle*, a habit which riled many opponents of the Sata administration. Although the Constitutional Court upheld the absolute unfetteredness of the DPP's powers, Mr Nchito's recourse to a *nolle* in his own personal case would eventually cost him his elevated position.

## *A time to reap*

Having acceded to the late Michael Sata's presidency, and firmly in possession of the instruments of prerogativist power, President Edgar Lungu wasted no time lashing out against his opponents within the Patriotic Front (Simutanyi & Hinfelaar 2018). President Lungu's mandate was both razor thin (a 1.5% margin over the United Party for National Development's [UPND] Hakainde Hichilema in the 2015 by-election), and short, with statutory elections scheduled to be held within 18 months. With a tight electoral contest again on the horizon, Mr Lungu was no doubt concerned about how his nemesis, journalist Fred M'membe, might use the popular *Post* newspaper to damage him politically. Since founding the *Post* in 1991, Mr M'membe had, in turn, tangled with each of Zambia's presidents.[20] A blunt editorialist, Mr M'membe had been arrested on politically motivated charges under the administrations of presidents Chiluba, Mwanawasa and Banda. On 23 September 2014, with President Sata on his deathbed, police officers and officials from the Zambia Revenue Authority (ZRA) laid siege to the *Post*'s offices in Lusaka. The raid was purportedly motivated by 26 million kwacha in tax liabilities owed by the *Post* to the Zambia Revenue Authority.[21] With Mutembo Nchito as his attorney, Fred M'membe fought doggedly to salvage the *Post*. Eventually, however, the Supreme Court ruled for the ZRA, and on 12 June 2016, on the final stretch to the statutory 2016 elections, the *Post* was shut down.[22] Five weeks

19 The unfettered nature of these powers was again tested and reaffirmed by the Constitutional Court in *Maambo v the People* (2017). For a commentary, see Kaaba and Sambo (2020).

20 The only exception is Michael Sata. The *Post*, however, often attacked Mr Sata (aka 'King Cobra') for his role as President Chiluba's minister without portfolio in the 1990s (see Larmer & Fraser 2007).

21 SCZ Judgment 18/2016, 610.

22 Mr M'membe, who is also president of the Socialist Party, has subsequently founded a new media outlet, *The Mast*.

later, Edgar Lungu was re-elected on the Patriotic Front ticket to a five-year term as Zambia's sixth president.[23]

Mutembo Nchito proved a harder nut for President Lungu to crack. As DPP, Mr Nchito enjoyed powerful constitutional protections. Then again, President Mwanawasa's dodgy dismissal of DPP Mukelabai Mukelabai – a process in which, ironically, the Nchito brothers had played a pivotal role (see Chapter 5) – had shown that constitutional immunity is not a failsafe shield against the ire of a prerogativist president. The assault on Mutembo Nchito began soon after the president's victory in the presidential by-election of 25 January 2015. On 12 February, a warrant for Mutembo Nchito's arrest was issued by a magistrate's court in Chongwe, a small township not far from the Lusaka airport. The warrant had been sought by former MMD Deputy Minister of Finance Newton Ng'uni, who had some months earlier applied unsuccessfully to the Supreme Court to have Edgar Lungu replace Vice-President Guy Scott as acting president. Mr Ng'uni accused Mr Nchito of abuse of office, fraud, forgery and other crimes committed between 2008 and 2013. High Court Judge Mwila Chitabo immediately quashed the arrest warrant, finding that the Chongwe court had no jurisdiction over crimes allegedly committed in Lusaka. Mr Ng'uni renewed his petition in Lusaka, and Mr Nchito found himself before Magistrate Judge Lamarck Mwale on 20 February 2015. Mr Nchito then made an audacious move. From the defendant's stand, DPP Nchito announced that he was issuing a *nolle prosequi*, discontinuing his own indictment. As with the Mahtani/Sangwa *nolle* three years earlier, there was a media uproar. When the hearing was resumed ten days later, Judge Mwale nonetheless affirmed that the director of public prosecutions had the right to discontinue a case, even when he is the accused (*Lusaka Times* 2015a). The matter did not end there, however.

On 10 March 2015, President Lungu dissolved the defunct Chikopa Tribunal, which had been investigating judicial misconduct by three High Court judges in the DBZ/Zambian Airways case against the Nchitos and Fred M'membe. Judges Kajimanga and Mutuna were reinstated to the bench.[24] At the same time, the president suspended Mr Nchito from the DPP's post and appointed a new tribunal, headed by retired Chief Justice Annel Silungwe to investigate Mutembo Nchito's alleged misconduct. The two other members of the tribunal were former Chief Justices Mathew Ngulube and Ernest Sakala, both of whom had some contentious history with Mutembo Nchito.[25] Among the eight items for scrutiny

23 The 50 + 1% provision in the Constitutional Amendment Act that Lungu signed into law on 6 January 2016 required that the winning presidential candidate receive more than half the popular vote. Lungu conveniently tallied 50.35% to Hakainde Hichilema's 47.63%, with a margin of 27,757 votes out of a total of nearly 3.8 million cast. According to the Electoral Commission of Zambia, 85,795 ballots were rejected in the poll.

24 Justices Kajimanga and Mutuna were both subsequently elevated to the Supreme Court.

25 The Zamtrop bank records that Mr Nchito had subpoenaed in connection with the 'Chiluba is a thief' trial in 2001 (see Chapter 7), revealed that Chief Justice Ngulube had accepted a monetary gift from President Chiluba. He subsequently stepped down from the bench

in the Silungwe Tribunal's terms of reference were directions to investigate five instances in which DPP Nchito had entered a *nolle prosequi* for cases 'in which he is alleged to have an interest of his own to serve,' including the discontinuation of his own case before Judge Lamarck Mwale. Also among the charges was Mr Nchito's 'act of intentional disrespect to judicial proceedings and to Mr. Justice Nigel Kalonde Mutuna' (*Lusaka Times* 2015a).[26] Overall, the charges before the Silungwe tribunal mirrored Newton Ng'uni complaints of the previous month.

Mutembo Nchito launched numerous legal gambits to have the Silungwe tribunal dismissed. He questioned the legality of the president's actions and protested the fact that two of the tribunal members were likely to hold a grudge against him. None of these initial petitions succeeded. Meanwhile, in August 2016, around the time of Edgar Lungu's electoral victory, Mr Silungwe submitted his tribunal's report to the president. Without an explanation, Mr Lungu did not make the report public. In any event, the president announced that Mutembo Nchito had indeed been found guilty on two counts of abusing his powers. Mr Nchito petitioned the Supreme Court to be furnished with a copy of the tribunal's allegedly damning report, but to no avail (more on this shortly).

Public announcements and media commentary highlighted Mutembo Nchito's issuing of a *nolle prosequi* in his own case in Judge Mwale's courtroom as the main cause of his undoing. President Lungu fired Mr Nchito immediately.[27] Having failed to get relief from the Supreme Court, Mr Nchito was left with one last avenue of appeal. The day after his dismissal, Mr Nchito challenged the constitutionality of his removal before the recently established Constitutional Court.[28] Mr Nchito's cause before the Constitutional Court meandered over the next four years, with the respondent (the Attorney General) challenging Mr Nchito's many petitions at every stage of the hearings. Over the course of this back and forth, the court whittled down the reliefs sought by Mr Nchito from the original eight demands to two. In the course of eliminating Mr Nchito's pleas for relief, the court also paraphrased Mr Nchito's original petition. For

(Mbewe 2018). Mutembo Nchito demanded that the judges recuse themselves from the tribunal. The tribunal itself dismissed the motion as without merit, while the Supreme Court ruled that this was an 'interlocutory ruling' and thus not amenable to judicial review.

26 Adding a surrealistic note, the tribunal was instructed to 'Investigate allegations that the DPP connived with and instigated officers from the Drug Enforcement Commission (DEC) to plant illicit drugs on Mr. Brebner Changala and Mrs. Agness Kawandami whereby the DEC swapped vermox tablets also call Mebendazole used for deworming human beings that were found in Mrs. Agness Kawandami's belongings at Mr. Changala's residence with what was said to be Metamphetamine or Ecstasy.'

27 In firing the DPP, the president committed a curious error. In his signed letter of dismissal, Mr Lungu invoked Article 144 of the 2016 constitution, according to which the removal of a DPP requires hearings by the Judicial Complaints Commission (JCC). In fact, the JCC played no role in the investigation into Mr Nchito's behavior, which was carried out under the auspices of the repealed Article 58 of the now defunct 1991 constitution.

28 The Constitutional Court panel comprised judges Mulenga, Mulembe, Mulonda, Munalula and Musaluke. See *Mutembo Nchito v AG*, 2016/CC/0029, ruling of 27 October 2020.

example, Mr Nchito's claim that 'the President's action of purporting to relieve the petitioner of his position as DPP pursuant to Article 144 of the Constitution is unconstitutional and therefore illegal, null and void,' was now refashioned into the question of

> (i) Whether the changes made to the Constitution of Zambia, 1991 by the Constitution Act No. 1 of 2016 and the Constitution of Zambia as amended [in 2016] affected the standing of the adhoc Tribunal appointed under the repealed Act 58 of the Constitution of Zambia, 1991 to probe the petitioner as DPP.

In other words, the court delimited its consideration of the constitutionality of the president's actions to the technical question of whether Mr Nchito was fired under the new constitution (as per the president's letter of dismissal), or under the pre-amendment constitution of 1991. The court disposed of this technical issue with little ado. Echoing the state's arguments, the court ruled (*Mutembo v AG*, §67) that 'repealed Article 58 is what applied in the case at hand.' While

> the reference to Article 144 of the Constitution as amended was misplaced ... the power exercised was covered by the repealed article 58 of the Constitution of Zambia, 1991. The President's action thus cannot be said to be unconstitutional, illegal or null and void as alleged by the petitioner.

The Constitutional Court thus took the narrow path to its conclusion. Having generously forgiven the president's erroneous reference to an incorrect authority in his letter of dismissal, the court had no difficulty affirming the legality of Mr Nchito's removal. The court found that in setting up a tribunal to investigate the DPP, President Lungu's act was constitutionally sound. Indeed, the court noted, given that the tribunal found the DPP guilty of misconduct, the president had no option but to fire him.

Arguably, no matter how one feels about the 'unfetteredness' of the DPP's powers, this is not what justice should look like.[29] Indeed, over four years of litigation, the legitimacy of the president's actions in firing the DPP was never given a proper airing. By bracketing key reliefs sought by Mr Nchito, the court avoided engaging with the substantive issue of the possible bias of two members of the Silungwe Tribunal. It sidestepped the question of whether the issuing of a *nolle prosequi* – a constitutionally conferred power that the court had itself recently upheld – could legitimately be considered 'misconduct' on the part of a DPP. Nor did it weigh in on the impeachability of Mr Nchito's alleged disrespect toward Judge Mutuna, given that the judge was on record as permitting the lawyer's exit from his court, and even in light of the fact that the judge was

29 UNZA law lecturers O'Brien Kaaba and Pamela Towela Sambo (2020) provide a compelling analysis of the Constitutional Court's 'manifestly troubling' reasoning in Mr Nchito's cause.

later shown to have lacked jurisdiction to hear the case in question. The key question hanging over this entire process concerns the provision or precedent upon which the tribunal's determination of Mutembo Nchito's alleged malfeasance was based. Here, again, is prerogativism at work. Its effect on the Nchito case resides in the president's refusal to reveal the legal basis of Mr Nchito's alleged misconduct. Strictly speaking, we only have the president's word (and the tribunal's public silence) to justify Mr Nchito's dismissal. According to state prosecutors, the substantive issues Mr Nchito flagged in his petitions should have been dealt with via judicial review of the tribunal's determinations in the High Court (NewsDiggers 2018). But Mutembo Nchito was refused access to the Silungwe tribunal's report – the basic precondition for him to prepare a case challenging its legitimacy. The contradiction inherent in this reasoning is further highlighted by the court's ruling concerning Mr Nchito's second plea which concerned his right of discovery, in other words Mr Nchito's right to see the tribunal report that made his dismissal possible.

## *Liberal absurdities*

The Constitutional Court's determination that Mr Nchito was legally relieved of his duties exhausted his path for relief. In light of this, the question of his right to see the tribunal's report was largely academic. As refashioned by the court, Mr Nchito's plea for discovery asked the judges to consider:

> (ii) Whether the petitioner having been a constitutional office holder and subjected to a constitutional removal process is entitled to the report of the adhoc Tribunal upon which the Republican President based his decision to relieve the petitioner of his duties as DPP.

Mr Nchito had already asked the court, back in 2016, to provide him with a copy of the Silungwe tribunal report. His petition led to an *ex parte* hearing[30] by a single judge, who rejected the request because he considered his authority was inadequate to pass judgment. This, claimed the judge, was due to the constitutional issues at stake (i.e., the interpretation of Article 58(3)(b)), which required the deliberation of a full bench. In its final ruling of October 2020 (§71), the court chides Mr Nchito for not petitioning the full court 'to address the issue of discovery of the Tribunal report,' implying that had he done so, his request for the report would have succeeded.[31]

The Supreme Court had already ruled that a tribunal's recommendations are subject to judicial review (*Attorney General v Mutembo Nchito* 2016). The

30 An *ex parte* hearing is one involving only one party to a dispute, and commonly focuses on procedural matters. Such a petition is conventionally heard by a single judge, and not a full bench which in the case of the Constitutional Court must involve at least three judges.

31 It is unclear why Mr Nchito did not pursue this option.

problem was that without the report, Mutembo Nchito had no way of knowing how the tribunal had reached its conclusions. This made formulating a case for judicial review virtually impossible. In its final judgment, the Constitutional Court was now sympathetic, albeit belatedly, to Mr Nchito's plight. Ruling in his favor, the court stated firmly (§84) that 'an affected party in a constitutionally ordained removal process... was entitled to a copy of the reasoned decision of such proceedings.'

Where the court had taken a 'literal' (or 'plain meaning') approach to the constitutionality of the DPP's dismissal, it now (§82) opted for a 'purposive' interpretation of the petitioner's right of discovery. The justification for this change in approach is that the literal reading of the constitution created an 'absurdity,' which the court was obliged to remedy.[32]

The absurdity in this case, in the court's view, was to deny Mr Nchito the means to defend himself through judicial review of the Silungwe tribunal's work. Thus, the court (§82) found that

> [i]f the framers of the Constitution had in mind the situation before us, they would have provided that the outcome of the investigation should also be provided or availed to the concerned office holder. This would enable the office holder to know the basis upon which the recommendation is made and to take appropriate action. This is what natural justice demands.

Despite its congenial pose, the Constitutional Court did not mandate any party to give the report to Mr Nchito (Kaaba & Sambo 2020). Nor did it specify where that responsibility should reside, other than affirming [§81] that 'the President as a recipient of the Tribunal report is under no obligation to avail a copy of the report to the affected secured officer.' Neither natural justice nor the purposiveness of the court's interpretation, it seems, extends to infringing on the autonomy of presidential prerogative. In Mr Nchito's case, the court's relief was effectively meaningless in that failure before the Constitutional Court exhausted his options for challenging the president's decision.

## Progress vs purpose

It is tempting to read the court's contrast of literalism versus purposiveness as a gesture to align its jurisprudence with contemporary theories of legal interpretation. The jurisprudence the court invokes suggests that when legislation or precedent is unduly inflexible, courts must stretch conventional boundaries to ensure that justice is served: No matter that the constitution does not explicitly guarantee Mutembo Nchito the right to learn how he has been judged, the court

32 This justification embellishes the Constitutional Court's own earlier ruling (in *Katuka v the Attorney-General*) which says '[i]t is only when the ordinary meaning leads to an absurdity that the purposive approach should be resorted to.'

can rise above this 'absurd' restriction to provide relief. Indeed, in my conversations with the Oasis Forum's legal experts a decade earlier, purposive reasoning was explicitly linked to a progressive, pro-democracy agenda. Dr Patrick Matibini (interview, 10 May 2007), for example, had this to say when reflecting on the purposiveness of two High Court rulings:

> Both [judges] attempt to capture and respond to context. Both define Zambia's democratic dispensation as the backdrop for their judgments. Both are anxious that their decisions conform with democratic ideals. One can even say that there is an element of judicial activism... If one takes a purposive approach, interpretation includes context. The courts should not make decisions in a vacuum. They should be alive to the aspirations of the people.

Such declarations appeal to the sentiments of political liberals. It is difficult, however, to see the Constitutional Court's alleged purposiveness in Mutembo Nchito's cause as a blow for popular democracy. Rather, the court's ruling walks a tight wire between conflicting efforts to invoke the prerogativist privileges of the president, on the one hand, and of the DPP, on the other. The court is careful to sustain 'confidence in the adjudicative mechanism' itself (§82), i.e., in the court's legitimacy. At the same time, it exercises caution not to undermine the 'doctrine of Executive supremacy' (Ndulo 2018, 22). These motives reflect a judicial instinct to preserve the status quo, not to find the most judicious solution available.

Perhaps one could rejoice in the fact that when judicial malfeasance is exposed in Zambia, it is generally due to incompetence, greed or coercion, and not to reactionary intent. Reactionary judicial activism does not seem to have a foothold in the Zambian politico-legal domain. There is, as far as I can discern, no judicial constituency actively scheming to unravel the constitution or to elevate unfettered autocracy to a legal virtue. Progressive judges, inasmuch as they exist, are hemmed in on several fronts. The bench's wariness to embrace new ideas reflects decades of operating under unmanageable backlogs and sloppy advocacy, both of which make the drafting of rulings tedious. The work is hard, resources are inadequate and opportunities to shine are rare (Masengu 2017). Activist lawyers – based at the University of Zambia's School of Law, working abroad, or employed domestically as consultants and lobbyists – see themselves as whistle-blowers, and are quick to expose possible betrayals of constitutional values (e.g., Kaaba 2018). Even judges at the pinnacle of juridical power are critical of day-to-day judicial performance. State Counsel and (since 2021) incumbent Chief Justice Mumba Malila (2020), for one, has bemoaned the 'ostensible timidity on the part of many individual judges to assert judicial independence probably for fear of victimization or reprisals by the executive which, not only appoints them, but disciplines and removes them too.' This timidity, Justice Malila suggests, begets 'judicial pusillanimity and the resultant self-restraint and lethargy.' On another flank, the executive and judiciary branches are not equal partners in government

– witness President Sata's assault on three High Court judges, and the dodgy dismissals, by Presidents Mwanawasa and Lungu, of their DPPs.

Why devote so much attention to this singular, maverick and contradictory crusader? What do Mutembo Nchito's politico-legal escapades tell us about the nature of Zambia's prerogativist order, and about the potential for disassembling it through juridical means? For all his contradictions, few other Zambian lawyers, with the possible exception of John Sangwa, have done more to expose the implications of prerogativist discretion for the politico-legal system. Ironically, Mutembo Nchito's contribution to revealing the contours of prerogativism has emerged more from his later efforts to harness its exceptional powers than from his earlier struggle to hold Mr Chiluba accountable. It is hard to assess the extent to which Mr Nchito's corrosive public persona contributed to his defeats in court. It is more interesting, in any case, to reflect on how his ascent into the solar glare of prerogativist power led to his politico-legal meltdown, and to his fall, Icarus-like, from grace.

I suspect that Mutembo Nchito's fall was at least partly a consequence of a misfounded faith in juristocracy (Hirschl 2009), i.e., in the idea that the law could shield him from politics. His legal acumen kept the creditors at bay, for a time at least, but it couldn't protect him from the president's ire, and even less so from the seductiveness of presidential powers, not just to wield the law, but to stand outside it. President Sata had defended his DPP's right to exercise unfettered discretionary powers in unprecedented ways. But with Mr Sata gone, Mutembo Nchito was left alone to bear the consequences of his actions.

Mutembo Nchito is above all a realist – both in his analysis of what is attainable through juridical means, and in his pragmatic legal maneuvers. Perhaps his by-any-means-necessary approach to legal contestation (and self-defense) reflects a fundamental confidence in his own ethical compass. This can be a dangerous thing, especially for those at the pinnacles of power. What's more, the serious financial troubles that cast a shadow over Mr Nchito's work as the Director of Public Prosecutions are not likely to have enhanced dispassionate ethical reflection. There was indeed, a growing sense of rashness informing his actions as DPP. Perhaps his newly found powers went to his head; he no doubt felt vindicated by President Sata's alleged 'allergy to corruption' (Mwewa 2019). As it turns out, there was probably too little time, and too many distractions, for him to sustain his focus in the shadow of President Sata's impetuous and inconsistent maneuvering. That said, the evidence arrayed above suggests that the ethics of his principled pragmatism became more fluid the closer to power Mr Nchito found himself.

As DPP, Mutembo Nchito emulated presidential privilege. He allowed the boundary between his private persona and his official embodiment to blur, emulating prerogativist hubris. It is indeed instructive to reflect on Mutembo Nchito's paradoxical attempt to fully embody prerogativist authority – pronouncing a *nolle* from the defendants' stand, and taunting a High Court judge to his face – while portraying himself as a champion of executive accountability. It is a thin wire to walk and Mr Nchito, like Mr Kabimba before him, fell from a remarkable height.

Was Annel Silungwe's tribunal correct to recommend Mr Nchito's dismissal? As in the Mukelabai Mukelabai case (Chapter 7), it is likely that the president's lack of trust made the DPP's removal unavoidable, and the tribunal simply acquiesced to this pragmatic fact.

Be that as it may, what might be said about Mr Nchito's discontinuation of Newton Ng'uni's legal harassment? Can it be justified? By dismissing Mr Ng'uni's accusations through a *nolle prosequi*, Mutembo Nchito quite evidently contravened a fundamental principle of natural law: *nemo judex in causa sua* (no one is a judge in their own cause). This is indeed how the incident appears from the perspective of liberal jurisprudence. On the other hand, the constitution is unequivocal. Granted, the provision affirming the DPP's discretion is a prerogativist provision, and sits uneasily with an ethos of government accountability. From Mutembo Nchito's point of view, however, the charges against him in Justice Mwale's courtroom were clearly part of a ploy to hound him out of office, driven by personal malice on the part of the new president. Why would he not use the powers vested in him by the constitution to protect himself, his office and his crusade? As Kaaba and Sambo (2020) attest, '[i]n granting nolle prosequi and discontinuing criminal matters, Nchito as then DPP was simply exercising his unfettered discretion, as propounded by the very Constitutional Court!' If an official's misconduct is backed up by the constitution, is it not the constitution that is at fault?

The parallel portraits of political legality in this and Chapter 9 may seem to speak to the narrative of the flawed postcolonial state (see Chapter 2); this is only a partial truth at best. To read these analyses as condemnations implies appraising the acts and outcomes of their protagonists by the ideals of political liberalism. Facets of liberal legality, as we have seen, play a significant role in the workings of Zambia's politico-legal system. Ideals of transparency, accountability, separation of powers, due process and so on are important rhetorical resources for lawyers, politicians and activists. Needless to say, the notion of constitutionalism, the empirical focus of this study, is a realm where liberal rhetoric has an amplified resonance. But while liberal sentiments cannot be ignored, they do not constitute the overall frame of action within which lawyers, activists and politicians pursue their aims. It may be more useful to ask how liberal ideas and aims intersect and blend with other principles in the constitution of the politico-legal domain.

This is not to extol the virtues of lawful illegality, nor of prerogativism more generally, as models of modern governance. Prerogativism is a colonial distortion that sustains the marginalization of popular constituent power. But there is a profound truth in the Foucauldian proposition that any form of power can exhibit both productive and destructive tendencies, and these are routinely intertwined in empirical governmental practices. Struggles for justice and equality must recognize the sources and characteristics of both. Whether or not one chooses to judge the world according to an idealized version of liberal principles, all those who bend these standards for political purposes are not enemies of justice.

# IV

# A new hope?

# 10 Decolonizing the republic

Throughout this study, I have examined how the legacy of imperial liberalism has shaped Zambia's politico-legal domain, normalizing a prerogativist strain of political legality. Postcolonial legality, as we have seen, serves to sustain a form of power predicated on the need for a 'unified command' in the face of internal and external threats to national security. This position evidently resonates with many Zambians. That said, it also stymies efforts to institutionalize a more popular form of democracy – one in which the *demos* is not merely an object of government, but its genuine subject. How this might come to pass, and what it would imply for Zambia's constitutional order is beyond the scope of the present inquiry. It may be noted, however, as law dean Carlson Anyangwe once argued (1997, 17) that the people alone

> have the sovereign right to effect a fundamental or radical change in the Constitution. They can do so peacefully by referendum as provided in the Constitution itself. Or they can do so by a revolutionary overthrow of the existing Constitutional order as dictated by the law of nature.

This chapter offers some provisional thoughts about the possibilities of such a radical transformation. What this entails, I submit, is the decolonization, at long last, of Zambia's republican order.

Zambia, of course, ceased being a colony with the enactment of the first republican constitution in 1964. That founding act of constitutionalization eradicated race-based discrimination and posited 'the people' and their will as the subject of its own government. These were landmark political achievements, but the ballast of colonial legality was not jettisoned overnight. Decolonization in the sense used here implies completing the process begun with that initial assertion of political and economic independence. It means realizing the ideal of a nation constituted, as Achille Mmembe (2021, 173) suggests, as 'a world seeking to exist by itself' – free, that is, of the 'received' politico-legal standards and modalities of power rooted in colonial subjectification.

This concluding chapter approaches the decolonization of the republic by revisiting two interwoven threads running through the study. These concern (a) the emancipatory potential of law; and (b) the constitutionalist status of

DOI: 10.4324/9780429198984-15

constituent power as an expression of the will of the people in constitution-making. Decolonizing the republic thus implies transcending the legacy of imperial liberalism by either dismantling the politico-legal culture of prerogativism or by transforming it into a form of power genuinely attuned to the will of the people. Such processes may begin with the law – i.e., through constitutional reform – or through popular political action. Postcolonial history offers myriad illustrations of both approaches: on the one hand, a recourse to 'transformative constitutionalism' (Klare 1998) to exorcise the politico-legal demons of apartheid rule in South Africa; on the other, the radical, if brief flourishing of 'constituent presidencies' (Bernal 2014) in Latin America. Both of these models, as we shall see, are fraught with contradictions, but their potential to advance justice have not, one hopes, been exhausted. If and when such paths fail to reach the desired destination of genuinely inclusive government, the only remaining resort is, as Carlson Anyangwe's epigram suggests, the revolutionary overthrow of the existing order. Popular revolution in postcolonial Africa has been a rare occurrence; then again, the postcolonial era is still relatively young.

## A constituent presidency?

Postcolonial jurisdictions across the globe have grappled in recent years with exorcising the legacy of colonial rule. One way that decolonialization has been framed invokes a politics of 'refounding.' This has been articulated most explicitly in connection with a trio of 'plebiscitary' (Conaghan 2008) or 'constituent' (Bernal 2014, Alterio 2019) presidencies in Latin America, i.e., those of Hugo Chávez of Venezuela, Evo Morales of Bolivia and Rafael Correa of Ecuador. All three of these presidents rose to power with the electoral support of disadvantaged and repressed majorities during the first decade of the current millennium. The experiences and outcomes of the political projects of these politicians varied, but each sought to harness, and extend, the extensive constitutional powers assigned to the presidency in order to pursue progressive socioeconomic transformation. According to Bernal (ibid., 440) these 'constituent' presidents

> have positioned their turn to constitutionalism not only through nationalistic rhetoric but specifically through the language of refounding, locating this return as an attempt to remake national identities, decolonize existing institutions and undemocratic governance structures, and establish a new political beginning on behalf of all those previously excluded from elitist political structures.

The radical notion of decolonization driving these efforts has been richly theorized as a 'political-epistemic insurgency' (i.e., Walsh 2010).[1] This refers to the

1 Among the key thinkers in this conversation have been Enrique Dussel (2000), Arturo Escobar (2010), Walter Mignolo (2000) and Anibal Quijano (2000). See Moraña (2010)

need not only to change the political system but also to reorient the conceptualization of history, race, gender and power from a subaltern perspective – thus acknowledging the experience of those disadvantaged by colonial and postcolonial oppression (Grosfoguel 2011). Echoing Arendt's (1958) notion of natality, Arturo Escobar (2010, 2) has characterized the politics of refounding in Latin America as '*un nuevo comienzo*' (a new beginning). At the heart of these movements are, in Escobar's account (ibid.), efforts to 'bring about a reinvention of democracy and development or, more radically still, the end of the predominance of liberal society of the past 200 years founded on private property and representative democracy.'

The rhetoric of radical political rupture notwithstanding, constitutionalism has been central to all of these Latin American political experiments. Indeed, a 'main vehicle for the refounding of the State and society has been the Constituent Assemblies' (Escobar 2010, 6), echoing the aspirations of the Oasis Forum's campaign for a 'people-driven' constitution during the Mwanawasa presidency. The Movement for Multiparty Democracy's (MMD) president, Mr Mwanawasa, whose administration overlapped with these Latin American experiments, resisted radical moves in general and the delegation of constitution-making power to a constituent assembly in particular. In contrast, Mr Mwanawasa's prime adversary, Michael Sata, embraced revolutionary rhetoric akin to that of the constituent presidents in Latin America. Like his categorical kinsfolk Chavez, Morales and Correa, Michael Sata might be considered a constituent president by virtue of his capacity to conjure constituent power into existence. In the mold of Hugo Chavez or Evo Morales, Mr Sata also worked to build a broad coalition by 'articulating, charismatically, urbanites' demands and grievances' (Sishuwa 2011, 4). After breaking with the MMD in 2001, Mr Sata set off on his own, founding the Patriotic Front (PF), and gradually building support over the course of three electoral campaigns. As the PF's platform evolved, the party underwent a radicalization of sorts – formulating a party manifesto which cast the PF as 'a revolutionary party of workers and peasants,' and seeking affiliation with the Socialist International (W. Kabimba, pers. comm.). Having lost narrowly to Mr Mwanawasa in 2006, and to Rupiah Banda in 2008, Michael Sata captured the republican presidency in 2011. His election was greeted with great popular enthusiasm, albeit not without some degree of trepidation by foreign donors and liberal elites, who were wary of Mr Sata's long and storied association with the illiberal aspects of presidents Kaunda and Chiluba, and his seeming imperviousness to established laws and conventions.

Michael Sata's alleged 'socialism' also raised eyebrows. And yet, Mr Sata's professed socialism was more about justice for the meek and downtrodden than about the eradication of private property. It was, in other words, a socialism more akin to the Catholic Church's social agenda than to a Marxist revolutionary

for an overview. In the African context, these sentiments resonate most clearly in the work of Sabelo Ndlovu-Gatsheni (2018).

movement. This message resonated with the platform of the justice activists within the Oasis Forum and represented a more direct political path to its realization. As many civil society activists rallied behind his campaign, Sata mobilized marginalized constituencies by projecting himself as the solution to their long-standing grievances. This skill can be termed 'populist,' in Laclau's (2005) sense of the term – Sata was indeed a 'floating signifier' capable of aggregating diverse grievances and demands within his political persona (cf. Fraser 2017, Sishuwa 2017). Yet, the pejorative label of populism masks the genuine connection Mr Sata forged with the plebian *sans-culottes* of the Third Republic in the run-up to the 2011 elections.

There is, arguably, a 'tendency of elites in Zambia to first look across at each other rather than downwards to their followers when it comes to strategies for maintaining power and seeking to influence the distribution of resources' (Pruce & Hickey 2016, 4). It was thus all the more remarkable that, as president, Mr Sata did initiate programs that delivered directly to the *demos*. The popular enthusiasm that swept Sata and the PF into power was based on genuine expectations of a shift in political priorities – away from the elite-driven neoliberalism of the MMD toward programs that would put 'money in the pocket' of the common citizen.[2]

At the same time, Mr Sata was also an unabashedly prerogativist president. In this, he also resembled his Latin American compatriots. Once in office, President Sata hunkered down to defend his prerogatives rather than investing in expanding the constituent power that brought him the presidency. As was the case with presidents Chavez (and later Maduro), Correa and Morales, the Patriotic Front administration was rife with lawful illegalities and, as detailed in earlier chapters, Mr Sata apparently had few qualms about subjugating legal institutions to his political ends. Lawyers in his administration who had earlier brandished their liberal principles proudly now signed onto Mr Sata's assertive brand of political legality.[3]

## *Another missed opportunity*

In its early years, Mr Sata's Patriotic Front flirted with the Oasis Forum's campaign for a constituent assembly but only embraced the Forum publicly when it threw its weight behind his demands for 50 + 1% electoral reform in the run-up to the 2006 elections. There is no indication that Mr Sata was committed to radically reforming the prevailing form of power (Prempeh 2017), although he recognized the political expediency of completing the cycle of constitution-making that had dragged on since the aborted efforts of the Mwanakatwe Constitutional Review

2 One dramatic gesture was the government takeover of a small-scale social cash transfer program, initiated by German donors, and upscaling cash transfers to poor households by 700% (Republic of Zambia 2014, Siachiwena 2016).

3 The legal assault on judges Mutuna, Kajimanga and Musonda (see Chapter 10) is a case in point.

Commission in Mr Chiluba's first term. Indeed, in his campaign speeches, Mr Sata presented himself as a 'champion of a new constitution' and 'repeatedly promised to bring to a swift conclusion the tortuous constitution-making process' (Simuchoba 2014).

In the 2011 election campaign against the MMD's Rupiah Banda, Mr Sata and his Patriotic Front lashed out at the MMD's failure to deliver a new constitution, and promised to deliver a 'people-driven constitution' within 90 days of assuming office (Munalula 2016). Once in State House, Mr Sata acted quickly on his promise but, against the recommendations of every constitutional review commission since 1991, he opted not to delegate constitution-making powers to a constituent assembly. This might be seen as a reasonable move in light of the fact that the prolonged and expensive National Constitutional Conference (NCC) – arguably a constituent assembly of sorts – had just submitted its draft for a new constitution; but it is also likely that Mr Sata, like all of his predecessors, was determined to keep any fundamental constitutional reforms under strict presidential oversight.[4]

Instead of a constituent assembly, President Sata appointed a 20-strong Technical Committee on the Drafting of the Zambian Constitution (TCDZC).[5] The TCDZC's draft constitution, submitted to the president in October 2013, included a number of provisions already endorsed by the NCC – such as a 50 + 1% electoral code, and the establishment of a Constitutional Court – which President Sata allegedly opposed (Collord 2014). Indeed, over the course of this process, signals began emanating from State House that suggested growing uneasiness toward the substance of the TCDZC's draft.

In August 2012, a year into the PF administration and in the midst of the TCDZC's extensive round of community consultations (Lungwangwa 2015), the Oasis Forum (2012a) issued a press statement questioning the government's political will to fulfill its commitment to quickly deliver a people-driven constitution. The Forum expressed concern over the lack of transparency in the TCDZC's work ('the importance of publishing the budget cannot be overemphasized') and the absence of a legal framework to govern how the new constitution will 'pass through a Referendum and eventually enactment by Parliament.' All in all, the

4 According to Neo Simutanyi (2012, 41), 'In 2006, Michael Sata of the PF advised UPND president Anderson Mazoka not to press for limiting presidential powers because they may both need them if they come to power.'

5 See Chapter 6. The TCDZC prepared the final draft of the 2016 constitution before its eventual modification and enactment by parliament. Among its terms of reference was the direction to 'Refer to the Mvunga Constitution Review Report; Review the Mwanawasa of Zambia, the 1993 Mwanakatwe Constitution Review Commission Report and Draft Constitution, the 2005 Mung'omba Constitution Review Report and Draft Constitution, and the 2010 National Constitution Conference Report and Draft Constitution' (Motsamai 2014, 5). The recommendations of the Mwanakatwe and Mung'omba reviews included the adoption of the constitution through a constituent assembly—positions strongly supported by the Oasis Forum.

Forum was anxious that 'the likelihood that the end product will be subject to some political manipulation is still there.'

These qualms proved valid. A year later, in November 2013, President Sata was reported in the online tabloid *Zambia Watchdog* to have 'u-turned on the enactment of the new constitution,' announcing at a rally in rural Mansa that 'Zambia does not need a new constitution but needs to amend the current one' (see Cheembe 2018, 134–5). This implied that the United National Independence Party (UNIP)-era Bill of Rights need not be revisited.

When the TCDZC submitted its second and final draft constitution in October 2013, President Sata's minister of justice, Wynter Kabimba, forbid its publication, and ordered that only ten copies be produced. According to veteran Zambian journalist Arthur Simuchoba (2014), Mr Sata also went on record asserting that

> The constitution-making process has been hijacked by individuals whose objective is to embarrass, humiliate and politically undermine the public will … It will be highly irresponsible for us … to authorize the release of this document before it goes through cabinet … the country already has a functional constitution and the state will not be pushed into fast and reckless conclusions.

The identity of the hijackers and their nefarious agenda was not specified, but the constitution-making process, once again 'stalled for over a year' (Munalula 2016).

This evident backpedaling by the PF incited an angry response from the Oasis Forum and allied civic organizations (Lusaka Voice 2014). Relations between the government and civil society deteriorated rapidly until

> [t]ensions reached new heights on February 27 [2014] when Justice Minister Wynter Kabimba, seen by many as Sata's closest ally, informed parliament that government lacked funds for a national referendum on the constitution, as requested by the NCC, and would prioritize more pressing social and economic concerns. (Collord 2014)

The government's dillydallying on the constitution had been widely blamed in the online tabloids on Mr Kabimba, who was the president's official point man on the constitution-making process. When the Lungu faction within the Patriotic Front succeeded in ousting Kabimba in August 2014, Lungu moved quickly to take control of the process. Just a week before Sata's death, Minister of Justice Lungu released the TCDZC draft to the public. This move may have been motivated by Mr Lungu's genuine commitment to constitutionalism; he was, and is, after all, a trained lawyer. But there were, no doubt, more immediate political considerations also at play. By releasing the draft that Sata had embargoed for 12 months, Minister Lungu seized ownership of the reform process, while signaling his independence from the forces within the Patriotic Front who had apparently been obstructing constitutional reform.

Having assumed the presidency in January 2015 through a by-election, Mr Lungu, 'resumed the constitution-making process in earnest' (Munalula 2016). A Constitution of Zambia (Amendment) Bill was tabled before parliament in July, revised and passed in December, and signed into law by Mr Lungu in January 2016 'in what was widely seen by Zambians as a milestone with unprecedented gains in the constitution building process' (ibid.). These milestones included a new section on national values and principles, a majoritarian presidency and a constitutional court, demands democracy activists had struggled for since the early years of the Third Republic.[6]

Mr Sata's brief presidency (from 2011 to 2014) ended before his progressive ambitions saw fruition, and there is no way of telling how his administration would have evolved. It is also unclear why Mr Sata's government backtracked on constitutional reform on the final stretch of his tenure. It is noteworthy that Edgar Lungu, who oversaw the enactment of the 2016 constitution and its progressive provisions, also appears to have had a change of heart, as his attempt to further amend the constitution through Bill 10 (see Chapter 6) attests. What is known, however, is that President Sata rose to power by galvanizing previously marginalized social groups, and initiated a process that revitalized the democratic thrust of constitutional jurisprudence. Granted, Mr Sata's saga falls well short of a full-blown political-epistemic insurgency, but it does suggest that even in Zambia's conservative politico-legal regime, political pathos can infuse law with progressive ethos under auspicious circumstances. The Patriot Front's tumultuous political trajectory thus provides valuable material to probe the ways that constituent power is instantiated and bound to an evolving constitutional order. From this perspective, we now turn to one of the most substantial innovations stemming from two decades of constitutionalist activism from the Civil Society Action Committee in the 1990s to the Oasis and Citizen forums of the 2000s: the young Constitutional Court. In light of its debt to these struggles, close attention to the work of the Constitutional Court provides grounds for considering the possibility of refounding Zambia's prerogativist politico-legal domain through legal means.

## A transformative jurisprudence?

The Oasis Forum's impassioned campaign for greater accountability in government was, albeit unsuccessful, not without long-term political effects. The Forum's liberal ethos clearly catalyzed the work of the NCC and, in particular, that of the TCDZC, which included a number of close Forum allies. The fact that concerted efforts to expand the UNIP-designed Bill of Rights failed to pass a mandatory referendum was an obvious disappointment, but the 2016 constitutional amendments did enact a majoritarian (50 + 1%) electoral system, as well as a

6 The Constitution Amendment Bill initially tabled before parliament was essentially the TCDZC's final draft. Before its enactment, parliament made a number of substantial revisions. For details, see Munalula (2016).

number of significant provisions impinging on the scope of executive powers. Most significantly, the 2016 constitution established a new apex bench, the Constitutional Court – first proposed by the Mwanakatwe Constitutional Review Commission in 1995 – of equal status to the already existing Supreme Court. Within the new court's purview are all legal matters related to the exercise of presidential power.[7] It represents, then, a potentially powerful tool to realign the entrenched interpenetration of legality and political convenience at the highest level of government. One way, then, to interrogate the legacy of the Forum's liberalism, as well as to test the emancipatory capacity of its 'legalized' forms of activism is to ask, how have these reforms played out? What trends or changes can we see in the politico-legal domain as a result of the Constitutional Court's labors? Do the new court's rulings and emerging jurisprudence redeem the Oasis Forum's and the Law Association's promise of contributing to the formulation of a people-driven constitution that will stand the test of time?

The birth of the new Constitutional Court engendered high expectations but, inevitably, also disappointments (e.g., Kaaba & Sambo 2020). It should nevertheless be noted from the outset that the young court has faced multiple challenges. In endeavoring to fulfill its constitutional remit, the Constitutional Court has been hobbled from the get-go by two fundamental contradictions. The first concerns jurisdiction: the court is obliged to read the constitution 'holistically,' and yet the entrenched Article 28(1) stipulates that if anyone 'alleges that any of the provisions of Articles 11 to 26 [the entrenched Bill of Rights] has been, is being or is likely to be contravened in relation to him, that person may apply for redress to the High Court.'[8] This effectively blocks the Constitutional Court from hearing cases, and issuing judgments, related to the Bill of Rights – an unusual and discomforting situation for any constitutional authority.

The second paradox concerns the executive. The court is mandated to rule on all matters related to the president, and through case-by-case analysis, it must transform the constitution's abstract provisions – some of which have never been

7 Article 128(1): Subject to Article 28 [of the 2016 Constitution], the Constitutional Court has original and final jurisdiction to hear—

(a) a matter relating to the interpretation of this Constitution;
(b) a matter relating to a violation or contravention of this Constitution;
(c) a matter relating to the President, Vice-President or an election of a President;
(d) appeals relating to election of Members of Parliament and councillors; and
(e) whether or not a matter falls within the jurisdiction of the Constitutional Court.

8 Articles 11 to 32 of Part III of the constitution [Protection of the fundamental rights and freedoms of the individual, i.e., the Bill of Rights] are 'entrenched' by virtue of Article 79(3) which states that 'A bill for the alteration of Part III of this Constitution or of this Article shall not be passed unless before the first reading of the bill in the National Assembly it has been put to a National referendum with or without amendment by not less than fifty per cent of persons entitled to be registered as voters for the purposes of Presidential and parliamentary elections.' The only attempt to amend Part III through referendum in August 2016 failed to garner sufficient support; see Annex A.

tested – into unambiguous stands on murky and contentious matters. Amid these challenges, the court's diverse bench[9] must seek to fabricate a consistent body of jurisprudence that addresses one of the republics' most critical and consequential issues: To what extent is 'unfettered' presidential discretion compatible with constitutionalism?

## *Professor Munalula dissents*

Over the course of its first five years, several of the court's early rulings have impinged on presidential powers. The record does not exude progressive ambition. The Constitutional Court has dealt with a presidential petition by the political opposition, contesting the outcome of a presidential election, which it dismissed on a technicality (*Hichilema v Lungu* 2016). It ruled that the constitutional provision limiting a president to two five-year terms did not prevent the incumbent president from standing for an election which, should he win, would allow him 13 years in office (*Pule v Attorney General* 2018; and again in *Legal Resources Foundation v Lungu* 2021; see Beyani et al. 2021). The court also condoned the president's dismissal of his Director of Public Prosecutions (DPP) based on a tribunal report which the president refused to allow the accused DPP see or to make public (*Nchito v Attorney General* 2020). In a separate case, the court nonetheless reaffirmed the immunity of the DPP to judicial oversight – thus, once again, sustaining the principle of unbridled executive discretion (*Maambo v the People* 2016). It also refused to intervene in the ruling party's haphazard efforts to introduce further amendments to the constitution – including the dilution of the majoritarian electoral clause (*LAZ v Attorney General* 2020). In its analyses, the court has presumably considered the scope of presidential powers 'without fear or favor.'[10] And yet scrutiny of the court's relevant rulings suggests rather a 'judicial politics of consensual institutional accommodation of the executive caprice,' as Upendra Baxi (2013, 46) has characterized such behavior. Bracketing the indemonstrable possibility of a compromised bench, the problem appears to be that the constitution gives the judges no effective tools for transcending the implicit prerogativist imperative at the core of the politico-legal culture.

If the court has been inclined to show deference to the head of state, this orientation has not been unanimous. In several of these cases, one Constitutional

9 The constitution prescribes a Constitutional Court of 13 members (or more). At this writing, with new appointments in April 2021, nine judges sit on its bench. Five are women and four are men. All have worked within the state legal apparatus, many within the Attorney General's chambers, and/or as in-house counsel or directors of parastatal agencies. All but one have served earlier on a superior bench. All have a firm legal education, but only one has the advanced academic merits of a PhD in law. One justice has extensive experience in both diplomacy and the non-profit world.

10 The Zambian judiciary's official website proclaims: 'We aim to provide effective and efficient administration of justice accessible to all people in Zambia … impartial and timely adjudication … without fear of favour.'

Court justice has submitted written dissents which clearly seek to imbue the court's jurisprudence with a more autonomous ethos. Mulela Margaret Munalula, officially addressed as the honorable lady justice, has vigorously defended the court's potential to advance Zambia's 'search for a new more democratic order' (dissenting opinion in *LAZ v Attorney General* 2020, 16). A series of tightly argued dissents, signed as *Professor* Munalula, proceed from the premise that the dispensation ushered in by the 2016 constitution signals a 'paradigm shift' in Zambia's legal domain (ibid., 2). Thus, Professor Munalula argues that

> [T]he Constitution of Zambia as amended in 2016 instituted a new constitutional order quite different from what prevailed in the past. The new order is the result of repeated efforts at constitution reform over the past 50 years. With the new order came a constitutional court to enforce it and inculcate a *new legal culture.* (emphasis added)

In Professor Munalula's view, the new court is a central pillar of this shift and in setting it up, she opines (ibid., 11),

> the People of Zambia made a fundamental break with Zambia's constitutional past in which the separation of powers favoured the Executive and Legislative branches of Government. The [Constitutional] Court was created to nurture and protect a new order which would deepen constitutionalism.

Professor Munalula thus places a great deal of faith in the potential of the court, empowered and emboldened by the 'the landmark 2016 constitutional amendments' (*Maambo* dissent, 1131) to address the politico-legal ballast of prerogativism. This implies many an uphill battle. Indeed, from her (one-voice minority) perspective (*LAZ v Attorney General*, 9–10),

> When there is an important constitutional question before it, a constitutional court cannot take refuge in precedent or technicalities nor shy away from making hard decisions that hold anyone and everyone including the court itself constitutionally accountable ... [Indeed,] a constitutional court should ... be prepared to push the boundaries to the outer limits of its constitutional mandate.

Tellingly, Professor Munalula has sought to advance this progressive agenda largely through solitary dissents to the court's majority rulings.[11] The *pathos* threading through Professor Munalula's opinions reflects disappointment in the nation's failure to enact a new Bill of Rights, thus stunting the court's jurisdiction and freezing core aspects of constitutional jurisprudence in the UNIP era. Indeed, she notes in one such dissent (in *LAZ v Attorney General*, 2), that

11 Professor Munalula was a member of the TCDCZ and thus has a stake of sorts in the success of these amendments.

> [i]n interpreting the Constitution … it is my firm belief that there is need to take into account the values embraced by the new order so as to minimize the impact of the impugned constitutional culture of the pre-2016 Constitution amendment era.
>
> To do this, of course, implies redressing past errors and injustices meted out by the very judiciary she serves.[12]

Through these prescriptive proclamations, Professor Munalula in effect declares herself a judicial activist. This is a controversial banner for a judge of an apex court to bear. The statutory Law Association made the radical departure of condoning its members' participation in the Oasis Forum's constitutionalist campaigns, and lawyers are expected to defend the (often partisan) interests of their clients. But cause activism on the bench is frowned upon in Zambia's politico-legal culture. As Supreme Court Justice Mumba Malila (2020, 394) notes, judicial activism is often 'viewed in a spirit of criticism rather than praise.' Indeed, "a judge, who makes his judgments beyond ordinary constitutional, statutory law considerations or legal precedent, is said to be 'legislating from the bench'." That said, Justice Malila is of a like mind with Professor Munalula when he expresses (ibid., 393) the 'full conviction that the judiciary can and should rightly play a pivotal role in developing a normative climate in which respect for human rights and constitutionality flourishes.' These, to be sure, are controversial positions in Zambia's conservative legal climate. In exhorting the court on which she sits to 'push the boundaries to the outer limits of its constitutional mandate,' Professor Munalula is herself straining the confines of conventional juridical propriety.[13]

### *Law's purposes*

As her submissions to the court record evince, Professor Munalula has been unhappy with unfettered executive discretion, and with the judiciary's history of deference to it. In the Constitutional Court's early years, however, Professor Munalula's efforts to subject executive actions to judicial review got tangled up in

12 In an earlier dissent (in *Milford Maambo and others v the People* (2016/CC/R001), Professor Munalula argued that provisions in the 2016 constitution (Article 267(4) read in conjunction with Article 180(7)) oblige the court to overturn a landmark Supreme Court judgment from 1977 (*DPP v Augustino*) which affirmed the unfettered powers of the Director of Public Prosecutions to issue a *nolle prosequi* without any justification. In her view (ibid., 1130–1), the earlier judgment erred in law due, perhaps, to the fact that it 'was made during the One Party State era, when Constitutional provisions were likely to be interpreted to erode rather than promote human rights.'

13 In her persistence, Professor Munalula perhaps finds consolation in Justice Malila's submission (ibid., 5) that 'perchance it is after all not too late for adjudicators in Zambia to begin to shake off the entrenched foundations of judicial pusillanimity and the resultant self-restraint and lethargy, especially when it comes to espousing human rights causes or deciding good governance issues.'

secondary debates around the court's approach to constitutional interpretation. These debates have pitted a 'literal' against a 'purposive' attitude toward statutory interpretation, with Professor Munalula consistently championing a purposive approach. Given the professor's activist mien, and the Constitutional Court's overall conservatism, one might ask whether disagreements over statutory interpretation signal elements of an ethico-legal fissure within the court? Or, to press the point, might one say that Professor Munalula's professed purposivism represents a more democratic variant of constitutionalism? Do demands for purposive interpretation represent, as some experts seem to argue (e.g., Kaaba 2018, Beyani et al. 2021), the seeds of a constitutional jurisprudence imbued with explicit democratic intent?[14] Or, is it rather the case that the technical disputes over purposive vs literal interpretation are simply a distraction from the court's primary concern of shielding its remit from the possibility of presidential disfavor?

Professor Munalula submitted her first extensive dissent as a Constitutional Court justice in a case concerning Director of Public Prosecutions Mutembo Nchito's use of the *nolle prosequi* to discontinue court proceedings.[15] In this case (*Maambo v the People*), three plaintiffs asked the court to determine whether DPPs are obliged to declare their reasons for issuing a *nolle*. The court's majority ruled (ibid.) that the DPP does, indeed, have unfettered powers under Article 180 of the 2016 constitution to enter a *nolle prosequi*. The majority ruling relies on this express provision of Article 180 of the constitution:

> (4) The Director of Public Prosecutions may—
> (c) discontinue, at any stage before judgment is delivered, criminal proceedings instituted or undertaken by the Director of Public Prosecutions or another person or authority.

In her dissenting opinion, Professor Munalula challenged the majority ruling, arguing that no official action, including that of a DPP, is immune to judicial review (ibid., 1110–39). Professor Munalula (ibid., 1112) framed her dissent as a purposive approach to interpreting the 2016 constitution, as opposed to what she termed the majority's 'legalist' reading of the law. Judicial interpretation, she acknowledged (citing Goldsworthy 2013, 689–90), is 'problematic and controversial, mainly because legitimate interpretation is difficult to distinguish from illegitimate change.' This is not a moot point, in her view, since judicial interpretation can (ibid.) 'have profound effects on the institutional structure of society, and the exercise of power within it.'

In Professor Munalula's view, the majority's legalist approach in *Maambo* obscures inconsistencies in the constitution. These inconsistencies, which affect 'the systematic checks and balance underpinning our constitution as a whole' had 'become acceptable in Zambia's legal system for historical reasons.' By this, she is

14 Recall, in this connection, Patrick Matibini's observation (see above, p. 230) that in the Zambian context, purposive interpretation implies 'an element of judicial activism.'
15 Mr Nchito's use of the *nolle prosequi* was discussed at length in Chapter 9.

clearly referring to the legacy of autocracy of the Kaunda era. At first blush, it appears that what is at stake in Professor Munalula's dispute with the majority is the way the constitution's intent or purpose should be understood. Judicial debates about legislative intent are, of course, ubiquitous.[16] Post–World War II appeals to purposive readings of law in the imperial metropole were initially presented in opposition to the prevailing literalism of English legal culture, rooted in 19th-century jurisprudence. According to these time-honored conventions, court rulings were expected to take their lead from the 'plain meaning' of legislative language. This approach derived from the doctrine of the legislative supremacy of parliament which, according to McLeod (2004, 1111) 'created a mindset on the part of judges that their role was to do what they were told by the supreme and, by the standards of the time, increasingly democratically validated Parliament.' Thus in 1892, one Lord Esher had declared before a London court that '[i]f the words of an Act are clear, you must follow them, even though they lead to a manifest absurdity. The court has nothing to do with the question whether the legislature has committed an absurdity.'[17]

Where literalists look to the plain meaning of an enactment, purposivists invoke what parliament would have wanted had it anticipated the contemporary circumstances of the case at hand (McLeod, op cit.). Initially, purposivism was conceived as a remedy for situations when (*pace* Lord Escher) the plain meaning of a legal text was ambiguous or led to an absurd conclusion.[18] In some iterations, however, purposive interpretations have been portrayed as the best or only valid approach, intended to supplant literalist interpretation. Ghanaian Supreme Court Justice Samuel Kofi Date-Bah (2015, 119), for example, endorses the view that 'a literal approach is always a flawed one, since even common sense suggests that a plain meaning interpretation of an enactment needs to be checked against the purpose of the enactment, if such can be ascertained.' Zambian legal scholar O'Brien Kaaba (2018, 15) goes one critical step further, claiming that '[t]he reasons advanced by the Constitutional Court for choosing the literal rule have no merit and in fact, it is respectfully submitted, the use of the literal approach in constitutional adjudication is unconstitutional.'

Purposivism spread to Africa in the postcolonial era (see e.g., Date-Bah, op.cit.). The first appeal to purposive interpretation in Zambia occurred in a Supreme

16 Disputes about legislative intent are at the core, for example, of the 'great debate' between originalism vs theories of a 'living' constitution (see, e.g., Solum 2018).

17 *Queen v Judge of the City of London Court*, 1 Q.B. 273; cited in McLeod (ibid.).

18 McLeod (2004) attributes the emergence of purposivism to two factors. One was the advent of a 'great deal of social legislation' after World War II, which McLeod suggests, obliged judges to read the law in a way that promoted popular political aims. A second factor was the entrance of the United Kingdom into the EEC in 1973, which necessitated a degree of harmonization between 'Community' and UK jurisprudence. Where the UK followed the common law tradition, which gives significant weight to *stare decisis* (judge-made precedent), European Community law was based on civil code, which ignored precedent, but allowed courts significant interpretative leeway. Purposivism aligned positively with this 'teleological' style of interpretation. It is noteworthy that MacLeod's narrative suggests that purposivism represents a more democratic approach to legal interpretation.

Court case from 1994,[19] but a Zambian jurisprudence of purposive interpretation has only begun to develop since 2016 through a series of Constitutional Court cases. That court initially delineated its rules of interpretation in a case where Mr Stephen Katuka, the secretary-general of the opposition United Party for National Development (UPND) petitioned the court to oust a set of presidential appointees.

That much-cited case (*Katuka v Attorney General* 2017) was ostensibly about political finances. The petitioners claimed, among other things, that the cabinet and provincial ministers appointed by the president had overstayed their term in office. In the petitioners' view, the ministers should have vacated their positions when President Lungu dissolved parliament, which he did, as per the constitution, 90 days before the August 2016 elections. Petitioner Stephen Katuka argued that according to the constitution, ministers are members of parliament and that MPs cease to hold office after dissolution of parliament. Thus, the MP/ministers must also vacate their cabinet and provincial assignments and forfeit the benefits associated with those positions.

The case, of course, was also about executive powers: The petitioners claimed (ibid., 961) that

> the failure by the President of the Republic of Zambia to dissolve his Cabinet following the dissolution of Parliament was a deliberate infringement of the Constitution and that, in so doing, the President has failed in his duties to, *inter alia*, respect, uphold and safeguard the Constitution and the sovereignty of the Republic and to promote democracy and enhance the unity of the nation and to uphold the rule of law.

Be this as it may, it is evident from the court proceedings that the constitution is ambiguous about whether the term of the cabinet is tied to that of parliament, prompting the court to ask (ibid., 1021): 'What is the effect of dissolution of Parliament on Ministers?' This is the substantive matter under review, but along the way the young court felt obliged to venture into a debate about how the constitution is to be read.

The respondents in *Katuka*, representing the ministers who were allegedly enjoying public funds illicitly, invoked provisions of the 2016 constitution which says that a cabinet or provincial minister remains in office until removed from office by the president or, among other things, 'another person assumes the office of President.'[20] The respondents' argument was that the term of parliament and the term of cabinet are two distinct things. The court (ibid., 1023–4) was not convinced. In its view, such a literal interpretation of the law

19 This was a case (*Attorney General v Mbikusita Lewanika* 1994) in which four MPs who resigned from the ruling MMD challenged the subsequent loss of their parliamentary seats. In this case, the court accepted the state's demand for a purposive ruling and sustained the rebel MPs' loss of their positions.

20 Articles 116(3)(e) and 117(2)(d) of the 2016 constitution.

> leads to absurdity because on one hand, the Constitution says Ministers will be appointed from among Members of Parliament and, yet, on the other, it appears to allow for the continuation of Ministers in their Cabinet portfolios following the dissolution of Parliament when the foundation upon which their ministerial positions stand, namely, membership of Parliament has been removed, once Parliament has been dissolved.

Noting that the expression, 'if another person assumes the office of President,' is 'capable of more than one [literal] meaning' (ibid.), the court sought recourse in purposive interpretation. This approach aligned with that of the petitioners, who had appealed to the court (ibid., 969) to 'apply a purposive and benevolent interpretation of the Constitution in accordance with the Bill of Rights and in a manner that promotes its purposes, values and principles and, contributes to good governance.' Beyond this, the petitioners prayed for a ruling that would take the prevailing politico-legal context into account. As the court noted (ibid., 974),

> We were urged not to turn a blind eye to the political realities in Zambia which is a multiparty democracy. Counsel [for the petitioners] submitted that it would be against the constitutional values of Zambia for the ruling party to advantage itself during the campaign period by allowing it to have its members occupy critical and influential positions in government during the campaigns when, constitutionally, they were required to vacate those positions.

Keeping ministers on the payroll during an election campaign is easily seen as a prerogativist maneuver by the incumbent president to skew the political playing field. In challenging an overbearing presidential maneuver, the petitioners felt a purposive interpretation best served their interest. They also argued that recent jurisprudence was on their side. In their view, the recent case of *Kabimba v Attorney General* (2011) clearly 'demonstrates the shift from the purely literal meaning towards the purposive construction of statutory provisions' (*Katuka*, 970).[21]

In *Katuka*, the president's lawyers did not dispute the validity of a purposive interpretation in the face of an obvious ambiguity (ibid., 994), thus ceding

21 In that instance, presiding Supreme Court Justice Albert Wood referred to an English case (*Seaford Court Estates ltd v Asher* 1949), in which the iconic Lord Denning had opined that

> The literal method is now completely out of date. It has been replaced by the approach which Lord Diplock described as the 'purposive approach' … in all cases now in the interpretation of statutes we adopt such a construction as will 'promote the general legislative purpose' underlying the provision. It is no longer necessary for judges to wring their hands and say: "There is nothing we can do about it." Whenever strict interpretation of a statute gives rise to absurdity and an unjust situation, the judges can and should use their good sense to remedy it by reading words in, if necessary, so as to do what Parliament would have done, had they had the situation in mind.

normative ground to the petitioners. In its unanimous ruling (ibid., 1013), to which Professor Munalula was a signatory, the Constitutional Court declared as official policy its preference for literal interpretation, but allowed that under certain circumstances – i.e., when 'absurdities' arise – a purposive approach may be warranted.[22] Comparing earlier drafts of the 2016 Constitution Amendment Act, the court (ibid., 1025) proceeded to find that having cabinet and provincial ministers remain in office after the dissolution of parliament 'is clearly not what Parliament could have intended.' The ministers in question were directed to vacate their positions and pay back any benefits accrued since the dissolution of parliament. The court did not expressly censure the president for abdicating his duties to uphold the constitution, however. Instead (ibid.), it enjoined parliament to resolve the ambiguity in the constitution which allowed for this dispute to arise.

Returning to Professor Munalula's dissent in *Maambo*, she contends (*Maambo*, 1112) that a purposive reading of the constitution indicates that 'in entering a *nolle prosequi*, the DPP's action is subject to judicial review and he (or she) must give reasons for entering the said *nolle prosequi*.' Professor Munalula anchors her analysis in Article 287 of the 2016 constitution, which reads, in part,

> (1) This Constitution shall be interpreted in accordance with the Bill of Rights and in a manner that—
>
> (a) promotes its purposes, values and principles;
> (b) permits the development of the law; and
> (c) contributes to good governance.

She agrees (ibid., 1115) that if Article 180(4)(c) of the constitution is 'read in isolation … it gives the DPP uniquely expansive and arbitrary power over the exercise of a *nolle prosequi*.' But Clause 7 of Article 180 includes this critical caveat:

> The Director of Public Prosecutions shall not be subject to the direction or control of a person or an authority in the performance of the functions of that office, *except* that the Director of Public Prosecutions *shall* have

22 The pertinent passage of the court's ruling reads as follows:

> In terms of the general or guiding principles of interpretation, the starting point in interpreting words or provisions of the constitution, or indeed any statute, is to first consider the literal or ordinary meaning of the words and articles that touch on the issue or provision in contention. This is premised on the principle that words or provisions in the constitution or statute must not be read in isolation. It is only when the ordinary meaning leads to absurdity that the purposive approach should be resorted to. The purposive approach entails adopting a construction or interpretation that promotes the general legislative purpose. This requires the court to ascertain the meaning and purpose of the provision having regard to the context and historical origins, where necessary. This exercise would sometimes require reading into the provision what the Legislature had intended

> regard to the public interest, administration of justice, the integrity of the judicial system and the need to prevent and avoid abuse of the legal process. (Munalula's emphases)

Professor Munalula further contends (ibid., 1117) that since Article 180 does not specifically immunize the Director of Public Prosecutions from judicial review, this shows that the constitution 'does not oust the court's oversight' over the DPP's actions. Indeed, the constitution's Article 267(4) says specifically that

> A provision of this Constitution to the effect that a person, an authority or institution *is not subject* to the direction or control of a person or an authority in the performance of a function, *does not preclude a court from exercising jurisdiction* in relation to a question as to whether that person, authority or institution has performed the function in accordance with this Constitution or other laws. (Munalula's emphases)

In *Maambo*, Professor Munalula's purposiveness does not involve any speculative extrapolation. It merely demands bringing all of the relevant bits of the constitution to bear on the case at hand. Her efforts at democratizing constitutional jurisprudence do not end here. Having lodged an unambiguous dissent over 'unfettered powers,' her next move is to insist that all constitutional interpretation must be approached through the constitution's newly enacted national values and principles.

## *The power of principles*

In August 2019, the Law Association of Zambia together with Chapter One Foundation Limited, a civic organization led by former LAZ president and Oasis Forum chairperson Linda Kasonde, commenced action in the Constitutional Court against the Attorney General. The purpose of the petition was to challenge the efforts of President Edgar Lungu's administration to further amend the 2016 constitution through the introduction of so-called Bill 10.[23] According to the petitioners, the ad hoc process by which the government pursued constitutional reform was itself unconstitutional, and they appealed to the Constitutional Court to quash the controversial bill, which was still under deliberation before the national assembly. The petition failed. It was, in any event, eventually rendered redundant when Bill 10 died in parliament. The significance of this minor case, then, is not in its legal outcomes so much as in the use Professor Munalula made of it to promote her vision of constitutionalism.

In its response to the petition in *LAZ v Attorney General*, the Attorney General argued that Bill 10 adhered strictly to the constitution's own protocol

23 Proposing the enactment of a new Constitution of Zambia (Amendment) Act; for background, see Chapter 6.

for revising the constitution, spelled out in Article 79. In a tersely worded dissent to the majority's dismissal of the petition, Professor Munalula (ibid., 7) rejected the state's claim on the basis that 'Article 79 is not the sole mandatory consideration in the process of amending the Constitution.' On the contrary, she argued (ibid., 5), Articles 8 and 9 of the constitution, which spell out Zambia's national values and principles 'are now a part of the constitutional requirements for amending the Constitution and therefore ought to be adhered to.' Professor Munalula grounded her dissent in an expansive argument about the purpose of the Constitutional Court. In setting up the court, she argues,

> the People of Zambia made a fundamental break with Zambia's constitutional past in which the separation of powers favoured the Executive and Legislative branches of Government. The Court was created to nurture and protect a new order which would deepen constitutionalism. (ibid., 11–12)[24]

Professor Munalula thus proposes that the cornerstone of this new legal order resides in the norms laid out in Articles 8 and 9 of the constitution,[25] and her dissent in *LAZ v Attorney General* seeks to imbue these metanorms with quasi-justiciable status. The aim seems to be to oblige the court to incorporate them in the fundamental tenets of constitutional jurisprudence, constituting a kind of surrogate Bill of Rights within the court's jurisdiction. In doing so, Professor Munalula's approach resonates with the views of Ethiopian legal scholar Berihun Gebeye (2017, 3) who argues that such metanorms, widely referred to as directive principles of state policies[26] are 'manifestations of, and relevant for, transformative

24 In this, Professor Munalula concurs with Chapter One Foundation petitioner Linda Kasonde, (ibid., J39), who submitted that 'this [Constitutional] Court is the last line of defence as Zambia has a long and checked [sic] history of constitution making and constitutional amendments from the Chona Constitution Review Commission all the way to the Mung'omba Commission and that successive governments have tried and so far have been successful in wrestling the power of the people of Zambia away from them.'

25 The Articles in question read as follows:

Article 8. Zambia's national values and principles are –

(a) morality and ethics;
(b) patriotism and national unity;
(c) democracy and constitutionalism;
(d) human dignity, equity, social justice, equality and non-discrimination;
(e) good governance and integrity; and
(f) sustainable development.

Article 9.The national values and principles shall apply to the

(a) interpretation of this Constitution;
(b) enactment and interpretation of the law; and
(c) development and implementation of State policy.

26 The notion of directive principles of state policy has been central to Indian constitutional jurisprudence, which was in turn inspired by the Irish independence constitution. Indian

constitutionalism in Africa.' Gebeye's position is that such directive principles should be seen as a tool of African constitutional jurisprudence (ibid., 33) 'not only [as] a means for constituting and constraining political power, but also [as] a mechanism for enabling societal transformation.' These sentiments and the concomitant concept of 'transformative' constitutionalism capture the *ethos* of Professor Munalula's jurisprudential philosophy succinctly.

Professor Munalula's efforts to elevate the status of national values and principles place the dispute over the style of judicial interpretation in a new light. Note how Professor Munalula's response to the *LAZ* petition makes it clear that the tensions within the court are *not* primarily about the relative validity of literalism versus purposivism in interpreting the constitution; by the same token, and despite Justice Munalula's profession of its virtues, recourse to 'purposivism' does not imply transformative intent.[27] Justice Munalula's disputes with her colleagues do not ultimately hinge on the *meaning* of the wording of specific provisions, but are rather about acknowledging the new democratic *ethos* of the 2016 constitution. This implies more than simply 'reading the Constitution as a whole,' or the edict that 'no singular provision should swallow or vanquish any other provision(s).'[28] Rather it means positing transformative outcomes as an overriding aim of all constitutional interpretation. What is at stake, then, is not the 'genuine intent' of a given provision, but rather how constitutionalism is itself understood. On the basis of its rulings on executive privilege thus far, it would appear that the court's majority is hostage to a prerogativist strain of constitutionalism. One might even say that the constitutionalism of the court's majority represents a coordinated defense of an unfettered presidency.

Professor Munalula champions a different vision. The honorable lady justice does not want the constitutional court to simply deliver reasonable rulings; she also prays (*Hichilema v Lungu* 2016, J7) that the court's 'well-reasoned decision[s]' could help to 'heal this nation.' Elsewhere (*LAZ v Attorney General*, 19), she pens these uplifting sentiments: 'The Constitution is hopeful and it is incumbent on this Court which holds the mandate to interpret and protect it to use all means constitutionally available to it to sustain that hope.' One can only wonder, is it not remarkable that Professor Munalula, alone within Zambia's judiciary, should acknowledge the indelible bond between injustice and suffering?

---

debates had a substantial impact on South African debates leading up to the 1994 interim constitution (see De Villiers 1992).

27 The ambivalence of purposivism concerning progressive judicial outcomes was already evident in the Supreme Court's ruling on *Attorney General v Mbikusita Lewanika* (1994) and has been reaffirmed in the arguments presented in the controversial constitutional court case of *Pule v Attorney-General* (2018) where the court was asked to give Article 106 of the constitution a 'generous and purposive' interpretation in order to affirm incumbent President Edgar Lungu's eligibility to stand for a third term as republican president (see Beyani et al. 2021).

28 As argued in *Katuka v the Attorney General* (2017, 994).

Seen in a broader context, Justice Munalula is far from alone. Without straying from our judicial context, one can find a rich and sophisticated discourse on the role of the courts in socioeconomic repair virtually next door, in South Africa. To put Professor Munalula's bold, albeit solitary campaign to reconfigure Zambia's constitutional jurisprudence into a wider perspective, one can turn to the literature on transformative constitutionalism in South Africa where similar arguments have circulated since the 1990s. It goes without saying that the structural injustices afflicting South African society are configured very differently than those in Zambia, where racialized discrimination has not been a prominent political cause since independence. These differences, to be sure, limit the comparability of the politico-legal dynamics at play in the two jurisdictions. Yet, while South Africa has gone much further than Zambia in attempting to use its Constitutional Court to decolonize the politico-legal domain, transformative judicial activism in South Africa has confronted obstacles similar to those that have stymied Professor Munalula's efforts in Zambia. In a heuristic spirit, then, the next section links Professor Munaluna's arguments about transformative legality to debates about the contribution of judicial activism to the reparation of systemic injustice.

## A postliberal legality?

The notion of transformative constitutionalism emerged in robust debates around South Africa's post-apartheid constitution of 1996, the legal foundations of a process that sought to dismantle the foundations of racial discrimination (see Klare 1998, Davis & Klare 2010, Vilhena et al. 2013, Kibet & Fombad 2017).[29] In a seminal essay that appeared soon after South Africa's fundamental constitutional reforms, American legal scholar Karl Klare (1998, 150) defined transformative constitutionalism as

> a long-term project of constitutional enactment, interpretation, and enforcement committed (not in isolation, of course, but in a historical context of conducive political developments) to transforming a country's political and social institutions and power relationships in a democratic, participatory, and egalitarian direction. Transformative constitutionalism connotes an enterprise of inducing large-scale social change through nonviolent political processes grounded in law.

In Klare's view (ibid., 147) the 'democratic transition in South Africa is intended to be a bridge from authoritarianism to a new culture of justification.' It is noteworthy that Klare's analysis was not focused on the specific provisions of the 1996 constitution but on the judicial *reasoning* undergirding legal judgment. Klare was concerned with interpretation, not legislation or enforcement, and he

29 Vilhena et al. (2013) extend debates around transformative constitutionalism to Brazil and India.

devoted much of his article to the possible contradiction between the new constitution's transformative intent and an entrenched, conservative legal culture. Klare's primary purpose was to suggest that realizing the transformative potential of the new constitution may require 'a revised, perhaps somewhat more politicized, understanding of the rule of law and adjudication that can consist with and support transformative hopes' (ibid., 150). Klare endorsed South African Judge Sydney Kentridge's view (in *State v Zuma* 1995, 17) that 'the Constitution does not mean whatever we might wish it to mean'; rather, in Klare's view (ibid.), transformative constitutionalism implies "a method of adjudication that is politically and morally engaged but that is *not* illicit 'judicial legislation,'" i.e., 'legislating from the bench,' as Justice Malila put it. The main target of Klare's scrutiny is thus the legacy of apartheid in the legal culture of judicial interpretation, and its impact on how South Africa's postliberal transformation will come to fruition. Though approached from a relatively narrow perspective, Klare is clearly addressing the question of whether emancipatory change can come about through judicial action.

Klare (1998, 150–1; emphasis in original) argued that in 1996, South Africans adopted what he termed a '*postliberal constitution*, one that may plausibly be read not only as open to, but committed to large-scale, egalitarian social transformation.' What he had in mind with this nod to constitutionalism beyond liberalism (i.e., Dowdle & Wilkinson 2017) was (op cit.) "a transformation vast enough to be inadequately captured by the phrase 'reform,' but something short of or different from 'revolution' in any traditional sense of the word." Postliberalism thus implies a clear break with the prevailing tradition of liberal legality but not, emphatically, with the prevailing form of power.

Transformative constitutionalism has had few overt detractors, but not everyone has embraced Klare's vision of postliberal constitutionalism. There are two main strands of critique, one staunchly liberal and the other more radical in approach. In the liberal vein, Theunis Roux (2013, 51) underscores transformative constitutionalism's continuity with conventional liberal values. Roux sees transformative constitutionalism as 'fundamentally a liberal constitutional project,' since

> '[First], the success of the project is tied to the maintenance of liberal political institutions, including universal adult franchise in a competitive multiparty political system, an independent judiciary and the rule of law.'

Second, argues Roux, transformative constitutionalism is a 'non-conservative' project because

> 'all social institutions, with the exception of the ones just mentioned, are susceptible to redefinition through the democratic process.'

Third, in Roux's view transformative constitutionalism

> 'eschews any grand theorising about the historical destiny of the masses, and instead concentrates on finding pragmatic solutions to social

> problems through an appropriate blend of technical expertise and democratic deliberation.'

Roux's liberal take on transformative constitutionalism, then, appears unconcerned with efforts to problematize the role of the *demos* and its constituent power in constitution-making, and puts its trust, rather, in the established liberal institutions and procedures of representative government, guided by legal technocrats, to redress decades of racial injustice. Unsurprisingly, radical critiques find that transformative constitutionalism is hobbled precisely by its links to the liberal tradition and its institutional apparatus. Many, like Terblanche Delport (2014, 117), find it problematic that transformative constitutionalism is framed as a specifically legal project:

> Transformative constitutionalism proposes that those who are already part of the discourse of the legal profession change their perspective from positivist to post-liberal while still not including the voices of those whose rights it is meant to protect ... Transformative constitutionalism is thus incompatible with a critical-liberatory position put forth by an ethics of liberation.

In a similar vein, Sanele Sibanda (2012, 44) argues that

> 'it is transformative constitutionalism's ostensible weddedness to liberal democratic constitutionalism that makes it ill-suited for achieving the social, economic and political vision it proclaims.'

While embracing the need for both social transformation and constitutional reform, radical critics problematize the kind of postliberal project transformative constitutionalism could be: One subordinated to the demands of an urban, middle-class in active pursuit of modernity; or one that actively encompasses 'the development of constitutional economics from a subaltern perspective' (Baxi 2013, 37)? Isaac Shai is aligned with the latter perspective. Shai (2019, 496) argues that

> any theorisation of radical transformation should at the very least reckon with the fact that while the impact of colonialism and apartheid ultimately is felt through material dispossession and raw economic exploitation, the more devastating, corrosive and long-lasting impact of colonialism continues to be ontological and epistemic.

Shai (ibid., 506) is skeptical of what he sees as Klare's essential premise, that 'it is possible to fill the law with humane content, and that legal culture can provide a context and a moral basis for resistance to injustice.' He is similarly unconvinced (ibid., 502) by the assumption embedded in the logic of transformative constitutionalism that law has the potential 'to resolve the legacies of colonialism and apartheid.' A radical postliberalism, from this perspective, requires changes well beyond the remit of the courts.

Such reservations concerning the emancipatory potential of law are, ironically perhaps, vindicated by Karl Klare's own empirical findings. A decade after Klare's original essay kicked off these debates, Klare and South African High Court Judge Dennis Davis (2010) undertook an assessment of the performance of the country's legal system in dismantling the legacy of apartheid. Their central concern was 'the potential of traditional South African legal culture to constrain the transformative project' (ibid., 403). The pivot of the authors' assessment is Sections 8(3) and 39(2) of the South African constitution – it's so-called 'development clauses' – which oblige courts to 'develop the common law' in accordance with the Bill of Rights. These provisions, the authors suggest, constitute a carte blanche for judicial activism in the battle to right the skewed distribution of assets and opportunities under apartheid – an algorithm still sustained by the prevailing legal culture. Davis and Klare (2010, 403) lament the conservativism of the South African bench in the face of this challenge, and express their disappointment, a decade into the 'postliberal' constitutional order, over

> the absence thus far of a coherent exploration of the Constitution's values or an explicit and sustained effort to develop new legal methodologies appropriate to transformative constitutionalism; the reluctance to interrogate the distributive consequences of private law rules in the routines of economic life, the emergence of a neo-liberal strand in constitutional application; and the lack of critical sharpness with respect to separation-of- powers issues.

The South African judiciary thus falls short, in the authors' view (Davis & Klare 2010, 404), of facilitating the constitution's vision of developing a 'democratic, egalitarian society committed to social justice and self-realisation opportunities for all.'

This politico-legal ethos resonates strongly with the social legalism of the Oasis Forum and with the many contributions to Zambia's various constitutional review processes over the past 30 years that found expression in the constitutional reforms of 2016. Professor Munalula's dissent in *LAZ v Attorney General* suggests that Articles 8 and 9 of the prevailing Zambian constitution might also be read as bench-empowering 'development clauses' but, as we have seen, Zambia's apex courts have resisted putting this insight into practice. Perhaps this is, as Kibet and Fombad (2017, 340) suggest, because in African legal systems the concept of transformative constitutionalism 'demands more from judges than has traditionally been understood.' As the record shows, buying into a transformative jurisprudence runs up against unspoken tenets of the prevailing politico-legal domain that judges seem disinclined to challenge.

Professor Munalula knows this as well as anyone. Although she does not, as far as I know, invoke Klare directly, one can sense ripples of the South African debates in her dissents. Klare argued that the 1996 South African constitution provided adequate tools to dismantle the material and cultural effects of apartheid, and exhorted South African judges to apply its provisions to that progressive task. Professor Munalula's discourse exudes a kindred *pathos*. Many liberal and radical critics alike have concurred with Klare and Davis' assessment of the South African courts' recalcitrant culture of statutory interpretation.[30] Professor Munalula's activism targets precisely this obstacle. Like Klare, Professor Munalula wants her fellow judges to take advantage of the constitution's unmined transformative potential, and to step up and read the constitution with the purpose of deepening democracy. For the time being, her colleagues are not listening. In any case, as the South African debates suggest, the common will of the people cannot be simply invoked, *sui iuris*, in a courtroom; it must be forged through political action. Excluded Zambians, it would seem to follow, must challenge the residual effects of imperial subjectification not only in court, but in, and possibly against, the workings of the institutions through which citizens govern themselves.

### *Postliberal trajectories*

In seeking to enhance the public and judicial scrutiny of executive actions, Professor Munalula's constitutional liberalism is progressive in context, a stark departure from the recent Supreme Court opinion that the president is 'the overall authority on everything' (*Attorney General v Mutuna* 2012), not to mention her own court's fresh ruling (in *Maambo*) on the 'unfettered' powers of the Director of Public Prosecutions. At the same time, Professor Munalula's position emboldens the status quo in its strict adherence to constitutional supremacy, i.e., to the view that law and its institutional apparatus are, in the words of Chapter One lawyer Linda Kasonde, the people's 'last line of defence' against a history of oppressive government. It is natural for a former president of the Law Association to appeal to such a doctrine, but as South African analyst Karin van Marle (2007, 412) notes, this gambit 'underscores law and supports a certain form of legal politics that holds the danger of overtaking politics as a form of resistance.'

Indeed, the Achilles' heel in Professor Munalula's position resides in her activism's (lack of) political entanglements. What this boils down to is the extent to which Zambians do, actually, assign transcendent powers to Articles 8 and 9 of the constitution. Such a sentiment of popular ownership must pertain to a tangible degree for Justice Munalula's crusade to make sense. Indeed, to legitimately hold the power to generate new constitutional meaning, the values and principles inscribed in the 2016 constitution must genuinely reflect the will of the people.

Professor Munalula's understanding of the people's will has both a theoretical and an empirical foundation. She is a widely published law professor and led the University of Zambia School of Law for many years. Beyond these academic

30 There have also been many positive views of the South African Constitutional Court's evolving jurisprudence, e.g., Himonga (2017), Parpworth (2017) and Gardbaum (2019). For a recent assessment of the court's transformative agenda, see Klug (2019).

merits, as a member of the Technical Committee on the Drafting of the Zambian Constitution, Professor Munalula was exposed to citizen testimony in the committee's multiple consultative forums and conventions. But even if each and every contributor to the committee's consultations affirmed some or all of what would become Article 8, these enunciations were not expressions of constituent power – rather, they were individual contributions to a process carefully managed by the government. And here we reach one limit of liberal legality vis-à-vis transformative justice. Justice Munalula's judicial activism is not validated through constituent power; it does not and, on its own terms, cannot make common cause with the *demos*. Her best hope, rather, is to carry her constituency on the bench with wile and irrefutable reason. If successful, this could, over time, undermine the legal culture of judicial deference to the presidency. This would, in principle, constitute a form of transformative constitutionalism, and could have far-reaching consequences for the prevailing form of power.

Ongoing struggles within the Constitutional Court over the substance of constitutionalism hinge upon opposing views of the court's mandate. The majority appears, thus far, to eschew departure from a jurisprudence anchored in the colonial past. Professor Munalula, in contrast, sees the new court as a socially ordained opportunity to shake things up for the better. Professor Munalula's dissents, which seek to democratize the court's reading of the constitution in an overt and systemic fashion, might be read in two different ways. On the one hand, her postliberal take on constitutionalism might be seen as an outlier, beyond what is legally and politically viable in Zambia's current context. In this scenario, the people's will is actually to defend a prerogativist form of power at the helm of their nation. If this is the case, there is a real threat that Professor Munalula's persistent lone-wolf objections to the majority's consensus may take her and her transformative ambitions 'out of the game,' so to speak.

On the other hand, it might also be so that Professor Munalula's arguments signal a latent possibility in the politico-legal domain, a fruit ripening for harvest. This fruit is the transformative potential of the constituent power upon which the founding republican constitution of 1964 was predicated. There is no predicting the ends to which the eruption of such popular political power might aspire, or achieve. Perhaps some indication of these aspirations were visible, however fleetingly, and perhaps with exaggerated optimism, in Mr Sata's embodiment of a constituent presidency. In any case, this latter premise points beyond the strict mandate of the court and invokes the possibility of seeing judicial action and popular political mobilization aligned in common cause. This book's concluding chapter considers this possibility in light of the empirical record thus far.

# 11 Coda

This book has been a work in progress for a long time. The constitution-making process I set out to study in 2003 only achieved some semblance of closure in 2016. Over the course of this process of studying, writing and reflecting, the world outside has undergone dramatic changes. Questions of constitutional legitimacy and the scope of presidential powers have, once again, become sites of heated debate. As have the challenges which our leaders must address, urgently, if our planet is to continue to be inhabitable for humans.

These final pages reflect on the political implications of my findings and analysis. What follows is written in a conversational and not an imperative tone. The contradictions inherent in writing about African politics from a White, male perspective are not lost on me; indeed, at times they feel overwhelming. At the same time, I feel an obligation to reciprocate, however inadequately, the generosity of so many people who made my work possible. I am, of course, anxious that I may have misunderstood or mangled the perspicacity of my learned interlocutors. On the other hand, I pray that they, and other readers, may find materials within these pages that could inspire them to initiate conversations on how to realize the promise and potential of Zambia as a land of milk and honey for all.

## The limits of liberal legality

Law, the foundation of government, exercises its emancipatory potential best when it is aligned with the will of the people. But how can the people's will be known? And how can it be institutionalized without abrogating its emancipatory potential? Earlier chapters have shown how popular intent is repeatedly claimed and instrumentalized by diverse social forces in postcolonial Zambia. The will of the people is invoked to legitimize state power, on the one hand, and to justify challenges to prerogativist excess, on the other. In practice, the constituent power of the Zambian *demos* has remained a muted force – implied in the process of constitutionalization at independence, but never given free rein to assert its scope and intent. Why is this?

One reason is that the relationship of law to constituent power is riven by a fundamental paradox. On the one hand, Zambia's 'received' law is fossilized in inescapable subsidiarity to its imperial roots. The logics of legality, enduring

DOI: 10.4324/9780429198984-16

reverberations of the embattled colonial state, project the political *ethos* of imperial liberalism, which is to say that postcolonial law was designed precisely to defend the discretionary powers of the sovereign in the face of real and perceived threats to a status quo predicated on systemic exclusion and injustice. The postcolonial legal order, in other words, is anathema to the unpredictability and potential volatility of constituent power. Law's champions persist in their defense of a colonial model of exclusive government, even when the markers of exclusion have 'evolved,' as Fanon (1967) predicted, from race to class.[1] Paradoxically, the achievement of independence from colonial rule – the basic condition for Zambia to 'exist by itself' – came about through an act of constitutionalization which posited 'the people' as the source of all power. If the constitution, then, is the vehicle and conduit of a colonial form of unfettered power, does it not also offers tools to discipline or harness it?

The key to why 'the people' have not wielded these tools more effectively in their own self-interest resides, to a large degree, in the alienation of law from the lived experience of the people. A crucial constraint on popular power is lodged in the political compartmentalization of the *demos* from affairs of the state through the systematic cordoning off of 'custom' from statutory 'law.' This has resulted not only in sustaining the colonial division of Zambians into two legal castes – those governed by modern statute, and those allegedly subject to archaic norms – but also in the bracketing of the constituent power embodied in inherited community leadership. Indeed, the power of so-called traditional authorities to constitute a 'people' has been portrayed from the outset as a threat to party/state hegemony (Inyambo Yeta, pers. comm., see also Chapter 3), and the contribution of chiefs to promoting the well-being of their subjects has been consistently underappreciated (Baldwin 2016). At the same time, the capacity of citizens to hold chiefs and their representatives accountable for their actions is routinely undermined by the intervention of the statutory legal system in the ways that customary authority governs itself, i.e., through impeachment and succession. Through generations of circular labor migration, from villages to towns and back again, the realm of custom has acquired urban forms, as well (Ogura 1991, Ferguson 1999). In terms of political recognition, the urban precariate and the rural poor are similarly suspect and marginal to statutory legality.

By sustaining these systemic mechanisms of elite appropriation and popular exclusion, the professional stewards of statutory legality – lawyers and judges – have been trapped in a paradoxical position – rhetorically compelled to uphold the will of the people, while harboring deep suspicion toward disorderly and unpredictable expressions of constituent power. By training and the regulatory framework governing their professional acts, the legal profession is inextricably aligned with the embattled state, eager to censure the mischief of individual authorities, but careful not to undermine the principles of prerogativist authority itself.

1 On this evolution, see also Burawoy (2014).

This paradox is evident in the experience of the Law Association's participation in the Oasis Forum (Chapter 6), which I have taken here as a test of the potential of law to serve transformative ends. The Forum was a vibrant expression of a liberal ethos that has arguably been prevalent among Zambian intellectuals since before independence (B.J. Phiri 2006, Macola 2010, Englund 2013). The Oasis Forum sought, and purported, to embody this ethos; its efforts to instate a non-partisan check on presidential prerogative were unprecedented. But where the Forum had successfully plugged into the people's will to help oust Chiluba, it lacked sufficient support to stymie President Mwanawasa's game plan to stall constitutional reform.

In the wake of President Chiluba's failed third-term campaign, and with Chiluba's party, the Movement for Multiparty Democracy (MMD), still in power, Lusaka's political climate seemed conducive to a constituent moment of radical change. This is how the Oasis Forum read the situation at the dawn of the new millennium, and this explains why its leadership maintained their coalition in order to challenge the Mwanawasa administration's (in)action on constitutional reform. The Forum, through its member organizations, was well positioned to incite support for a radical refounding of the republic, but its strategists' strict adherence to legalism held this process back. The Forum espoused apolitical, non-partisan adherence to statute to shore up its legitimacy, but legalization didn't incite popular support; on the contrary, the predominance of 'suits' in the Forum's leadership further alienated the *demos.*

As the Law Association of Zambia's (LAZ) representative to the Forum at the time, future Attorney General Musa Mwenye noted in an early conversation (16 April 2003):

> lawyers are the spoilsports in the Oasis Forum. When the others want to push ahead, we always see a problem. Where the others are pushy, aggressive, we say but such action is illegal or otherwise problematic or wrong. Areas of dispute relate to tactics, not to principle; for example, the activists would want to hold a rally tomorrow, but we would slow things down by demanding that we adhere to the notification demands in the Public Order Act.

Lawyerly conservatism has impacted on the emergence of transformative constitutionalism both in the courts and in the streets, since – as one future constitutional court justice (interview, 20 April 2004) observed at the time – 'lawyers run the show.' Then, as now, public law practitioners oversaw the judiciary, and thus ruled on critical political issues, such as presidential petitions; they were in charge of crucial statutory bodies, such as the Electoral Commission, the Lands Commission and the Anti-Corruption Commission; they held pivotal constitutional offices, such as that of the Attorney General and the Director of Public Prosecutions.

The built-in epistemic limits of liberal legality were thus a formidable constraint on the Oasis Forum's strategic imagination. The Forum's demand for a constituent assembly to adopt the constitution was timely, but without intense bottom-up pressure, it stood no chance of success. As recounted in Chapter 4, the Forum's lawyers resisted a strategy of 'going to the people' to generate such pressure. This was not only partially out of a false confidence in the coalition's ability to bend the president's will, but also out of a deeply felt repugnance toward fomenting 'confusion,' i.e., violence by or against the *demos*. Perhaps the activists also feared that the people would not heed their call, thus undermining the Forum's carefully cultivated edifice of popular legitimacy. One cannot fault this sense of caution. Unleashing popular unrest is an unpredictable affair, and the course of an uprising is impossible to plot or contain. On the other hand, it is hard not to infer that the lawyers' exaggerated sense of procedural decorum undercut popular mobilization explicitly aimed at radical changes to the structure of government.

Instead of going to the people, the Forum acquiesced to what might be termed a 'stakeholder' version of constituent power – epitomized by the ideal of a 'broadly representative' (Matibini 2008, 11) constituent assembly culled together in accordance with a conception of popular power that is always already fully institutionalized and subject to the constraints of bureaucratic expediency. This technocratic instinct to compartmentalize unfettered constituent power was seen by its architects, no doubt, as practical and expedient. But beneath the veneer of convenience lies a font of suspicion. As Markus Böckenförde (2017, 31) observes,

> '(f)or some there is a considerable distrust of the direct involvement of the people at the end of the [constitution making] process, due to their potential irrationality or even inability to understand inherently complex issues.'[2]

This innate distrust of the *demos* is not a simple instinct. It is the unacknowledged residual of imperial rule, a legacy of the embattled state which predisposes elites to view the *demos* and their constituent power as dangerously, rather than creatively, unfettered. This perception is reflected in the view, articulated by Colón-Ríos (2010, 242), that

> a constituent assembly, as repository of the constituent power, has no limits to its competencies and can make any change in the constitutional regime, no matter how fundamental. It can even result in the abolition of democracy and in the alteration of the very amendment formula that provides for its convocation, although if it does, it would destroy its very democratic legitimacy together with that of the constitutional regime.

At the same time, to distinguish oneself from the masses is central to the quest for modernity, a core ambition of the emerging elite classes for which a legal degree is a coveted merit. Much attention is paid to class distinction in lawyers' rituals of professional socialization, with its exaggerated emphasis on comportment. It

2 Böckenförde is referring here specifically to the use of referenda to elicit popular assent to constitutional reform, but my findings suggest that such socio-epistemic discrimination intervenes in each aspect of constitution-making.

would seem, then, that the legalist mindset at the helm of constitutionalist activism did not grasp the real-life embodiments of the people, with their unschooled beliefs and untempered grievances, as vital to the creation of a constitution that would stand the test of time. Instead, the Forum and their legal activists conflated their intuitive liberal inclinations with an allegedly homogeneous popular will. In other words, the activists took their own legitimacy for granted; they felt that their view of constitutionalism reflected, if not 'the will of all (what the people will),' at the very least 'the general will (the option that the people should will, whether they actually do or not)' (Honig 2009, 17). They had, they felt, through their own self-constitution, achieved that most difficult task of making a singularity of a plurality.

This is not to say that the Oasis Forum's activists were armchair cosmopolitans. They incited and organized mass demonstrations on behalf of a constituent assembly. These met staunch government resistance – a demonstration in December 2004 turned violent as police arrested 68 activists, including 11 journalists (*Post*, 6 January 2005). Yet, as the 2006 elections approached, there were no mass mobilizations, no popular uprising demanding the immediate enactment of a majoritarian electoral code. Mr Mwanawasa was re-elected with 43% of the vote. That Mr Mwanawasa is likely to have prevailed in a hypothetical second round against the Patriotic Front's Michael Sata (who polled 29% of the vote) is both pure speculation and beside the point. The will that the people expressed with their ballot acquiesced to Mwanawasa's prerogativist maneuvers.

Elitist legal conservatism proceeded to dominate the state-managed constitution-making process. When LAZ broke with the Oasis Forum's other members to participate in Mr Mwanawasa's National Constitutional Convention (NCC), the legalists cut themselves off from the moral guidance of the Church and the women's movement, whose representatives had long and consistently clamored for a transformative constitutionalism. Instead of staying on board with this agenda, the Forum's lawyers – as NCC draftspersons, committee chairs and ordinary delegates – championed a strategy of, at best, incremental adjustment to postcolonial legality.

As its momentum ebbed in the run-up to the 2006 elections, the liberal activism of the Oasis Forum turned its focus to regime change, not to remaking the form of presidential power. That said, the Oasis Forum was not entirely silent concerning the president's unchecked authority. In its strategic plan for 2002–2004 (Oasis Forum 2002), the Forum outlined a number of 'Priority areas of Intervention.' The first of these regarded 'Presidentialism and Separation of Powers.' The document provides a brief, if realistic survey of the unlimited scope of presidential powers, and bemoans the ineffectiveness of existing checks and balances in the face of the president's unbridled discretion. Its recommendation (ibid., 11–12), however, is remarkably timid:

> 'The Forum believes that the unflinching autonomy of the legislature and the judiciary arms of government, devoid of executive influence therefore, may lie in restructuring the legal framework within which they operate.'

Hardly a revolutionary call to arms – especially given the fact that no means of 'restructuring the legal framework' are spelled out, while substantive demands for constitutional reform are deferred to a hypothetical constituent assembly. Forum activists were, of course, fully aware of the extent that 'presidentialism' dominates the contours of government. The Forum's strategists were, and are, quite capable of assessing what is politically and juridically feasible through civic leverage.

Be this as it may, the Forum eschewed radical juridical maneuvers. No proposals were tabled that would have, for example, advocated for the (nominally illegal) nullification of the 1991 constitution, and the instigation of a radically new legal order on the far shore of the resulting constitutional rupture. Within the framework of the Forum's conservative legalism, such an approach was inconceivable; demands for breaching the constitutional order to override structural impediments to liberal reforms would have been squashed by the Law Association in short order. The task of purging obstacles to a radical reworking of the Bill of Rights, the anchor of prerogativism, was beyond the political imagination of the moment. Continuity in the legal order, it was argued, must be maintained. At the end of the day, the legalism upon which the Oasis Forum relied to rescue the nation from arbitrary presidential discretion pre-empted the flourishing of constituent power; or, to put it less ornately, the space of politics.

The Forum's legalist strategy was not for naught. Eventually, in 2016, the Zambian constitution was amended to require that the president represent the majority of the electorate. The Oasis Forum cannot claim sole credit for this, but it certainly did mobilize broad popular awareness of the need to restructure the republic's legal framework. The courage, self-sacrifice and intelligence with which they did so should be an inspiration to current and future generations of democratic dreamers.

That said, the lean achievements of Zambia's decades-long struggle with constitution-making highlight the fragility of the liberal legalism project in the face of prerogativist power. Does this imply that the only recourse to arbitrary government lies in a popular uprising? Perhaps so, but the lesson of this analysis is that power is made, not seized. The crucial precondition of a democratic order is not one of baptism through blood or fire, but for a *demos* – in the full range of its plurality – to constitute itself as a political force that cultivates its intrinsic plurality within a shared sense of the common good. What paths might there be to such a dispensation? What forms of politics and what modes of legality would be commensurate with such a constitutional order? What form of power?

Of all Zambia's leaders in the Third Republic, Michael Sata most clearly articulated a vision of a refounded Zambia. Michael Sata's populist political vision did not, at the end of the day, embrace the ideals of the Oasis Forum and other progressive constitutionalists. He was comfortable with the imperial form of power – sustained by prevailing constitutional provisions, and explicitly upheld by the Supreme Court – and saw it as vital for the perpetuation of his regime. This was a lesson Mr Sata may have absorbed back in the day from Kenneth Kaunda. At some point, the nature of power as an end in itself eclipsed its potential as an instrument for justice. Justice, after all, is a long-term goal, while staying in power, as messrs Kabimba and Nchito learned the hard way (Chapters 8 and 9), is a day-to-day concern.

It is tempting to blame lawyers for the decay of democratic ideals. Even if they could not stop the proverbial train of politics, they were instrumental to its momentum. Surely some variety or degree of legal activism would suffice to better align 'rule of law' with the 'will of the people'? Surely the professional stewards of the law have the means to remake the prerogativist legacy of imperial legality in the service of just ends? Such demands on how lawyers *ought* to deploy their juridical capital are simply made. We commit a disservice, however, if we insist that African lawyers must be for or against the liberal agenda, 'either missionaries of the rule of law, or mercenaries of neo-colonialism' (Ballakrishnen & Dezalay 2021, 2). This juxtaposition demands that we see African lawyers as simple projections of a Euro-American agenda, as backwater residents, caged in by the categories of the imperial script of our times. In reality, as we have seen, lawyers can be both, which suggests they can also be something else entirely.

## A constituent politics of refounding?

A radical refounding of the republic appears attractive for some jurisdictions struggling with their colonial legacies (Bernal 2014). Zambia, as we have seen, cannot seem to find a constitutional path to decolonize its Bill of Rights and dismantle the unfettered presidential powers it protects; at the same time, it is hard to imagine a means to genuine social justice that does not involve a sweeping challenge by the *demos* to elite entitlements. Refounding, understood as a moment of natality (Arendt 1963), implies that the *demos* rises to a genuine constituent moment (Frank 2010). Historically, constituent power has found expression through popular insurrection. Is this, then, the only option for delivering justice to Zambia's excluded majority?

Political historian Miles Larmer (2011, 17) has argued that "[c]ontrary to a well-established view, in both academic circles and 'common sense' discourse in Zambia," effective control of the one-party state under President Kaunda and the United National Independence Party (UNIP) was 'limited, consistently under challenge and frequently insecure.' If this was true for the Second Republic, it is no doubt equally valid in the Third Republic. Larmer's claim speaks to the ethos of an embattled postcolonial state and helps explain the governing elite's deference to prerogativist discretion. But it also begs the question of why popular discontent has never coalesced into a radical challenge to a patently unjust status quo. Throughout the postcolonial era, Zambians have been remarkably compliant, and have not demonstrated an appetite for the violent overthrow of power.[3] Perhaps the closest thing to a revolutionary moment

3 The single-party Second Republic (1973–91) faced periodic unrest at the University of Zambia campus, as well as still-born coup attempts in 1980, 1988 and 1990. A low-key if prolonged insurrection on the north-west border region with Angola, led by dissident Adamson

occurred in 1986, when riots erupted along the line of rail in reaction to a sharp rise in the cost of food. This short-lived uprising, which resulted in 6 fatalities and 1,000 arrests (Apnews 1986), evinced the population's distress over prolonged economic hardship. It triggered a military response as well as the closing of the national borders (ibid.), but it did not spawn an organized rebellion against the UNIP regime. When the next opportunity came for a constitutional change of government, in 1991, Zambians went peacefully to the polls and elevated a new political force, the Movement for Multiparty Democracy, to power.[4]

Indeed, Larmer's image of an insecure and wobbly state is difficult to reconcile with Zambia's protracted political stability, and with the jurisdiction's continuity of constitutional power. Confronted with this conundrum, the 'common-sense' explanation cites the role of the state's intelligence and security service (ZSIS) in pre-empting threats to the hold of government on power. This was probably the case under presidents Kaunda and Chiluba, when the ruling party exercised hegemonic control over the security apparatus (Chapter 7). With an increasingly fragmented political dispensation since 2001, characterized by a divided parliament and rotating factions at the helm of power (Gould 2023). It is harder to imagine a consummate role for the intelligence and security forces in policing the political realm.

Be that as it may, I am inclined to look elsewhere for an explanation for Zambia's long-term politico-legal continuity. This study shows, I submit, that the imperial form of power inherited at independence is so deeply entrenched in Zambian politico-legal culture that its radical overthrow falls outside the Zambian political imaginary. This is certainly true of the shallow elite strata that control the state apparatus and may pertain to the deep ranks of *demos* as well. Paradoxically, acquiescence (if indeed this term captures the complex sentiments involved) to unfettered power finds expression in the recurrent adherence to constitutionalism in Zambian political discourse. Granted, as we have seen, there is no unitary or universally accepted consensus on what constitutionalism entails, but these findings suggest that Zambian elites believe that the constitution is a dike holding back a tsunami of chaos and confusion. This anxiety is conveyed in assurances that respect for the constitution ensures that the will of the people will ultimately prevail, even in the face of evidence that some politicians seek to usurp power for unscrupulous ends. For the most part, this constitutionalism represents the discursive glue that binds together popular political culture. This

---

Mushala, was put down in 1982 (Larmer op cit., Wele 1987, 1995). A coup attempt by a junior military officer was also quickly quelled in 1997 (see Chapter 6).

4 In 1990, citizens in Lusaka rioted over UNIP's austerity measures, leaving 23 dead, and inspiring 30-year-old Army Lieutenant Mwamba Luchembe to seize a radio station and announce the overthrow of government (Chisala 1991). Luchembe's coup attempt was limited to the capital and easily crushed. It may have hastened President Kaunda's decision to revoke the one-party constitution, but it was far from a revolutionary uprising.

dispositive obviously serves elite interests, but it also provides a framework for thinking about the possibility of transforming the politico-legal domain.

### *The incrementalist option*

The conservative nature of Zambian political culture speaks for a politics of incrementalism in redesigning the form of power. While some Oasis Forum activists yearned for a rapid transformation of the politico-legal domain after Mr Chiluba's retreat from power (see Chapter 4), the subsequent trajectory of Zambia's politico-legal framework has evolved via baby steps. President Sata's constituent presidency initially promised radical constitutional reform, but the eventual amendments endorsed by his party in 2016 were modest at best. Indeed, despite Professor Mulela Margaret Munalula's faith in the transformative power of the newly enacted constitutional values and principles (see Chapter 9), it is clear that any opportunities that these provisions may afford for remaking the form of power on a case-by-case basis are likely to play out in a temporal frame of decades, if at all.

The evidence thus far indicates that the repurposing of the constitution's entrenched and unfettered power will not originate within the politico-legal domain. Legal actions guide the actions of legislatures and partisan organs alike, and progressive court rulings can cultivate a culture of republicanism (the notion of a common good). The rub is that the legal system is saturated with entrenched post-imperial epistemic habits. If lawyers are indoctrinated to serve as guardians of prerogativism, they are also expected to act as the rhetorical oracles of political liberalism. This is a constitutive paradox of the postcolonial politico-legal domain; in my understanding, actors who successfully navigate its halls and chambers do not experience these two imperatives as contradictory. Neither, for that matter, did the colonial governor. Is it not likely that this 'flexibility' in the face of contradictory normative codes allows ostensibly liberal legality to produce illiberal effects?

Professor Munalula aptly articulates the frustrations that this paradox evokes among liberal constitutionalists, but she cannot conjure the means to re-engineer the system. There are, as yet, few grounds for expecting that her brand of judicial activism will turn the tide of constitutional interpretation. These frustrations beg the question of how the politico-legal system might be altered in such a way that it encourages the agents of unfettered discretion to invest in justice, as against mere self-preservation. Professor Munalula, like the Oasis Forum's activists before her, invoked the will of the people as the fulcrum of change, but they all erred, I feel, in believing that simply exercising constitutional norms to their full extent will suffice to align elite courts with 'what the people actually will.'

If, then, constitutional activists are mistaken to invest their energies in liberal legality, perhaps the terms of a progressive strategy need rethinking. What if politico-legal 'flexibility' – the capacity to reconcile prerogativist power with liberal aspirations – was to be re-imagined as an asset, as a tool with transformative potential, and not simply as a problem to be resolved? This, one might argue, is the promise inherent in the notion of the constituent presidency (Chapter 10). From that vantage point, prerogativism is not an obstacle to be dismantled, but an object subject to political design. Within this framework, progressive strategists would not ask how to overcome discretionary power, but how to harness it. The issue becomes: Given that this is how our republic is constituted, and that this form of power is the cornerstone of our politico-legal order, how then do we harness it to the ends of greater equity and justice? President Kaunda's unfettered discretion was invaluable in stemming the politicization of ethnicity in the Second Republic, and for the ultimate overthrow of apartheid in Southern Africa. Similar powers are arguably necessary to arrest the skewed distribution of wealth; for imposing regulatory measures vital to curbing $CO_2$ emissions; and for ensuring that the inevitable impacts of climate change are shared justly. Constitutional issues remain, and progressive judicial activists can play an important role in the coming transformation. But from a strategic perspective, constituent politics would seem to be the primary site of struggle: Instead of seeking out yet another charismatic populist to mesmerize the nation, the challenge is of making the politico-legal domain itself an object of scrutiny and creative engagement.

This task is not without precedent. As president, Michael Sata demonstrated the *possibility* of mobilizing political support for a politics of refounding, of making the voice of *demos* central to political practice. President Sata's will to repurpose the form of power to transformative ends, if genuine, faltered with his declining health, but the dream did not dissipate. The hypothetical task, then, may not be to exorcise prerogativism, which seems beyond the realm of political possibility, but to reconcile it with the common good. This requires fundamental transformations in the relationship between elites and the *demos*. At the minimum, the residual ethos of embattlement that both justifies and fuels a prerogativist form of power would need to give way to genuine political reciprocity between the rulers and the ruled, based on mutual trust and identification.

## The case for a progressive postliberalism

As discussed in Chapter 10, Karl Klare's vision of a postliberal legal order flirted with the notion of an activist court, but refrained from exploring the political conditions for a postliberal order to flourish. A postliberal dispensation is not innately progressive; there also exists a clearly reactional strain, which is fundamentally hostile to inclusivity and popular justice. A 'Right' postliberalism, increasingly familiar from its avant-garde in Hungary, Poland, Turkey, the United States and elsewhere embraces an exclusive, Schmittian notion of politics obsessed with creating enemies. For contemporary Right postliberalism, politics is about communities of the faithful, 'movements of patriots' pitted against the enemies of 'freedom.'

A 'Left' postliberalism, in contrast, embraces a different orientation. It recognizes that the imperial roots of liberalism hinder the development of a progressive politico-legal culture – one that respects communal (as against individualized) forms of difference, the plurality of the *demos*, age-old principles of natural justice. Progressive postliberalism invests its faith in the will*s* of the people*s*; its democratic ethos implies dialogue and constructive engagement with power. Such popular engagement can be agonistic as needs be, but it is anchored neither in elite paranoia nor elite privilege.

In Zambia's case, a Left postliberalism would need to approach the prevailing form of power pragmatically. Prerogativism can be a tool of repressive rule, but also a tool with powerful transformative potential. In this, Left postliberalism parts ways with the mainstream political liberalism that typically portrays the governing style of Zambia's presidents as intrinsically repugnant. A Left postliberalism not only acknowledges the duality of presidential personhood, but also recognizes the ways in which the postcolonial politico-legal framework allows presidents to juxtapose their mortal and their transcendent personae. This recognition can serve to demystify presidential power, and open space for honest deliberation of how it might be deployed to progressive ends.

Chabal and Daloz's seminal essay (1999) obscures the transformative potential of a genuinely constituent presidency. The authors argued that African government 'works' because it is functionally dysfunctional – poor governance is a cultural predilection that persists because it allows for corruption and the fraudulent abuse of state resources to escape detection. There is truth in this, for some governments and in some circumstances, but it misses the larger point that 'plunder' is not all that prerogativism enables presidents to achieve.

Liberal political analysts stamped Mr Sata as a disingenuous 'ethnopopulist,' with nothing in mind but his own power (Cheeseman & Larmer 2013). While Mr Sata was capable of appealing to themes of ethnic abandonment in his campaign rhetoric (Sishuwa 2021), his subsequent administration was not dedicated to regional favoritism. I would argue, instead, that it makes sense to see in Mr Sata (and, to some extent, in his mentor/nemesis Mr Chiluba) a prototypical Left postliberal figure.[5] Mr Sata had a sophisticated understanding of the form of power, and expressed the will to harness its expansive capacities to a long-term progressive political agenda – including poverty reduction.[6] This agenda was the primary source of his immense popular appeal.

Despite Mr Sata's political acumen, it was an uphill struggle. The state apparatus is difficult to wield to one's will, and even the president's most trusted lieutenants – not to mention his conniving allies – entertained contrary agendas. By focusing on the real-life issues confronting disadvantaged sections of the population, Mr Sata opened space for a convergence of political interests between politicians and progressive activists. He resuscitated the national ethos, which had decayed under his predecessor. Sadly, these transformative gambits

5 Presidents Sata and Chiluba both arose from poverty and were, arguably, of the people. They did not, initially at least, fear the *demos*. Therein lies their potential as constituent presidents.

6 The memoir of Mr Sata's vice-president (Scott 2019) lends considerable credence to this claim.

were short-lived. Mr Sata's mortal body faltered and with it, his control over the presidency's transcendent powers. As he weakened, his powers dissipated, and were not resurrected in a bodily form that shared Mr Sata's personal magnetism and transformative agenda.

The essence of progressive postliberalism, one might argue, lies in the recognition of the irrevocable unfetteredness of postcolonial presidential power, coupled with a will to deploy these powers for the general good. This perspective may share features with the 'developmental authoritarianism' that Hilary Matfess (2015, 181) attributes to Ethiopia and Rwanda, but Zambia's economy and its politico-legal history have little in common with either of these states. Neither is progressive postliberalism akin to the 'developmental neoliberalism' (Harrison 2019; cf. Mkandawire 2001) that relies on autocratic practices to shore up economic subsidiarity to international capital. A constituent president is attuned first and foremost to the people; their grievances are both heard and channeled, but citizens must also be led judiciously. Such an orientation is better served by economic nationalism, as difficult as this has been since Kaunda's time. A progressive postliberal executive does not seek to stifle the other branches of government (albeit this was not one of Mr Sata's primary virtues). Instead, it encourages creativity in both law-making and judicial judgments in support of an inclusive agenda.

This leads to a critical hypothesis, flagged earlier in Chapter 4. A radical repurposing of the prevailing form of power demands a *countervailing political force* to temper the centripetal impulses of unfettered power. The Oasis Forum both sought and purported to embody a non-partisan check on presidential excess. In its successes with the No Third Term campaign, it demonstrated the potential of such a socio-political force. But where the Forum initially channeled popular hostility to Chiluba's lawful illegalities, it failed to take the bolder step of institutionalizing constituent power in the service of radical constitutionalist ideals.

Granted, to do so would have demanded a fundamental shift of political mindset. For all of its non-partisan credentials, Oasis Forum activists were captive to the pervasive perception of politics as a question of party dominance. Beneath their non-partisan constitutionalist rhetoric, Forum strategists were plainly fed up with the MMD and wanted to see another party take over. They were not, for the most part, politicians – they craved neither the privileges nor responsibilities of government, and resisted frequent exhortations to form an opposition party of their own. Still, their imagination encompassed only two forms of politics – the *campaign*, centered on one-off public demonstrations; and the *election*, through which a partisan political organization could accede to power. What was missing was a vision of *institutionalized* public resistance, a domain of non-elite civic bodies and networks, capable of applying pressure to pull down solutions to the everyday dilemmas of survival in an unpredictable economic environment, as well as curbing executive excess, if needed. The Forum's reluctance to 'go to the people' reflected this lacuna in their political imagination, as well as, perhaps, a lack of willingness on the part of the lawyers to invest the time and labor that grasswork organizing entails.

How, then, might such a countervailing force emerge which could anchor prerogativism in a transformative agenda? The transformative potential of a progressive postliberalism must apply to 'the construction of autonomous spaces from below' (Escobar 2020, xix). If elite civil society is an inappropriate platform for fomenting the institutionalization of autonomous spaces and countervailing force, would some form of ***community-based authority*** be a conceivable option? There are, roughly, two sites where such authority thrives. One is the so-called traditional leadership in rural communities, while vestiges of another reside in urban and peri-urban neighborhoods (compounds) of the precariate.

The postcolonial history of the relationship between rural chiefs and the state has been one of an endless, largely inconclusive attempt to compartmentalize traditional authority through the 'codification' of customary norms. This, as Pnina Werbner (2020, 1077) notes "is bound to fail, since the very act of transcription negates the 'living' aspect of customary law: its responsiveness to changing circumstances." The epistemic obstacles to empowering rural power brokers are, of course, formidable. Already, Fanon's *Wretched of the Earth* articulated progressives' deeply entrenched skepticism regarding indigenous political structures. As Tejas Parasher (2015, 17), channeling Fanon, points out while

> those within urban centers are able to participate (however limitedly) within political, economic, and educational institutions we might identify as being modern or at least formed in conversation with capitalist modernity, the majority of the rural population is made comparatively impoverished and kept at a remove from accessing the Europeanized world.

Where Fanon faulted urban elites for excluding the impoverished masses from politics, Mahmood Mamdani's (1996) characterization of customary leaders as 'decentralized despots' shifted the blame to postcolonial chiefs. Recent literature continues to underscore the 'invented' nature of customary norms (e.g., Comaroff & Comaroff 2018), undermining any claims that chiefs might have to legitimate political or moral authority. And yet, the issue here is not about exposing a disingenuous 'politics of custom' (Zenker & Hoehne 2018), but about the willingness of excluded populations to channel their hopes for a fair share through leaders with organic ties to their communities. What is at stake, in other words, is the 'genuine faith held by local people in the antiquity, authenticity and, hence, legitimate authority of customary law and leadership' (Werbner, loc cit.).

Whether such faith exists is an empirical, not a theoretical question. One should not be so naïve as to assume that decades of colonial and postcolonial manipulation, from 'indirect rule' to myriad external interventions in succession procedures, would not have compromised local perceptions of chiefly authority. But this is not the point; certainly, perceptions of the *demos* concerning the legitimacy of statutory power are no less perverted. That said, could traditional power structures not provide the *demos* with an instrument of oversight through the immediate political embodiment of their popular will?

The situation among the urban and peri-urban precariate is less clearly structured. Efforts at the compartmentalization of urban resistance have historically been centered on keeping urban councils under partisan control, and on cultivating clientelistic bonds between government and trade unions. The demise of the mining sector and its eventual privatization in the 1990s undermined union membership as well as its influence on the government. With the decline and fragmentation of salaried labor, and its progressive informalization, the only channel of political influence for residents in poor urban neighborhoods has been through political parties, and largely only in election season. Most neighborhoods have myriad networks and committees to bridge the yawning gap between municipal provisioning and local needs. As yet, as far as I am aware, these groups do not exert a mode of concerted political pressure that can effectively aggregate demands and unite similarly disadvantaged citizens between residential areas.

I say 'as far as I know,' because the institutionalization of precariate mobilization is regrettably under-researched. Or rather, there has been considerable interest in the 'heterogeneous interests of informal workers' (Hinfelaar et al. 2020, 26), but such studies invariably focus on the success of competing political parties in attracting the votes of the disadvantaged and the so-called middle classes. Such research feeds the conception of politics as a struggle for party dominance, but the obsession with party fortunes obscures more fundamental political dynamics. Obviously, in Zambia's winner-take-all dispensation, party dominance is a cogent issue. But it is also important to look beyond electoral dynamics to the daily grind of interest articulation and aggregation at the grassroots and at the dynamics of coalition formation *among* the disadvantaged. Such inquiry would require a sophisticated rethinking of the received category of 'class' in contemporary Africa. Studies elsewhere in the region (e.g., Metsola 2018, McGregor & Chatiza 2020) demonstrate a robust, if fragile, process of coalition formation around issues of water and sanitation, housing and care. Valuable work on, for example, the pollution of household water sources by pharmaceutical discharges (e.g., Ngumba et al. 2020) indicates critical threats to community health, but parallel studies of how communities are responding to such threats are lacking. Time will tell whether civic coalitions of the disadvantaged will emerge to confront such risks and, if so, whether they could be the seeds of a countervailing force to political abandonment in a postliberal future.

## In closing

I have argued throughout this book that the role of the will of the people in the design of Zambia's republican constitution is fundamentally flawed. At no point since independence in 1964 have the Zambian people constituted themselves as a *demos* in order to articulate their will and encode it in the provisions of the supreme law of the land. Carefully examining the gestation of all five constitutions to date underscores the extent to which constitution-making has been a process managed by socio-political elites and consistently manipulated to protect prerogativist powers.

As clear as the evidence is, there is a 'but': While specific constitutional provisions cannot be shown to reflect the people's will, a politico-legal *ethos* of 'constitutionalism' arguably does. This conclusion can be drawn, for example, from the positive public response to consultative hearings organized by the Mwanakatwe and Mung'omba constitutional review commissions, by the National Constitutional Convention and by the Technical Committee to Draft the Constitution of Zambia. Constitutionalism was also at the core of the Oasis Forum's Green Ribbon campaign against President Chiluba's third term, which galvanized the public. It is also noteworthy how *The Post* newspaper rose to such journalistic prominence from the end of the 1990s until its demise in 2016 on an editorial platform heavily anchored in the defense of constitutionalism.

Constitutionalization at the moment of Zambia's independence created the notion of 'the people' and the associated postulate of a coherent popular 'will' at the heart of the politico-legal domain. Struggles over the normative substance of constitutionalization, so central to the Oasis Forum's project, might thus be seen as struggles of that latent popular will to find its means of realization. These facts suggest that Zambian citizens are not aloof to the virtues of having an overriding legal framework that defines the ways that governmental power should, and should not, be exercised. Of course, constitutionalism is at best a floating signifier, the substance and effects of which shift according to the contingencies of political context, as well as to the commitments and perspectives of its various champions. Zambia's many and diverse constituencies can and do embrace normative positions that may at times be incongruent with the provisions of the prevailing constitution. Such is the legacy of imperial liberalism, and its corollary, postcolonial legality.

There remains, then, a fraughtness – a dialectical tension, perhaps – between an apparent popular commitment to constitutionalism in the politico-legal culture of the nation, on the one hand, and the contours of real-life constitutionalism, on the other. When real-life constitutionalism expresses an elite ideology tied to the state and its biopolitical practices, the tension between popular ideals and politico-legal reality can be stretched to breaking point. This can be seen in the multiple ways in which legal professionals – lawyers and judges – provide the lubricant that keeps the governmental machinery running – not altogether smoothly, but in ways that sustain the exclusion of the majority from its rightful share (Ferguson 2015). One day, this lubricant may no longer suffice to ward off the rupture teeming below the surface of the political system.

Decades of politico-legal culture cannot be swept away in one fell swoop. It is important then, to think of ways that the essential features of the politico-legal domain can be harnessed to progressive ends. In the words of Afro-British artist Shabaka Hutchings (NYT 11 March 2020), '[w]e need to start articulating our utopias, articulating what needs to be burned and what needs to be saved.' What is essential for political outcomes is not the form of power per se, but the ends a leader pursues. If we accept this proposition, the normative assessment of prerogativism becomes a secondary issue, and we can turn our attention to deliberating its productive potential. Political theorists from Carl Schmitt (1922) to Oren Gross (e.g., Gross & Ní Aoláin 2006) have argued that unbridled executive power has the potential to bring about progressive transformation of the political economy. Glimpses of this potential were indeed evident in the Kaunda, Chiluba and Sata presidencies, albeit that the transformative capacity of prerogativist power has consistently fallen short of its potential.

That said, one shouldn't lose sight of the fact that even in its failure to realize its ideals of liberal constitutionalism, Zambian political society has sustained the *paradigm* of a government constituted not by autocracy, but by the will of the people. Moments of organized resistance – in 1991 against Kaunda and in 2001 against Chiluba – demonstrate the will of the Zambian peoples to hold their leaders accountable. What has not (yet) erupted is popular mobilization bent on deepening positive and productive reciprocities between governors and governed. Without these bonds, democratic government committed to the will of the people is an empty slogan. Whether one is suffering from the skewed distribution of wealth, or worried that structural injustice is a threat to the hard-won achievements of modernity, it should be clear that the politico-legal domain needs a qualitative overhaul, from below, a democratic refounding of a different quality than that of the elite-driven projects examined here.

These findings suggest that a more just Zambia requires the radical remaking of the ways that political power is constituted. It also demands a recalibration of the political imagination – a political-epistemic insurgency, perhaps. This implies a shift in political, and legal, justifications away from a mythical will of the people, toward the collective deliberation of progressive ends. This cannot happen overnight. As John Sangwa (cited in Malunga 2020) rightly notes, "Zambia is a train in motion, you can't stop it and say 'let's fix this.'" The euphemisms of modernity and development – i.e., poverty eradication and sustainable goals, contingent on the terms of foreign aid and investment – have not served the nation well. A fairer future demands the pursuit of popularly endorsed *ends*, rather than campaigns for more liberal *means* – not merely abstract demands for transparency and accountability, but concrete designs for redressing real and urgent grievances concerning livelihoods, health, education, poverty and the environment. Such designs can only come from below, from the peoples that postcolonial legality has persistently left behind.

# Annexes

## Annex A: A note on Article 79

Article 79 of the Zambian constitution sets out quite draconian constitutional amendment procedures. So strict are they that Article 79 has proved to be an unsurmountable 'constitutional handcuff' (Albert 2010) on comprehensive constitutional reform. Article 79 does not render any part of the constitution 'unamendable,' but its provisions for constitutional amendment render Section III, aka the Bill of Rights, virtually impossible to repeal. This has led to a situation where the hastily drafted document of 1991 may remain Zambia's constitutional framework in perpetuity. This is not necessarily a bad thing in itself; but in Zambia's case, it does mean that the nation's understanding of legal rights will remain frozen in the Second Republic. It also implies that certain provisions related to the president's opaque powers are beyond democratic oversight.

Article 79 requires that any changes to Section III of the constitution (comprising provisions for individual rights and freedoms, but which also lays the foundations for the president's vast discretionary powers) as well as to Article 79 itself, must be approved through a national referendum in which more than half of all *eligible* voters assent to the changes. The one time that this was attempted, in August 2016, only about one-quarter of eligible voters assented to the proposed changes. This probably had less to do with the desire of Zambian citizens to update their rights and freedoms than to the practical difficulties in mobilizing widely dispersed rural voters to the polls. Reform fatigue and general mistrust of government intentions may also have played a part in the low turnout.

Article 79 descends from Article 72 of Zambia's 1964 constitution which 'entrenches' both Section III (on rights and freedoms) as well as Section VII (concerning the judicature). I haven't found any record of the reasoning behind these provisions, but I think it is a good guess that the authors of Zambia's first constitution wanted to protect the liberal principles of the sections in question (explicit individual rights, an independent judiciary) from opportunistic manipulation by the new indigenous government.

The provisions of Article 72 were removed in connection with the one-party constitutional reform of 1973 as 'unnecessary' (the Kaunda administration did not envision any need for referenda in a one-party state). The current Article 79 was introduced in its present form in the 1991 constitution. The justification, according to one lawyer (interview, 19 October 2004), who sat on the constitutional review commission that drafted the 1991 constitution, was 'protection':

> You see, we were going to avail an unknown and unpredictable future. We didn't want anybody to play around with the Bill of Rights. We didn't want anybody to feel that [the Constitution] was as easy as that to amend.

The 'anyone' referred to here points to any post-United National Independence Party (UNIP) president, and to the Movement for Multiparty Democracy (MMD) leader Frederick Chiluba in particular. It seems reasonable to infer that in both 1964 and 1991, what Albert (2010, 666) terms a 'preservative' entrenchment clause was imposed in order to tie the hands of a volatile political unknown – Kaunda's Black African government in 1964 and Chiluba's anti-UNIP regime in 1991.

## Annex B: A map of constitution-making in Zambia

### *Colonial constitutions*

Northern Rhodesia Order in Council 1911
Northern Rhodesia Order in Council 1924 (repeals the 1911 OiC)
Northern Rhodesia Legislative Council, 1945
Northern Rhodesia Legislative Council, 1958
Northern Rhodesia Legislative Council, 1959
Northern Rhodesia Legislative Council, 1962
Northern Rhodesia Legislative Council, 1963 (Order in Council)

### *Republican constitutional legislation*

Zambia Independence Order/Zambia Independence Act 1964
Constitution of Zambia Act 1973
Constitution of Zambia Act No. 1 of 1991
Constitution of Zambia Amendment Act Nos. 17 & 18 of 1996
Constitution of Zambia Draft 2005 (not enacted)
Constitution of Zambia Bill 2010 (not enacted)
Constitution of Zambia Amendment Act Nos. 1 & 2 of 2016
Zambia Bill of Rights Enhancement Act 2016
The National Dialogue (Constitution, Electoral Process, Public Order and Political Parties) Act, 2019

### *Constitutional review bodies*

Mainza Chona Constitutional Review Commission, 1973 (appointed by President Kenneth Kaunda)
John Mwanakatwe CRC, 1993–5 (President FTJ Chiluba)
Wila Mung'omba CRC, 2003–5 (President Levy Mwanawasa)
National Constitutional Convention, 2007–10 (President Mwanawasa)
Technical Committee on Drafting the Zambian Constitution, 2013 (President Michael Sata)
National Dialogue Forum, 2019 (President Edward Lungu)

# Source materials

## Official and legislative documents

Great Britain. Colonial Office 1952. *Digest of Colonial Statistics.* London: His Majesty's Stationary Office.

Laws of Zambia. Electoral Act (Chapter 13).

Laws of Zambia. Legal Practitioner's Act (Chapter 30).

Laws of Zambia. The Zambia Law Development Commission Act (Chapter 32).

Laws of Zambia. Inquiries Act (Chapter 41).

Laws of Zambia. State Proceedings Act (Chapter 71).

Laws of Zambia. Penal Code Act (Chapter 87).

Laws of Zambia. Criminal Procedure Code (Chapter 88).

Laws of Zambia. Lands Act (Chapter 184).

National Assembly of Zambia. 2007. The National Constitutional Conference Act (No. 19 0f 2007, amended by Act 5 of 2010). Lusaka: Government Printers. Accessed from: http://www.parliament.gov.zm.

National Assembly of Zambia. 2019a. The National Dialogue (Constitution, Electoral, Public Order and Political Parties) Act. No. 1 of 2019. Lusaka: Government Printers. Accessed from https://www.parliament.gov.zm/7942

National Assembly of Zambia. 2019b. The Constitution of Zambia (Amendment) Bill. Lusaka: Government Printers. Accessed from http://www.parliament.gov .zm/node/8067

Northern Rhodesia. 1926. Colonial Reports - Annual: No.1292 Northern Rhodesia Report for 1924–25. London: His Majesty's Stationary Office.

Republic of Zambia. 1972. Report of the National Commission on the Establishment of a One-Party Participatory Democracy in Zambia; Summary of Recommendations Accepted by Government. Lusaka: Government Printers [Chona Constitution Review Commission Report].

Republic of Zambia. 1991a. Summary of the Main recommendations of the Constitution Commission of Inquiry Together with the Government Reactions to the Recommendations. Government Paper No. 2 of 1991. Lusaka: Government Printer (Mvunga Constitution Review Commission Report).

Republic of Zambia. 1991b. Constitution of Zambia Act 1991.

Republic of Zambia. 1995. Summary of the Recommendations of the Mwanakatwe Constitutional Review Commission and Government Reaction to the Report. Lusaka: Government Printers (Mwanakatwe Constitution Review Commission Report).

Republic of Zambia. 1996. Constitution of Zambia (Amendment) Act No. 18 of 1996.

Republic of Zambia. 1996. *Government White Paper on the Mwanakatwe Constitutional Review Commission.* Lusaka: Government Printers.

Republic of Zambia. 2007. Speech Delivered by His Excellency Dr. Levy Patrick Mwanawasa, SC on the Occasion of the Official Opening of the National Constitution Conference at Mulungushi Conference Centre, Lusaka, 5 August.

Republic of Zambia. 2009. *Report on the Sittings of the Executive Committee of the National Constitutional Conference* held from 12th January to 10th February. Lusaka: Government Printers (archival source held by the African Studies Centre in Leiden).

Republic of Zambia. 2010. *National Constitutional Conference: Final Report of the National Constitutional Conference.* Lusaka: Government Printers.

Republic of Zambia. 2011. *Terms of Reference for Technical Committee on Drafting the Zambian Constitution.* Accessed from: https://wiredproject316.files.wordpress.com/2011/11/terms-of-reference.pdf.

Republic of Zambia. 2014a. National Social Protection Policy: 'Reducing Poverty, Inequality and Vulnerability'. Lusaka: Ministry of Community Development, Mother and Child Health.

Republic of Zambia. 2014b. *Wynter Kabimba Tribunal Report.* Accessed from http://www.laz.org.zm/wp-content/uploads/2014/04/Wynter-Kabimba-Tribunal-Report.pdf

Republic of Zambia. 2016. Constitution of Zambia (Amendment) Act No. 2 of 2016.

## Judicial documents

### *Zambian jurisdiction*

*Akashambatwa Mbikusita-Lewanika and Others v Chiluba.* Accessed from https://www.zambiadailynation.com/2013/09/06/lessons-from-justice-mulengas-ruling-in-dora-sililo-mwale-case/.

*Attorney General & Movement for Multiparty Democracy v Akashambatwa Mbikusita-Lewanika and others.* (S.C.Z. Judgment No.2 of 1994) [1994] ZMSC 3 (9 February 1994). Accessed from https://zambialii.org/node/2329.

*Attorney General v Mutembo Nchito*, Selected Judgment No 1 of 2016.

*Attorney General v Nigel Kalonde Mutuna, Charles Kajimanga & Phillip Musonda* 2012 [Appeal No. 88/2012, SCZ/8/185/2012]. At https://www.zambiawatchdog.com/full-supreme-court-ruling-on-judges-tribual-in-case-you-have-the-time/.

*Dr Daniel Pule, Wright Musoma, Pastor Peter Chanda & Robert Mwanza v Attorney General & Davies Mwila (in his capacity as Secretary General of the Patriotic Front)* (2017/CC/004) [2018] ZMCC 10 (6 April 2018). Accessed from https://zambialii.org/node/13243.

*Development Bank of Zambia v JCN Holdings, Post Newspapers Ltd & Mutembo Nchito* (2009/HPC/0322; judgment 19 April 2012).

*Director of Public Prosecutions v Mbayoo Mutwala Augustino* (1977/ZR 287) [1977].

*Dr Sishuwa Sishuwa & Another v Luo & 16 Others* (2021/CCZ/0028/0032) [2021] ZMCC 10 (11 June 2021). Accessed from https://zambialii.org/node/15611.

*Fred M'membe and Bright Mwape v Speaker of the National Assembly, Commissioner of Prisons & Attorney General* (1996/HCJ/X).
*Hakainde Hichilema & Geoffrey Bwalya Mwamba v. Edgar Chagwa Lungu, Inonge Wina, Electoral Commission of Zambia & Attorney General* 2016 [CC/0031], 05 SEP 2016. Accessed from https://zambialii.org/node/12445.
*JCN Holdings vs Development Bank of Zambia* (Appeal no. 87 2012) [2013] ZMSC 22 (17 December 2013)
*Law Association of Zambia & Chapter One Foundation Limited v. Attorney General* [2019/CCZ/0013, 2019/CCZ/0014, ruling on 03 July 2020]. Accessed from https://zambialii.org/node/14748.
*Legal Resources Foundation, Dr Sishuwa Sishuwa & Chapter One Foundation Limited v Edgar Chagwa Lungu & Attorney General* 2021 [2021/CC/0025, 2021/CC/0027], 11 JUN 2021.
*Leonard Banda & Cuthbert Phiri v Dora Siliya* (2011/HP/EP/11 & 39; judgment 13 April 2012).
*Leonard Banda v Dora Siliya* (SCZ/8/127/2012; SCZ Judgment No. 20 of 2013).
*Milford Maambo, Ziwa Malilo Ziwa & Chanda Chabala v. the People* 2016/CC/R001) [2017] ZMCC 9 (11 July 2017); Justice Munalula's dissent (1110–39). Accessed from https://zambialii.org/node/13003.
*Mutale & Phiri v. The People* (1995–1997, ZR 277).
*Mutembo Nchito v. The Attorney General* (2016/CC/0029) [2020] ZMCC 7 (28 October 2020). Accessed from https://zambialii.org/node/15036.
*Nkumbula v The Attorney-General* (1972 ZR 206).
*Speaker of the National Assembly, Commissioner of Prisons & Attorney General v. Fred M'membe* [1996] - (1996 HCJ X).
*Steven Katuka and Another v the Attorney General and Others* (2016/CC/0010/0011) [2017] ZMCC 7 (17 November 2017). Accessed from https://zambialii.org/node/13065.
*The People v Shamwana and Others (HP/166/1981) [1983] ZMHC 1* (19 January 1983)
*The People v. Frederick Chiluba, Faustin Kabwe & Aaron Chungu* (SSP/124/2004).
*Wynter Kabimba v Attorney General* [3Z.R. 492/2011] (2011/HP/744) [2011] ZMHC 83 (8 August 2011). Accessed from https://zambialii.org/node/3306.
Zambia Revenue Authority v Post Newspapers Limited (Appeal 36 of 2016 [2016] ZMSC 182 (13 June 2016).

## *UK jurisdiction*

*Queen v. Judge of the City of London Court*, 1 Q.B. 273.
*Vedanta Resources PLC and another (Appellants) v Lungowe and others (Respondents)* (2019 UKSC20, Hilary Term).
*Zambia v. Meer, Desai & Care and Others* ([2007] EWHC 952 (Ch)). Accessed from https://www.bailii.org/ew/cases/EWHC/Ch/2007/952_2.html.
*Council of Civil Service Unions and Other Appellants and Minister for the Civil Service Respondent* [1984] UKHL 9, [1985] AC 374, [1984] 3 All ER 935, [1984] 3 WLR 1174, [1985] IRLR 28, [1985] ICR 14.
*Seaford Court Estates ltd v Asher* [1949] 2 K. B. 481.

### *South African jurisdiction*

*State v Zuma and Others* (CCT5/94) [1995] ZACC 1; 1995 (2) SA 642; 1995 (4) BCLR 401 (SA); 1995 (1) SACR 568; [1996] 2 CHRLD 244 (5 April 1995). Accessed from http://www.saflii.org/za/cases/ZACC/1995/1.html.

## *Printed sources*

Abrahamsen, Rita. 2000. *Disciplining Democracy: Development Discourse and Good Governance in Africa*. London: Zed Books.

Abrams, Philip. 1988. Notes on the Difficulty of Studying the State (1977). *Journal of Historical Sociology* 1(1), 58–89. https://doi.org/10.1111/j.1467-6443.1988.tb00004.x.

Agamben, G. 1998. *Homo Sacer: Sovereign Power and Bare Life*. Stanford, CA: Stanford University Press.

Agamben, Giorgio. 1991. *Language and Death: The Place of Negativity*. Theory and History of Literature: 78. Translated by K. E. Pinkus & M. Hardt. Minneapolis, MN: University of Minnesota Press.

Agamben, Giorgio. 2005. *State of Exception*. Chicago, IL: University of Chicago Press.

Alterio, Ana M. 2019. Reactive vs Structural Approach: A Public Law Response to Populism. *Global Constitutionalism* 8(2), 270–296. https://doi.org/10.1017/S2045381719000029.

Anderson, Perry. 1974. *Lineages of the Absolutist State*. London: Verso.

Andersson, Per-Åke & Manenga Ndulo. 1994. Hyperinflation, Stabilization and the New Economic Recovery Program in Zambia. *Macroeconomics Studies* 51, Stockholm: Swedish International Development Co-operation Agency.

Andersson, Per-Åke, Arne Bigsten & Håkan Persson. 2000. *Foreign Aid, Debt and Growth in Zambia*. Uppsala: Nordiska Afrikainstitutet.

Anyangwe, Carlson. 1997. The Zambian Constitution and the Principles of Constitutional Autochthony and Supremacy. *Zambia Law Journal* 29, 1–32. Accessed from http://saipar.org/wp-content/uploads/2013/09/Law-Journal-1997.pdf.

Arato, Andrew. 2000. Good-Bye to Dictatorships? *Social Research* 67(4), 925–955.

Arato, Andrew. 2016. *Post Sovereign Constitution Making: Learning and Legitimacy*. Oxford and New York: Oxford University Press.

Arditi, Benjamin. 2008. Arguments about the Left Turns in Latin America: A Post-Liberal Politics? *Latin American Research Review* 43(3), 59–81. https://doi.org/10.1353/lar.0.0061.

Arendt, Hannah. 1958. *The Human Condition*. Chicago, IL: University of Chicago Press.

Arendt, Hannah. 1963. *On Revolution*. London: Penguin Books.

Arendt, Hannah. 1968 [1951]. *The Origins of Totalitarianism*. New York: Harcourt.

Ashar, Sameer M. 2007. Public Interest Lawyers and Resistance Movements. *California Law Review* 95(5), 1879–1926.

Baczko, Bronislaw. 1988. The Social Contract of the French: Sieyès and Rousseau. *The Journal of Modern History* 60, Supplement: Rethinking French Politics in 1788, S98–125. https://www.jstor.org/stable/1880372.

Bakhtin, Mihail. 1981. *The Dialogic Imagination: Four Essays*, edited by Michael Holquist. Translated by Caryl Emerson & Michael Holquist. Austin, TX: University of Texas Press.

Balakrishnan, Gopal. 2000. *The Enemy: An Intellectual Portrait of Carl Schmitt*. London and New York: Verso.

Ballakrishnen, Swethaa & Sara Dezalay. 2021. Introduction: Law, Globalisation and the Shadows of Legal Globalisation. In their (eds.) *Invisible Institutionalisms: Collective Reflections on the Shadows of Legal Globalisation*. Oxford and New York: Hart Publishing, 1–24.

Baldwin, Kate. 2016. *The Paradox of Traditional Chiefs in Democratic Africa*. Cambridge: Cambridge University Press.

Ballacci, Giuseppe. 2019. Deliberative Agonism and Agnostic Deliberation in Hannah Arendt. *Theoria* 66(161), 1–24. https://doi.org/10.3167/th.2019.6616101.

Banakar, Reza. 2015. *Normativity in Legal Sociology: Methodological Reflections on Law and Regulation in Late Modernity*. Switzerland: Springer International Publishing. https://doi.org/10.1007/978-3-319-09650-6.

Barak, Aharon. 2005. *Purposive Interpretation in Law*, translated by Sari Bashi. Princeton, NJ and Oxford: Princeton University Press.

Bartlett, David M. C. 2000. Civil Society and Democracy: A Zambian Case Study. *Journal of Southern African Studies* 26(3), 429–446.

Bates, Robert H. & Paul Collier. 1995. The Politics and Economics of Economic Reforms in Zambia. *Journal of African Economies* 4(1), 115–143, https://doi.org/10.1093/oxfordjournals.jae.a036822

Baxi, Upendra. 2013. Preliminary Notes on Transformative Constitutionalism. In Oscar Vilhena, Upendra Baxi & Frans Viljoen eds., *Transformative Constitutionalism: Comparing the Apex Courts of Brazil, India and South Africa*. Pretoria: Pretoria University Law Press, 19–48.

Bayart, Jean-Francois. 1993. *The State in Africa: Politics of the Belly*. New York: Longman.

Beckstein, Martin. 2011. The Dissociative and Polemical Political: Chantal Mouffe and the Intellectual Heritage of Carl Schmitt. *Journal of Political Ideologies* 16(1), 22–51. https://doi.org/10.1080/13569317.2011.540941.

Bell, Duncan. 2016. *Reordering the World: Essays on Liberalism and Empire*. Princeton, NJ: Princeton University Press.

Bemong, Nele & Pieter Borghart. 2010. Bakhtin's Theory of the Literary Chronotope: Reflections, Applications, Perspectives. In Nele Bemong et al. eds., *Bakhtin's Theory of the Literary Chronotope: Reflections, Applications, Perspectives*. Ghent: Ginkgo-Academia Press, 3–16.

Benhabib, Seyla. 1992. *Situating the Self: Gender, Community, and Postmodernism in Contemporary Ethics*. New York: Psychology Press.

Benhabib, Seyla. 1996. *The Reluctant Modernism of Hannah Arendt*. London: Sage.

Benhabib, Seyla. 1994. Judith Shklar's Dystopic Liberalism. *Social Research* 61(2), 477–488.

Benton, Laura. 2002. *Law and Colonial Cultures: Land Regimes in World History 1400–1900*. Cambridge: Cambridge University Press. https://doi.org/10.1017/CBO9780511512117.

Berman, Paul Schiff. 2012. *Global Legal Pluralism: A Jurisprudence of Law Beyond Borders*. New York: Cambridge University Press.

Bernal Angelica, M. 2014. The Meaning and Perils of Presidential Refounding in Latin America. *Constellations* 2(4), 440–456. https://doi.org/10.1111/1467-8675.12130.

Bessner, Daniel & Nicolas Guilhot, eds. 2018. *The Decisionist Imagination: Sovereignty, Social Science and Democracy in the 20th Century*. New York and Oxford: Berghahn Books.

Beyani, C. 1998. International Law and the Lawfulness of Derogations from Human Rights during States of Emergency in Zambia. *Zambia Law Journal*, Special Edition, 103–119.

Bhorat, Haroon, Nomsa Kachingwe, Morné Oosthuizen & Yu Derek. 2017. *Understanding Growth-Income Inequality Interactions in Zambia* (Final Report S-41304-ZMB-1). London: International Growth Centre, London School of Economicand Political Science. Accessed at www.theigc.org.

Bierschenk, Thomas & Jean-Pierre Olivier de Sardan. 1997. Local Powers and a Distant State in Rural Central African Republic. *Journal of Modern African Studies* 35(3), 441–468.

Bigsten, Arne & Steve Kayizzi-Mugerwa. 2000. The Political Economy of Policy Failure in Zambia. *Working Papers in Economics (No 23)*. Göteborg University, Department of Economics.

Blokker, Paul & Chris Thornhill, eds. 2017. *Sociological Constitutionalism*. Cambridge: Cambridge University Press. https://doi.org/10.1017/9781316403808.

Böckenförde, Markus. 2017. Letting the Constituent Power Decide? Merits and Challenges of Referenda in Constitution-Making Processes in Africa. In Tania Abbiate, Markus Böckenförde & Veronica Federico eds., *Public Participation in African Constitutionalism*. London: Routledge, 26–39.

Bork, Robert H. 2005. Slouching Towards Miers. *Wall Street Journal*, October 19. https://www.wsj.com/articles/SB112968557638772718.

Bourdieu, Pierre. 1987. The Force of Law: Toward a Sociology of the Juridical Field (Translation and Introduction by Richard Terdiman). *Hastings Law Journal* 38(5), 814–854.

Burawoy, Michael. 2014. The Colour of Class Revisited: Four Decades of Postcolonialism in Zambia. *Journal of Southern African Studies* 40(5), 961–979. https://doi.org/10.1080/03057070.2014.946213.

Burawoy, Michael. 1998. The Extended Case Method. *Sociological Theory* 16(1), 4–33.

Burgess, Glenn. 1992. The Divine Right of Kings Reconsidered. *English Historical Review* 107(425), 837–861. https://doi.org/10.1093/ehr/CVII.CCCCXXV.837.

Burnell, Peter. 2005. From Low-Conflict Polity to Democratic Civil Peace: Explaining Zambian Exceptionalism. *African Studies* 64(2), 107–133.

Campbell, Tom. 2008. Emergency Strategies for Prescriptive Legal Positivists: Anti-terrorist Law and Legal Theory. In V. V. Ramraj ed., *Emergencies and the Limits of Legality*. Cambridge: Cambridge University Press, 201–228.

Canovan, Margaret. 2000. Arendt's Theory of Totalitarianism: A Reassessment. In Dana Villa ed., *The Cambridge Companion to Hannah Arendt*. Cambridge: Cambridge University Press, 25–43.

Carbado, Dean W. 2019. States of Continuity or State of Exception: Race, Law and Politics in the Age of Trump. *Constitutional Commentary* 34(1), 1–16.

Carothers, Thomas. 2002. The End of the Transition Paradigm. *Journal of Democracy* 13(1), 5–21.

Chabal, Patrick & Jean-Pascal Daloz. 1999. *Africa Works: Disorder as Political Instrument*. James Curry Publishers.

Chaisty, P., N. Cheeseman & T. Power. 2014. Rethinking the 'Presidentialism Debate': Conceptualizing Coalitional Politics in Cross-Regional Perspective. *Democratization* 21(1), 72–94. https://doi.org/10.1080/13510347.2012.710604.

Chaisty, P., N. Cheeseman & T. Power. 2018. *Coalitional Presidentialism in Comparative Perspective. Minority Presidents in Multiparty Systems*. Oxford: Oxford University Press.

Chakrabarty, Dipesh. 2000. *Provincializing Europe: Postcolonial Thought and Historical Difference*. Princeton, NJ: Princeton University Press.

Chalfin, Brenda. 2010. *Neoliberal Frontiers: An Ethnography of Sovereignty in West Africa*. Chicago, IL: University of Chicago Press.

Chama, Brian. 2017. Anti-Corruption Tabloid Journalism in Zambia. In his (ed.) *Anti-Corruption Tabloid Journalism in Africa*. London: Palgrave Macmillan, 21–37.

Chambers, Raymond L. 1977. The Executive Power: A Preliminary Study of the Concept and of the Efficacy of Presidential Dictates. *Presidential Studies Quarterly* 7(1), 21–37. www.jstor.org/stable/27547326.

Chanda, Alfred W. 1986. The Legal Basis of Emergency Powers in Zambia. *Zambia Law Journal* 18, 19–34.

Chanda, Alfred W. 1996. Zambia's Fledgling Democracy: Prospects for the Future. *Zambia Law Journal* 25, 125–154.

Chanda, Alfred W. 1997. The State Security Act vs Open Society: Does a Democracy Need Secrets? *Zambia Law Journal* 29, 33–47.

Chanock, Martin. 2001. *The Making of South African Legal Culture 1902–1936: Fear, Favour and Prejudice*. Cambridge: Cambridge University Press.

Chanock, Martin. 1985. *Law, Custom, and Social Order: The Colonial Experience in Malawi and Zambia*. Cambridge: Cambridge University Press.

Chatterjee, Partha. 1993. *The Nation and Its Fragments: Colonial and Postcolonial Histories*. Princeton, NJ: Princeton University Press.

Cheembe, Boniface. 2018. People and Constitutions: The Case of Zambia. In Tania Abbiate et al. eds., *Public Participation in African Constitutionalism*. London: Routledge, 128–141.

Cheeseman, Nic & Marja Hinfelaar. 2010. Parties, Platforms, and Political Mobilization: The Zambian Presidential Election of 2008. *African Affairs* 109(434), 51–76. https://doi.org/10.1093/afraf/adp070.

Cheeseman, Nic & Miles Larmer. 2013. Ethnopopulism in Africa: Opposition Mobilization in Diverse and Unequal Societies. *Democratization* 22(1), 22–50. https://doi.org/10.1080/13510347.2013.809065.

Cheeseman, Nic. 2018a. Introduction: Understanding African Politics: Bringing the State Back In. In his (ed.) *Institutions and Democracy in Africa*. Cambridge: Cambridge University Press, 1–38.

Cheeseman, Nic. 2018b. Rule-of-Law Ethnography. *Annual Review of Law and Social Science* 14(1), 167–184.

Cheyeka, A. M. 2003. Challenging the State: Catholic Clergymen as Political Actors in Zambia, 1991–2002. *Zango* 24(14), 35–54.

Chiluba, Frederick. n.d. [2009]. *Here I Stand: Verbatim Testimony of the Second Republican President Dr. Frederick Chiluba before Ndola High Court Deputy Registrar Jones Chinyama Sitting as Magistrate in Lusaka 27/01/2009.* Lusaka: ZDS Press Services.

Chisala, Beatwell. 1991. *Lieutenant Luchembe Coup Attempt.* Lusaka: Multimedia.

Choudry, Aziz & Dip Kapoor. 2013. *NGOization: Complicity, Contradictions and Prospects.* London: Zed Books Ltd.

Civil Society Action Committee (CSAC). 1996. *The Citizens' Convention Report* (by the Steering Committee of the CSAC). Accessed from http://constitutionnet.org/vl/item/citizens-convention-report.

Clough, G. D. 1924. The Constitutional Changes in Northern Rhodesia and Matters Incidental to the Transition. *Journal of Comparative Legislation and International Law* (Third Series) 6(4), 278–282. www.jstor.org/stable/752781.

Collord, Michaela. 2014. President Sata and Zambia's 'People-Driven' Constitution, *Democracy in Africa*, March 22, 2014. http://democracyinafrica.org/zambia-president-sata-people-driven-constitution/.

Colón-Ríos, Joel. 2010. Legitimacy of the Juridical: Constituent Power, Democracy, and the Limits of Constitutional Reform. *Osgoode Hall Law Journal* 48(2), 199–245.

Colón-Ríos, Joel. 2012. *Weak Constitutionalism: Democratic Legitimacy and the Question of Constituent Power.*London & New York: Routledge.

Colón-Ríos, Joel. 2017. Primary Assemblies, Constituent Power, and the Imperative Mandate. In Hanna Lerner & David Landau eds., *Elgar Handbook of Comparative Constitution-Making.* Cheltenham: Edward Elgar Publishing, 1–33. Accessed from SSRN-id3392115.pdf.

Comaroff, Jean & John Comaroff, eds. 2006. *Law and Disorder in the Postcolony.* Chicago, IL: Chicago University Press.

Comaroff, John L. & Jean Comaroff, eds. 2018. *The Politics of Custom: Chiefship, Capital and the State in Contemporary Africa.* Chicago, IL and London: Chicago University Press.

Conaghan, C. M. 2008. Ecuador: Correa's Plebiscitary Presidency. *Journal of Democracy* 19(2), 46–60.

Cooper-Knock, Sarah J. & George H. Karekwaivanane. 2016. Law and Social Order in Africa: Introduction. *Africa* 86(1), 33–36. https://doi:10.1017/S0001972015000807.

Corrigan, Philip & Derek Sayer. 1985. *The Great Arch: English State Formation as Cultural Revolution.* Oxford: Basil Blackwell.

Cotterrell, Roger. 2013. Rethinking 'Embeddedness': Law, Economy, Community. *Journal of Law and in Society* 40(1), 49–67. https://doi.org/10.1111/j.1467-6478.2013.00612.x.

Cownie, Fiona & Anthony Bradley. 2013. Socio-Legal Studies: A Challenge to the Doctrinal Approach. In D. Watkins & M. Burton eds., *Research Methods in Law.* London and New York: Routledge, 34–54. https://doi.org/10.4324/9780203489352.

Craig, J. T. 1973. Presidential Power and Procedural Error. *Zambia Law Journal* 5, 139–168.

Cristi, Renalto. 1998. *Carl Schmitt and Authoritarian Liberalism: Strong State, Free Economy.* Cardiff: University of Wales Press.

Das, Veena & Deborah Poole, eds. 2004. *Anthropology in the Margins of the State.* Santa Fe, NM: School for Advanced Research Press.

Das, Veena. 2011. State, Citizenship and the Urban Poor. *Citizenship Studies* 15(3–4), 319–333. https://doi.org/10.1080/13621025.2011.564781.
Date-Bah, Samuel Kofi. 2015. *Reflections on the Supreme Court of Ghana*. JCL Studies in Comparative Law No 14. London: Wildly, Simmonds and Hill Publishing.
Davies, C. A. 2012. *Reflexive Ethnography: A Guide to Researching Selves and Others*. London & New York: Routledge.
Davis, Dennis & Karl Klare. 2010. Transformative Constitutionalism and the Common and Customary Law. *South African Journal on Human Rights* 26(3), 403–509. [University School of Law Research Paper No. 68-2011]. https://doi.org/10.1080/19962126.2010.11864997.
De Brabandere, Eric. 2010. The Responsibility for Post-Conflict Reforms: A Critical Assessment of Jus Post Bellum as a Legal Concept. *Vanderbilt Journal of Transnational Law* 43(1). Available at https://ssrn.com/abstract=1569990.
de la Cadena, Marisol. 2015. *Earth Beings: Ecologies of Practice across Andean Worlds*. Durham, NC and London: Duke University Press.
De Roeck, Mathias & Ronan Van Rossem. 2015. *Fifty Shades of Grey? Conceptualizing and Measuring Political Regimes Using Theories of Democracy, 1972–2010*. Institute of Development Policy (IOB) Working Papers 2015.05. Universiteit Antwerpen.
de Villiers, Bertus. 1992. Directive Principles of State Policy and Fundamental Rights: The Indian Experience. *South African Journal on Human Rights* 8(1), 29–49. https://doi.org/10.1080/02587203.1992.11827851.
Delport, Terblanche. 2014. An Ethical (Anti-)Constitutionalism? Transformation for a Transfigured Public. *Acta Academica* 46(3), 104–121. Accessed from https://journals.ufs.ac.za/index.php/aa/article/view/1462/1436.
Deng, F. M. 2008. *Identity, Diversity, and Constitutionalism in Africa* (in collaboration with D. J. Deng, D. K. Deng & V. Jiménez). Washington, DC: United States Institute of Peace.
Depoorter, Ben & Paul H. Rubin. 2017. Judge-Made Law and the Common Law Process. In Francesco Parisi ed., *Oxford Handbooks in Economics: Volume 3: Public Law and Legal Institutions*. Oxford: Oxford University Press. https://doi.org/10.1093/oxfordhb/9780199684250.013.001.
Dezalay, Sarah & George Karekwaivanane. 2015. Juristes, faiseurs d'état. *Politique africaine* 138. Paris: Karthala. Accessed from http://orca.cf.ac.uk/id/eprint/99505.
Dillion-Malone, Clive M. 1989. *Zambian Humanism, Religion, and Social Morality*. Berkeley: University of California Press.
Dinh, Viet D. 2002. Freedom and Security after September 11. *Harvard Journal of Law and Public Policy* 25(2), 399–406.
Disch, Lisa. 2011. How Could Hannah Arendt Glorify the American Revolution and Revile the French? Placing *On Revolution* in the Historiography of the French and American Revolutions. *European Journal of Political Theory* 10(3), 350–371. https://doi.org/10.1177/1474885111406389.
Dodge, Doris J. 1977. *Agricultural Policy and Performance in Zambia: History, Prospects and Proposals for Change*. Berkeley Research Series No. 32. University of California: Institute of International Studies.
Douzinas, Costas & Adam Gearey. 2005. *Critical Jurisprudence: The Political Philosophy of Justice*. Oxford: Hart Publishing.
Dowdle, Michael W. & Michael A. Wilkinson, eds. 2017. *Constitutionalism beyond Liberalism*. Cambridge: Cambridge University Press.

Dussel, Enrique. 2000. Europe, Modernity, and Eurocentrism. *Nepantla: Views from South* 1(3), 465–478. https://www.muse.jhu.edu/article/23901.

Dyzenhaus, David, ed. 1998. *Law as Politics: Carl Schmitt's Critique of Liberalism.* Durham, NC and London: Duke University Press.

Eisenstadt, S. N. 1973. *Traditional Patrimonialism and Modern Neopatrimonialism.* Beverly Hills, CA: Sage Publications.

Ellet, Rachel. 2013. *Pathways to Judicial Power in Transitional States: Perspectives from African Courts.* London and New York: Routledge.

Elster, Jon. 1995. Forces and Mechanisms in the Constitution-Making Process. *Duke Law Journal* 45(2), 364–396. https://doi.org/10.2307/1372906.

Englund, Harri. 2006. *Prisoners of Freedom: Human Rights and the African Poor.* Berkeley: University of California Press.

Englund, Harri. 2011. *Human Rights and African Airwaves: Mediating Equality on the Chichewa Radio.* Bloomington, IN: Indiana University Press.

Englund, Harri. 2013. Zambia at 50: The Rediscovery of Liberalism. *Africa* 83(4), 670–689. Https://doi.org/10.1017/S0001972013000508.

Englund, Harri. 2015. Multivocal Morality: Narrative, Sentiment, and Zambia's Radio Grandfathers. *HAU: Journal of Ethnographic Theory* 5(2), 251–273. https://doi.org/10.14318/hau5.2.015.

Engster, Daniel. 2001. *Divine Sovereignty: The Origins of Modern State Power.* DeKalb, IL: Northern Illinois University Press.

Erdmann, Gero & Ulf Engel. 2006. *Neopatrimonialism Revisited – Beyond a Catch-All Concept.* Hamburg: German Institute of Global and Area Studies.

Escobar, Arturo. 2010. Latin America at a Crossroads: Alternative Modernizations, Post-liberalism, or Post-development? *Cultural Studies* 24(1), 1–65. https://doi.org/10.1080/09502380903424208.

Escobar, Arturo. 2020. *Pluriversal Politics: The Real and the Possible.* Durham, NC: Duke University Press.

Evans, Richard. 1983. From Hitler to Bismarck: 'Third Reich' and *Kaiserreich* in Recent Historiography. *The Historical Journal* 26(2), 485–497.

Fanon, Franz. 1967 [1952]. *Black Skins, White Masks.* New York: Grove Press.

Fanon, Franz. 2005. *The Wretched of the Earth*, translated by R. Philcox. New York: Grove Press.

Ferguson, James. 1999. *Expectations of Modernity: Myths and Meanings of Urban Life on the Zambian Copperbelt.* Berkeley, CA: University of California Press.

Ferguson, James. 2015. *Give a Man a Fish: Reflections on the New Politics of Distribution.* Durham, NC and London: Duke University Press.

Figgis, J. Neville. 1922 [1896]. *The Divine Right of Kings* (2nd edition with three additional essays). Cambridge: Cambridge University Press.

Fitzpatrick, P. 2005. Bare Sovereignty: Homo sacer and the Insistence of Law. In A. Norris ed., *Politics, Metaphysics, and Death. Essays on Giorgio Agamben's Homo sacer.* Durham, NC: Duke University Press, 49–73.

Fix-Fierro, Héctor & Pedro Salazar-Ugarte. 2012. Presidentialism. In Michel Rosenfeld & András Sajó eds., *Oxford Handbook of Comparative Constitutional Law.* Oxford: Oxford University Press, 628–652. https://doi.org/10.1093/oxfordhb/9780199578610.013.0031.

Fombad, Charles Manga. 2008. Post-1990 Constitutional Reforms in Africa. In: Alfred Nhema & Paul Tiyambe Zeleza eds., *The Resolution of African Conflicts:*

*The Management of Conflict Resolution & Post-conflict Reconstruction*. Athens, OH: Ohio University Press, 179–196.

Foucault, Michel. 1982. The Subject and Power. *Critical Inquiry* 8(4), 777–795. http://doi.org/10.1086/448181.

Frænkel, Ernst. 1969 [1941]. *The Dual State: A Contribution to the Theory of Dictatorship*. Oxford: Oxford University Press.

Frank, Jason. 2010. *Constituent Moments: Enacting the People in Postrevolutionary America*. Durham, NC: Duke University Press.

Fraser, Alastair & Miles Larmer, eds. 2010. *Zambia, Mining, and Neoliberalism: Boom and Bust on the Globalized Copperbelt*. Basingstoke: Palgrave Macmillan.

Fraser, Alistair. 2017. Post-Populism in Zambia: Michael Sata's Rise, Demise and Legacy. *International Political Science Review* 38(4), 456–472. https://doi.org/10.1177/0192512117720809.

Gann, L. H. 1977. Review of Andrew Roberts 1976. *The Zambian Past. A History of Zambia. Journal of African History* 18(3), 458–459.

Gardbaum, Stephen. 2019. Pushing the Boundaries: Judicial Review of Legislative Procedures in South Africa. *Constitutional Court Review* 9(1), 1–18. https://doi org/10 2989/CCR 2019 0001.

Gebeye, B. A. 2017. The Potential Role of Directive Principles of State Policies for Transformative Constitutionalism in Africa. *Africa Journal of Comparative Constitutional Law* 2017(1), 1–34.

Gertzel, C. & M. Szeftel, eds. 1984. *The Dynamics of the One-Party State in Zambia*. Manchester: Manchester University Press.

Getachew, Adom 2020. *Worldmaking after Empire: The Rise and Fall of Self-Determination*. Oxford: Princeton University Press.

Gewald, Jan-Bart, Marja Hinfelaar & Giacomo Macola, eds. 2011. *Living the End of Empire: Politics and Society in Late Colonial Zambia* [Afrika-Studiecentrum Series 21]. Leiden: Brill Academic Publishers.

Ghai, Yash. 1987. Law, Development and African Scholarship. *Modern Law Review* 50(6), 750–776. Accessed from https://www.jstor.org/stable/1096031.

Gluckman, Max. 1955. *Custom and Conflict in Africa*. Oxford: Basil Blackwell.

Goldring, E. & M. Wahman. 2016. Democracy in Reverse: The 2016 General Election in Zambia. *Africa Spectrum* 51(3), 107–121.

Goldsworthy, J. 2013. Constitutional Interpretation. In András Sajo & Michel Rosenfeld eds., *The Oxford Handbook of Comparative Constitutional Law*. Oxford: Oxford University Press, 689–717.

Gordon, David M. 2012. *Invisible Agents: Spirits in a Central African History*. Athens, OH: Ohio University Press.

Gordon, R. J. 2018. *The Enigma of Max Gluckman: The Ethnographic Life of a 'Luckyman' in Africa*. Lincoln: University of Nebraska Press.

Gould, Jeremy. 2002. Contesting Democracy: The 1996 Zambian Elections. In M. Cowen & L. Laakso eds., *Multi-Party Elections in Africa*. Oxford: James Currey, 299–324.

Gould, Jeremy. 2006. Strong Bar, Weak State? Lawyers, Liberalism and State Formation in Zambia. *Development and Change* 37(4), 921–941. https://doi.org/10.1111/j.1467-7660.2006.00507.x.

Gould, Jeremy. 2007. Zambia's 2006 Elections: The Ethnicization of Politics? *New South from the Nordic Africa Institute* 1/2007, 5–9.

Gould, Jeremy. 2010. *Left Behind: Rural Zambia in the Third Republic.* Lusaka: Lembani Trust.
Gould, Jeremy. 2012. Postcolonial Liberalism and the Legal Complex in Zambia: Elegy or Triumph? In T. Halliday et al. eds., *Fates of Political Liberalism in the British postcolony.* Cambridge: Cambridge University Press, 412–454.
Gould, Jeremy. 2015. Les juristes, le politique et la fabrique de la légalité postcoloniale. Un cas d'étude zambien. *Politique Africaine* 138(2), 71–92.
Gould, Jeremy. 2023. Zambia: Security Intelligence as a Special Branch of Presidentialism. In Ryan Shaffer ed., *Handbook of African Intelligence Cultures.* Lanham, MD: Rowman & Littlefield, 717–729.
Gould, J. & J. Ojanen. 2005. Tanzania: Merging in the circle. In J. Gould ed., *The New Conditionality: The Politics of Poverty Reduction Strategies.* London: Zed Books, 17–65.
Gould, Jeremy & Katja Uusihakala, eds. 2016. *Tutkija peilin edessä: Refleksiivisyys ja etnografinen tieto* [*The Scholar's Mirror: Reflexivity and Ethnographic Knowledge*]. Helsinki: Gaudeamus.
Graeber, David & Marshall Sahlins. 2017. *On Kings.* Chicago, IL: HAU Books.
Griffiths, Anne. 2011. The Power of Paradigms in a Global World. *Journal of Legal Pluralism* 64, 173–202.
Griffiths, John. 1986. What Is Legal Pluralism? *Journal of Legal Pluralism and Unofficial Law* 18(24), 1–55. https://doi.org/10.1080/07329113.1986.10756387.
Grosfoguel, Ramón. 2011. Decolonizing Post-Colonial Studies and Paradigms of Political-Economy: Transmodernity, Decolonial Thinking, and Global Coloniality. *Transmodernity: Journal of Peripheral Cultural Production of the Luso-Hispanic World* 1(1). https://doi.org/10.5070/T411000004.
Gross, Oren. 2000. The Normless and Exceptionless Exception: Carl Schmitt's Theory of Emergency Powers and the 'Norm-Exception' Dichotomy. *Cardozo Law Review* 21, 1825.
Gross, Oren & Fionnuala Ní Aoláin. 2006. *Law in Times of Crisis: Emergency Powers in Theory and Practice.* Cambridge: Cambridge University Press.
Guha, Ranajit. 1997. *Dominance without Hegemony: History and Power in Colonial India.* Cambridge, MA: Harvard University Press.
Gupta, Akhil & Aradhana Sharma, eds. 2009. *The Anthropology of the State: A Reader.* Hoboken, NJ: John Wiley & Sons.
Gupta, Akhil. 2012. *Red Tape: Bureaucracy, Structural Violence, and Poverty in India.* Durham, NC and London: Duke University Press.
Hadfield, Percival. 1949. *Traits of Divine Kingship in Africa.* London: Watts & Co.
Hall, Richard. 1969. *The High Price of Principles. Kaunda and the White South.* New York: Africana Publishing Corporation.
Halliday, Terence C., Lucien Karpik & Malcolm M. Feeley, eds. 2007. *Fighting for Political Freedom: Comparative Studies of the Legal Complex and Political Liberalism.* London: Hart Publishing.
Halliday, Terence C., Lucien Karpik & Malcolm M. Feeley, eds. 2012. *Fates of Political Liberalism in the British Post-Colony: The Politics of the Legal Complex.* Cambridge: Cambridge University Press. https://doi.org/10.1017/CBO9781139002981.
Hansungule, M. 2003. Zambian Constitution: A Plea for Genuine Reforms. [Paper Presented for a Public Discussion at the Constitutional Review Workshop

Organized by the Non-Governmental Organization Coordination Committee (NGOCC), Lusaka 18–19 March 2003]. Mimeo.

Haraway, Donna. 1991. *Simians, Cyborgs and Women: The Reinvention of Nature.* London: Routledge.

Harrison, Graham. 2019. Authoritarian Neoliberalism and Capitalist Transformation in Africa: All Pain, No Gain. *Globalizations* 16(3), 274–288. https://doi.org/10.1080/14747731.2018.1502491.

Hatchard, J. 1995. Undermining the Constitution by Constitutional Means: Some Thoughts on the New Constitutions of Southern Africa. *Comparative and International Law Journal of Southern Africa* 28(1), 21–35.

Herbst, J. 2014. *States and Power in Africa: Comparative Lessons in Authority and Control.* Princeton: Princeton University Press.

Hessebon, Gedion T. 2013. Some Major Themes in the Study of Constitutionalism and Democracy in Africa. *Vienna Online Journal on International Constitutional Law* 7(1), 28–48.

Higgins, Rosalyn. 1977. Derogations under the Human Rights Treaties. *British Yearbook of International Law* 48(1), 281–319. https://doi.org/10.1093/bybil/48.1.281.

Himonga, C. 2017. The Constitutional Court of Justice Moseneke and the Decolonisation of Law in South Africa: Revisiting the Relationship between Indigenous Law and Common Law. *Acta Juridica* 2017(1), 101–123.

Himonga, Chuma N. 1991. Family Law Reform and the Integration of the Laws of Succession in Zambia. *Verfassung und Recht in Übersee/Law and Politics in Africa, Asia and Latin America* 24(4), 340–361. Accessed from www.jstor.org/stable/43110858.

Hinfelaar, Hugo. 1991. Women's Revolt: The Lumpa Church of Lenshina Mulenga in the 1950s. *Journal of Religion in Africa* 21(2), 99–129. http://www.jstor.org/stable/1580801.

Hinfelaar, Hugo. 2004. *History of the Catholic Church in Zambia.* Lusaka: Bookworld Publishers.

Hinfelaar, M. 2008. Introduction. In J. Komakoma & M. Hinfelaar ed., *The best of Fr. Joe Komakoma's Ruminations.* Ndola: Mission Press, iii–iv.

Hinfelaar, M., D. Renick & S. Sishuwa. 2020. Cities and Dominance: Urban Strategies for Political Settlement Maintenance and Change – Zambia Case Study. *ESID Working Paper N. 136.*

Hirschl, R. 2004. The Political Origins of the New Constitutionalism. *Indiana Journal of Global Legal Studies* 11(1), Article 4. Accessed from https://www.repository.law.indiana.edu/ijgls/vol11/iss1/4.

Hirschl, R. 2008. The Judicialization of Politics. In K. E. Whittington, D. R. Kelemen & G. A. Caldeira eds., *Oxford Handbook of Law and Politics.* Oxford and New York: Oxford University Press, 119–141.

Hirschl, R. 2009. *Towards Juristocracy: The Origins and Consequences of the New Constitutionalism.* Cambridge: Harvard University Press.

Hobbes, Thomas. 1651. *Leviathan.* Accessed from http://www.woldww.net/classes/General_Philosophy/Hobbes_on_the_state_of_nature.htm.

Honig, Bonnie. 1991. Declarations of Independence: Arendt and Derrida on the Problem of Founding a Republic. *American Political Science Review* 85(1), 97–113. https://doi.org/10.2307/1962880.

Honig, Bonnie. 1993. *Political Theory and the Displacement of Politics*. Ithaca, NY: Cornell University Press.

Honig, Bonnie. 2009. *Emergency Politics: Paradox, Law, Democracy*. Princeton, NJ: Princeton University Press.

Hopkins, Christopher. 2010. *Getting Behind the Patriotic Front in Zambia: The Organisation and Mobilisation of an Opposition Party*. M.A. Thesis. University of Oxford.

Hountondji, Paulin J. 1970. Comments on Contemporary African Philosophy. *Diogenes* 18(71), 109–130. https://doi.org/10.1177/039219217001807108.

Hudson, J. 1999. *A Time to Mourn: Personal Account of the 1964 Lumpa Church Revolt in Zambia*. Lusaka: Book World.

Huntington, Samuel P. 1991. The Third Wave: Democratization in the Late Twentieth Century. *Journal of Democracy* 2(2), 12–34.

Hussain, Nasser. 2003. *The Jurisprudence of Emergency: Colonialism and the Rule of Law*. Ann Arbor, MI: University of Michigan Press. http://www.jstor.org/stable/10.3998/mpub.17774.

Hutchinson, Terry. 2014. *Valé* Bunny Watson? Law Librarians, Law Libraries, and Legal Research in the Post-internet Era. *Law Library Journal* 106(4), 579–592. https://doi.org/10.5553/ELR.000055.

Hutchinson, Terry. 2015. The Doctrinal Method: Incorporating Interdisciplinary Methods in Reforming the Law. *Erasmus Law Review* 38(3). https://doi.org/10.5553/elr.000055.

Ihonvbere, Julius O. 1995. The 'Zero Option' Controversy in Zambia: Western Double Standards Vis A Vis Safeguarding Security? *African Spectrum* 30(1). https://www.jstor.org/stable/40174562.

Isanga, Joseph M. 2016. African Judicial Review, the Use of Comparative African Jurisprudence, and the Judicialization of Politics. *George Washington International Law Review* 49(4), 749–800.

Jackson, A., 2004. *Governing Empire: Colonial Memoirs and the History of HM Overseas Civil Service* (book review). *African Affairs* 103/412, 471–491.

Jeffries, Charles. 1972. *Whitehall and the Colonial Service: An Administrative Memoir*. London: The Athlone Press.

Joseph, Richard. 1992. Zambia: A Model for Democratic Change. *Current History* 91(565), 199.

Kabimba, Wynter. 2016. The Constitutional (Amendment): Does It Settle the Constitutional Question? *Lusaka Times*, January 14. https://www.lusakatimes.com/2016/01/14/the-constitutional-amendment-does-it-settle-the-constitutional-question/.

Kalusa, W. T. 2017. The Politics of the Corpse: President Levy Mwanawasa's Death, Funeral and Political Contestation in Post-Colonial Zambia. *Journal of Southern African Studies* 43(6), 1137–1155.

Kalyvas, Andreas. 2008. *Democracy and the Politics of the Extraordinary: Max Weber, Carl Schmitt, and Hannah Arendt*. Cambridge: Cambridge University Press.

Kantorowicz, Ernest. 2016 [1957]. *The King's Two Bodies. A Study in Mediaeval Political Theology*. Princeton, NJ and Oxford: Princeton University Press.

Karekwaivanane, George H. 2011. 'It Shall be the Duty of Every African to Obey and Comply Promptly': Negotiating State Authority in the Legal Arena, Rhodesia 1965–1980. *Journal of Southern African Studies* 37(2), 333–349. https://doi.org/10.1080/03057070.2011.579440.

Karekwaivanane, George H. 2016. 'Through the Narrow Door': Narratives of the First Generation of African Lawyers in Zimbabwe. *Africa* 86(1), 59–77. https://doi.org/10.1017/S0001972015000789.

Karekwaivanane, George H. 2017. *The Struggle over State Power in Zimbabwe: Law and Politics Since 1950.* Cambridge: Cambridge University Press. https://doi.org/10.1017/9781316996898.

Karpik, L. & T. C. Halliday. 2011. The Legal Complex. *Annual Review of Law and Social Science* 7(1), 217–236.

Kaswende, Kingsley. 2012. Political Meddling and Poor Management Cripple Zambia's Airlines. *Bulletin & Record*, December 2011/January 2012, 9–11.

Katz, Elai. 1995. On Amending Constitutions: The Legality and Legitimacy of Constitutional Entrenchment. *Columbia Journal of Law and Social Problems* 29(2), 251.

Kaunda, Kawache & T. C. Kabwe. 1994. *Cuthbert Ng'uni: Torture and Death of an Honourable M.P. in Zambia.* Lusaka: Own Voice Publishers.

Kaunda, Kenneth. 1973. *Letter to My Children.* London: Longman.

Kibet, Eric & Charles Fombad. 2017. Transformative Constitutionalism and the Adjudication of Constitutional Rights in Africa. *African Human Rights Law Journal* 17(2), 340–366. https://doi.org/10.17159/1996-2096/2017/v17n2a1.

Killingray, David. 1986. The Maintenance of Law and Order in British Colonial Africa. *African Affairs* 85(340), 411–437. https://doi.org/10.1093/oxfordjournals.afraf.a097799.

Kirchheimer, Otto. 1961. *Political Justice: The Use of Legal Procedures for Political Ends.* Princeton, NJ: Princeton University Press.

Kirk-Greene, Anthony, ed. 1979. *The Transfer of Power: The Colonial Administrator in the Age of Decolonisation* [Africa in the Colonial Period Series]. Oxford: Oxford University Press.

Kirk-Greene, Anthony. 1980. The Thin White Line: The Size of the British Civil Service in Africa. *African Affairs* 79(314), 25–44.

Kirk-Greene, Anthony. 1991. His Eternity, His Eccentricity, or His Exemplarity? A Further Contribution to the Study of H. E. the African Head of State. *African Affairs* 90(358), 163–187.

Kirk-Greene, Anthony. 1999. *On the Crown Service: History of the Colonial Service.* London and New York: I.B. Tauris.

Kirk-Greene, Anthony. 2000. *Britain's Imperial Administrators, 1958–1966.* New York: St Martin's Press.

Klare, Karl E. 1998. Legal Culture and Transformative Constitutionalism. *South African Journal on Human Rights* 14(1), 146–188. https://doi.org/10.1080/02587203.1998.11834974.

Koskenniemi, Martti. 2002. Between Impunity and Show Trials. *Max Planck Yearbook of United Nations Law Online* 6(1), 1–35. https://doi.org/10.1163/18757413-00601002.

Kostal, R. W. 2005. *A Jurisprudence of Power: Victorian Empire and the Rule of Law.* Oxford: Oxford University Press.

Klug, H. 2019. Transformative Constitutions and the Role of Integrity Institutions in Tempering Power: The Case of Resistance to State Capture in Post-Apartheid South Africa. *Buffalo Law Review* 67(3), 701–742.

Klug, H. 2021. The Judicialization of Politics? In Shauhin Talesh et al. eds., *Research Handbook on Modern Legal Realism.* Cheltenham: Edward Elgar Publishers, 295–308.

Kydd, Jonathan. 1988. Coffee after Copper? Structural Adjustment, Liberalisation, and Agriculture in Zambia. *Journal of Modern African Studies* 26(2), 227–251. Accessed from www.jstor.org/stable/161056.

Laclau, Ernesto. 2005. *On Populist Reason.* London and New York: Verso.

Larmer, Miles. 2011. *Rethinking African Politics: A History of Opposition in Zambia.* London and New York: Routledge.

Larmer, Miles & Alastair Fraser. 2007. Of Cabbages and King Cobra: Populist Politics and Zambia's 2006 Election. *African Affairs* 106(425), 611–637. https://doi.org/10.1093/afraf/adm058.

Latour, Bruno. 2010. *The Making of Law: An Ethnography of the Conseil d'État* [translated from French by Marina Brilman and Alain Pottage]. Cambridge: Polity.

Lazar, Naomi Claire. 2009. *States of Emergency in Liberal Democracies.* Cambridge: Cambridge University Press.

Lederman, Shmuel. 2014. Agonism and Deliberation in Arendt. *Constellations* 21(3), 327–337. https://doi.org/10.1111/1467-8675.12096.

Lee, John Michael. 1967. *Colonial Development and Good Government: A Study of the Ideas Expressed by the British Official Classes in Planning Decolonization, 1939–1964.* Oxford: Clarendon Press.

Levitsky, S. & L. A. Way. 2010. *Competitive Authoritarianism: Hybrid Regimes after the Cold War.* Cambridge: Cambridge University Press.

Lewis, Arthur W. 1965. *Politics in West Africa.* Toronto and New York: Oxford University Press.

Lewis, Paul. 2009. Shifting Legitimacy: The Trials of Frederick Chiluba. In E. Lutz & C. Reiger eds., *Prosecuting Heads of State.* Cambridge: Cambridge University Press, 130–150. https://doi.org/10.1017/cbo9780511575600.010.

Li, Tania Murray. 2007. *The Will to Improve: Governmentality, Development, and the Practice of Politics.* Durham, NC and London: Duke University Press.

Liljeström, Marianne & Salla Peltonen. 2017. On Feminist Epistemic Habits and Critique. *Feminist Encounters* 1(1), 2.

Lichterman, P. 2017. Interpretive Reflexivity in Ethnography. *Ethnography* 18(1), 35–45.

Linz, Juan José. 1990. The Perils of Presidentialism. *Journal of Democracy* 1(1), 51–69. https://doi.org/10.1353/jod.1990.0011.

Lorde, Audre. 2018. *The Master's Tools Will Never Dismantle the Master's House.* London: Penguin Modern.

Losurdo, Domenico. 2011. *Liberalism: A Counter History*, translated by Gregory Elliot. London: Verso.

Loughlin, Martin. 2003. *The Idea of Public Law.* Oxford: Oxford University Press.

Loughlin, Martin. 2007. Constituent Power Subverted: From English Constitutional Argument to British Constitutional Practice. In Martin Loughlin & Neil Walker eds., *The Paradox of Constitutionalism: Constituent Power and Constitutional Form.* Oxford: Oxford University Press, 27–49.

Loughlin, Martin. 2014. The Concept of Constituent Power. *European Journal of Political Theory* 13(2), 218–237. https://doi.org/10.1177/1474885113488766.

Loughlin, Martin. 2017. On Constituent Power. In Michael W. Dowdle & Michael A. Wilkinson eds., *Constitutionalism beyond Liberalism*. Cambridge: Cambridge University Press, 151–175.
Loughlin, Martin & Neil Walker. 2007. Introduction. In Martin Loughlin & Neil Walker eds., *The Paradox of Constitutionalism: Constituent Power and Constitutional Form*. Oxford: Oxford University Press, 1–8.
Lucey, Francis E. 1941. Jurisprudence and the Future Social Order. *International Social Science Review* 16(3), 211–217.
Lungwangwa, Vincent. 2015. *Constitution Making Process: The Zambian Experience*. Doctoral dissertation (Law). University of Zambia.
Lutz, Ellen L. & Caitlin Reiger, eds. 2009. *Prosecuting Heads of State*. Cambridge: Cambridge University Press. https://doi.org/10.1017/CBO9780511575600.
McGregor, J. & K. Chatiza. 2020. Partisan Citizenship and Its Discontents: Precarious Possession and Political Agency on Harare City's Expanding Margins. *Citizenship Studies* 24(1), 17–39.
Macola, Giacomo. 2010. *Liberal Nationalism in Central Africa: A Biography of Harry Mwaanga Nkumbula*. New York: Palgrave Macmillan.
Malila, Mumba. 2020. Righting the Wrongs: Justice Clever Mule Musumali's Legacy of Judicial Activism Revisited. *International Journal of Research and Innovation in Social Science* 4(12), 392–408. Accessed from https://www.rsisinternational.org/journals/ijriss/Digital-Library/volume-4-issue-12/392-408.pdf.
Mamdani, Mahmood. 1996. *Citizen and Subject. Contemporary Africa and the Legacy of Late Colonialism*. Princeton, NJ: Princeton University Press.
Marcus, George E. 1995. Ethnography In/of the World System: The Emergence of Multi-sited Ethnography. *Annual Review of Anthropology* 24(1), 95–117. www.jstor.org/stable/2155931.
Masengu, Tabeth. 2015. Standing on the Sidelines Watching: Women and Zambia's Constitutional Processes. In Jaap de Visser et al. eds.,*Constitution-Building in Africa*. Belleville: University of Western Cape, 48–74.
Masengu, Tabeth. 2017. The Vulnerability of Judges in Contemporary Africa: Alarming Trends. *Africa Today* 63(4), 3–19. Accessed from https://biblio.ugent.be/publication/8555855.
Matfess, Hilary. 2015. Rwanda and Ethiopia: Developmental Authoritarianism and the New Politics of African Strong Men. *African Studies Review* 58(2), 181–204. https://doi.org/10.1017/asr.2015.43.
Matibini, Patrick. 2008. Constitution-Making Processes – The Case of Zambia. *Zambia Law Journal* 39, 231–250.
Mazrui, Ali. 1967. The Monarchical Tendency in African Political Culture. *British Journal of Sociology* 18, 231–250.
Mbao, M. L. M. 2011. Prevention and Combating of Corruption in Zambia. *Comparative and International Law Journal of Southern Africa* 44(2), 255–274. https://doi.org/10.2307/23253099.
Mbao, Melvin. 2010. The Politics of Constitution-Making in Zambia: Where Does the Constituent Power Lie? In Charles Fombad & Christina Murray eds., *Fostering Constitutionalism in Africa*. Pretoria: Pretoria University Law Press, 87–117.
Mbembe, Achille. 1992. Provisional Notes on the Postcolony. *Africa: The Journal of the International African Institute* 62(1), 3–37. Accessed November 3, 2020. http://www.jstor.org/stable/1160062.
Mbembe, Achille. 2001. *On the Postcolony*. Berkeley: University of California Press.

Mbembe, Achille. 2019. *Necropolitics*, translated by Steve Corcoran. Durham, NC and London: Duke University Press.

Mbembe, Achille. 2021. *Out of the Dark Night: Essays on Decolonization*. New York: Columbia University Press.

Mbikusita-Lewanika, Akashambatwa & Derrick Chitala. 1990. *The Hour Has Come*. [Proceedings of the National Conference on the Multi-party Option held at the Garden House Hotel, Zambia, 20-21 July].

McCormick, John, ed. 2007. *The European Superpower*. New York: Palgrave Macmillan.

McKie, Kristin. 2019. International Donor Funding and Social Movement Demobilization: The Barabaig Land-Rights Movement in Tanzania. *Africa Today* 66(1), 72–95. https://doi.org/10.2979/africatoday.66.1.04.

McLeod, Ian. 2004. Literal and Purposive Techniques of Legislative Interpretation: Some European Community and English Common Law Perspective. *Brooklyn Journal of International Law* 29(3), 1109–1134. Available at: https://brooklynworks.brooklaw.edu/bjil/vol29/iss3/5.

Médard, J. F. 1982. The Underdeveloped State in Tropical Africa: Political Clientelism or Neo-Patrimonialism. In C. Clapham ed., *Private Patronage and Public Power: Political Clientelism in the Modern State*. London: Macmillan, 162–192.

Meierhenrich, Jans. 2008. *The Legal History of South Africa in the Longue Durée. The Legacies of Law: Long-Run Consequences of Legal Development in South Africa, 1652–2000*. Cambridge and New York: Cambridge University Press.

Meierhenrich, Jens. 2017. An Ethnography of Nazi Law: The Intellectual Foundations of Ernst Frænkel's Theory of Dictatorship in E. Frænkel, *The Dual State: A Contribution to the Theory of Dictatorship* (J Meierhenrich ed.). Oxford: Oxford University Press, xxvii–llxxxi.

Meierhenrich, J. 2018. *The Remnants of the Rechtsstaat: An Ethnography of Nazi Law*. Oxford: Oxford University Press.

Mérieau, Eugenie. 2016. Thailand's Deep State, Royal Power and the Constitutional Court (1997–2015). *Journal of Contemporary Asia* 46(3), 445–466. https://doi.org/10.1080/00472336.2016.1151917.

Mérieau, Eugénie. 2019. *La dictature, une antithèse de la démocratie ? 20 idées reçues sur les régimes autoritaires*. Paris: Editions Le Cavalier Bleu.

Merry, Sally Engel. 2002. Ethnography in the Archives. In June Starr & Mark Goodale eds., *Practicing Ethnography in Law: New Dialogues, Enduring Methods*. New York and St. Martin: Palgrave, 128–142.

Metsola, L. 2018. Incremental Dependencies: Politics and Ethics of Claim-Making at the Fringes of Windhoek, Namibia. In C. Ammann & T. Förster eds., *African Cities and the Development Conundrum*. Leiden: Brill Nijhoff, 162–187.

Mignolo, Walter. 2000. *Local Histories/Global Designs: Coloniality, Subaltern Knowledges, and Border Thinking*. Princeton, NJ: Princeton University Press.

Mill, John Stuart. 1963. On Liberty. In J. M. Robson & R. F. McRae eds., *Collected Works*, Vol 18. Toronto: University of Toronto Press.

Mitchell, Timothy. 1999. Society, Economy, and the State Effect. In George Steinmetz ed., *State/Culture: State Formation after the Cultural Turn*. Ithaca, NY and London: Cornell University Press, 76–97.

Mkandawire, Thandika. 2001. Thinking about Developmental States in Africa. *Cambridge Journal of Economics* 5(3), 289–314. Accessed from https://rrojasdatabank.info/Mkandawireafrica.pdf.

Mkandawire, Thandika. 2015. Neopatrimonialism and the Political Economy of Economic Performance in Africa: Critical Reflections. *World Politics* 67(3), 563–612. https://doi.org/10.1017/S004388711500009X

Møller, J. & S.-E. Skaaning. 2010. Beyond the Radial Delusion: Conceptualizing and Measuring Democracy and Non-Democracy. *International Political Science Review* 31(3), 261–283. https://doi.org/10.1177/0192512110369522.

Momba, Jotham. 2007. The Intersection between Politics and Corruption in Zambia. *South African Journal of International Affairs* 14(1), 115–125.

Mommsen, Hans. 1985. The Reichstag Fire and Its Political Consequences. In H. W. Koch ed., *Aspects of the Third Reich*. London: Palgrave, 62–95.

Moore, S. F. 1972. Law and Social Change: The Semi-Autonomous Social Field as an Appropriate Subject of Study. *Law & Society Review* 7, 719.

Morganthau, Hans. 1964 [1955]. *Politics among Nations: The Struggle for Power and Peace*. New York: Alfred A. Knopf.

Morris, Douglas. 2020. *Legal Sabotage: Ernst Frænkel in Hitler's Germany*. New York: Cambridge University Press.

Mouffe, Chantal. 1993. *The Return of the Political*. London and New York: Verso.

Mouffe, Chantal, ed. 1998. *The Challenge of Carl Schmitt*. London and New York: Verso.

Muldoon, James. 2015. Arendt's Revolutionary Constitutionalism: Between Constituent Power and Constitutional Form. *Constellations: An International Journal of Critical and Democratic Theory* 22(4), 596–607. https://doi.org/10.1111/1467-8675.12179.

Mulenga, Kampamba. 1998. *Blood on Their Hands*. Lusaka, Zambia: ZEPH.

Mulford, D. C. 1967. *The Politics of Independence, 1957–1964*. Oxford: Oxford University Press.

Munalula, Mulela Margaret. 1989. Gender, Bureaucracy and Law: The Search for Change. *African Law Journal*, 21–24, 48–60.

Munalula, Mulela Margaret. 2004. *Legal Process: Zambian Cases, Legislation, and Commentaries*. Lusaka: UNZA Press for the School of Law.

Mutesa, Fred. 2005. *The Nexus between Management Reforms and Neo-patrimonial Politics*. [Draft Contribution for the Conference on *Political Dimensions of poverty Reduction: The Case of Zambia*, Mulungushi Conference Centre, Lusaka, Zambia, March 9–11], Mimeo.

Muthu, Sankar. 2003. *Enlightenment against Empire*. Princeton, NJ: Princeton University Press.

Mutua, Makau. 2008. Human Rights in Africa: The Limited Promise of Liberalism. *African Studies Review* 52(1), 17–39. https://doi.org/10.1353/arw.0.0031.

Mwanakatwe, John. 1994. *End of Kaunda Era*. Lusaka: Multimedia Publications.

Mwanakatwe, John. 2003. *Teacher Politician Lawyer: My Autobiography*. Lusaka: Bookworld Publishers.

Mwewa, Charles. 2019. *Allergic to Corruption: The Legacy of President Michael Sata* (independently published).

Nair, S. 2011. Sovereignty, Security, and the Exception: Towards Situating Postcolonial *Homo sacer*. In G. Delanty & S.p. Turner eds., *Routledge International Handbook of Contemporary Social and Political Theory*. London: Taylor and Francis, 386–394.

Ndlovu-Gatsheni, Sabelo. 2013. *Coloniality of Power in Postcolonial Africa: Myths of Decolonization*. Dakar: Codesria.

Ndlovu-Gatsheni, Sabelo. 2018. *Epistemic Freedom in Africa: Deprovincialization and Decolonization.* London: Routledge.

Ndulo, Muna. 2002. Presidentialism in the Southern African States and Constitutional Restraint on Presidential Power. *Vermont Law Review* 26(4), 769–802.

Ndulo, Muna B. & Robert B. Kent. 1996. Constitutionalism in Zambia: Past, Present and Future. *Journal of African Law* 4(2), 256–278. https://doi.org/10.1017/s0021855300007816.

Ndulo, Muna B. & Robert B. Kent. 1998. The Constitutions of Zambia. *Zambia Law Journal* 30(11), 1.

Negretto, G. L. & J. Rivera. 2000. Liberalism and Emergency Powers in Latin America: Reflections on Carl Schmitt and the Theory of Constitutional Dictatorship. *Cardozo Law Review* 21(5–6), 1797–1824.

Ngumba, E., A. Gachanja, J. Nyirenda, J. Maldonado & T. Tuhkanen. 2020. Occurrence of Antibiotics and Antiretroviral Drugs in Source-Separated Urine, Groundwater, Surface Water and Wastewater in the Peri-Urban Area of Chunga in Lusaka, Zambia. *Water SA* 46(2), 278–284.

Nkrumah, Kwame. 1962. Ghana. *Journal of African Law* 5(2), 103–112. Accessed from https://www.jstor.org/stable/745009.

Ntomba, Reginald. 2016. *The Mwanawasa Years: An Analysis of His Presidency.* Lusaka: Gadsden Publishers.

Nwabueze, B. O. 1974. *Presidentialism in Commonwealth Africa.* New York: St. Martin's Press.

O'Donnell, G. & P. C. Schmitter. 1986. *Transitions from Authoritarian Rule: Tentative Conclusions about Uncertain Democracies.* Baltimore: John Hopkins University Press.

Oasis Forum. 2012. *Constitutionalism and Constitution Development in Zambia. Strategic Plan for 2002–2004* (mimeo).

Obarrio, Juan. 2014. *The Spirit of the Laws in Mozambique.* Chicago, IL: University of Chicago Press.

Obermaier, Frederik & Bastian Obermayer. 2016. *The Panama Papers: Breaking the Story of How the Rich and Powerful Hide Their Money.* London: Oneworld Publications.

Ochoa Espejo, Paulina. 2011. *The Time of Popular Sovereignty: Process and the Democratic State.* University Park, PA: Pennsylvania State University Press.

Ogura, M. 1991. Rural-Urban Migration in Zambia and Migrant Ties to Home Villages. *Developing Economies* 29(2), 145–165.

Ohtonen, Saija. 2005. *Opportunities, Alliances and Passionate Agents: The Political Role and Strategies of the Women's Movement in Zambia.* M.A. thesis (Development Studies). University of Helsinki.

Oklopcic, Zoran. 2014. Three Arenas of Struggle: A Contextual Approach to the Constituent Power of 'the People'. *Global Constitutionalism* 3(2), 200–235. https://doi.org/10.1017/S2045381714000069.

Okoth–Ogendo, H.W.O. 1991. *Constitutions without Constitutionalism: Reflections on an African Political Paradox.* In Shivji, I.G. (ed.) *State and Constitutionalism: An African debate on democracy.* Harare: SAPES Trust.

Olivier de Sardan, J. P. 2014. The Delivery State in Africa. Interface Bureaucrats, Professional Cultures and the Bureaucratic Mode of Governance. In Thomas Bierschenk et al. eds., *States at Work: Dynamics of African Bureaucracies.* Leiden: Brill, 399–429.

Oloka-Onyango, J. 2017. *When Courts Do Politics: Public Interest Law and Litigation in East Africa.* Cambridge: Cambridge Scholars Publishing.

Orwell, George. 1945. *Animal Farm.* London: Secker & Warburg.

Oya, Carlos. 2007. Agricultural Maladjustment in Africa: What Have We Learned after Two Decades of Liberalisation? *Journal of Contemporary African Studies*, 25(2), 275–297. https://doi.org/10.1080/02589000701396355.

Pain, J. H. 1978. The Reception of English and Roman-Dutch Law in Africa with Reference to Botswana, Lesotho and Swaziland. *Comparative and International Law Journal of Southern Africa* 11(2), 137–167.

Parker, Collins 1980. Control of Executive Discretion under Preventive Detention Law in Zambia. *Comparative and International Law Journal of Southern Africa*, 13(2), 159–176.

Parpworth, N. 2017. The South African Constitutional Court: Upholding the Rule of Law and the Separation of Powers. *Journal of African Law* 61(2), 273–287.

Patel, Rajeev & Philip McMichael. 2004. Third Worldism and the Lineages of Global Fascism: The Regrouping of the Global South in the Neoliberal Era. *Third World Quarterly* 25(1), 231–254. https://doi.org/10.1080/0143659042000185426.

Perrings, Charles 1977. Consciousness, Conflict and Proletarianization: An Assessment of the 1935 Mineworkers' Strike on the Northern Rhodesian Copperbelt. *Journal of Southern African Studies* 4(1), 31–51

Pettman, Ralph. 1974. Problems in Australian Foreign Policy, January to June 1974. *Australian Journal of Politics and History* 20(3). https://doi.org/10.1111/j.1467-8497.1974.tb01119.x.

Phiri, Bizeck J. 2005. Strengthening Parliamentary Democracy in Southern Africa. Country Studies: Zambia. *South African Journal of International Affairs* 12(1), 205–218.

Phiri, Bizeck J. 2006. *A Political History of Zambia: From Colonial Rule to the Third Republic, 1890–2001.* Trenton: Africa World Press.

Phiri, Isaac. 1999. Why African Churches Preach Politics: The Case of Zambia. *Journal of Church and State* 41(2), 323–348.

Phiri, Isabel Apawo. 2003. President Frederick J. T. Chiluba of Zambia: The Christian Nation and Democracy. *Journal of Religion in Africa* 33(4), 401. http://doi.org/10.1163/157006603322665332.

Pitts, Jennifer. 2005. *A Turn to Empire: The Rise of Imperial Liberalism in Britain and France.* Princeton, NJ and Oxford: Princeton University Press.

Pletcher, James. 2000. The Politics of Liberalizing Zambia's Maize Markets. *World Development* 28(1), 129–142. https://doi.org/10.1016/S0305-750X(99)00120-5.

Plowden, Edmund. 1816. *Commentaries or Reports.* London: S. Brooke, Paternoster-Row.

Prempeh, H. Kwasi. 2007. Africa's 'Constitutionalism Revival': False Start or New Dawn? *International Journal of Constitutional Law* 5(3), 469–506. https://doi.org/10.1093/icon/mom016.

Prempeh, H. Kwasi. 2008. Presidential Power in Comparative Perspective: The Puzzling Persistence of Imperial Presidency in Post-authoritarian Africa. *Hastings Constitutional Law Quarterly* 35(4), 761–833.

Prempeh, Kwasi. 2017. Does Participation Help to Foster Constitutionalism in Africa? In Tania Abbiate, Markus Böckenförde and Veronica Federico eds., *Public Participation in African Constitutionalism.* London: Routledge, 296–307.

Priest, Graham. 2002. Paraconsistent Logic. In D. M. Gabbay & F. Guenthner eds., *Handbook of Philosophical Logic*. Dordrecht: Springer. https://doi.org/10.1007/978-94-017-0460-1_4.

Pruce, Kate & Sam Hickey. 2016. *The Politics of Promoting Social Protection in Zambia, WIDER Working Paper, No. 2016/156*. Helsinki: UNI-WIDER. GRZ. http://doi.org/10.35188/UNU-WIDER/2016/200-7.

Puta-Chekwe, Chisanga. 2017. *Cobra in the Boat: Michael Sata's Zambia*. London: Adonis & Abbey Publishers Ltd.

Quijano, A. 2000. Coloniality of Power, Eurocentrism, and Latin America. *International Sociology* 15(2), 215–232. https://doi.org/10.1177/0268580900015002005.

Rakner, Lise & Lars Svåsand. 2005. Stuck in Transition: Electoral Processes in Zambia 1991–2001. *Democratization* 12(1), 85–105. http://doi.org/10.1080/1351034042000317970.

Rakner, Lise. 2003. *Political and Economic Liberalization in Zambia 1991–2001*. Uppsala: Nordic Africa Institute. http://doi.org/10.1353/at.2005.0064.

Ramose, Mogobe B. 1999. *African Philosophy through Ubuntu*. Harare: Mond Books.

Ramraj, Victor V., ed. 2008. *Emergencies and the Limits of Legality*. Cambridge and New York: Cambridge University Press.

Ranger, Terence. 1980. Making Northern Rhodesia Imperial: Variations on a Royal Theme, 1924–1938. *African Affairs* 79(316), 349–373. Accessed October 31, 2020. http://www.jstor.org/stable/722045; https://doi.org/10.1093/oxfordjournals.afraf.a097229.

Rawls, John. 1972. *A Theory of Justice*. Oxford: Oxform University Press.

Rawls, John. 1993. *Political Liberalism*. New York: Columbia University Press.

Rikalainen, Noora. 2006. *Churches Preaching Politics: The Changing Role and Shifting Opportunities of the Catholic Church in Politics in Zambia*. M.A. thesis (Political Science). University of Helsinki.

Roberts, Andrew D. 1969. White Judges under Attack: Growing Pressure for a One-Party State. *The Round Table* 236(236), 423–426.

Roberts, Andrew D. 1976. *A History of Zambia*. London: Holmes & Meier.

Roberts, Simon. 2005. After Government? On Representing Law Without the State. *Modern Law Review* 68(1), 1–24. Accessed from https://www.jstor.org/stable/3699110.

Rorty, Richard. 1989. *Contingency, Irony, and Solidarity*. Cambridge: Cambridge University Press.

Rotberg, Robert. 1966. *The Rise of Nationalism in Central Africa: The Making of Malawi and Zambia 1873–1964*. Cambridge, MA: Harvard university Press.

Rotberg, Robert. 1977. *Black Heart: Gore-Browne and the Politics of Multi-racial Zambia*. Berkeley, CA: University of California Press. https://doi.org/10.1017/s0364168600001560.

Roux, Theunis. 2013. A Brief Response to Professor Baxi. In Oscar Vilhena, Upendra Baxi & Frans Viljoen eds., *Transformative Constitutionalism: Comparing the Apex Courts of Brazil, India and South Africa*. Pretoria: Pretoria University Press, 48–51.

Ruedisili, S. 1996. Zambia's Elusive Search for a Valid Public Order Act: An Appraisal. *Zambia Law Journal* 25–28, 1–65.

Saïd, Edward. 1978. *Orientalism*. New York: Pantheon.

Sangwa, J. 2000. Constitution-Making and Experience with Constitutional Rule in Zambia Since 1990. *Transnational Law and Contemporary Problems* 10(2), 483–515.

Santos, Boaventura de Sousa. 2002. *Toward a New Legal Common Sense: Law, Globalization, and Emancipation.* London: Butterworths LexisNexis.

Sardanis, A. 2003. *Africa: Another Side of the Coin. Northern Rhodesia's Final Years and Zambia's Nationhood.* London and New York: I.B. Tauris.

Sartori, Giovanni. 1962. Constitutionalism: A Preliminary Discussion. *American Political Science Review* 56(4), 853–864.

Schaap, Andrew. 2007. Political Theory and the Agony of Politics. *Political Studies Review* 5(1), 56–74. https://doi.org/10.1111/j.1478-9299.2007.00123.x.

Scheppele, Kim Lane. 2004. Constitutional Ethnography: An Introduction. *Law and Society Review* 38(3), 389–406. https://doi.org/10.1111/j.0023-9216.2004.00051.x.

Scheppele, Kim Lane. 2017. *Constitutional Ethnography, Counter-constitutions, and the Study of Form, Sediment and Trajectory.* Lecture at the Old Observatory, Leiden, January 13.

Scheuerman, W. E. 1996. Carl Schmitt's Critique of Liberal Constitutionalism. *Review of Politics* 58(2), 299–322. https://doi.org/10.1017/s0034670500019392.

Scheuerman, W. E. 2000. Social Democracy and the Rule of Law: The Legacy of Ernst Frænkel. In P. C. Caldwell & W. E. Scheuerman eds., *From Liberal Democracy to Fascism.* Humanities Press, 74–105.

Scheuerman, William E. 2008. Presidentialism and Emergency Government. In V. V. Ramraj ed., *Emergencies and the Limits of Legality.* Cambridge: Cambridge University Press, 258–286.

Schmitt, Carl. 2005 [1922]. *Political Theology, Four Chapters on the Concept of Sovereignty.* Studies in Contemporary German Social Thought. Translated by George Schwab. Cambridge, MA: MIT Press.

Schmitt, Carl. 1931. *Der Hüter der Verfassung.* Tübingen: Mohr.

Scott, G. 2002. Zambia: Structural Adjustment, Rural Livelihoods and Sustainable Development. *Development Southern Africa* 9(3), 405–418.

Scott, Guy. 2019. *Adventures in Zambian Politics: A Story in Black and White.* Boulder, CO: Lynne Rienner Publishers, Inc.

Seidman, Ann et al (eds). 2007. *Africa's Challenge: Using Law for Good Governance and Development.* Trenton: Africa World Press.

Shai, Isaac. 2019. The Right to Development, Transformative Constitutionalism and Radical Transformation in South Africa: Post-colonial and De-Colonial Reflections. *African Human Rights Law Journal* 19(1), 494–509. http://doi.org/10.17159/1996-2096/2019/v19n1a23.

Sharma, Aradhana & Akhil Gupta, eds. 2009. *The Anthropology of the State: A Reader.* Oxford: Blackwell Publishing.

Shklar, Judith. 1964. *Legalism: Law, Morals and Political Trials.* Cambridge, MA: Harvard University Press.

Siame, M., N. Mulikita, S. Longwe & R. Clarke. 1998. *Beyond Inequalities: Women in Zambia.* Lusaka and Harare: ZARD/SARDC.

Sibanda, Sanele. 2012. Not Purpose-Made! Transformative Constitutionalism, Post-Independence Constitutionalism and the Struggle to Eradicate Poverty. In S. Liebenberg & G. Quinot eds., *Law and Poverty: Perspectives from South Africa and Beyond.* Cape Town: Juta & Company Ltd., 482–500.

Sikkink, Kathryn. 2011. *The Justice Cascade: How Human Rights Prosecutions Are Changing World Politics*. New York: W.W. Norton & Co.

Simutanyi, Neo. 1996. The Politics of Structural Adjustment in Zambia. *Third World Quarterly* 17(4), 825–839. https://doi.org/10.1080/01436599615407.

Simutanyi, Neo. 2012. The Politics of Constitutional Reform in Zambia: From Executive Dominance to Public Participation? In Danwood M. Chirwa & Lia Nijzink eds., *Accountable Government in Africa: Perspectives from Public Law and Political Studies*. Cape Town: UCT Press, 26–41.

Singhal, Ashish Kumar & Ikramuddin Malik. 2012. Doctrinal and Socio-Legal Methods of Research: Merits and Demerits. *Educational Research Journal* 2(7), 252–256.

Sipalo, Ngenda. 1978. *Constitutional Development in Zambia 1890–1975*. LLM dissertation. University of Zambia, School of Law. Accessed from http://dspace.unza.zm/handle/123456789/957.

Sishuwa, Sishuwa. 2011. *The Making of an African Populist: Explaining the Rise of Michael Sata, 2001–2006*. M.A. thesis [History]. University of Oxford.

Sishuwa, Sishuwa. 2017. *'I am Zambia's redeemer': Populism and the Rise of Michael Sata, 1955–2011*. Doctoral thesis [History]. University of Oxford.

Sishuwa, Sishuwa. 2018. Step by Inevitable Step: Lungu's Strategic March to 2021 and Beyond. *African Arguments*, December 4, 2018. https://africanarguments.org/2018/12/zambia-2021-lungu-strategic-march/.

Sishuwa, Sishuwa. 2019. 'A White Man Will Never Be a Zambian': Racialised Nationalism, the Rule of Law, and Competing Visions of Independent Zambia in the Case of Justice James Skinner, 1964–1969. *Journal of Southern African Studies* 45(3), 503–523. https://doi.org/10.1080/03057070.2019.1626190.

Sishuwa, Sishuwa. 2020. Surviving on Borrowed Power: Rethinking the Role of Civil Society in Zambia's Third-Term Debate. *Journal of Southern African Studies* 46(3), 471–490. https://doi.org/10.1080/03057070.2020.1730644.

Sishuwa, Sishuwa. 2021. Roots of Contemporary Political Strategies: Ethno-Populism in Zambia during the Late Colonial Era and Early 2000s. *Journal of Southern African Studies*, 1–21. https://doi.org/10.1080/03057070.2021.1940602.

Sleat, M. 2011. Liberal realism: A liberal response to the realist critique. *The Review of Politics* 73(3), 469–496.

Smolenski, Jan. 2012. Substantive Equality, Popular Sovereignty, and Antagonistic Politics: An Introduction to Carl Schmitt's Democratic Theory. CEU Political Science Journal 7(3), 269–289. Available at SSRN: https://ssrn.com/abstract=2189485.

Solum, L. B. 2018. Originalism Versus Living Constitutionalism: The Conceptual Structure of the Great Debate. *Northwestern University Law Review* 113(6), 1243–1296.

Spencer, Jonathan. 1997. Post-colonialism and the Political Imagination. *Journal of the Royal Anthropological Institute* 3(1), 1–19.

Spivak, Gayatri. 1988. Can the Subaltern Speak? In Cary Nelson & Lawrence Grossberg eds., *Marxism and the Interpretation of Culture*. Basingstoke: Macmillan Education, 271–313.

Spivak, Gayatri. 1993. *Outside in the Teaching Machine*. London: Routledge.

Stein, A. R. 1985. Forum Non Conveniens and the Redundancy of Court-Access Doctrine. *University of Pennsylvania Law Review*, 133(4), 781–846.

Steinmetz, G. ed. 1999. *State/Culture: State-Formation after the Cultural Turn*. Ithaca: Cornell University Press.
Stepan, A. & C. Skach. 1993. Constitutional Frameworks and Democratic Consolidation: Parliamentarianism versus Presidentialism. *World Politics* 46(1), 1–22. https://doi.org/10.2307/2950664.
Stern, Philip J. & Carl Wennerlind. 2014. Introduction. In their (eds.) *Mercantilism Reimagined: Political Economy in Early Modern Britain and Its Empire*. New York: Oxford University Press, 3–22.
Sunstein, Cass R. 2006. Justice Breyer's Pragmatic Constitutionalism. *Yale Law Journal* 115, 1719.
Suntrup, Jan Cristoph. 2020. Between Prerogative Power and Legality – Reading Ernst Frænkel's *The Dual State* as an Analytical Tool for Present Authoritarian Rule. *Jurisprudence: An International Journal of Legal and Political Thought* 11(3), 335–359. https://doi.org/10.1080/20403313.2020.1734337.
Sylvester, Christine. 2006. Bare Life as a Development/Postcolonial Problematic. *Geographical Journal* 172(1), 66–77.
Szeftel, Morris. 2000. 'Eat with Us': Managing Corruption and Patronage under Zambia's Three Republics, 1964–99. *Journal of Contemporary African Studies* 18(2), 207–224. https://doi.org/10.1080/713675624.
Thomas, Philip A. 1971. Legal Education in Africa: With Special Reference to Zambia. *Northern Ireland Legal Quarterly* 22(1), 3–37.
Thomson, Alex. 2009. Polemos and Agon. In A. Schaap ed., *Law and Agonistic Politics*. Edinburgh: Glasgow Law and Society Series. Farnham: Ashgate Publishing, 105–118.
Tordoff, William. 1974. *Politics in Zambia*. Berkeley, CA: University of California Press.
Trubek, D. M. 1972. Toward a Social Theory of Law: An Essay on the Study of Law and Development. *Yale Law Journal* 82(1), 1–50. https://doi.org/10.2307/795251.
Trubek, L. G. 1991. Critical Lawyering: Toward a New Public Interest Practice. *Boston University Public Interest Law Journal* 1, 49–56.
Tunander, Ola. 2009. Democratic State vs Deep State - Approaching the Dual State of the West. In Eric Wilson & Tim Lindsey eds., *Government of the Shadows: Parapolitics and Criminal Soveregnty*. London: Pluto Press, 56–72.
Valverde, Mariana. 2015. *Chronotopes of Law: Jurisdiction, Scale and Governance*. London: Routledge.
Van de Walle, N. 2003. Presidentialism and Clientelism in Africa's Emerging Party Systems. *Journal of Modern African Studies* 41(2), 297–321. Accessed October 31, 2020. http://www.jstor.org/stable/3876122.
van Donge, Jan Kees. 1995. Zambia: Kaunda and Chiluba. Enduring Patterns of Political Culture. In John A. Wiseman ed., *Democracy and Political Change in Sub-Saharan Africa*. London: Routledge, 205–231.
van Donge, Jan Kees. 2009. The Plundering of Zambian Resources by Frederick Chiluba and His Friends: A Case Study of the Interaction Between National Politics and the International Drive Towards Good Governance. *African Affairs* 108(430), 69–90. https://doi.org/10.1093/afraf/adn073.
Van Marle, K. 2007. "The Spectacle of Post-Apartheid Constitutionalism." *Griffith Law Review* 16(2), 411–429. https://doi.org/10.1080/10383441.2007.10854597.
Verheul, Susanne. 2013. 'Rebels' and 'Good Boys': Patronage, Intimidation and Resistance in Zimbabwe's Attorney General's Office after 2000." *Journal of*

*Southern African Studies* 39(4), 765–782. https://doi.org/10.1080/03057070.2013.858544.
Vilhena, Oscar, Upendra Baxi & Frans Viljoen, eds. 2013. *Transformative Constitutionalism. Comparing the Apex Courts of Brazil, India and South Africa.* South Africa: Pretoria: Pretoria University Law Press.
Vinx, Lars, ed. and trans. 2015. *The Guardian of the Constitution. Hans Kelsen and Carl Schmitt on the Limits of Constitutional Law.* Cambridge: Cambridge University Press. https://doi.org/10.1017/CBO9781316136256.
Vinx, Lars. 2019. Ernst-Wolfgang Böckenförde and the Politics of Constituent Power. *Jurisprudence* 10(1), 15–38. https://doi.org/10.1080/20403313.2018.1442257.
Volk, Christian. 2017. *Arendtian Constitutionalism: Law, Politics and the Order of Freedom.* Oxford: Bloomsbury Hart Publishing.
von Bogdandy, Armin. 2012. National Legal Scholarship in the European Legal Area—A Manifesto. *International Journal of Constitutional Law* 10(3), 614–626. https://doi.org/10.1093/icon/mos023.
Wai, Zubairu. 2012. Neo-Patrimonialism and the Discourse of State Failure in Africa. *Review of African Political Economy* 39(131), 27–43. https://doi.org/10.1080/03056244.2012.658719.
Waldron, Jeremy 1987. Theoretical Foundations of Liberalism. *Philosophical Quarterly* 37(147), 127–150.
Wallerstein, Immanuel. 2001 [1991]. *Unthinking Social Science. The Limits of Nineteenth-Century Paradigms* (2nd ed.). Philadelphia, PA: Temple University Press.
Walsh, Catherine. 2010. Political-Epistemic Insurgency, Social Movements and the Refounding of the State. In Mabel Moraña & Bret Gustafson eds., *Rethinking Intellectuals in Latin America.* Frankfurt a. M., Madrid: Vervuert Verlagsgesellschaft, 199–212. https://doi.org/10.31819/9783954871698-010.
Weber, Max. 1968. *Economy and Society*, edited by Guenther Roth & Claus Wittich. Berkeley, CA: University of California Press.
Wele, Patrick. 1987. *Kaunda and Mushala Rebellion: The Untold Story.* Lusaka: Multimedia Publications.
Wele, Patrick. 1995. *Zambia's Most Famous Dissidents: From Mushala to Luchembe.* Solwezi: PMW Publishers.
Werbner, Pnina. 2020. Review of *the State and the Paradox of Customary Law in Africa. Journal of Southern African Studies* 46(5), 1076–1078. https://doi.org/10.1080/03057070.2020.1792173.
Williams, Stephanie. 2011. *Running the Show: The Extraordinary Stories of the Men Who Governed the British Empire.* London: Penguin. Viking.
Woodman, George R. 1998. Ideological Combat and Social Observation: Recent Debate about Legal Pluralism. *Journal of Legal Pluralism and Unofficial Law* 30(42), 21–59. https://doi.org/10.1080/07329113.1998.10756513.
Wunsch, J., Michael Bratton & Peter Kareithi. 1992. *Democracy and Governance in Zambia: An Assessment and Proposed Strategy.* Prepared for USAID/Zambia. Burlington, VT: Associates in Rural Development.
Young, Crawford. 1994. *The African Colonial State in Comparative Perspective.* New Haven, CT and London: Yale University Press.
Zakaria, Fareed. 1997. The Rise of Illiberal Democracy. *Foreign Affairs* 76(6), 22–43. https://doi.org/10.2307/20048274.

Zenker, Olaf & Markus Virgil Hoehne, eds. 2018. *The State and the Paradox of Customary Law in Africa*. London and New York: Routledge.

Zimba, Jack. 2012. Wynter Kabimba: Rabble-Rouser or Truth Seeker? *Bulletin & Record*. [Lusaka], August 2012, 6–10.

Zinn, Jens O. 2020. 'A monstrous threat': How a State of Exception Turns into a 'New Normal'. *Journal of Risk Research* 23(7), 1083–1091. https://doi.org/10.1080/13669877.2020.1758194.

Zukas, Simon. 2002. *Into Exile and Back*. Lusaka: Bookworld Publishers.

Zulu, A. G. 2007. *Memoirs of Alexander Grey Zulu*. Ndola: Times Printpak Zambia Ltd.

## Internet resources

AP News. 1986. Six Dead, 1,000 Arrested, in Zambian Food Riots. *AP News*, December 10, 1986. https://apnews.com/article/e165610b1aa7e554b5ffed4d1ff551df.

BBC. 1999. Congo Peacebroker Calls for un Force. *BBC News*, September 22. http://news.bbc.co.uk/1/hi/world/africa/454245.stm.

BBC. 2007. Chiluba Attacks "Racist" UK Court. *BBC News*, May 10. http://news.bbc.co.uk/2/hi/africa/6644261.stm.

BBC2008. Zambia Seizes 'Chiluba Millions', at http://news.bbc.co.uk/2/hi/africa/7392911.stm.

BBC. 2017. Zambia opposition leader Hakainde Hichilema released https://www.bbc.com/news/world-africa-40945825

Beyani, C. et al. 2021. Is Lungu Eligible to Stand for a Third Term? The Submission of Zambian Constitutional Law Experts as Filed in the Constitutional Court. *Lusaka Times*, June 10, 2021. https://www.lusakatimes.com/2021/06/10/is-lungu-eligible-to-stand-for-a-third-term-the-submission-of-zambian-constitutional-law-experts-as-filed-in-the-constitutional-court/.

Brooks, David. 2019. The Lawyers Who Did Not Break. *The New York Times*, February 21. https://www.nytimes.com/2019/02/21/opinion/trump-investigation-robert-khuzami.html.

Chirwa, Joseph. 2020. The Nolle Prosequi in Zambia: A Political Tool or a Prosecutor's Necessity? https://www.linkedin.com/pulse/nolle-prosequi-zambia-political-tool-prosecutors-necessity-chirwa

Funga, Mukosha. 2018. Mutembo Presses ConCourt to Hear His Evidence. *NewsDiggers*, February 23. https://diggers.news/courts/2018/02/23/mutembo-presses-concourt-to-hear-his-evidence/.

Geertz, Clifford. 1998. Deep Hanging Out. *The New York Review*, October 22, 1998. https://www.nybooks.com/articles/1998/10/22/deep-hanging-out/.

Goodley, Simon & Mark Hollingsworth. 2012. Zambian Minister under Investigation over Trafigura Contract. *The Guardian*, December 3. https://www.theguardian.com/world/2012/dec/03/trafigura-zambia-bribery-allegations.

Hamalengwa, Munyonzwe & Charles Mwewa. 2014. Submission to the Legal and Justice Sector Reform Commission of Zambia. *Pambazuka News*, September 18, 2014. https://www.pambazuka.org/governance/critical-notes-legal-system-zambia.

Holder, Christina. 2011. Zambia's Constitutional Review Process Has Thwarted Meaningful Public Patricipation. *HuffPost*, August 31. Accessed from https://www.huffpost.com/entry/zambias-constitutional-re_b_700494?ncid=engmodushpmg00000006.

Human Rights Watch. 1996. Zambia: Elections and Human Rights in the Third Republic. *Human Rights Watch Africa* 8(4). https://www.hrw.org/reports/1996/Zambia.htm.

Human Rights Watch. 1999. *Human Rights Watch World Report 2000 – Zambia*, December 1. Accessed August 21, 2020. https://www.refworld.org/docid/3ae6a8c74c.html

IFEX. 2002. Editor-In-Chief M'membe "Put On His Defence" Over "Chiluba is a Thief" Editorial. https://ifex.org/editor-in-chief-mmembe-put-on-his-defence-over-chiluba-is-a-thief-editorial/.

International Commission of Jurists (ICJ). 2012. *Zambia Mission Report, May 16–19, 2012.* https://www.icj.org/wp-content/uploads/2018/10/Zambia-Mission-Publications-Reports-Mission-reports-2012-ENG.pdf.

Jere, Dickson. 2017. The Nolle Prosequi Question. *Lusaka Times*, August 17. Accessed on December 12. https://www.lusakatimes.com/2017/08/17/nolle-prosequi-question/.

Jurecic, Quinta. 2017. Body Double: What Medieval Executive Theory Tells Us about Trump's Twitter Accounts. *Lawfare*. April 24, 2017. Accessed from https://www.lawfareblog.com/body-double-what-medieval-executive-theory-tells-us-about-trumps-twitter-accounts.

Kaaba, O'Brien. 2018. Milford Maambo and Others v The People 2016/CC/R001 [2017]. *SAIPAR Case Review* 1(2), Article 12. Available at: https://scholarship.law.cornell.edu/scr/vol1/iss2/12.

Kaaba, O'Brien & Pamela Towela Sambo. 2020. Mutembo Nchito v Attorney General (2016/CC/002927 October 2020). *SAIPAR Case Review* 3(2), Article 4. Available at: https://scholarship.law.cornell.edu/scr/vol3/iss2/4.

Kaaba, O'Brien & Pamela Towela Sambo. 2020. Where Exactly Is the ConCourt Taking Zambia? A Comment on the Mutembo Nchito Judgment. *The Mast*, December 2, 2020. https://www.themastonline.com/2020/12/02/where-exactly-is-the-concourt-taking-zambia-a-comment-on-the-mutembo-nchito-judgment/.

Kalunga, Felicity. 2019. The Proposed 2019 Constitution Amendment Bill: A Threat to Zambia's Democracy? *Commonwealth Lawyers Association*, September 24. Accessed from https://www.commonwealthlawyers.com/africa/the-proposed-2019-constitution-amendment-bill-a-threat-to-zambias-democracy/.

Kenyans for Peace with Truth and Justice. 2014. *A Guide to Public Interest Litigation in Kenya*. Accessed from http://kptj.africog.org/wp-content/uploads/2015/03/PIL-24032015.pdf.

Law Society of England and Wales. 2007. *Zambia v Meer Care & Desai. The Law Society*. Accessed from https://web.archive.org/web/20101228130111/http://www.lawsociety.org.uk/newsandevents/news/view=newsarticle.law?NEWSID=340538.

LAZ. 2013. Press Statement by Judiciary Not Legally Binding – LAZ. Accessed from https://www.lusakatimes.com/2013/08/09/press-statement-by-judiciary-not-legally-binding-laz/.

Locke, John. 2005 [1690]. *Two Treatises of Government*, accessed at *The Federalist Papers Project* www.thefederalistpapers.org.

Lumina, Cephas. 2020. Zambia's Proposed Constitutional Amendments: Sowing the Seeds of Crisis? http://constitutionnet.org/news/zambias-proposed-constitutional-amendments-sowing-seeds-crisis.
Lusaka Times. 2008. In Honour of Zambia's First Minister of Justice [Obituary for James John Skinner], November 24, 2008. Accessed from https://www.lusakatimes.com/2008/11/24/in-honour-of-zambias-first-minister-of-justice/.
Lusaka Times. 2015a. Mutembo Nchito's Self Nolle Prosequi Is Valid-Magistrate Mwale. *Lusaka Times*, March 2. https://www.lusakatimes.com/2015/03/02/mutembo-nchitos-self-nolle-prosequi-valid-magistrate-mwale/.
Lusaka Times. 2015b. President Lungu Sets Terms of Reference for DPP Mutembo Nchito Tribunal. *Lusaka Times*, March 11, 2015. https://www.lusakatimes.com/2015/03/11/president-lungu-sets-terms-reference-dpp-mutembo-nchitotribunal/.
Lusaka Voice. 2014. Oasis Forum Demands Release of Draft Constitution. *Lusaka Voice*, June 11, 2014. https://www.lusakavoice.com/2014/06/11/oasis-forum-demands-release-draft-constitution/.
Mail & Guardian. 2009. Chiluba's Wife Jailed, March 3, at http://www.mg.co.za/article/2009-03-03-chilubas-wife-jailed.
Maingaila, Francis. 2016. Zambia: Bill of Rights Referendum 'Unsuccessful'. *Anadolu Agency*. August 19, 2016. https://www.aa.com.tr/en/africa/zambia-bill-of-rights-referendum-unsuccessful/631627.
Malunga, Julia. 2020. Zambia Is a Train in Motion, You Can't Stop It to Fix It – Sangwa. *NewsDiggers*, September 8, 2020. https://diggers.news/local/2020/09/08/zambia-is-a-train-in-motion-you-cant-stop-it-to-fix-it-sangwa/.
Mbewe, Zondiwe. 2018. Mutembo Exposes Former Chief Justice Ngulube, Sakala. *NewsDiggers*, October 8, 2018. https://diggers.news/courts/2018/10/08/mutembo-exposes-former-chief-justices-ngulube-sakala/.
Mbikusita-Lewanika, Akashambatwa. 1993. Let the People Determine a Democratic Constitution. *Weekly Post*. December 17.
Mbikusita-Lewanika, Akashambatwa. 2017. Mulena Inyambo Ilute Yeta Celebrates 40 Years on Throne. *Zambia Daily Mail Limited*, October 7. http://www.daily-mail.co.zm/mulena-inyambo-ilute-yeta-celebrates-40-years-on-throne/.
Media Institute of South Africa (MISA). 2002. Editor-in-Chief M'membe "Put On His Defence" Over "Chiluba Is a Thief". *IFEX*, February 25, 2020. https://ifex.org/editor-in-chief-mmembe-put-on-his-defence-over-chiluba-is-a-thief-editorial/.
Motsamai, Dimpho. 2014. Zambia's Constitution-Making Process. *ISS Africa*. January 15, 2014. Accessed from https://issafrica.org/research/situation-reports/zambias-constitution-making-process.
Munalula, Mulela Margaret. 2016. The 2016 Constitution of Zambia: Elusive Search for a People Driven Process. *ConstitutionNet*, January 26. Accessed from http://constitutionnet.org/news/2016-constitution-zambia-elusive-search-people-driven-process.
Munshya, E. 2013. Lessons from Justice Mulenga's Ruling. In Sililo Dora & Mwale Case eds., *Daily Nation*, September 6. https://www.zambiadailynation.com/2013/09/06/lessons-from-justice-mulengas-ruling-in-dora-sililo-mwale-case/.
Mwale, Simson. 2004. Zambia's Economic, Social and Cultural Rights: Why Should They Be in the New Constitution? Research Report. Jesuit Centre for Theological Reflection Social Conditions Research Project (Lusaka). https://repository.jctr.org.zm/bitstream/handle/123456789/94/ZAMBIA%27S%20ESCR%20WHY

%20SHOULD%20THEY%20BE%20IN%20THE%20NEW%20CONSTITUIT .pdf?sequence=1&isAllowed=y.

Mwiinga, Jowie. 1994. Chill for Chiluba. *Africa Report* 39(2), 58–61.

Ndulo, Muna B. 2018. *Attorney General v Mutuna and Others (Appeal No. 088/2012) [2013] ZMSC 38. SAIPAR Case Review* 1, Issue 2 (May 2018). Accessed from https://scholarship.law.cornell.edu/cgi/viewcontent.cgi?article=1014&context=scr.

Ndulo, Muna B. 2019. A Comment by Prof Ndulo on the National Dialogue. *Lusaka Times*, April 2. https://www.lusakatimes.com/2019/04/02/a-comment-by-prof-ndulo-on-the-national-dialogue/.

Ndulo, Muna B. 2020. Bill 10, If Enacted, Will Install a Constitutional Dictatorship and Undermine Democracy in Zambia. *Southern African Journal of Policy and Development* 5(1), 31–43. https://scholarship.law.cornell.edu/sajpd/vol5/iss1/7.

New People African Feature Service. 1999. Zambia: Mung'omba Down but Not Out. *New People African Feature Service*, Issue 83, February 1999. Accessed from http://ospiti.peacelink.it/npeople/feb99/primafeb99.html (consulted 13.07.09).

NewsDiggers. 2018. Mutembo Presses ConCourt to Hear His Evidence. https://diggers.news/courts/2018/02/23/mutembo-presses-concourt-to-hear-his-evidence/.

Oasis Forum. 2019. Press Statement by the Oasis Forum on the Constitution of Zambia (Amendment) Bill No. 10 of. 2019 and Legal Reforms [8th August 2019]. Accessed from http://www.laz.org.zm/wp-content/uploads/2019/08/Press-Statement-by-the-Oasis-Forum-on-the-Constitution-Amendment-Bill-2019.pdf.

Oasis Forum. 2012a. Press Statement on the Constitution by the Oasis Forum Issued at Kapingila House. Wednesday, 22 August 2012 http://www.parliament.gov.zm/index.php?option=com_content&task=view&id=1851&Itemid=1.

Oasis Forum. 2012b. Press Statement by the Oasis Forum on Constitution Amendment Bill 2019. Oasis Forum, August 20, 12. https://www.zambiawatchdog.com/oasis-forum-disappointed-by-pf/.

Olcott, M. & M. Ottaway. 1999. *Challenge of Semi-Authoritarianism*. Carnegie Endowment for International Peace. Accessed from https://policycommons.net/artifacts/977401/challenge-of-semi-authoritarianism/1706528/ on 27 Nov 2022. CID: 20.500.12592/3txc63.

O'Loughlin, E. 1998. Killing of Minister Alarms Zambia. *Independent* [London], November 19. https://www.independent.co.uk/news/killing-of-minister-alarms-zambia-1185872.html.

Oloka-Onyango, Joe. 2017. *Law, Policy and Human Rights in Oil and Gas-Producing Regions of East Africa: A Focus on Local Communities*. Available at https://ssrn.com/abstract=3617307 or http://dx.doi.org/10.2139/ssrn.3617307.

Parasher, Tejas. 2015. Legal Rights and Structural Inequality: Reading Human Rights Historiography through Fanon. Unpublished paper. Pozen Family Center for Human Rights, University of Chicago. https://s3.amazonaws.com/pozen/system/ckeditor/attachments/274/legal_rights_and_structural_inequality_-_parasher.pdf.

Phiri, Chris. 2019. CSOs Oppose Dialogue Bill. *Zambia Reports*, March 29. Accessed from https://zambiareports.com/2019/03/29/csos-oppose-dialogue-bill/.

Post. 2005. Zambia: Civil Society Rejects Third Term. *AllAfrica Global Media*, January 19, 2005. https://allafrica.com/stories/200501190811.html.

Reuters. 2013. Zambia Strips Ex-President of Immunity from Prosecution. *Reuters*, March 15. https://www.reuters.com/article/us-zambia-banda-prosecution/zambia-strips-ex-president-of-immunity-from-prosecution-idUSBRE92E0WA20130315.

Ryder, Katherine E. 2011. Making Hay While the Sun Shines: Experiences with the Zambian Task Force on Corruption. *U4 Anti-Corruption Resource Centre Practice Insight* 4.

Schlesinger, Arthur M. 1973. The Imperial Presidency. *The Atlantic*. Accessed February 28, 2020. https://www.theatlantic.com/magazine/archive/1973/11/the-runaway-presidency/306211/.

Siachiwena, Hangala. 2016. Social Protection Policy Reform in Zambia during the Sata Presidency, 2011–2014. CSSR Working Paper No. 380.

Sieyès, Abbé. 1789. *What Is the Third Estate?* Accessed from https://pages.uoregon.edu/dluebke/301ModernEurope/Sieyes3dEstate.pdf.

Silwamba, Eric. 2009. Silwamba Explains Dora Siliya's Judgment. *Lusaka Times*, June 17. http://www.lusakatimes.com/2009/06/17/lusaka-lawyer-eric-silwamba-explains-dora-silayas-judgment/.

Siliya, Dora. 2011. Dora Speaks Out on Corruption [Citation at 02:33-02:53]. Accessed from https://www.youtube.com/watch?v=cz3XgVjnlgQ.

Simuchoba, Arthur. 2014. Zambia: Sata's Constitutional Tricks Risk Electoral Backlash. *African Arguments*, April 14, 2014. https://africanarguments.org/2014/04/zambia-satas-constitutional-tricks-risk-electoral-backlash-by-arthur-simuchoba/.

Simutanyi, Neo & Maria Hinfelaar. 2018. *Understanding Zambia's Black Box [Discussion Paper Series No.3]*. Southern Africa's Institute for Policy and Research.

TIME. 1969. Zambia: Justice on Trial. August 15, 1969. Accessed from http://content.time.com/time/magazine/article/0,9171,901234,00.html.

Vinx, Lars, 'Carl Schmitt', *The Stanford Encyclopedia of Philosophy* (Fall 2019 Edition), Edward N. Zalta (ed.), URL = <https://plato.stanford.edu/archives/fall2019/entries/schmitt/>.

VOA. 2009. Former Zambian President Chiluba's Graft Trial Begins Monday. *Voice of America*, November 1. https://www.voanews.com/archive/former-zambian-president-chilubas-graft-trial-begins-monday.

Waldron, Jeremy. 1987. Theoretical Foundations of Liberalism. *Philosophical Quarterly* 37(147), 140

Waluchow, Wil. 2018. "Constitutionalism", The Stanford Encyclopedia of Philosophy (Spring 2018 Edition), Edward N. Zalta (ed.), URL = <https://plato.stanford.edu/archives/spr2018/entries/constitutionalism/>.

World Bank Group. 2018. *Republic of Zambia Systematic Country Diagnostic*. Washington, DC: World Bank. https://openknowledge.worldbank.org/handle/10986/29702

ZANIS. 2013. Judge Wood Testifies in Chikopa Tribunal How Judge Kajimanga Conducted Himself Unprofessionally. *Lusaka Times*, July 15. https://www.lusakatimes.com/2013/07/15/judge-wood-testifies-in-chikopa-tribunal-how-judge-kajimanga-conducted-himself-unprofessionally/?fb_source=pubv1.

Zulu, Jack Jones. 2006. *Zambia after the HIPC 'Surgery' and the Completion Point*. Policy Brief. Lusaka: Jesuit Centre for Theological Reflection. https://repository.jctr.org.zm/bitstream/handle/123456789/103/ZAMBIA%20AFTER%20THE%20HIPC%20SURGERY%20AND%20THE%20COMPLETION%20POINT.pdf?sequence=1.

# Index

Kolibri 360 GmbH
Ferdinand-Jühlke-Straße 7
99095 Erfurt, Deutschland
produktsicherheit@kolibri360.de